THE
COLLEGE
PRESS
NIV
COMMENTARY

NEW TESTAMENT
INTRODUCTION

THE
COLLEGE
PRESS
NIV
COMMENTARY

NEW TESTAMENT
INTRODUCTION

DAVID A. FIENSY, Ph.D.

New Testament Series Co-Editors:

Jack Cottrell, Ph.D.
Cincinnati Bible Seminary

Tony Ash, Ph.D.
Abilene Christian University

COLLEGE PRESS
PUBLISHING COMPANY
Joplin, Missouri

We gratefully acknowledge:
M.M. Parvis, "Ephesus in the Early Christian Era," *Biblical Archaeo-logist* 8 (1945) 61-73 for the map of Ephesus.
C.F. Pfeiffer and G. Vos, *The Wycliffe Geography of Bible Lands* (Chicago: Moody Press, 1967) for the maps of Antioch and the Roman Forum.
J. Finegan, *Archaeology of the New Testament* Vol. II: *The Mediterranean World of the Early Christian Apostles* (Boulder, CO: Westview Press, 1981) for the maps of Rome and Philippi.
J. Strange and H. Shanks, "Has the House Where Jesus Stayed in Capernaum Been Found?" *Biblical Archaeology Review* VIII/6 (1982) 31 and the Studium Biblicum Franciscanum for the artist's reconstruction of the house(s) in Capernaum.

Sources of information in several other charts are as noted in the text. (See Bibliographies.)

The abbreviation "NIV" in the series title is used by permission of the International Bible Society, 1820 Jet Stream Drive, Colorado Springs, CO 80921-3696.

All Scripture quotations in this volume are the author's own translation, unless otherwise noted.

International Standard Book Number: 0-89900-642-6
Library of Congress Catalog Number: 93-74824

PREFACE

I warmly welcome this reprint of my monograph published in 1994. We have been able to correct some of the errors in the first printing, add maps and tables that could not be included earlier, and supply an index. These changes should make the volume more useful to the reader.

This book is aimed at both college students and the interested Christian reader. Teachers may wish to give assignments from C.K. Barrett, *The New Testament Background* (*NTB*) to supplement the understanding of the New Testament environment. To this end, suggested readings have been added in many of the bibliographies.

The idea for this book began in a series of lessons delivered on Sunday evenings at the Grape Grove Church of Christ in Jamestown, Ohio where I ministered. It was truly a blessing to share in this community of believers and especially to write this book in such a fellowship of faith and love. I also would like to express my appreciation to my present place of ministry, Kentucky Christian College, for their support of Christian writing.

To three very important people in my life, my wife, Molly, and my daughters, Amanda and Jeannie, I say thank you for being you.

Finally I thank God for giving me the opportunity to write, teach, and preach about our Lord, Jesus Christ.

David A. Fiensy
Kentucky Christian College
January 1997

DEDICATION

TO MY MOTHER AND IN MEMORY OF MY FATHER
Prov. 1:8

ABBREVIATIONS

ANF . . . . Menzies, *Ante Nicean Fathers*

Ant. . . . . Josephus, *Antiquities*

b. . . . . Babylonian Talmud

BA . . . . *Biblical Archaeologist*

BAGD . . . . . . Bauer, Arndt, Gingrich, and Danker, *A Greek English Lexicon of the New Testament*

BAR . . . . *Biblical Archaeology Review*

CHJ . . . . Finkelstein and Davies, *Cambridge History of Judaism*

Danby . . . . . . Danby, *The Mishnah*

FBK . . . . Feine, Behm, and Kuemmel, *Introduction to the New Testament*

Guthrie . . . . . Guthrie, *New Testament Introduction*

IDB. . . . . *Interpreter's Dictionary of the Bible*

IEJ . . . . *Israel Exploration Journal*

ISBE o.s. . . . . *International Standard Bible Encyclopedia* (Old Series)

JQR . . . . *Jewish Quarterly Review*

LCL . . . . Loeb Classical Library

LSJ . . . . Liddell, Scott, Jones, and McKenzie, *Greek Lexicon*

m. . . . . Mishnah

MBA. . . . . *Macmillan Bible Atlas*

NTA . . . . Hennecke, Schneemelcher, Wilson, *New Testament Apocrypha*

NTB . . . . Barrett, *New Testament Background* (1989 edition)

NTS . . . . *New Testament Studies*

OCD . . . . *Oxford Classical Dictionary*

OTP . . . . Charlesworth, ed., *The Old Testament Pseudepigrapha*

RA . . . . Montefiore and Loewe, *Rabbinic Anthology*

SVM . . . . Schurer, Vermes, Miller, *The History of the Jewish People in the Age of Jesus Christ*

t. . . . . Tosephta

TDNT . . . . . . Kittel, et al., *Theological Dictionary of the New Testament*

WHJP . . . . . . *World History of the Jewish People*, Vol. VI Schalit, *The Hellenistic Age*; Vol. VII Avi-Yona, *The Age of Herod*

WHG . . . . Pfeiffer and Vos, *Wycliff Historical Geography*

y. . . . . Jerusalem Talmud

TABLE OF CONTENTS

CHAPTER 1

PALESTINE FROM THE PTOLEMIES TO BAR KOSIBA

THE PTOLEMIES AND SELEUCIDS IN PALESTINE, 323–166 B.C.

Bibliography: E.R. Bevan, *The House of Ptolemy*; Idem, *The House of Seleucus*; M. Cary, *A History of the Greek World from 323-146 B.C.*; E. Eddy, *The King is Dead*; E. Ferguson, *Backgrounds of Early Christianity*; D.A. Fiensy, *The Social History of Palestine in the Herodian Period*; S. Freyne, *Galilee from Alexander to Hadrian*; M. Grant, *From Alexander to Cleopatra*; R.M. Haywood, *Ancient Greece and the Near East*; M. Hengel, *Judaism and Hellenism*; SVM; W.W. Tarn, *Hellenistic Civilization*; V. Tcherikover, *Hellenistic Civilization and the Jews*.

Primary Sources: 1 and 2 Maccabees; Polybius, *Histories*; Josephus, *Antiquities*.

The death of Alexander the Great touched off a frenzy of greed and ambition. When the dust finally settled in 275 B.C. three successors in the main had carved out kingdoms for themselves from Alexander's empire: Antigonas in Macedonia, Seleucus and his heirs in Syria, and Ptolemy in Egypt.

Palestine was mainly under the control of the Ptolemies until 198 B.C. when it passed to the descendant of Seleucus, Antiochus III. Alexander's dream of Hellenization began to be realized almost everywhere in his empire. Palestine was no exception. Economically a new method was at work under Alexander's successors, the Ptolemies and the Seleucids. The Greek language began to spread especially among the urban dwellers. Greek philosophy and literature were cultivated and prized highly by many Jews in Jerusalem.

But the process of Hellenization did not move fast enough for

13

Antiochus IV called Epiphanes (illustrious), who ruled Syria from 175-164 B.C. Antiochus was a true apostle of Hellenism. He was born in Athens and received much of his education in that city which so epitomized what it meant to be a Greek. He determined to Hellenize and thus unify his kingdom. This in turn would reduce the chances of disturbance or rebellion.

Antiochus's calculation was wrong, however. As Eddy has brilliantly shown, the process of forced Hellenization in general met with resistance from the local natives, especially the rural folk. The same was true in Palestine where they were totally unimpressed with Greek culture and saw Greek religion as apostasy.

Of course there were always a select few self-styled progressives who eagerly adopted Hellenization. In Palestine Onias III, the High Priest, was strictly orthodox, but many Jews living in Jerusalem, including his own brother, Jason, wanted to be accommodating toward Hellenism. When Jason offered Antiochus IV a larger tribute than Onias and more openness toward Greek culture to boot, the king made Jason the new High Priest in 174 B.C. This action understandably infuriated the orthodox Jews.

Jason immediately set to work in his program of making Jerusalem a Greek city by building a gymnasium. A gymnasium in the Greek world was not just a place of exercise; it was also closely associated with pagan religion (see *OCD* and *IDB*). Not only that, but since the athletic participants trained naked, their Jewish circumcision became obvious to all. The embarrassment over circumcision led many Jews to endure a painful operation to make them look like a Greek. The pious Jews, however, resented the gymnasium deeply as a religious symbol of apostasy.

By 171 B.C Antiochus was ready to sell the high priesthood to an even higher bidder, Menelaus, not a Levite but a Benjamite. Thus he was of illegitimate lineage to be the High Priest.

In 168 B.C. Antiochus launched a forced Hellenization campaign in Jerusalem. This, as many historians have speculated, was perhaps out of anger over his humiliation by Rome. When Antiochus was marching south to do battle with Ptolemy of Egypt, the Roman legate, Popilius Laenas, met him and gave him the decree of the Roman Senate which ordered him to turn around.

When Antiochus said he would need time to consider the matter, Popilius drew a circle around him in the sand and replied, "Decide here." Antiochus decided not to oppose Rome — which had just defeated Macedonia — and thus apparently vented his anger on Judea.

Antiochus sent an official named Apollonius to enforce his designs. A pagan cult of the Greek deity, Zeus, was set up in the temple. Pigs were offered as sacrifices to Zeus on the altar once used for Yahweh. An idol of Zeus was actually erected in the Holy of Holies. Temple prostitutes practiced within the sacred precincts. Circumcision, keeping the Sabbath and reading the Torah were now prohibited by decree. Menelaus continued as High Priest, but now he was the High Priest of Zeus.

It was during this year and the following year that Jews witnessed a horrible persecution. For example, an elderly scribe named Eleazar was flogged to death for refusing to eat pork; a mother and her seven sons were butchered for refusing to pay homage to Zeus; two mothers who had circumcised their sons were driven through the city and cast headlong from the temple wall.

THE HASMONEANS 166 B.C. TO 63 B.C.

Bibliography: E. Bevan, *Jerusalem Under the High Priests*; E. Bickerman, *From Ezra to the Last of the Maccabees*; G.H. Box, *Judaism in the Greek Period*; S. Cohen, *From Maccabees to Mishnah*; W. Foerster, *From the Exile to Christ*; J.A. Goldstein, *1 Maccabees*; Idem, *2 Maccabees*; L.L. Grabbe, *Judaism from Cyrus to Hadrian*; M. Pearlman, *The Maccabees*; D.S. Russell, *The Jews from Alexander to Herod*; SVM; S. Zeitlin, *The Rise and Fall of the Judean State*.

Primary sources: 1 and 2 Maccabees; Josephus, *Antiquities*; *NTB* 116-123.

The family of Mattathias of the clan of Hasmon now stepped on to the stage of world history. Mattathias was of priestly (but not High Priestly) descent and lived in a small village 17 miles northwest of Jerusalem called Modin. He would have gone up to Jerusalem to perform his priestly duties twice a year, but otherwise lived as a peasant farmer with his five sons, John, Simon, Judas (called Maccabeus[1], the "hammer"), Eleazar, and Jonathan.

Hellenization must have always met with the most resistance in the countryside. To be sure, many residents of Jerusalem objected to it as the equivalent of apostasy from the Law and from Yahweh. But the country folk, for whom city ways were always worthy of suspicion, must have been especially difficult to convince that Hellenism meant progress.

Some time in the year of 167 B.C. officers of Antiochus IV came to Modin to compel the residents to sacrifice to Zeus. Mattathias was asked to lead the way in this ritual. When he refused, another Jew in the village started to sacrifice. Mattathias grabbed a sword from one of the officers standing nearby, killed the would-be sacrificer and then killed the officer. The incident began an irreversible and perhaps inevitable series of events that would lead eventually to Jewish independence.

Mattathias and his sons fled to the hills and others quickly joined them, among them the Hasidim ("pious ones") said to be "mighty warriors, everyone a volunteer for the Torah" (1 Macc 2:42). How long prior to this the Hasidim had existed as a group we cannot know, but it appears that they and perhaps others that were loyal to the Torah had only awaited a spark to ignite rebellion.

In every rebellion there is at first a convulsion of revenge. Now Mattathias and his band of rebels attacked and killed Hellenizing Jews and forced Jewish boys to be circumcised. They also tore down pagan altars and "drove the haughty before them" (1 Macc 2:47). Years of anger were vented in those first weeks.

The importance of this period for understanding the New Testament cannot be overemphasized. The commitment to the Torah which cost some Jews their lives left a deep impression on subsequent generations. The pious *hasid* who maintained loyalty to Torah regardless of environmental or cultural influences became a

---

[1]Judas's alias has been used to refer to this entire period (167-134 B.C.) when he and his brothers ruled Judea. It is thus called the Maccabean period.

heroic type. Thus the apostle Paul met with very hostile resistance when he preached and lived without the Torah.

GENEALOGY OF THE HASMONEANS

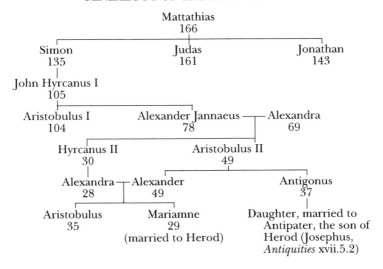

Mattathias died shortly after the rebellion began and the leadership fell to his son Judas Maccabeus. Judas proved to possess a native fighting genius which harked back to the days of King David. He was daring, yet clever and he knew perfectly how to fight in the Judean hill country. His successes over the next few years in keeping at bay one of the most formidable armies in the ancient world was due to three factors. The first was his own genius as a tactician; the second was the recklessness of some of the Syrian military commanders; and the third was the chaotic infighting of the Syrians after Antiochus's death.

The Syrian military, trained in the Macedonian style of fighting, employed the phalanx, that frightening formation of death used to devastate the Persians. But in hilly and rocky country such as Judea the phalanx proved helpless. Judas seemed to sense that for he usually attacked them with short swords and in narrow wadis where the long pikes could not be maneuvered.

Judas's own genius was aided by the folly of several Syrian generals who thought the Judean rebels only a band of disorganized ruffians and no real threat. They were continually being surrounded or splitting up their forces only to have Judas defeat one half and then the other. Judas's amazing string of successes — which included killing Apollonius, the general who was supposed to enforce Hellenization — culminated in his capture of the temple in 164 B.C. and its subsequent cleansing and rededication (Hanukkah).

During the turmoil following the death of Antiochus IV in 164, Judas was able to gain concessions. The general Lysias, one of the contenders for the throne, granted complete religious freedom and executed Menelaus, the apostacized High Priest, in 163 B.C. But Judas was not invincible. The Hasmoneans decided that religious freedom was not enough and to fight on for political freedom as well. Although Judas won a stunning victory in early 161 and negotiated a treaty with Rome, he met his end later that same year. In spite of the fact that his army had dwindled to only 800 men, he attempted a suicidal attack on a large Syrian force. He was struck down and his body carried to Modin to be buried with his father and his brother Eleazar, who had earlier died in battle.

The leadership was now given to Jonathan. Jonathan was not the military hero his brother had been but he knew how to play off opposing sides. By killing all the Hellenists he found in the rural areas by night and courting the favor of the populace by day he soon established himself as the political power to be reckoned with.

Both Demetrius (Antiochus's nephew) and Alexander Balas (who claimed to be Antiochus's illegitimate son) needed Judea to strengthen their claim to the throne. So Demetrius allowed Jonathan to march an army into Jerusalem unmolested. Alexander sent a letter to Jonathan promising him the High Priesthood. Demetrius sent him the counter offer of allowing Judea to be nearly tax free. Jonathan chose to accept Alexander's offer and tipped the balance scales. From now on the Hasmonean ruler in Palestine would be the High Priest. This action infuriated and scandalized certain of the orthodox Jews in Jerusalem because the Hasmoneans, although priests, were not of High Priestly lineage. This year probably marks the beginning of the Essene sect.

Jonathan died of treachery in 142 when he was captured by Tryphon, another claimant for the throne. His brother, John, had also died in battle just before this. Thus of Mattathias and his five sons only Simon was left.

Simon made a treaty with Demetrius II — the rival of Tryphon — to avenge his brother's death. Demetrius granted Judea in return complete political independence. Not since the Babylonian defeat of Judah in 586 B.C. had Judea known the feeling of freedom. Simon also was elected to the position of High Priest.

In 134 Simon was assassinated by his ambitious son-in-law and his son, John Hyrcanus (ruled 134-104) succeeded him. His noteworthy actions were first his conquering the Idumeans to the south and forcing them to be circumcised and his annexation of Samaria. But he broke with the sect of the Pharisees — who are mentioned here for the first time in Josephus — and favored the Sadducees.[2]

Hyrcanus's eldest son, Aristobulus, only reigned one year before he died of a painful disease. His brief reign is distinguished by his annexation and forced circumcision of the residents of Galilee. The other notable event of Aristobulus's reign was his open assumption of the title of king, the first Jewish king since Zedekiah before the exile (586 B.C., see 2 Kings 24).

Alexander Jannaeus (reigned 103-77 B.C.), the brother of Aristobulus, was a man of war and violence. His unpopularity with the masses and his hostility toward the Pharisees led to conflicts, riots, and eventually civil war. Once while sacrificing during the feast of Tabernacles — for he was not only king, of course, but High Priest — the crowd began to pelt him with their citrons — part of the required articles for Tabernacles. His soldiers took revenge by slaughtering many in the crowd. Later after a failed attempt at revolution, Alexander took revenge on the leaders, many of whom were Pharisees. He executed 800 men along with their wives and children. At that time 8000 of Alexander's enemies fled from

---

[2]An old legend — found both in Josephus (*Antiquities* 13.288-98) and the Talmud (b. Kiddushin 66a) — says that Hyrcanus had asked the Pharisees what else he might possibly do to insure that he was exact in the Law. An ill-tempered Pharisee answered, "Give up the High Priesthood." The reason was that gossip said Hyrcanus's mother had been a captive during the reign of Antiochus IV (and thus was possibly defiled). Hyrcanus was furious with this answer and thus disavowed Pharisaism.

Jerusalem. Many historians believe a sizeable part of this group went to Qumran to join the Essene community.

When Alexander Jannaeus died he left the throne to his wife, Alexandra (77-68 B.C.). Since she could not also be High Priest, she appointed her eldest son, Hyrcanus II, to that office. Her reign was marked by peace and consolidation. Syria was becoming ever weaker and was thus in no position to bother with Palestine. At home, Alexandra reconciled with the Pharisees and even made them leaders in her government.

Hyrcanus II was Alexandra's rightful heir but his younger brother, Aristobulus II, quickly deposed him and managed to rule for some five years (68-63 B.C.). His reign was cut short, however, by the coming of the great Roman general, Pompey.

In 64 B.C. Pompey defeated the Seleucid monarchy in Syria. While staying in Damascus, Pompey received both Hyrcanus II and Aristobulus II, each of whom argued he should be king instead of the other. There was also an embassy of Jews requesting that neither remain as king. Pompey put off his decision but later when Aristobulus seemed to be preparing for war, Pompey pursued him and put him into prison. Aristobulus's followers fled to the temple for refuge. Pompey laid siege and took it in three months. He subsequently reinstalled Hyrcanus as High Priest — but not king — under the authority of the new Roman governor of Syria and took away much of the territory the Hasmoneans had acquired.

This period — from Mattathias's uprising in 167 B.C. to the coming of Pompey in 63 — witnessed the rise of the three most important religious-political sects: Pharisees, Sadducees, and Essenes. It produced a taste for freedom and a tradition of armed resistance against foreign foes from which later groups, in the middle of the first century A.D., would gain inspiration. The Hasmonean illegal assumption of the High Priesthood left a desire for religious reform, just as their acceptance of the title "king" strengthened the yearning for a Davidic king or Messiah. Finally, the personal danger which loyalty to the Torah had often involved, resulted in extreme fanaticism. Neglect of the Torah was viewed by some groups as the worst of crimes. This 100-year era, then, shaped the Jewish religious and ideological soul which is found in the time of Jesus.

THE HERODS

Bibliography: M. Avi-Yonah, *The Herodian Period* (*WHJP*, VII); R.J. Bull, "Caesarea Maritima — The Search for Herod's City" *BAR* 8/3 (1982) 24-41; *CAH* Vol. X; H.W. Hoehner, *Herod Antipas*; A.H.M. Jones, *The Herods of Judea*; E. Netzer, "Searching for Herod's Tomb" *BAR* 9/3 (1983) 30-51; R. Otto, "Herodes" *PW*; S.H. Perrowne, *The Life and Times of Herod the Great*; Idem, *The Later Herods*; S. Sandmel, *Herod: Profile of a Tyrant*; *SVM*; Y. Yadin, *Masada*.

Primary sources: Josephus; The Gospels and Acts; *NTB* 127-132.

Although Hyrcanus II was stripped of his formal political power by Pompey, a certain amount of political influence always accompanied religious power in the Middle East. By virtue of his being the High Priest he was still a powerful man in Jewish society. But Hyrcanus seemed always incapable of wielding such authority. He needed someone to prompt him, even push him along, first his mother and later the opportunist, Antipater of Idumea.

The people of Idumea — a territory just south of Judea — had been subdued and circumcised by compulsion under Hyrcanus's grandfather, John Hyrcanus. The Idumean family of Antipater begins to find mention in Josephus after Pompey's conquest of Palestine when Antipater became advisor and confidant to Hyrcanus II. Although Hyrcanus had been allied with Pompey against Julius Caesar in the Roman civil war, Antipater counselled Hyrcanus to align himself quickly to Caesar after Pompey's death in 48 B.C. Later when Antipater joined forces with Caesar to defeat Ptolemy of Egypt — to wrench the throne from Ptolemy in favor of his sister, Cleopatra — Caesar was so pleased he restored full political power to Hyrcanus and gave Antipater Roman citizenship along with the title of "finance manager" (ἐπιτρόπος, *epitropos*) of Palestine, and later the title of governor of Southern Syria.

The wily Antipater now had his claws on all of Palestine and he never let go, for Hyrcanus ruled in name only. Antipater's two sons, Phasael and Herod, managed the country in Jerusalem and Galilee respectively.

But the political situation in Rome from 49-30 B.C. made it difficult to become too comfortable. No sooner had the civil war between Pompey and Caesar settled than Caesar was himself assassinated (in 44 B.C.) by a conspiracy led by Brutus and Cassius. Antipater and Herod were very helpful to Cassius — they could change sides at a moment's notice — when he came to Syria to raise an army.

In 42 B.C., however, Brutus and Cassius were defeated and killed by Octavian and Mark Antony. The two divided up the Roman world, Octavian taking the west and Antony the east. By this time Antipater had died of poisoning and Herod and Phasael were ruling Palestine. Although a delegation of Jews came to Antioch to implore Antony to banish the two sons of Antipater from Palestine and although they had sided with Brutus and Cassius, Antony decided to retain them.

From 40 to 37 B.C. — while Antony dallied in Egypt with Cleopatra — Palestine again was in turmoil when the Parthians from the east overran Syria and swept down into Palestine. Along the way the son of Aristobulus II, Antigonas (Hyrcanus II's nephew), who had been a prisoner in Antioch, convinced the Parthians to bring him along. They surrounded Herod, Phasael, and Hyrcanus in Jerusalem and promised to come to terms with them. But when Phasael and Hyrcanus went to the Parthians' camp they were placed in chains. Phasael committed suicide while Antigonas cut off his uncle Hyrcanus's ears to prevent him from qualifying any longer as High Priest (Lev 21:17). The Parthians departed and took Hyrcanus with them, leaving Antigonas as High Priest and king (40 to 37 B.C.).

Herod managed to escape and made his way first to Alexandria, then to Rome seeking Antony to plead for a new army. By 38 B.C. he had obtained all of Palestine except Jerusalem. After marrying Mariamne, granddaughter of Hyrcanus II, he completed the siege of Jerusalem in 37 B.C. Antigonas was captured and sent to Antony in Antioch where he was executed. Now Herod was in total control of Palestine.

Herod was granted the title of king by Rome and ruled over the territories of Idumea, Judea, Samaria, Galilee, Perea and Gaulanitis

from 37 to 4 B.C. In the first period of Herod's reign he faced opposition from mainly two sources: the remnants of the Hasmonean
family and Cleopatra, the famous queen of Egypt. If Herod ever
thought that marrying into the Hasmonean family — by Mariamne —
would solve any problem he might have from that quarter, he was
mistaken. First, Hyrcanus II returned from Parthia. Then his mother-
in-law, Alexandra, lobbied for her son, Aristobulus III, to become
the High Priest, and Herod finally consented — only to realize how
politically dangerous such an appointment could be. Third, Herod
was the victim of his own continual jealousy and suspicion concerning his wife, the beautiful Mariamne. Herod solved these problems
in what would become characteristic in his reign. One by one they
were all murdered, Aristobulus III in 35, Hyrcanus II in 30,
Mariamne in 29, and Alexandra in 28 B.C. His troubles from the
Hasmoneans were only temporarily solved, however, because
Mariamne had born to Herod two sons, Alexander and Aristobulus
IV. He would later have to deal with them in a similar fashion.

Cleopatra was a constant source of irritation for Herod. Allegedly
Herod had once spurned her amorous advances, leaving her set on
revenge. At any rate, she often had teamed with Alexandra, Herod's
mother-in-law, before the latter's death, to lodge complaints against
him to Mark Antony. She persuaded Antony to take away Herod's
most lucrative agricultural estate, the balsam and date palm planta-
tions around Jericho. His problems with Cleopatra ended, however,
with the watershed sea battle of Actium in 31 B.C. in which Antony
— now in a civil war against Octavian — was defeated and later
killed. Cleopatra subsequently committed suicide.

One might think Antony's defeat a problem for Herod since he
had been such a close ally, but the cunning of the Herods once again
came to the fore. He had hedged his bets by preventing a group of
gladiators from coming to Antony's aid. That action plus the charm
and bravado Herod showed when interviewed by Octavian convinced Octavian to retain him as a vassal king in Palestine.

After Actium the entire Mediterranean world settled into a *Pax
Romana* (Roman Peace) including Palestine. This peace lasted until
the death of Nero in A.D. 68. Herod, now firmly in control of
Palestine, was free to build the kind of kingdom he envisioned. He

made Jerusalem a magnificent city with his own palace, an amphitheater, a hippodrome, a new military guard house called the Tower of Antonia (named after Antony), and especially by a newly built temple. The latter structure, begun in 20 B.C., was finished well after Herod's lifetime and only a few years before the great war against Rome in A.D. 66.

Herod also built new cities such as Antipatris, Caesarea Maritima (see R.J. Bull) and Sebaste, and strengthened and lavished fortified places such as Masada (see Yadin), Machaerus, and Herodium (see Netzer). In addition he gave gifts of money to various Greek cities. Such building required a huge income. Most historians have concluded — from Herod's will — that his annual income was 1000 talents or 10,000,000 Attic Greek drachmas of silver.

The old family problems arose once again toward the end of Herod's life. His two sons by Mariamne, Alexander and Aristobulus IV, he executed in 7 B.C. They had never reconciled with the other members of the Herod family and always resented their mother's murder. A third son, Antipater, he executed as well in 4 B.C. only a few days before his own death. In Rome they said, "It is better to be Herod's pig (ὗς, *hus*) than his son (υἱός, *huios*)."

Shortly before his death Herod gave orders to his government ministers to execute the most distinguished men in his kingdom on the day of his death. His rationale for such an order was that he wanted there to be great lamentation at his death. The order was never carried out, however. He died in 4 B.C., shortly after changing his will one more time, and was buried at Herodium. Though archaeologists have excavated at Herodium, his tomb has not yet been discovered.

Herod left his kingdom primarily to three of his sons. To Archelaus he bequeathed Idumea, Judea, and Samaria and the title of king. Rome later changed his title to "ethnarch" (leader of a nation). To Antipas he left Galilee and Perea, and to Philip he willed Gaulanitis, Batanea, Trachonitis, and Auranitis. Antipas and Philip were called "tetrarchs" (literally, "leaders of a fourth" but meaning here leaders of a territory). According to the expected annual income, Archelaus received the greatest wealth, Antipas the next, and Philip the least.

COLLEGE PRESS NIV COMMENTARY

Archelaus ruled his territories from 4 B.C. to A.D. 6. He was a brutal and ruthless ruler like his father. The emperor of Rome, Octavian — now called Augustus — finally banished him to Gaul where he remained until his death. After him — except for a brief time under Agrippa I — a Roman procurator under the authority of the Syrian proconsul governed these regions.

Antipas ruled from 4 B.C. to A.D. 39. He evidently possessed the cunning of his father, Herod, because Jesus called him on one occasion, "that fox" (Luke 13:32). Antipas scandalized the Jews by casting off his first wife, the daughter of Aretas, king of Arabia, and marrying Herodias, his brother's wife. Aretas would later defeat Antipas in battle (in A.D. 36) partly out of anger over the treatment of his daughter.

Antipas is best known for his execution of John the Baptist. The Gospels (Mark 6:17-28) indicate that John was beheaded at the prodding of Herodias (and her daughter Salome) because John condemned Antipas's marriage. Josephus writes that Antipas executed John because he feared he was becoming too popular. Doubtless both considerations played a role in Antipas's decision.

Antipas, like his father Herod, was a builder. His two greatest achievements were the cities Tiberias and Sepphoris, both in Galilee. The latter city, called "the ornament of all Galilee" by Josephus, lay only three miles from Nazareth.

Antipas incurred the displeasure of emperor Caligula in A.D. 39 when the emperor heard a series of accusations made against him. He therefore exiled Antipas in Gaul, as Archelaus before him, and gave his territories to Herodias's brother, Agrippa I.

Philip enjoyed a long reign (4 B.C. to A.D. 34) over the territories of northeast Palestine. Not much is known about him except that he built the well decorated city of Caesarea Philippi. When he died, Agrippa I received his territories as well.

Agrippa I was given the title of king in A.D. 34 and reigned until his death in 44. He was the grandson of Herod the Great and Mariamne and the son of Aristobulus IV. He had spent much time in Rome, where he was a personal friend of Caligula. The emperor gave him various territories in piece-meal fashion, first those of Philip in 34, then of Antipas in 40, and finally the territories

Samaria, Judea and Idumea in A.D. 41. He lived only until 44 when he succumbed to a sudden illness. Thus from A.D. 41 to 44 he ruled as king over roughly the same area as his grandfather, Herod.

Although Agrippa's moral debauchery was well known in Rome, while in Palestine he at least pretended to be a devout Jew and seems to have been quite popular as a ruler. Both Josephus and the Mishnah speak highly of him. He sought to please the Jewish leadership by persecuting Christianity and thus executed the apostle James (Acts 12:1-3). His death is described both in Josephus and Acts 12:20-23.

Upon Agrippa's death, the entire kingdom was again assigned to a Roman procurator and was called Judea. Thus Galilee, Perea, and the northeast territories of Philip came under direct Roman rule for the first time in A.D. 44. This situation continued until in 53 Agrippa's son, Agrippa II, was made king and received the former territories of Philip which he ruled until his death in A.D. 93. This was the Agrippa before whom Paul made his plea in Acts 26. Agrippa II was the last of the Herods to rule.

THE PROCURATORS

Bibliography: F.F. Bruce, *New Testament History*; W.R. Farmer, *Maccabees, Zealots and Josephus*; E. Ferguson, *Backgrounds of Early Christianity*; D.A. Fiensy, *The Social History of Palestine in the Herodian Period*; M. Hengel, *The Zealots*; R.A. Horsley and J.S. Hanson, *Bandits, Prophets, and Messiahs*; H. Kreissig, *Die sozialen zusammenhänge des judäischen Krieges*; D. Rhoads, *Israel in Revolution*; S. Safrai and M. Stern, *The Jewish People in the First Century*; SVM; E.M. Smallwood, *The Jews Under Roman Rule*.

Primary sources: Josephus, *War of the Jews*; The Gospels and Acts; Tacitus, *Annals*; NTB 133-134.

The Roman procurators who governed Judea until A.D. 41 and after A.D. 44 governed all of Palestine, began in violence and ended the same way. These administrators had three main duties: military (command a standing army in Judea), judicial (serve as the supreme court), and fiscal (administer the finances). They resided at Caesarea Maritima but made occasional visits to Jerusalem.

The first procurator, Coponius, immediately made a census of the population.[3] Rome always sized up her expected income from a new land at the very beginning of its rule. A census was taken in Egypt every fourteen years and presumably Syria would have done the same. Every male between the ages of 14 and 65 and every female between 12 and 65 was expected to pay a poll-tax in Syria. The average amount of the poll-tax for the poor was, according to Stenger, probably around one denarius per person (Mark 12:13-17). But in addition, an assessment would have been made of the agricultural potential of Judea to assess the tax on the soil, usually around 12% per year (see Chapter 3).

The Jews were outraged by this census and one Jewish scholar named Judas[4] decided the situation was intolerable. He said only cowards would submit to these taxes after serving God alone and that his fellow Jews should not tolerate men as their masters. Judas formed a movement — called a "philosophy" by Josephus — which actively and violently opposed the census. Although Coponius rather quickly disposed of him and the disturbance, it was only the beginning of a series of violent clashes between Jewish idealists and Roman procurators, clashes that ultimately in A.D. 66 developed into total war.

The effect of Judas's uprising is now difficult to assess. Some historians (e.g., Hengel) speculate that a secret society, the Zealot movement, began at this time and was active behind the scenes until the war broke out. Others (e.g., M. Smith)[5] argue that the Zealots did not exist as a movement or party until the war began. At least

---

[3]The difficult question of Luke's reference to a census (Luke 2:1-3) cannot be handled here. Among the voluminous literature on this topic see *SVM*, Vol. I, Excursus I; and R. Brown, *The Birth of the Messiah*, Appendix VII.

[4]This was not of course Judas Iscariot, the man who betrayed Jesus. That Judas would have been much too young in A.D. 6. The name Judas was common for descendants of the tribe of Judah, especially since the Hasmonean hero, Judas Maccabeus.

[5]See M. Smith's influential article, "Zealots and Sicarii, Their Origins and Relation," *HTR* 64 (1971) 1-19. Smith follows K. Lake (in K. Lake and F. Jackson, *Beginnings of Christianity*).

one can say that the bitter memory of that encounter remained vivid and played a role in fanning flames later.

The next procurator of note was Pontius Pilate, who not only executed Jesus of Nazareth but aroused the ire of the Jews in a number of ways. First he attempted to put in Jerusalem a flag or standard which had a figure of the Roman emperor (Tiberius) on it. This action obviously angered orthodox Jews who saw it as a transgression of the second commandment (Exod 20:4). A protest and riot in Caesarea over Pilate's activities resulted in the slaughter of a great many Jews.

Pilate provoked yet another riot when he appropriated temple funds to pay for an aqueduct for Jerusalem. From Pilate's perspective, the Jews should pay for this aqueduct themselves and where else could he get the money but the temple treasury? But to pious Jews he had committed sacrilege by robbing the temple. Many Jews died in this riot in Jerusalem.

Finally, after Pilate's murder of a band of Samaritans which was traveling to Mt. Gerizim (see Chapter 2 for Samaritans) he was dismissed as procurator.

In A.D. 40 the emperor Caligula ordered his own image erected in the temple as Antiochus IV had done with the statue of Zeus. Worshiping the Roman emperor as a god began in the east after Augustus's death (see Chapter 7) and usually only involved emperors who had died and subsequently had been "deified." Some, however, began pushing the deification before their own deaths. Caligula's order almost caused a total rebellion. Jewish peasants threatened not to plant any more crops and leaders such as Agrippa I and Petronius feared a "harvest of banditry." Only the urgent pleading of Agrippa and Petronius convinced Caligula of the folly of his vengeful decision. This occasion is one of the few in which a procurator — or in this case proconsul — exhibited an enlightened rule.

In A.D. 44 a Jewish pretender named Theudas excited a large following. He claimed to be a prophet and promised he could do an outstanding miracle as proof of his office. He would part the waters of the Jordan river — as Joshua had done — then lead his followers to a victory against Rome. Fadus, the procurator, however, caught up with this mob and its leader and massacred most of them, including Theudas.

While Cumanus was procurator in A.D. 49, a Roman soldier caused a riot during one of the Jewish feasts. He was standing atop the tower of Antonia, which overlooked the temple area, when he made a crass and obscene gesture which was visible to many of the participants below. Many Jews were killed in the subsequent violent protest. In revenge a Jewish group attacked a Roman official. The tension also led a Roman soldier to tear up a copy of the Torah.

Cumanus had further trouble in 52 when a group of Samaritans murdered some Jews who were passing through Samaria on their way to a feast in Jerusalem. When Cumanus refused to punish the offenders, some Jews secured the services of a notorious brigand, Eleazar ben Dinai. After they had taken their revenge, however, many of the brigands were captured by Cumanus and crucified. The Syrian proconsul at this point dismissed Cumanus for his blatant anti-Judaism.

The next procurator, Felix, came with strong contacts in Rome. His brother, Pallas, was the finance minister of emperor Claudius and a very powerful man. But even that connection could not prevent Felix from being recalled in A.D. 60 because he caused such hostile feelings toward Rome.

Felix's treachery and brutality provoked drastic violence on the part of the Jews. A group formed which devoted itself to assassination. They carried small daggers (called in Latin *sicae*) which could easily be concealed and thus received the nickname *sicarii*. They murdered not only Romans but pro-Roman Jews. Thus Jonathan, the High Priest, was cut down by them.

Also during Felix's procuratorship an Egyptian Jew — Josephus does not give his name — in the manner of Theudas before him claimed to be a prophet. He would offer a great sign of his authority by causing the walls of Jerusalem to collapse at his command. After that sign he would defeat and drive out the Romans. Felix met the unfortunate crowd before it arrived in Jerusalem and slaughtered a great number. The Egyptian, however, escaped.

Felix is also mentioned in the New Testament as the dishonest and greedy procurator who hoped the apostle Paul would pay him a bribe (Acts 24:26). Felix in the end left office like so many procurators before him: due to the strong anti-Roman feelings he caused among Jews, he was recalled.

Festus, who succeeded Felix, is also mentioned in Acts (Acts 25-26). He is the procurator to whom the apostle Paul declared his desire to plead his case before Caesar (Emperor Nero). His brief management of Judea, which was ended by his death, saw further conflicts with the violent sicarii. There was also another prophetic pretender, unnamed in Josephus, who led a group of followers into the desert. Festus, in typically Roman fashion, dealt with the band of men by killing some and scattering the rest.

According to Josephus, Festus's successor, Albinus, was one of the greediest and most unscrupulous procurators. Roman officials customarily enriched themselves when they served in foreign lands, but too much graft would always incite the anger of the locals. Albinus seems to have overstepped the bounds of seemly plunder. To make matters worse he had no qualms about taking bribes from both sides, from the pro-Roman faction of Jews and from the anti-Roman faction. Thus he even accepted bribes from the sicarii. Anarchy and chaos prevailed.

Josephus indicates that Florus, the last procurator, was also the worst. He openly stole funds from cities and even the temple treasury. He allowed banditry if the bandits gave him a cut of the booty. The situation under Florus was intolerable and the result predictable.

On one occasion, when Florus sent two cohorts of soldiers into Jerusalem to keep the peace, the anger of the Jews was beyond control. A riot this time turned into all-out war. Jewish revolutionaries quickly captured the temple in Jerusalem. Soon other fortifications throughout Palestine were taken by Jews, among them Masada. A.D. 66 marks the beginning of the great rebellion.

THE GREAT JEWISH WAR, A.D. 66–73 (74)

Bibliography: G. Cornfeld, *Josephus: The Jewish War*; R. Furneaux, *The Roman Siege of Jerusalem*; R.A. Horsley and J.S. Hanson, *Bandits,*

Prophets and Messiahs; M. Hengel, *The Zealots*; D.M. Rhoads, *Israel in Revolution*; *SVM*; E.M. Smallwood, *The Jews Under Roman Rule*; Y. Yadin, *Masada*.

Primary sources: Josephus, *The Jewish War*; Dio Cassius, *Histories*; *NTB* 138-144.

It is appropriate here to pause to review the causes of this war. We must remember that no war begins out of only one cause. There is always an interwoven complexity of reasons and motivations. None of these causes listed below then is sufficient in itself to explain fully why the war began. The motives of individuals and groups were complex and the number and variation of groups were probably greater than Josephus explicitly indicates. Those modern scholars who tend to focus on only one cause for the war (religious ideals or socio-economic reasons, e.g.) are really imposing their own philosophy of history on the sources.

Further, the degree of enthusiasm for the war also varied greatly from pro-Roman to "moderate" — those hoping to withstand the Roman attack and then make a treaty — to Zealot and like groups, in favor of all-out war until they had utterly defeated the pagans.

The following motives can safely be assigned to most of the groups and movements fighting in the war:

1) Poor procurators. This was Josephus's implication in rehearsing the actions of the procurators, especially those that managed Judea just before the war. No doubt their greed and ineptness contributed largely to Jewish frustration and hopelessness under the Romans.

2) Jewish leaders. Again Josephus alleged that it was Jewish "imposters" and "deceivers" that led the hapless masses into a suicidal war and then engaged in such infighting that the defense of the homeland was impossible. The story he tells does seem feasible, though these leaders cannot have been the villains Josephus claimed. It is highly doubtful that the riot in Jerusalem when Florus was procurator (see below) would ever have become a full rebellion without proper leadership. The peasant masses have never been able to organize themselves for such endeavors. They needed capable leaders from the aristocracy. Most of those to whom

Josephus refers were exactly that: aristocratic leaders.

3) Religious motives. Rhoads lists several religious motives behind the rebellion. Among these motives are: defense of the law, exclusion of aliens, defense of the temple, and eschatological hopes. The war was a "holy war" (Hengel) led by Messianic pretenders such as Menahem and Simon bar Giora. The fact that the Zealots chose a new High Priest — to replace the Roman appointee (*War* 2.441, 4.153) — and that they believed strongly that God would give them victory (*War* 5.459) argues that these rebels were strongly religiously motivated.

4) Socio-economic motives. On the other hand, the modern reader must be aware that religion and socio-economics were inseparable in ancient Israel. One had a religious obligation to help the poor and oppressed and God would punish the oppressor. Further, it is clear (Horsley and Hanson; Kreissig) that the revolutionaries did sense economic oppression, not just at the hands of the Romans but especially at the hands of wealthy Jews. The sicarii burned the debt records of Jerusalem (*War* 2.427) and a group tried to do the same thing in Galilee (*Life* 375). The poor masses burned the mansions of Agrippa II and the High Priest — who had been appointed by Rome — and pursued and killed many prominent Jewish citizens and large landowners. The war then could be seen as a class war among the Jews themselves.

The riot that Florus began in Jerusalem had turned into unmanageable violence. The proconsul of Syria, therefore, sent Cestius Gallus to Jerusalem with an army and orders to quell the uprising. Such uprisings had happened before — Judas of Galilee, Theudas, the Egyptian — and had always been easily handled. The untrained Jewish peasants were never any match for Roman legionaries. Cestius, however, was unable this time to subdue Jerusalem and was even forced to march back to Antioch. On the way home the rebels ambushed him — in Maccabean fashion — and he took flight. The Jews had their first victory.

The Romans clearly at first underestimated the strength of the rebellion. The Jews began to organize their defenses and train for war. At first the aristocrats of Palestine, elected by a popular assembly, led them. Jerusalem was defended by recruits led by Josephus ben Gorion and Ananus (the High Priest). Idumea was headed by

Jesus ben Sappias and Eleasar ben Ananias (both of the High Priestly family). Galilee was under the command of Josephus, the historian. As the war progressed, however, this picture changed dramatically. Ananus was executed by the Zealots and a new High Priest was chosen by lot. Josephus had continual problems from John of Gischala in Galilee. The low-born leader Simon bar Giora became one of the main players in the rebellion.

The Roman attack began in Galilee in A.D. 67. Emperor Nero had given the war over to Vespasian, a successful and respected general. Vespasian had little trouble subduing Galilee. The fortresses at Jotapata and Gamala were destroyed; Tiberias opened its gates to Vespasian's son, Titus. By the end of 67, all of northern Palestine was again under Roman domination.

Josephus himself was captured by Vespasian. He and other officers had fled to a cistern to hide from the Romans after the fall of Jotapata. They had made a suicide pact and Josephus was to take his life after the others had died. Josephus, however, instead of committing suicide along with the others, surrendered and was brought before Vespasian. With amazing chutzpah, he prophesied that Vespasian would some day be emperor, a prophecy that not only pleased the general, but proved to be correct a year later. His life was spared and thus began the career of the great historian, for he began making notes about the war almost immediately.

After Vespasian had subdued Perea and while he was preparing for the siege of Jerusalem in A.D. 68, he heard of the death of Nero. In quick succession came three other emperors: Galba, Otho, and Vetellius. All were killed shortly after they were proclaimed emperor. In A.D. 69 the armies of the eastern empire proclaimed Vespasian emperor. He therefore set out for Rome and left his son Titus in charge of the siege.

By A.D. 70 the picture in Jerusalem had changed. The city was commanded by three Jewish parties or factions. Simon bar Giora, a Messianic pretender, controlled most of the city outside the temple area. John of Gischala in Galilee had led his army into the city and controlled the temple mount. Eleasar ben Simon had charge of the temple itself.

Titus had four legions which he placed at various strategic

points around the city. In the spring of A.D. 70 the third north wall was breached first, then the second north wall. These two breaches had taken only 20 days to accomplish with battering rams, but the rest of the siege took considerably longer. The other walls were stronger and had to be battered for weeks to punch a hole through them. The guard house, called the Tower of Antonia, was captured and from there the temple was seized and torn to the ground. Next, Titus broke through the first north wall of the city and captured it with great carnage. The whole siege took five months.

Three fortresses still remained in Jewish hands: Herodium, Masada, and Machaerus (east of the Dead Sea). Lucilius Bassus, the new procurator, was given the task of capturing these strongholds. Herodium and Machaerus surrendered with little resistance but the rebel forces of Masada seemed determined to hold on to the end. Bassus died soon after undertaking this assignment and the command passed to Flavius Silva. Silva found only one way to take such a fortress: he built a giant ramp of earth up to the top of the butte. It was an engineering feat of enormous proportions on the Roman side, but held the prospect of death on the Jewish side.

The Jews made a suicide pact just before the Romans stormed the fortress and thus systematically began killing their own families and each other. The last ten plus Eleazar drew lots to see who would kill whom. Archaeologists have discovered the bits of pottery on which these eleven wrote their names. Masada, the last Jewish stronghold, fell in A.D. 73 or 74. The war was over.

THE TIME BETWEEN THE WARS

Bibliography: J. Neusner, *A Life of Yohanan ben Zakkai*; Idem, *First Century Judaism in Crisis*; *SVM*; E.M. Smallwood, *The Jews Under Roman Rule*; S. Zeitlin, *The Rise of the Judean State*.

Primary sources: Rabbinic sources; Eusebius, *Ecclesiastical History*; Dio Cassius, *Roman History*.

The Great War of A.D. 66-73 (74) left the Jewish nation decimated and the Jewish religion without a center. An estimated one third of the Jewish population of Palestine died in the war. Jerusalem was a leveled ruin and the temple was completely demolished. A standing army — the Tenth Legion — would from now on guard against insurrection. The land now belonged to the emperor (Vespasian) and the peasants on it became his tenants. Since the temple was gone, the temple tax now went to the Roman god, Jupiter Capitolinus, in Rome.

It was a time of physical and emotional devastation. Some coped by turning to visions. The apocalyptists, especially 4 Ezra and 2 Baruch, promised that God would soon rebuild the temple and smite the Romans. The anguish in these two writings is obvious.

The Sadducees disappeared from history. Without the temple as their power base, the mostly priestly Sadducees had no reason to exist as a group. Thus the destruction of the temple meant the end of this way of living as a Jew.

The scribes and Pharisees turned from the temple to the Torah. Their spiritual descendants, the rabbis, now focused on making the Torah the center of Jewish religious life and applying and interpreting its precepts. Post 70 Judaism, thus, became in the main rabbinic Judaism, the Judaism of the Torah. The temple was not needed to study the Torah, thus rabbinic Judaism could survive.

The leader of the rabbinical movement was Johanan ben Zakkai. Born in Galilee, he escaped from Jerusalem by stealth during the Roman siege, with five disciples. He later won from emperor Vespasian the right to start an academy in the coastal town of Jamnia. Johanan and his disciples were soon joined by other scholars and thus the Jamnia council began. Over the course of the following years they reorganized Judaism. The liturgy was standardized, various legal rulings were emended, a new Greek translation of the Old Testament was made by a Jewish proselyte named Aquila, and the canon of the Old Testament was debated. The period at Jamnia is formative for the direction Judaism would take after the Great War.

There was also further violence from A.D. 115 to 117, from the end of Emperor Trajan's reign to the beginning of Hadrian's. Jews lashed out in violence in Egypt, Cyrene, Cyprus, Mesopotamia, and probably to some extent also in Palestine. The causes of the violence are unknown but it left great slaughter and destruction. Rome of course dealt extremely harshly with the insurrectionists and had all of them subdued within a few months after Hadrian began to reign as emperor.

THE BAR KOSIBA WAR

Bibliography: G. Alon, *History of the Jews in Palestine in the Period of Mishnah and the Talmud*; Y. Harkabi, *The Bar Kokhba Syndrome*; H. Mantel, "The Causes of the Bar Kokba Revolt" *JQR* 58 (1967-8) 224-42, 274-96; *SVM*; Y. Yadin, *Bar Kochba*.

Primary sources: Eusebius, *Ecclesiastical History*; Justin, *I Apology*; Dio Cassius, *Roman History*; The Bar Cochba letters (published in P. Benoit, J.T. Milik, and R. de Vaux, *Discoveries in the Judean Desert II*); *NTB* 122-124.

It is one of the misfortunes of history that the second great Jewish rebellion, which lasted from A.D. 132 to 135, had no story teller like Josephus to record the events. Consequently, we are left with only bits and pieces from several sources and these sources often contradict one another. Another consequence of this paucity of information is the relative lack of attention this war has received as if it were only a minor conflict. But as Schurer has concluded, this war was at least as violent and destructive as that of A.D. 66. In terms of human lives, it may have been more costly.

Most historians cite two causes for the war: Emperor Hadrian's prohibition of circumcision and his plans to rebuild — perhaps already begun when the war broke out — Jerusalem as a Gentile city called Aelia Capitolina (named after himself, Aelius Hadrian). Hadrian believed circumcision was barbaric and should not be practiced within the empire. Jews were not the only practitioners of circumcision, of course. Some parts of Egypt and Arabia practiced it as well. But to the Jews this seemed like an attempt to destroy their religion, not unlike the attempt of Antiochus IV.

Further, the plan to build a pagan city and to erect a temple to Zeus on the same location as the destroyed temple of Yahweh was an obvious sacrilege which few Jews could tolerate. Hadrian intended to do what Antiochus IV had failed to do. The result was predictable.

Y. Harkabi suggests that the rebels prepared for years before they began the revolt. How long these preparations took is not clear. It is also not clear whether or not the preparations began before Hadrian's decree about circumcision. If so, then, a certain segment within Palestinian Judaism acted out of additional motives — desire for freedom? Messianism? socio-economic reasons? — to plan for war.

The leader of the revolt was Simon bar Kosiba. His name "son of Kosiba" was changed by his followers to bar Kochba, "son of the Star" (Num. 24:17), a Messianic title.[6] He was hailed as the Messiah by many Jewish leaders, among them Rabbi Akiba, one of the great scholars of the Torah. The newly discovered documents from his time — including some of his own correspondence — indicate that the Jews saw his leadership as beginning a new era. These documents date themselves "year one of the freedom of Israel," that is, the first year of the new era. He had coins minted — indicating political independence — and on one side of the coins was the picture of palm branches, a Messianic symbol. Other coins have a picture of a star standing over the temple. Christian sources (Justin) indicate that Jewish Christians were persecuted by Bar Kosiba because they would not accept him as Messiah.

Bar Kosiba was followed not only by the great rabbis of his day but also by Eleazar the Priest who it seems was his second in command. The new government, it has been suggested, intended to rebuild the temple with Eleazar as High Priest. This suggestion is undoubtedly true since no Jewish freedom movement could have forgotten about the temple.

Violence broke out in A.D. 132 but never developed into an all-out battle. Bar Kosiba's strategy was to wage guerrilla war, hiding in

---

[6]Later, after the war had been lost and hundreds of thousands had died following him, his Jewish detractors called him bar Koziba, "son of the Lie."

caves and striking by ambush. At first Bar Kosiba must have been successful. He probably controlled much of Judea and may even have recaptured the ruins of Jerusalem.

The Romans under general Julius Severus were content to fight a war of attrition. Gradually their superior numbers and better supplies and arms wore down the Jews.

The major fighting seems to have taken place in Judea. Galilee either participated not at all or in a minor way. The Romans destroyed almost one thousand villages in Judea and killed close to 600,000 people — perhaps one half of the Jewish population of Palestine. Judea was practically depopulated of Jews.

Most historians conclude that the Romans also received heavy casualties in the war, though the numbers are not given by ancient historians. The war was a blood bath on both sides.

The last stronghold to fall to the Romans was Bathar, a few miles southwest of Jerusalem. Here in A.D. 135 Bar Kosiba was killed along with thousands of others. Many of the great rabbis, including Akiba, had already been martyred. It was a sad end and bitter disappointment for the Jews.

Hadrian did build his city, Aelia Capitolina, and his pagan temple to Zeus (Jupiter). He forbade Jews to enter the city on penalty of death and maintained the prohibition against circumcision. Emperor Antoninus Pius in A.D. 138 rescinded the ban on circumcision, but not until the fourth century under Constantine were Jews once more allowed to enter the holy city.

JOSEPHUS AS A HISTORICAL SOURCE

Bibliography: P. Bilde, *Flavius Josephus between Jerusalem and Rome*; S.J.D. Cohen, *Josephus in Galilee and Rome*; L.H. Feldman and G. Hata, eds., *Josephus, the Bible, and History*; T. Rajak, *Josephus*; H. St. John Thackery, *Josephus, the Man and the Historian*; *NTB* 192-195.

Josephus ben Mattathias (A.D. 37-100?) was born of a priestly family. His mother was of Hasmonean descent. At a young age (16) he studied the main Jewish sects and then became for three years a disciple of a desert hermit named Bannus. He claims that later he joined the Pharisees but many modern scholars doubt it.

He was swept up into the war in A.D. 66 and given the command of Galilee. After losing Jotapata, he surrendered and was accepted by Vespasian as a mediator and interpreter during the remainder of the war.

He wrote an account of the war in Aramaic shortly after it ended and it was subsequently translated into Greek. Twenty years later he wrote his most extensive work, the *Antiquities*, which tells the story of Jewish history from the patriarchs to the start of the war. To this latter work he attached his own biography. Last of all, he wrote the *Against Apion*, a defense of Judaism against the calumnies of a pagan named Apion.

Josephus has been maligned as a historian for the past two hundred years. Scholars have alleged that he often flatters Vespasian and his son Titus, he defends Judaism, and mostly he justifies himself. But while it is true that Josephus does all of these things, that does not necessarily destroy his basic credibility as a historian. Archaeological and other literary evidence have helped to confirm his history and modern scholars are concluding that Josephus' biases are not as strong as some have claimed in the past. Thus Josephus' works are a major historical source for this period.

CHAPTER 2

JEWISH INSTITUTIONS, SECTS, AND RELIGIOUS MOVEMENTS

INSTITUTIONS

The Temple

Bibliography: A. Edersheim, *The Temple*; E. Ferguson, *Backgrounds of Early Christianity*; D. Gowan, *Bridge Between the Testaments*; J. Jeremias, *Jerusalem in the Time of Jesus*; P. Levertoff, "Sanhedrin" *ISBE* o.s.; H. Mantel, *Studies in the History of the Sanhedrin*; S. Safrai, "The Temple and the Divine Service" *WHJP*, Vol. VII; E.P. Sanders, *Judaism: Practice and Belief 63 B.C.E.–66 C.E.*; E.M. Smallwood, "High Priests and Politics in Roman Palestine" *Journal of Theological Studies* 13 (1962) 114-34; M. Stern, "Aspects of Jewish Society: The Priesthood and Other Classes" *The Jewish People in the First Century* I.2; W.F. Stinespring, "Temple of Jerusalem" *IDB*.

Primary sources: m. Tamid, m. Sanhedrin, m. Middoth; Josephus, *Antiquities*; Gospels and Acts; *NTB* 174-186, 207-209, 124-126.

It is difficult for us now to appreciate the importance of the temple in the life of Judaism in the first century A.D. Certainly synagogues had appeared in most Jewish villages and cities, but these had never replaced the role of the temple. The temple and the land gave Judaism its center and focus. The Torah was important but not yet as central as the other two elements.

Judaism was still a religion of sacrifice and offering, holy place and priest. Each day bloody offerings of animals were made in the temple. People made regular pilgrimages from various parts of Palestine and even outside of Palestine to worship in its sacred precincts. Nearly every Jew paid the yearly temple tax as well as tithes to priests and Levites. The temple was the glue that held all

Jews together.

The structure in the first century A.D. was magnificent. Herod the Great had disassembled the beggarly temple of Zerubbabel to build one more in line with his taste for extravagance. The work, begun around 20 B.C., was essentially completed in a few years, but certain of the embellishments and trimming were only completed a short while before the temple was destroyed in A.D. 70.

By all accounts, Herod's temple was something to behold. It consisted of, first, a sacred precinct — also called the court of the Gentiles — a platform which Herod had built up around the upper part of Mt. Zion (or Mt. Moriah). In this area Jews and Gentiles alike could gather for prayer, study, or exchanging money and buying sacrificial animals (see Plan, p. 41).

The court of women marked the dividing point between Jews and Gentiles since no Gentile could cross beyond that point. This area (135 x 135 cubits) was the location for public worship for all Israelites. Here the High Priest read the Torah on the Day of Atonement. Women could not proceed beyond this area.

The inner court, consisting of the court of Israel for all male Israelites, and the priests' court, was the location of most of the temple rituals. The Levites stood to sing in the priests' court. Here the altar of sacrifices stood and the laver for purification of the priests and their sacrifices. Within this area also stood the sanctuary itself, which measured 100 cubits long, 70 cubits wide and 100 cubits high. The sanctuary was divided into two parts, the Holy Place and the Holy of Holies, with a curtain between the two chambers. In the Holy Place stood the Golden Altar (for incense), the Golden Table of Shewbread, and the Golden Lampstand. Only the priests could enter the Holy Place. In the Holy of Holies stood, in place of the lost Ark of the Covenant, a stone. Only the High Priest entered this chamber and then only on the Day of Atonement to sprinkle blood.

The temple officials consisted in the main of priests and Levites. The non-aristocratic priests — those not of a High Priestly family — were divided into twenty-four divisions and served in the temple for one week at a time, thus about twice a year. The rest of the time they might engage in a craft or farming. Many lived outside

Jerusalem in Judea and Galilee.

During their week of duty in Jerusalem, the priests offered the sacrifices and burned the incense in the temple. They kept themselves in a state of ritual purity by washing in ritual baths in the temple and wore white garments as symbolic of their purity. They determined their various duties of the day by casting lots in the morning (m. Tamid 3:1).

The Levites were mainly involved as gatekeepers and singers/instrument players. As gatekeepers they insured that no one unclean could enter the temple area. As singers they sang the special Psalms during sacrifices and feast days and played lyres, harps, and cymbals. They too were divided into twenty-four divisions and served one week at a time in the temple.

Over the entire procedure of the temple stood the High Priest. The High Priest permanently resided and worked in Jerusalem but did not usually conduct the sacrifices except on Sabbaths and feast days. His prestige as religious head of the nation and his wealth as recipient of tithes and probably owner of large tracts of lands made him the second most powerful man in Palestine, after the political ruler. In addition to presiding over the temple cultus, the High Priest was president of the Sanhedrin.

Second to the High Priest in authority was the captain of the temple (called *sagan*, סְגָן, in Hebrew). He is mentioned not only in the Mishnah but in the New Testament (Acts 4:1; 5:24-26). He was also a member of the ruling High Priestly family and evidently was responsible for the daily routine of the temple.

The temple opened and closed each day with the offering of a lamb and the recitation of the *shema* (שְׁמַע, from the first word of the verse, Deut 6:4). In addition were the feast day ceremonies: the water procession at Tabernacles, the lamb slaying at Passover, the release of the Red Heifer and the blood sprinkling on the Day of Atonement, and so forth. The ritual for each of these feasts is described in the Mishnah and is presumably in the main correct.

But the people would bring sacrifices in addition to these. They might bring sin offerings or guilt offerings to expiate some offense or they could give free will offerings out of thanksgiving. Some of these offerings were holocausts and thus the entire animal — except for certain parts going to the priests — was burned. Most offerings were only partially burned on the altar with the rest eaten by the pilgrim and his party in a solemn meal.

Such daily ritual required a good supply of sacrificial animals as well as a supply of salt (Lev 1:13) since most sacrifices had to be accompanied with it. Obviously the temple needed a great quantity of wood for the altar and a quantity of water as well for washing down the area and for the purification of the participants, for blood was splattered everywhere.

Another important function connected with the temple and presided over by the High Priest was the Sanhedrin. The Sanhedrin was a body of 71 distinguished justices which judged civil and criminal cases.[1] On the council were members of the High Priest's family, scribes — i.e., experts in the Old Testament Law — and so-called elders or aristocratic laymen, with the High Priest as chief justice. Men both of the Sadducean and Pharisaic parties served on the Sanhedrin but the Pharisaic party was probably in the minority.

The origin of this court is shrouded in silence, but it is likely that it began under the Ptolemies and Seleucids. We read about a "council" (γερουσία, gerousia) which decided important matters at that time (1 Macc 12:6; 2 Macc 1:10; 4:44) although it was not called a Sanhedrin.

The Sanhedrin met in the Hall of Hewn Stone adjacent to the temple (see plan, opposite) usually during the time of daily sacrifice, but not on Sabbaths or feast days. The members sat in a semi-circle to enable them to see one another and the accused stood in the middle. The court was evidently prohibited by the Romans from deciding capital cases, except in the case of a Gentile desecrating the temple.

Finally, we must mention the temple treasury and bank. The temple had its own treasury funded by the yearly temple tax of one half shekel on all male Israelites. This fund paid for the upkeep of

---

[1]The Rabbinic sources describe a council, bet-din (בֵּית־דִּין), which was led by Pharisees and decided religious matters as well. Whether there were two deliberative bodies, a criminal court and a religious court — which is doubtful — or only a criminal court, we cannot certainly decide. One must always be cautious, however, in using the Talmud uncritically as a historical source.

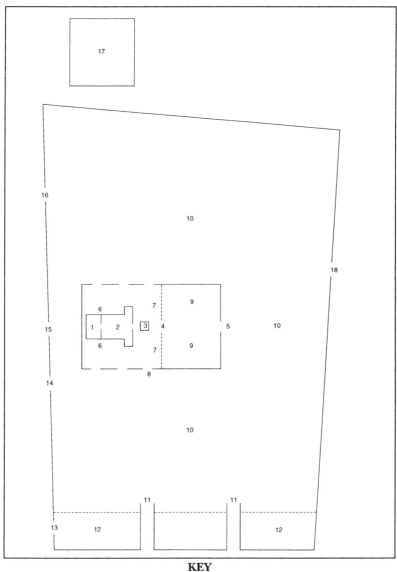

KEY

1. Holy of Holies	7. Court of Israel	13. Robinson's Arch
2. Holy Place	8. Hall of Hewn Stone	14. Wilson's Arch
3. The Altar	9. Court of Women	15. Warren's Gate
4. Nicanor's Gate	10. Court of the Gentiles	16. West Gate
5. Gate Beautiful	11. Huldah Gates (tunnels)	17. Tower of Antonia
		(military garrison)
6. Court of the Priests	12. Solomon's Portico	18. Golden Gate

(For greater detail, see the works of Safrai and Stinespring) the temple buildings, purchased the daily offering, as well as, no doubt, financing the Sanhedrin — although presumably most members of this body were wealthy. From time to time the treasury also paid for repairs and buildings throughout the city of Jerusalem.

In addition the temple may have served as a bank or currency exchange. Money could be exchanged from one currency — Tyrian, Attic, Roman, etc. — to another for a fee. This exchange was both for the temple, since one could only pay the temple tax in Tyrian coinage, and for business in general.

The main reason anyone came to the temple in Jerusalem of course, was to celebrate the feasts. The most important feast, Passover, was celebrated for seven days in the Jewish month of Nisan. Passover included eating the passover lamb, unleavened bread, and bitter herbs in Jerusalem to commemorate the exodus from Egypt. The lamb would first have to be slaughtered in the temple precincts, then taken to a place of residence to be roasted (see Exod 12:1-13:16). The Passover is referred to often in the New Testament (John 2:13; 6:4; 12:1; Acts 12:3).

The feast of Weeks or Pentecost was a one-day feast, kept in the month of Sivan. It marked the end of the grain harvest (Lev 23:15-21). It was during Pentecost that the church began (Acts 2:1).

The feast of Tabernacles took place in the month of Tishri and lasted seven days. It commemorated Israel's wandering in the wilderness for forty years when they lived in tents or tabernacles (Lev 23:33-43; Num 29:12-32). This feast is mentioned in John 7:2.

In addition to the three main feasts found in the Old Testament Law, Judaism had added two more by the New Testament period. The feast of Dedication or Hanukkah celebrated the dedication of the temple after it was liberated by Judas Maccabeus (see Chapter 1 and 1 Macc 4:52-59). This feast is referred to in John 10:22 and was celebrated in the month Chislev.

The second new feast, Purim, was celebrated in the month Adar. It recalled the deliverance of the Jews from Haman by Esther and Mordecai (Esther 9:24-28). This feast is not alluded to in the New Testament unless John 5:1, which mentions an unidentified feast, is referring to it.

In addition to the feasts there was one fast, Yom Kippur or the

Day of Atonement, held in the month Tishri. This was a day of repentance and expiation (see Lev 23:26-32; Num 29:7-11). The Day of Atonement is mentioned in Acts 27:9 and Hebrews 9:7.

All of these special days required presence in the temple in order to celebrate them. Thus most Jews living at some distance from Jerusalem celebrated them irregularly. Yet at feast time the city would swell with thousands of pilgrims.

Jewish Months

1. Nisan (March-April)
2. Iyyar (April-May)
3. Sivan (May-June)
4. Tammuz (June-July)
5. Ab (July-August)
6. Elul (August-September)
7. Tishri (September-October)
8. Marcheshvan (October-November)
9. Chislev (November-December)
10. Tebeth (December-January)
11. Shebat (January-February)
12. Adar (February-March)

The Synagogue

Bibliography: D.A. Fiensy, *Prayers Alleged to be Jewish*; J. Heineman, *Prayer in the Talmud*; J. Mann, *The Bible as Read and Preached in the Old Synagogue*; S. Safrai, "The Synagogue" in *The Jewish People in the First Century*; S. Sandmel, *Judaism and Christian Beginnings*; H. Shanks, *Judaism in Stone.*

Primary sources: Rabbinic sources; archaeology; the Gospels and Acts; *NTB* 187-194.

The second great Jewish institution was the synagogue. Although it seems reasonable that the synagogue began during the exile as many of the older scholars have maintained, this assumption is by no means proven. All that we can say with certainty is that regardless of when synagogues began appearing — during the exile, after the exile, or in the Hasmonean period — they were widespread by the first century A.D., existing throughout Palestine and the Diaspora.

While the temple was run by priests, the synagogue was operated by the general populace.[2] They selected a head of the synagogue (m. Sota 7:7; Luke 13:14) who administered its services. He would have been a fairly well-educated man who could judge the abilities of the Torah readers and preachers who might be on hand for Sabbath services. The head of the synagogue was usually a man of some financial means and thus was not paid for this service but enjoyed the honor of it.

The synagogue had two main functions: prayer and study. It was first and foremost a house of prayer. They would recite the *Shema* (Deut 6:4) as in the temple but in addition there gradually developed a rather fixed set of prayers called the Eighteen Benedictions. Though the final form of these prayers was not set until a century later, the prototypes of these Eighteen Benedictions were already present.

One of the prayers that probably was recited in the first century synagogue is as follows:

"Blessed are you, O Lord our God, and God of our fathers, God of Abraham, Isaac and Jacob. . . . Blessed are you, O Lord, Shield of Abraham."

Another prayer emphasizes belief in the resurrection: "Blessed are you, O Lord, who makes the dead alive."

Another prayer reflects language from Isaiah 6 to extol the greatness of God:

"Holy, holy, holy, Lord of Hosts, all the earth is full of your glory. . . . There is no God beside you. Blessed are you, O Lord, the Holy God."

The prayers were recited while standing with someone

---

[2]The frequent assertion that the Pharisees presided over the synagogue is untenable. It would have taken extraordinary organization and intercommunication for one religious party to control the thousands of synagogues.

appointed to lead the congregation, perhaps the head of the synagogue or an assistant.

The second main function of the synagogue was study both for children and adults. Younger children were taught to read Hebrew and older children the content and exposition of the Old Testament. The teacher in this would have been a sage or scribe employed by the village or perhaps paid by tuition fees. Most scholars agree that Jewish children generally were taught to read, but one must not assume that there were not many exceptions. Children from extremely poor families probably had to work.

Girls were most likely not invited to the synagogue school. Although there are references to female Torah scholars, they were apparently few in number. One famous rabbi is supposed to have declared, "There is no wisdom for a woman except at the spindle" (see Safrai).

Adults continued their study of Torah during Sabbath worship.[3] In addition to the prayers said on Sabbath, someone would read a selection of Scripture from the Torah scroll which was kept in a chest and unrolled with great ceremony. At a later time, the lectionaries were standardized so that the entire Torah/Pentateuch would be read every three years. It is not certain, however, if that sort of standardization existed in Palestine in the first century. In addition to reading the Torah passage someone would read from the prophets. After the Torah was read from the Hebrew text, someone would translate it — usually in a paraphrase rather than literally — in the local vernacular. In Palestine therefore one translated the text into Aramaic. These Aramaic paraphrases also became standardized and were later written down as the Targums. (See Appendix 3.) In most parts of the Diaspora, on the other hand, a Greek version was used, at first the Septuagint, later Aquila's version (see Chapter 1). After the translation, someone — often a scribe, but anyone who wished and whom the head of the synagogue approved — made comments about the text or preached a sermon on it.

It is not clear whether most synagogues in the first century had a special building for their meetings or if other public buildings were

---

[3]It is also possible that worship and study took place on Mondays and Thursdays.

used. The ruins of most of the oldest synagogues found in Palestine indicate they were built in the latter part of the second century A.D. Synagogue ruins from the first century, however, have been found at Masada, Herodium — both of which were in Herodian fortresses and not village synagogues — and at Gamala. In addition, some archaeologists believe the synagogue building in Capernaum, which is from the second century, rests on foundations from Jesus' time. Thus surely some synagogue buildings did exist in the first century but many villages probably met on the Sabbath in private houses or perhaps in other public buildings.

SECTS

Essenes

Bibliography: R.T. Beckwith, "The Pre-History and Relationships of the Pharisees, Sadducees, and Essenes: A Tentative Reconstruction" *Revue de Qumran* 11 (1986) 3-46; F.F. Bruce, *Second Thoughts on the Dead Sea Scrolls*; J.H. Charlesworth, "The Origin and Subsequent History of the Authors of the Dead Sea Scrolls: Four Transitional Phases Among the Qumran Essenes" *Revue de Qumran* 10 (1979-81) 213-233; F.M. Cross, *The Ancient Library of Qumran*; P.R. Davies, *Behind the Essenes*; D. Gowan, *Bridge Between the Testaments*; G. Jeremias, *Der Lehrer der Gerechtigkeit*; K. Kohler, "Essenes" *JE* (pre-Qumran article); W.S. LaSor, *The Dead Sea Scrolls and the New Testament*; J. Murphy-O'Connor, "The Essenes and Their History" *Revue Biblique* 81 (1974) 215-244; H. Ringgren, *The Faith of Qumran*; L.H. Schiffman, "The Significance of the Scrolls" *Bible Review* (October 1990); Idem, "New Light on Insights from the Dead Sea Scrolls" *Bible Review* (June 1992); J.E.H. Thompson, "Essenes" *ISBE* o.s. (a pre-Qumran article); R. de Vaux, *Archaeology and the Dead Sea Scrolls*; G. Vermes and M.D. Goodman, *The Essenes*; G. Vermes, *The Dead Sea Scrolls*; Idem, *The Dead Sea Scrolls in English*; B.Z. Wacholder, *The Dawn of Qumran*.

Primary sources: Josephus, *War, Antiquities*; Philo; Pliny the Elder, *Natural History*; Hippolytus of Rome; the Dead Sea Scrolls (see Appendix 3); *NTB* 210-224, 135-137.

There has never been unanimity about the Essenes.[4] In the older works (before 1947) scholars wrestled with the discrepancies found among the classical sources (Josephus, Pliny, Philo, Hippolytus) and came to sometimes very different conclusions about the origin and nature of this Jewish sect. Then in 1947 the Dead Sea Scrolls were discovered at Qumran and things have only gotten more confused. There was for a while a consensus of a sort about the Essenes but now that consensus is being challenged by re-evaluation of the sources. To make matters worse (or better) new documents from Qumran — most notably one labeled 4QMMT — which are now published, promise to add more confusion.

At this point we can only present what the consensus has been and await further developments. The writings of Vermes, with some modifications from Jeremias and Davies, can represent what had been agreed upon rather broadly and perhaps will even remain the commonly accepted view after the newer documents are out.

First, the community at Qumran, described in the Dead Sea Scrolls and whose material remains have been left behind in the settlement at Qumran, were Essenes. Too much evidence exists — the similarity in theology and practice between the scrolls and what the classical sources say — to conclude otherwise. Thus one can (cautiously) use certain of the scrolls in combination with the classical sources to construct the history and characteristics of the Essenes.

Second, the origin and history of the Essenes were as follows: Sometime after the exile, probably in the early second century B.C., the sect began. Many scholars claim an affinity between the Essenes and Pharisees and with the Hasidim (see Chapter 1). If that is true, both sects were derivatives from the Hasidim. (But Schiffman believes the Essenes were an offshoot from the Sadducees.) At any rate the early Essenes followed an interpreter of the Torah who laid down new halakah (legal precepts) about marriage, the calendar, and other rules. At some point this charismatic teacher/interpreter — called the Teacher of Righteousness — arose in the community. He was of High Priestly, Zadokite, lineage and thus opposed

---

[4]Even the name is debated. Does the name Essenes mean the "pious ones" or the "healers"?

Jonathan, the Hasmonean, who erroneously accepted the High Priesthood for himself. Jonathan is known in the scrolls as the "Wicked Priest." At this point (about 150 B.C.) the Essenes led by the Teacher of Righteousness went into the desert to Qumran and pronounced the temple cultus in Jerusalem invalid (because its High Priest was of improper lineage). Essenes also lived at many other villages and apparently one group lived near the southwest gate of Jerusalem. Philo reported that there were 4000 Essenes in Palestine in his day.

The exile of at least some of the Essenes in the desert at Qumran may also mark the formal split between the Essenes and Pharisees, for the Pharisees accepted the new High Priestly order. Henceforth the Pharisees are called by the Essenes the "seekers after smooth things." The Teacher of Righteousness was opposed at some point within the community by a figure called the "Man of Lies" who may have become the leader of the Pharisees.

The Essene community at Qumran, and presumably the other Essenes scattered all over Palestine, rejoiced when the Hasmoneans were conquered by Rome in 63 B.C. But later the community changed its attitude toward Rome and regarded Rome as the eschatological enemy. When the war broke out in A.D. 66, some of the Essenes fought against the Romans, notably John the Essene, one of the Jewish commanders (see Josephus, *War*) and the Essenes present at Masada (whom archaeology has identified).

Third, the practices of the Essenes were as follows:

1. A one-year, followed by a two-year probationary period were required for one to become a member of the sect.

2. Only adult males were admitted to the sect though children were taken in to educate.

3. The members were celibate except for one sub-group within the Essenes that practiced marriage.

4. The members surrendered all of their possessions to the community and lived in personal poverty.

5. They forbade the practice of slavery.

6. They forbade the use of oaths (as did Jesus).

7. They bathed in cold water before each meal.

8. They wore white robes like the priests in the temple.

9. The eating of a meal together as a community was considered highly important. The priests of the community prepared the meal according to their purity rules, they took their ritual bath, then assembled for the meal. No uninitiated person could participate.

10. They practiced healing and cultivated the knowledge of medicinal herbs.

11. The Essenes also believed they had prophetic gifts, and Josephus offers several examples of their prophecies that came true.

Essene beliefs are best discovered in the Dead Sea Scrolls. Their theology begins with belief in the absolute providence and sovereignty of God. Everything that happens is predestined or "appointed" by God. This predestination includes nature, history, and individual actions and thoughts. God has created two spirits or powers: good and evil. Man's behavior depends on belonging to the domain of one of these spirits. Those belonging to the domain of the good are called "Sons of Light" and those belonging to the bad "Sons of Darkness."

God's plan, his predestination for the universe, is a secret (Aramaic: רז, *raz*). He has appointed a time for evil to predominate and then it will be destroyed. These mysteries are partly in the Old Testament but one must interpret it properly to see the mysteries. Thus God has given insight to the Teacher of Righteousness and has caused him to know the secrets. God has, then, made his esoteric teaching known to his elect through the Teacher of Righteousness.

The New Testament and the Essenes

Bibliography: M. Black, *The Scrolls and Christian Origins*; J.H. Charlesworth, ed., *John and Qumran*; D. Howlett, *The Essenes and Christianity*; J. Murphy-O'Connor, ed., *Paul and Qumran*; W.S. LaSor, *The Dead Sea Scrolls and the New Testament*; K. Stendahl, *The Scrolls and the New Testament*.

The Essenes are never mentioned in the New Testament but that has not prevented speculation about their influence. Various scholars allege that John the Baptist and even Jesus were Essenes, were reared by Essenes, or were influenced by Essenes. Others suggest that the early Christian community — or the "Hellenists" in that community (Acts 6) — was largely Essenic or influenced by Essenes (see the survey of these ideas in LaSor). Still others see Jesus as refuting specific Essene ideas or understand Paul or the Johannine writings as standing theologically opposed to Essenism (see Charlesworth and Murphy-O'Connor). This is not to mention the unusual and bizarre theories that the Dead Sea Scrolls have inspired.[5]

What we can say with confidence about the Essenes and the New Testament is as follows: Certainly Jesus and John the Baptist knew Essenes. Essenes were too numerous for them not to have known them. Possibly some Essenes were converted to earliest Christianity and were thus a part of the Jerusalem church described in Acts. One can understand Johannine and Pauline concepts (e.g., flesh and spirit) better by comparing and contrasting them with the concepts in the scrolls.

But if John the Baptist and Jesus ever had been Essenes — which is certainly doubtful — they were no longer so by the time we encounter them in the Gospels. John and Jesus invited sinners freely to repentance and Jesus even ate with them. Both of these actions are very unlike Essenes. The early church did at times hold all possessions in common but not in the same way as the Essenes (see Chapter 6).

Pharisees

Bibliography: L. Baeck, *Pharisees*; S. Cohen, *From Maccabees to Mishnah*; W.D. Davies, *Introduction to the Pharisees*; E. Ferguson, *Backgrounds of Early Christianity*; L. Finkelstein, *The Pharisees*; D. Gowan, *Bridge Between the Testaments*; R.T. Herford, *The Pharisees*; G.F. Moore, *Judaism*; J. Neusner, *From Politics to Piety*; Idem, *Rabbinic Traditions about the Pharisees Before 70*; E. Rivkin, *A Hidden Revolution*; A.J. Saldarini, *Pharisees, Scribes, and Sadducees*; SVM.
Primary sources: Josephus; the Mishnah; Gospels and Acts; *NTB* 135, 153-154.

---

[5]See the reference to J. Allegro's publications and allegations in LaSor.

The name Pharisee means "separated." That much is agreed upon. But scholars debate from what this group separated itself. Did they separate themselves from the common folk, from the Hasmoneans, from the Sadducees, or from the Hasidim? Further, were the Pharisees a political party or a religious sect? The answers to these questions depend on how one constructs the history of this sect.

The historical reconstruction of Neusner is still probably the best and most of the other recent attempts to understand the Pharisees borrow from or interact with him. Thus we will offer his view of the history of the sect.

We first meet with the Pharisees in Josephus in the High Priesthood of John Hyrcanus when he dismissed them from his government because of a remark made at a banquet (see Chapter 1). Instead of Pharisees as the dominant political party, Hyrcanus now installed the Sadducees. This hostility was reversed under Queen Alexandra who reinstated the Pharisees in government. This series of events leads us to conclude that the Pharisees were originally a "political action group" (Saldarini's term) which competed with other like groups, especially the Sadducees, for power within the Hasmonean government. Naturally, the Pharisees were also concerned with religious matters – in a government in which the High Priest was also the king, how could they not? – but political power was the main item on their agenda. Moreover, they seem to have been, usually, the dominant party.

Under Herod the Great this emphasis changed. This was the era of one of the greatest Pharisees, named Hillel. Neusner concludes that Hillel changed the direction of the group from political party to pietist sect. Herod would hardly countenance meddling in his political affairs by a troublesome group of religionists, bent on having its way. Thus the group retired from politics and devoted itself entirely to matters of halakah. The Pharisees became a "table-fellowship sect." They moved from "politics to piety," where they remained until the Jewish war of A.D. 66. After the war, the Pharisees emerged again as the politically dominant party within Judaism. Thus during the Herodian period (37 B.C.-A.D. 70), the time of Jesus and the early church, the Pharisees were a quietist sect concerned with table fellowship, purity laws, and tithing. In

Josephus's day the sect numbered 6000 members.

During the reign of Herod the Great two great Pharisees, Hillel and Shammai, became the founders of rival schools. The two schools debated the issues most dear to Pharisees (laws of purity, Sabbath, festivals, and table fellowship) almost always disagreeing with one another. Yet in spite of their many disagreements, they apparently did not split into two separate sects but remained merely two schools of interpretation within Pharisaism.

Many of the stories told about the founders of the schools are probably legendary but they may indicate at least something about the two schools. Hillel was said to be less strict and more progressive; Shammai was known as strict and conservative. A gentile allegedly once told Shammai that he would convert to Judaism if Shammai could explain the Torah to him while he (the gentile) stood on one foot. The irascible Shammai drove him away with a stick. When the same gentile approached Hillel, the great Pharisee responded, "Don't do to others what is hateful to you. This is the Torah and all the rest is commentary."

The many references in the Mishnah to the two schools demonstrate that Pharisaism was not always the same. It changed not only as it moved through history but as one moved from one school to the next. Thus it is erroneous to characterize all Pharisees as agreeing on all matters of the Torah.

Neusner has nothing to say about the origins of the Pharisees and their history before the time of John Hyrcanus. For this information we must depend mostly on the Dead Sea Scrolls and a few references in the Apocrypha (i.e., 1 and 2 Maccabees). Many scholars see the origin of the Pharisees and Essenes as follows:

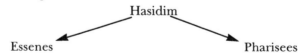

Although this suggestion seems reasonable, there is really no evidence to prove it. Any suggestions about the origin of the Pharisees remain for the present pure speculation.

The general characteristics of the Pharisees are as follows:

1. Primary among the characteristics was the belief in and devotion to the oral Torah. Both Josephus (*Antiquities* 13.297, 408) and

the New Testament (Mark 7:3) refer to the "traditions" (Greek: παραδόσεις, *paradoseis*) that the Pharisees followed and which were handed down from their forefathers. The Mishnah (m. Hagiga 2:2; m. Aboth 1:1-18) and the Tosephta (t. Hagiga 2:8) give lists of tradents who passed on the oral Torah to the next generation. This oral Torah, which the rabbis claimed originated with Moses on Mt. Sinai, was actually an interpretation of the written Torah (the Pentateuch) and a supplementation of it. The adherence to the oral Torah was the main point of contention between Pharisees and Sadducees.

2. The Pharisees taught the general resurrection of the dead and the retribution of the wicked after death, doctrines the Sadducees rejected (*War* 2.163; *Ant* 18.16; Mark 12:18).

3. They believed in the existence of angels and spirits, which the Sadducees denied (Acts 23:8).

4. Josephus writes something about divine sovereignty and free will that is not totally comprehensible. It appears, however, that the Essenes believed in total predestination and absolute divine sovereignty, that the Sadducees rejected these doctrines and that the Pharisees were somewhere in between. God is sovereign, but humans also have free will according to Pharisees (*War* 2.163).

5. The Pharisees concerned themselves much about dietary and purity laws and about tithing. They wanted to be in a state of ritual purity or cleanness as the priests in the temple and so were meticulous about what rendered the hands and garments unclean and the washing of hands (m. Yadaim 4:6; m. Hagiga 2:7; Mark 7:3). Likewise they ate not only kosher food but only grain from which the proper tithes had already been given (m. Demai 6:6; Matt 23:23).

6. The Pharisees were, according to Josephus, the most popular of the Jewish sects. They had the complete confidence of the masses (*Ant* 18.15-17).

7. Finally, we must say a word about the general assumption that all Pharisees were hypocrites, inwardly evil, while appearing outwardly to be pure. Jesus' denunciation of the Pharisees (Matt 23) should not be taken as applying to all Pharisees and thus by extension to all Jews. The Pharisees were in the main a pious sect seeking to live out the will of God as best they could. That Jesus strongly

disagreed with *some* of them is clear but he also seems to have been friends with others of this sect (see Chapter 4).

We can now answer the questions we raised above. From whom did the Pharisees separate themselves? Undoubtedly they separated themselves from the Sadducees (as Rivkin maintains). A group as popular as this could not have separated itself from the masses (as the Essenes did). Were they a political party or a religious sect? Although politics and religion were closely intertwined in ancient Palestine, and even at times inseparable, one can say that the emphasis was on politics before the time of Herod the Great but on religious matters after that.

Sadducees

Bibliography: S. Cohen, *From Maccabees to Mishnah*; D. Gowan, *Bridge Between the Testaments*; A.J. Saldarini, *Pharisees, Scribes, and Sadducees*; *SVM*; M. Simon, *Jewish Sects at the Time of Jesus*.

Primary sources: Josephus; the Mishnah; Gospels and Acts; *NTB* 135.

The origin of the Sadducees is even more mysterious than that of the Essenes and Pharisees. Virtually nothing is known about it. Further, although we have the Dead Sea Scrolls, which presumably represent some of the Essenes, and the Mishnah, which represents at least the descendants of the Pharisees, we have no literature from the Sadducees at all. None of the sources which refer to them are sympathetic or positive. Thus we are even more in the dark in describing the sect.

The name Sadducee undoubtedly derives from the name Zadok, the priest (1 Kings 2:35; Ezek 40:46). The Sadducees saw themselves as the true sons of Zadok, the true priests. They were closely affiliated, then, with the priesthood. But some priests were Pharisees and many belonged to no sect at all; thus the group of priests was certainly not equal to the Sadducees. Since Josephus indicates that they were aristocrats, we should probably think of the Sadducean influence especially among the High Priestly families. They were a group of wealthy High Priests, relatives of the High

Priests and friends of the High Priests. They also had many differences from the Pharisees in interpreting the written Torah and differences in theology.

The characteristics of the Sadducees were as follows:

1. They were aristocrats. Josephus wrote that they could persuade only the rich to their point of view (*Ant* 12.298). One is tempted to add that they only *wanted* to persuade the rich. Aristocrats are seldom concerned about increasing membership. Thus one should think of a rather small, but disproportionately powerful, politico-religious group.

2. They rejected the oral Torah of the Pharisees (*Ant* 13.297). Only the written regulations (i.e., the Pentateuch) were considered binding. It is probably not true, however, that the Sadducees rejected the prophetical books of the Old Testament, as the early church writers sometimes alleged. Josephus does not mention that and it would have been very unusual for any Jew to have done so (the half-Jewish Samaritans did so, however).

3. In penal laws the Sadducees were usually severe and strict, keeping the letter of the law, and the Pharisees were lenient, even putting up legal roadblocks to harsh punishments (*Ant* 20.199; m. Yadaim 4:7; but see by way of contrast m. Makkoth 1:6).

4. The Sadducees did not believe in the resurrection, the immortality of the soul, or afterlife (*War* 2.165; *Ant* 18.16; Mark 12:18; Acts 23:8). They thus deny penalty and reward after death.

5. They denied the existence of angels (Acts 23:8).

6. Finally, the Sadducees denied entirely the operation of predestination on the will of mankind. Men and women are completely free to choose their own conduct, they believed (*War* 2.164).

The Sadducees continued to wield enormous power over the life of the Jewish community until the destruction of the temple in A.D. 70. After that, with the power base of the High Priesthood gone, the sect had no unifying symbol and no source of authority and thus ceased to function.

Zealots, Fourth Philosophy and Sicarii

Bibliography: S.G.F. Brandon, *Jesus and the Zealots*; D. Gowan,

Bridge Between the Testaments; W.R. Farmer, *Maccabees, Zealots and Josephus*; M. Hengel, *The Zealots*; Idem, *Was Jesus a Revolutionist?*; R.A. Horsley and J.S. Hanson, *Bandits, Prophets and Messiahs*; R.A. Horsley, "The Zealots" *Novum Testamentum* 28 (1986) 159-192; D.M. Rhoads, *Israel in Revolution: 6-74 C.E.*; M. Smith, "Zealots and Sicarii, Their Origins and Relation" *Harvard Theological Review* 64 (1971) 1-19.

Primary sources: Josephus, *NTB* 138.

The so-called Fourth Philosophy (Josephus's term) began with Judas of Galilee in A.D. 6. The Sicarii arose to prominence in the fifties and sixties of the first century, and the Zealots are mentioned by Josephus in connection with their activities in A.D. 67-70. We will describe each of these movements below and then determine if they were related to each other in any way.

The Fourth Philosophy, by which Josephus meant the fourth Jewish sect (after the Essenes, Pharisees, and Sadducees), began with Judas the Galilean or Gaulanite. In A.D. 6 when Quirinius, proconsul of Syria, assessed Judea for taxation, Judas incited many Jews to rebel. He took a hard line in his devotion to Yahweh alone as Master and Lord. If Jews paid this tax, he maintained, it would be cowardice and apostasy from their commitment to God.

Judas is called a sophist (sage, teacher or scholar) by Josephus. Thus he was no poor man from the masses but a well-educated teacher of the Torah. He was aided by a man named Saddok, a Pharisee, and Josephus writes that this sect agrees with Pharisaism in other respects but adds to these teachings a passion for liberty and serving God alone as master. The adherents of the Fourth Philosophy thought nothing of submitting to death themselves or seeing their relatives and friends die in the service of their cause.

Judas's armed uprising was apparently defeated and he was killed by Quirinius (Acts 5:37) but his Fourth Philosophy continued its influence. His sons, James and Simon, were executed later by the procurator, Alexander, for their seditious activities. Another relative (called a "son" by Josephus) of Judas, Menahem, was one of the leaders of the Jewish revolt in A.D. 66. Still another kinsman, Eleazar, led the sicarii that held Masada until A.D. 73 (74). Furthermore, Josephus says that Judas and his sect sowed the seeds of rebellion which led eventually to the disaster in A.D. 66-73 (74). Finally, the fact that Josephus called Judas's movement a philosophy and sect indicates it lasted beyond Judas's lifetime as an organized group.

The sicarii arose under the procurator Felix (A.D. 52-60), and were especially troublesome by the time Festus began as procurator (A.D. 60-62). They were so named because of the dagger (called *sica* in Latin) which they concealed under their garments in order to carry out assassinations. They later participated as regular soldiers in the Jewish war and remained bitter enemies of Rome to the very end. The resistance fighters on Masada were mainly sicarii.

The Zealots were first mentioned by name in connection with the Jewish war. We meet them initially in Josephus when the High Priest, Ananus, a moderate (i.e., neither pro-Roman nor fanatically in favor of war), hopes to delay in prosecuting the war and thus possibly turn the fanatical Zealots to a wiser course. The Zealots are always represented as bent on slaughter and killing, unyielding in their lust for war with Rome and feared by any of the Jews that might wish to surrender to Rome. Although we should not necessarily see a continuous Zealot movement and underground resistance in the first century A.D., surely they did not spring up suddenly as the war began. An organized group with a name for itself surely argues for a history prior to A.D. 67.

The three groups were probably not the same sect or movement. There may have been many such movements beginning and ending throughout first century Palestine, a place infested with varying degrees of fanaticism and violence. Jesus may not have had the actual Zealots in mind in any of his teachings or debates, but he almost certainly encountered those who resembled them.

Samaritans

Bibliography: F.M. Cross, "Aspects of Samaritan and Jewish History" *Harvard Theological Review* 59 (1966) 201-211; D. Gowan, *Bridge Between the Testaments*; J. MacDonald, *The Theology of the Samaritans*; J.A. Montgomery, *The Samaritans, the Earliest Jewish Sect.*

Primary sources: The Samaritan Chronicle.

The next two groups we will consider, the Samaritans and scribes, were not strictly speaking Jewish sects. The Samaritans had a separate ethnic identity and different religious history. The scribes were more a guild than a sect. Nevertheless, the two groups are usually discussed in relation to the sects, and it is convenient to do so here.

The Samaritans were the racial and religious descendants of the ten northern tribes which were conquered by the Assyrians in 722 B.C. The aristocrats and the elite were sent by the Assyrians into exile and other conquered peoples were resettled in the Samaritan cities. But the country folk, the villagers, remained mostly untouched by the changes. The Samaritans of Jesus' day represented the first century version of the ten tribes left behind. They practiced in a way an older form of Yahwism which was not influenced by the Babylonian exile of Judah.

But Samaritanism too had made its changes by the first century. The Samaritans had their own High Priesthood and their own account of the origin of this priesthood which differed markedly from the Biblical account (cf. 2 Kgs 17:24-41 with the Samaritan Chronicle). This priestly succession has continued down to the present day. A small group of Samaritans still exists with its priests in modern Israel.

The Samaritan points of doctrine are as follows:

1. They believe in Yahweh as the only God and are thus fiercely monotheistic (not somewhat paganistic as some have alleged).

2. They accept the five books of Moses only (the Pentateuch), rejecting the prophets and the writings.

3. They once had a temple, which was destroyed in the Jewish War of A.D. 66-73 just as the Jewish temple was destroyed. The Samaritans also took part in the Jewish war. Josephus recorded that 11,600 of them were massacred on Mt. Gerizim when their temple was leveled. Samaritans still perform sacrifices on the mountain even though the temple is no longer standing.

4. They believe in a coming day of vengeance and recompense (in other words, a judgment day).

The animosity between Jews and Samaritans is clear both from Josephus and the New Testament. But both Jesus and the early church showed great interest in evangelizing the Samaritans. Jesus portrayed the Samaritans in a favorable light (Luke 10:33) and the early Christian community welcomed them into the church (Acts 8:5-17).

Scribes

Bibliography: M. Back, "Scribes" *IDB*; G.F. Moore, *Judaism*; A.J. Saldarini, *Pharisees, Scribes and Sadducees*; E.E. Urbach, "Class-Status and Leadership in the World of the Palestinian Sages" *Proceedings of the Israel Academy of Science and the Humanities* 2 (1968) 38-74.

Primary sources: Josephus; the Gospels; Rabbinic literature.

A scribe (Greek γραμματεύς, *grammateus*; Hebrew: סופר, *sofer*) was one learned in the Torah and other wisdom. Saldarini rightly traces the history of this profession from the Old Testament pre-exilic period. They were highly educated government ministers and personal secretaries. Scribes were present in the Maccabean era and one of them, Eleazar (2 Macc 6:18), died a martyr's death for the Torah. The apocryphal book written by Jesus ben Sirah (c. 180 B.C.), who was himself a scribe, describes how one trained for this profession (38:24-39:11). It required knowledge of wisdom, parables, and the Torah, and it necessitated travel to other lands to gain insight. The scribe was of course, according to Ben Sirah, a very devout Yahwist. Josephus also referred to scribes, both high level officials of the government and the village scribes of low status (*War* 1.479). Likewise the New Testament depicts scribes as Torah scholars. They seem to have been located mainly in Jerusalem but were also present in villages.

Saldarini speculates that the village scribe probably could read and write and knew how to compose letters, contracts and petitions for the villagers. At the middle level of the social ladder were the scribes with positions in the government. These latter were educated bureaucrats. At the highest level would have been the highly educated and well-trained scribes described by Ben Sirah. These last scribes were the highest level government ministers.

The scribes then were not a religious sect, a political party or a social class. They were a profession. No organization or group formation can be detected though they may have had guilds. They could be wealthy or poor, politically powerful or insignificant. They were often highly educated but may at times have known only how to write and compose official documents.

Although scribes were not a religious sect they could belong to one. Some belonged to the Pharisees (Mark 2:16; Acts 23:9) and presumably others were Sadducees.

Conclusion

The numerous Jewish sects indicate that Judaism was very pluralistic in antiquity. Pharisaic Judaism apparently won the competition for popularity after A.D. 70 and so made Judaism thereafter normative but before that the scene was confused. Many different sects, theologies and practices vied for followers. Many different sects are listed in the sources — not counting the Samaritans and scribes — but there were undoubtedly more. How many sects perhaps had only ten or twenty members? How many were so secretive that almost no one outside the sect knew of its existence? One can only guess how large the iceberg is by looking at its tip.

RELIGIOUS MOVEMENTS

Prophetic Movements

Bibliography: F.F. Bruce, *New Testament History*; M. Hengel, *The Zealots*; R. Horsley and J.S. Hanson, *Bandits, Prophets and Messiahs*; R. Meyer, "προφήτης" in *TDNT*; G. Vermes, *Jesus the Jew*.

Primary sources: Josephus, *War*.

One could conclude from passages in the apocryphal book of 1 Maccabees (4:46; 9:27; 14:41) and in the Rabbinical literature (t. Sota 13:2) that no prophet existed after Haggai, Zechariah and Malachi. But the evidence shows that at least some claimed to be prophets.

The Essenes were especially cultivators of prophecy (i.e., inspired utterances). Josephus (*War* 2.159) says they claimed to foretell the future as a result of a lifetime of study of the sacred books and adds that few of their prophecies ever were wrong. If the Dead Sea Scrolls found at Qumran were indeed the product of Essenes, as we maintained above, then the so-called Teacher of Righteousness was such an Essene prophetic figure. He was clearly considered inspired by the Essenes. They believed he had been given the Spirit of God and the ability to make known interpretations of Scripture (e.g., Habakkuk) which contained knowledge for the end-time or eschaton.[6]

The Pharisees too had their prophets, though prophecy was not as important among this sect. Sameas, the Pharisee, predicted also that Herod the Great would someday be king (*Ant* 14.174). A group of Pharisees years later predicted that Herod's kingdom would be taken from him (*Ant* 17.43) provoking Herod to execute the predictors. Josephus notes that these Pharisees were believed to have foreknowledge of things. Josephus, who said he was a Pharisee, also claimed prophetic powers. He reported a dream he had (*War* 3.351-354) which he was able to interpret as a prediction of the tragic outcome of the Jewish war. Later, when captured, he predicted that Vespasian would soon be emperor of Rome. Likewise important rabbinic figures such as Hanina ben Dosa, Eliezer ben Hyrcanus and Johanan ben Zakkai supposedly had foreknowledge of certain events.

This evidence must be analyzed carefully. Predictions about future kings or rulers seem to have been common. These may have been only flattery and later turned into prophecy after the flattery came true. Josephus's self-serving claims must always be viewed with scepticism. Nevertheless, there clearly was significant "prophetic" activity among the Essenes and some among the Pharisees.

---

[6]See 4QpHab, the Qumran commentary on Habakkuk.

The troubled period from A.D. 6 to 73 witnessed the coming of many prophetic troublers. Josephus wrote that many imposters and deceivers promised to show great signs in the wilderness and incited the mob into a frenzy. Josephus described in some detail the activity of three such false prophets and more briefly about a fourth one. The first was a Samaritan who did his mischief during the procuratorship of Pontius Pilate (c. A.D. 35). The Samaritan promised he could show the mob where on Mt. Gerizim Moses had buried the holy vessels of the Tabernacle. The excited crowd came with arms evidently expecting revolution to follow quickly (*Ant* 18.85-87).

The next was Theudas (A.D. 45) who promised he could part the Jordan river as Joshua had done. Many of the simple peasant folk gathered their belongings and followed him to the river (*Ant* 20.97-98).

Another false prophet, whom Josephus called the Egyptian, around A.D. 56 promised to make the walls of Jerusalem fall down at his command. He then would overpower the Roman garrison there and take charge of the city (*Ant* 20.169-71; *War* 2.261-63).

Finally, one of the numerous prophets that delivered encouraging promises of success during the Jewish War made a disastrous prediction in A.D. 70. He claimed, incorrectly, that God had decreed that everyone should go to the temple where God would deliver them from the Romans (*War* 6.283-85).

In every case the gullible crowd met with disaster. Hundreds were slaughtered by the unmerciful Romans. In the last case, Josephus writes that 6000, including women and children, died when the Romans burned the temple area. These false prophets kept the mobs stirred up and ultimately led them to their deaths. The prophets themselves — except for the Egyptian who escaped — were caught and executed by the Romans.

One final prophet must be mentioned. Jesus ben Ananias[7] began prophesying in A.D. 62 or 63 that Jerusalem and the temple would be destroyed. He was a man of humble, peasant origins and evidently affected a very strange manner. He walked up and down the streets of Jerusalem day and night shouting his dire words like Jeremiah of old. Although he was flogged within an inch of his life,

---

[7]The name Jesus (Aramaic ישׁוע, *yeshu'a*) was common in this period.

he refused to stop this behavior. Finally, the war started and then came the siege of Jerusalem. Jesus ben Ananias was struck by a missile and killed while walking around the walls of the city (*War* 6.300-309):

> For seven years and five months he continued his wail, his voice as strong as ever and his vigor unabated, till, during the siege, after seeing the fulfillment of his foreboding, he was silenced. He was going his rounds, shouting in penetrating tones from the wall, "Woe, woe once more to the city, and the people and the Temple;" then, when he added a last word, "and woe to me also!" a stone hurled from the ballista struck him, killing him on the spot. Thus, with those same forebodings still upon his lips, he met his end.[8]

Thus prophetic activity was not lacking from 200 B.C. through the fall of Jerusalem. Most of these prophetic figures were persecuted or killed by the Jewish leadership or by the Roman authorities. It was into this situation that John the Baptist and Jesus came preaching the Kingdom of God and they were treated as violently as many of these prophets we have just named.

Miracle Workers

Bibliography: D.R. Cartlidge and D.L. Dungan, *Documents for the Study of the Gospels*; D.C. Duling, "Testament of Solomon" *OTP*, Vol. I; H.C. Kee, *Miracle in the Early Christian World*; M. Smith, *Jesus the Magician*; R.C. Trench, *Notes on the Miracles of Our Lord*; G. Vermes, *Jesus the Jew*.

Primary sources: Rabbinic literature; Josephus.

There were many healers and exorcists in the ancient world. We will discuss in Chapter 6 their presence in Greco-Roman society but for now we could mention the famous healer Apollonius of Tyana and the numerous Greek magical papyri (*NTB* 30, 86-88) which attest of exorcisms.

---

[8]Translation in G. Cornfeld, *Josephus: The Jewish War*, p. 428.

The same phenomena were present among the Palestinian Jews. Solomon had evidently become for them the patron of exorcism, as the pseudepigraphal book, The Testament of Solomon, indicates. Josephus also relates the case of an exorcism performed by a certain Eleazar who lived in the first century A.D. and cast out a demon using secret knowledge he thought came from Solomon:

> He put to the nose of the possessed man a ring which had under its seal one of the roots prescribed by Solomon, and then, as the man smelled it, drew out the demon through his nostrils, and when the man at once fell down, adjured the demon never to come back into him, speaking Solomon's name and reciting the incantations which he had composed (*Ant* 8.46-47).[9]

There were also Jewish miracle workers. Honi the Circle Drawer (first century B.C.), called Onias the Righteous by Josephus, was said to have performed miraculous acts. His most noteworthy miracle was an Elijah-type prayer for rain. Both Josephus (*Ant* 14.22-24) and the Mishnah (m. Taanith 3:8) remembered the miracle. Honi prayed for rain during a time of drought, but it did not rain. Therefore he drew a circle, stood in it, and informed God that he would not move from the circle until God made it rain. At first only a drizzle came, and Honi complained that the rain was not enough. Finally, a good rain descended.

Another great Jewish miracle worker was Rabbi Hanina ben Dosa, who lived in the latter first century A.D. He came from a small village near Sepphoris in Galilee (about ten miles from Nazareth). Reportedly, a poisonous snake once bit Hanina while he was deep in prayer. The snake died but Hanina was unharmed (t. Ber 2:20). On another occasion, R. Johanan ben Zakkai's son was ill, and he asked Hanina to pray for him. Hanina put his head between his knees and prayed and the boy lived (b. Ber 34b). Hanina's most remarkable miracle was when he healed R. Gamaliel II's son from a distance. Emissaries came to Galilee to request prayer, and Hanina ascended into his upper room. After returning, he announced that the boy had been healed in Jerusalem (b. Ber 34b).

---

[9]Translation in G. Vermes, *Jesus the Jew*, p. 63.

That there were miracle workers — charismatic figures called חסיד (*ḥasid*) by the rabbis — in ancient Judaism is clear. Whether they healed or performed miracles by the power of suggestion or actually by the Spirit of God is not clear. God may have empowered certain Jews just as he did in the Old Testament days. But the differences between these alleged miracles and Jesus' miracles — John the Baptist did none — is that Jesus' miracles were signs pointing to his message and validating his message. By his assumed knowledge of secret roots, the exorcist Eleazar practiced knowledge the Jews thought had been passed down, from generation to generation, from Solomon. Jesus' exorcisms meant that the Kingdom of God was breaking into this age and that Satan was being bound (see Chapter 4). Thus the purpose of Jesus' miracles was quite different.

Apocalyptic Authors

Bibliography: J.J. Collins, *Apocalypse, the Morphology of a Genre*; P.D. Hanson, *The Dawn of Apocalyptic*; K. Koch, *The Rediscovery of Apocalyptic*; L. Morris, *Apocalyptic*; G.W. Nickelsburg, *Jewish Literature Between the Bible and the Mishnah*; H.H. Rowley, *The Relevance of the Apocalyptic*; D.S. Russel, *The Method and Message of Jewish Apocalyptic*; M.E. Stone, *Jewish Writings of the Second Temple*; W. Schmithals, *The Apocalyptic Movement*.
Primary sources: *OTP*, Vol. I; *NTB* 260-274.

Apocalyptic literature is somewhat easier to recognize than define. Nevertheless, the best definition is probably that of J.J. Collins which we paraphrase here: An apocalypse is a written document which describes how a revelation was made from God to a human being through an angel. The revelation can be about the future (temporal revelation) or about the heavens as they are now (spatial revelation).

D.S. Russel, in his now classic description of apocalyptic literature, lists four important characteristics:

1. Apocalypses are "esoteric in character." That is, they claim to be disclosing secrets. The secrets often were, it is alleged, written on

heavenly tablets (1 Enoch 81:2, 103:2; Testament of Asher 7:5).

2. Apocalypses are literary in form. They are written documents. While the prophetic movements in the first century were oral, the apocalyptic movement was literary. Writing down the revelation, the secrets, is usually commanded of the recipient (Testament of Moses 1:16).

3. These literary products are highly symbolic in language. Many of the symbols are taken from the Old Testament and others from ancient Near Eastern mythology. There are sea monsters (Testament of Asher 7:3; 1 Enoch 60:7-9; 4 Ezra 6:49-52), great beasts (4 Ezra 13:2), bulls (1 Enoch 85-86), sheep (1 Enoch 89:16), and many other animals. There are stars and other cosmic luminaries (1 Enoch 87:2; Testament of Levi 8:2) and numbers (especially the numbers 3, 4, 7, 10, and 12 and multiples of these numbers. See 2 Enoch and 2 Baruch *passim*). Writing in symbols made it possible for only the initiated or those familiar with apocalypses to understand the message, and it gave the book an attractive vividness and even scariness.

4. Invariably the apocalypses are pseudonymous. That is, they attribute authorship to a hero of the past such as Enoch, Moses, Abraham, Ezra, or Baruch (Jeremiah's secretary). The apocalypse alleges that this ancient figure received this revelation, wrote it down and passed it on to succeeding generations. Why was this literature pseudonymous? Three main suggestions have been offered: a) The real author wanted to protect himself from persecution. b) The author thought that the name of a famous person would insure that the apocalypse would be read. c) Most interesting is Russel's suggestion that the real authors thought they shared something distinctive ("corporate personality") with the ancient heroes. Thus the authors did not regard themselves as original writers but as "inheritors and interpreters" of what the hero of the past had already received. The authors stood in the same tradition as the heroes and were inspired by the same Spirit, they thought.

Collins divides the apocalypses into two categories: apocalypses with historical reviews and apocalypses with heavenly journeys — of course some apocalypses contain both. The first type contains in prophetic form, and often in highly symbolic language, a review of the major events from the exile to the author's own time (see e.g., 4 Ezra). The second type describes a journey through the various levels of heaven (see e.g., 2 Enoch).

According to Collins, there are approximately fifteen apocalypses imbedded in nine documents which have survived from this period.[10] They are published in collections of pseudepigrapha. J.H. Charlesworth, however, has published nineteen apocalypses (*OTP*, Vol. I) in his now standard collection. The size of the apocalyptic corpus will vary from scholar to scholar but all agree that the most important apocalypses are 1 Enoch, 2 Enoch, 2 Baruch, 3 Baruch, 4 Ezra, the Apocalypse of Abraham, and parts of the Testaments of the Twelve Patriarchs.

What historical and social conditions produced this literature? Much of it clearly has been written in a period of stress. Jews were either being persecuted or recovering and healing after the destruction of their nation. During such tremendous stress, the cosmic picture with its vivid symbols and the underlying message of all these apocalypses — that God is the sovereign of the cosmos — must have been reassuring. But some of the apocalypses were apparently not written in such times. They represent not a desperate cry for relief from suffering but a way of looking at reality that is very much centered on a lofty and elevated God who controls the course of history. These apocalypses are a call to otherworldliness and to righteousness.

The influence of these writings, especially the historical apocalypses, on the Jewish masses must have been substantial. For example, Josephus reports that in A.D. 66 at the Passover some silly people claimed the altar in the temple glowed brightly and others alleged that a cow gave birth to a lamb in the temple. A few days later some people said they saw war chariots in the sky. These were interpreted as apocalyptic signs that the end-time was near and the Romans would be overthrown. In A.D. 70, during the siege of Jerusalem, some said they saw a star in the shape of a sword standing over Jerusalem, and a comet appeared in the sky for many days

---

[10] 1 Enoch for example is actually a composite of five main parts and several other small parts. Each of these sections must have existed at one time as separate apocalypses.

(*War* 6.288-299). The apocalypses stirred people up to look for such signs. They pictured in colorful symbolism the slaying of monsters which represented the Romans (or in earlier apocalypses, represented the Macedonians). They predicted Israel's return to righteousness. And many apocalypses spoke of the mysterious one who was to come: the Messiah.

Messianism

Bibliography: R.H. Charles, *Eschatology*; J.H. Charlesworth, ed., *The Messiah*; A. Edersheim, *The Life and Times of Jesus the Messiah*; R. Horsley and J.S. Hanson, *Bandits, Prophets, and Messiahs*; J. Klausner, *The Messianic Idea in Israel*; S. Mowinckel, *He That Cometh*; J. Neusner, *Messiah in Context*; G.W.E. Nickelsburg, *Resurrection, Immortality and Eternal Life in Intertestamental Judaism*; R. Patai, *The Messiah Texts*; H. Ringgren, *The Messiah in the Old Testament*; D.S. Russel, *The Method and Message of Jewish Apocalyptic*; SVM.

Primary sources: Apocrypha and Pseudepigrapha; Dead Sea Scrolls; Josephus; Rabbinic Literature; *NTB* 271-274.

Many passages in the Old Testament indicate that Yahweh would some day intervene in history to establish his kingdom in a new and final way (Micah 5; Isa 11; Ezek 40-48). Often the Scriptures indicate that God's agent in this kingdom would be an anointed one (מָשִׁיחַ, *mašiaḥ*), a prince (נָשִׂיא, *naśi'*), the righteous branch, the son of David, or the king (מֶלֶךְ, *melek*; see Jeremiah 23:5f; Zechariah 9:9; Daniel 9:25f; Isaiah 9:6f).

In addition to the royal Messiah predicted in the Old Testament there is a reference in Isaiah (49:1-9; 52:13-53:12) to a "servant" who suffers for his people. His suffering brings salvation and reconciliation between God and Israel.

A third kind of figure in the Old Testament is the "Son of Man" (Daniel 7:13) who is an exalted, heavenly person.

The Messianic expectations during the time of Jesus derive from such Old Testament passages as well as from other influences. These expectations were part of the cultural life of the people Jesus and the early church preached to and are thus very important to understand if anyone would interpret the New Testament.

For the sake of convenience, we will follow the outline given in *SVM*, keeping in mind that the speculation about the Messiah on the part of many ancient Jews was much more varied than presented here. Still this outline can serve as a useful organization of the material.

Usually, before the Messiah comes in the Jewish literature of our period of study, there is a time of tribulation. This is what the Rabbinic literature terms "the birth pangs of the Messiah." Many cosmic events will indicate this time has arrived: the sun and moon will be darkened; swords will appear in the sky; blood will drip from wood; and sin will run rampant. Next, it was believed, the forerunner Elijah will come. He will establish peace on earth and bring order. Some groups (at Qumran) may have also looked for an end-time Prophet like Moses. The Dead Sea Scrolls mentioned this figure, and R. Akiba served in that capacity for Bar Kosiba.

Then comes the Messiah, the King, the Son of David. He will conquer all the ungodly nations and allow no unrighteousness. He will be an earthly king, a warrior, but will have special gifts and powers because he will be endowed with the Holy Spirit. The main functions of the Messiah would be — according to the Jewish literature of antiquity — to punish ungodly Gentiles, to gather Israel into its homeland, and to establish justice and righteousness (all taken from Old Testament prophecies).

The clearest statement as to the work of the Messiah is found in the pseudepigraphical Psalms of Solomon 17:21-32, written in the mid-first century B.C.:

> See Lord and raise up for them their king, the son of David, to rule over your servant Israel in the time known to you, O God. Undergird him with the strength to destroy the unrighteous rulers, to purge Jerusalem from gentiles who trample her to destruction; in wisdom and in righteousness to drive out the sinners from the inheritance; to smash the arrogance of sinners like a potter's jar; to shatter all their substance with an iron rod; to destroy the unlawful nations with the word of his mouth; At his warning the nations will flee from his presence; and he will condemn sinners by the thoughts of their hearts.

> He will gather a holy people whom he will lead in righteous-
> ness; and he will judge the tribes of the people that have been
> made holy by the Lord their God. . . . And he will be a right-
> eous king over them, taught by God. There will be no unright-
> eousness among them in his days, for all shall be holy, and
> their king shall be the Lord Messiah.[11]

The Messiah smashes the Gentiles as a rod of iron shatters clay
pots. He is then a military hero, a mighty warrior. This concept certainly seems to have been at play in the examples of would-be
Messiahs that are referred to in the historical records. Horsley and
Hanson list six examples from Josephus: Judas, son of Hezekiah
(not the same as Judas the Galilean), Simon, and Athronges led
respective rebellions in 4 B.C. at the death of Herod the Great.
According to Josephus, at least one of these Messianic claimants,
Athronges, was unusually large, often considered an important
characteristic for a king in the Ancient Near East. Two other
Messianic hopefuls were Menahem, the son or grandson of Judas of
Galilee, founder of the Fourth Philosophy, and Simon Bar Giora.
Both of these men led military forces during the Jewish war of A.D.
66-73. Finally, Bar Kosiba was military commander of a later Jewish
war, A.D. 132-135.

Thus, all the known examples of Jewish Messiah claimants,
except Jesus of Nazareth, were militaristic men of battle who led
forces of war and were themselves probably fierce fighters. They
sought further to conquer the Romans, the godless Gentiles, and to
establish justice in the land.

Note should be made, however, of three exceptions to the
general pattern. First, texts were found at Qumran that mention,
alongside the Davidic-warrior Messiah, the expectation of an
Aaronic-priestly Messiah (see 1QS and 1QSa). Thus the Essenes
expected two Messiahs, one to wage war and the other to officiate
in the temple. The same phenomenon is in the Testaments of the
Twelve Patriarchs.

Second, the title Son of Man, from Daniel 7, is taken in one
section of 1 Enoch as the more important title for the Messiah and

---

[11]Translation by R.B. Wright in *OTP*, Vol. II.

his heavenly origin is emphasized. This passage (1 Enoch 37–71) describes the Son of Man as the exalted judge of all the earth. But apart from 4 Ezra, this messianic title is not employed elsewhere in Jewish literature. Jesus, however, used it often to refer to himself.

Third, the idea of Suffering Servant from Isaiah is rare, though certain late Rabbinic texts do indicate an expectation that the Messiah would suffer for the sins of humanity. But the warrior Messiah was a more popular concept in Jesus' day. The Suffering Servant idea, however, was basic for Jesus' self-understanding.

After the Messiah appeared, according to popular Jewish speculation, there would be one final and major assault on him by the Gentile powers. The leader of this assault would be a chief adversary, an antichrist figure according to the literature. The hostile powers and their leader would be annihilated in battle either by actual fighting or, as some texts have it, "by the word of (the Messiah's) mouth."

After the great battle would come the time of renewal, restoration, and gathering of the dispersed Israelite tribes. There would be great wealth, prosperity and joy in Israel, and the Messiah would establish peace. Everyone will enjoy good health, and women will bear children without pain. The new kingdom will be devoted to obedience to God and thus is called the Kingdom of God. The Messiah will not allow unrighteousness. The following passage from 2 Baruch 29 captures the expectant joy of this age:

> And it will happen that when all that which should come to pass in these parts has been accomplished, the Anointed One (Messiah) will begin to be revealed. . . . The earth will also yield fruits ten thousandfold. And on one vine will be a thousand branches, and one branch will produce a thousand clusters, and one cluster will produce a thousand grapes, and one grape will produce a cor of wine. And those who are hungry will enjoy themselves and they will moreover, see marvels every day. For winds will go out in front of me every morning to bring the fragrance of aromatic fruits and clouds at the end of the day to distill the dew of health. And it will happen at that time that the treasury of manna will come down again from on high, and they will eat of it in those years because

these are they who will have arrived at the consummation of time.[12]

The temple ritual would also be maintained in the Messianic Kingdom of God. Even the Essenes who withdrew from the temple cultus believed proper worship there would be restored. Life in the kingdom would be mostly taken up in service to God.

Not only would Israelites already alive at the time of the Messiah participate, but also those that had died. They would arise from their graves to share in this glorious prosperity and peace. (Only the Sadducees denied the resurrection.) The wicked would remain dead according to some texts, but according to others they would also be raised in order to be judged and punished.

For some, the Messianic kingdom was everlasting, though the Messiah himself was not usually thought of as immortal. For others, the kingdom was but the last phase of this world. After a lengthy period of prosperity, this kingdom would end, and God would create a new heaven and earth for eternity.

Much of this typical Jewish expectation about the Messiah was taken, of course, from Old Testament prophecies. The excessive emphasis on material property and wealth in the kingdom, however, comes from Jewish speculation more than from Scripture. Likewise, the view of the Messiah as a kind of superman, mighty in battle but very mortal, was based more on the culture of the time than the Old Testament.

It was doubtless because of such expectations about the Messiah that Jesus urged his disciples not to tell anyone at first that he was the Messiah (Mark 8:30). Much of Jesus' ministry and teaching was devoted to redefining who the Messiah was.

Religious Practices Among the Common Folk

Bibliography: J.H. Charlesworth, "Jewish Astrology in the Talmud, Pseudepigrapha, The Dead Sea Scrolls, and Early Palestinian Synagogues" *Harvard Theological Review* 70 (1977) 183-200; L.

---

[12]Translation by A.F.J. Klijn in *OTP*, Vol. I.

Finkelstein, *The Pharisees*; A. Oppenheimer, *The Am Ha-Aretz*; R. Redfield, *Peasant Society*; S. Safrai, "Religion in Everyday Life" *Judaism in the First Century*; J.F. Strange, "Archaeology and the Religion of Judaism in Palestine" *ANRW* II.19.1 (1979) 646-680.

Primary sources: m. Demai; archaeology.

One might get the impression that everyone in Palestine belonged to one of the religious sects in the first century A.D. That impression is, of course, not true. There were only 6000 Pharisees, 4000 Essenes, and a few hundred Sadducees in the mid-first century, out of a total Jewish population of between two and three million. Thus the vast majority of the masses belonged to no sect. Indeed, they had neither time nor inclination to worry about the niceties of interpretation. Their energy was spent in growing and seeking food.

In every peasant culture, there is a view of things among the educated elite and another view among the uneducated masses. The educated had time and ability to study the Torah, but the poor farmers and craftsmen often did not. The ordinary peasant therefore practiced his adherence to Torah in ways different from the educated. This is clear both from the literature and from archaeology.

The most important distinction between the peasant and the Pharisees was the failure to surrender the tithes. There were two agricultural tithes due plus a wave offering. The peasant almost always, it would seem, gave the wave offering (1/40 to 1/50), but he was often reluctant to surrender 20% of his grain harvest.

Second, the ordinary peasants were lax about keeping the Sabbatical year. Every seventh year, according to Deuteronomy 15, the land had to lie fallow. The Jews of Palestine[13] often tried to obey this law, as the ancient sources show, but there were always suspicions that the ordinary folk had sown and were reaping their fields in that year.

In addition to the general laxity concerning the agricultural laws, a number of practices have been noted by J.F. Strange, from his

[13]The tithes and the Sabbatical year laws only applied to Palestine. Jews living in the Diaspora, or outside the land, did not pay tithes or leave their land fallow.

analysis of the ancient Jewish cemetery at Beth Shearim in Galilee. First, Strange notes that the tombs of "holy men" or pious Jews were venerated. Religious pilgrims would visit them to pray and often left inscriptions as records of their visit. Second, there were holy caves where important events allegedly took place, such as the cave where Elijah lived. Third, was the practice of astrology (see also Charlesworth on this). On many tombs were signs of the zodiac, and the Talmud and Dead Sea Scrolls have numerous references to astrology. Fourth, there is evidence of healing cults as later pilgrims to Palestine noted. These cults centered around places such as springs or trees where it was believed healing had occurred. The pool of Bethesda in Jerusalem (see John 5) may have been such a cult center.

These four practices listed by Strange are also well known from pagan Greek and Roman folk religion. They were surely frowned upon by Jewish religious leaders (priests, scribes, and Pharisees) but practiced by some of the common folk nonetheless.

Conclusion

We cannot speak of "Judaism" when speaking about the era of Jesus and the early church. We must speak of "Judaisms" in the plural. There were many competing sects, many competing beliefs, and many competing leaders. What we can say about this period is that Jews everywhere in Palestine struggled to understand what it meant to obey the Torah in a land occupied by Romans and ruled often by the Idumean Herods. It was this question more than others which underlay many of the controversies of Jesus' ministry. Judaism was still very much centered on the temple, but was already becoming a religion of the book.

CHAPTER 3

SOCIAL LIFE AND ECONOMIC CONDITIONS IN PALESTINE

SOCIO-ECONOMIC STRUCTURE OF PALESTINE

Bibliography: N. Avigad, *Discovering Jerusalem*; E. Ferguson, *Backgrounds of Early Christianity*; D.A. Fiensy, *The Social History of Palestine in the Herodian Period*; S. Freyne, *Galilee from Alexander to Hadrian*; J. Jeremias, *Jerusalem in the Time of Jesus*; G.E. Lenski, *Power and Privilege*; A.N. Sherwin-White, *Roman Society and Roman Law in the New Testament*; *SVM*, Vol. II.

Primary sources: Josephus.

Palestine had become by the time of Jesus a society with many social and economic classes. A few people, namely the royal families and other entrepreneurs, had amassed large landed estates. These groups formed an elite class of wealthy and powerful aristocrats which stood over against the class of peasants and those horrifyingly poor classes which had lost their land. Palestine was a typical ancient agrarian society. To understand what such societies were like we will be guided in this chapter by Lenski's important work on such societies.

At the very top of this society during the period of time we are considering was the king (Herod the Great, Agrippa I or Agrippa II), the procurator (when Rome ruled all or part of Palestine directly) or the tetrarch/ethnarch (Archelaus, Antipas, Philip). These leaders exceeded all other members of the elite class not only in political power, but probably also in wealth.

Also powerful were the Herodians. The Herodians were members of Herod's extended family and their descendants. Most of them must have inherited great wealth. The Herodians lived mainly in the cities of Palestine such as Jerusalem, Caesarea Maritima, Sebaste, and later, Tiberias, Sepphoris, Caesarea Philippi, and Bethsaida Julias where they built royal palaces for themselves. The palaces of Herod, his successors, and his descendants were by all accounts lavish displays of wealth.

The High Priestly families were another group within the elite class. These were the members of the noble families from which the High Priests were selected (see *SVM*). The High Priestly families were not only a social group but a caste into which one had to be born. Most of the High Priests in the Herodian period came from one of four powerful families. The sons or sons-in-law from these dynasties probably entered the High Priesthood already from a high social standing with respect to the wealth and prestige of their families. The fact that these four families were able to maintain a virtual monopoly on the High Priesthood shows their extraordinary power and influence.

Most of the members of this caste/social group must have lived in the upper western part of Jerusalem. Ananias, the High Priest when the revolt began in A.D. 66, had a house there, evidently near the palace of Agrippa II (*War* 2.426f). This section is also where the "Burnt House" was found by the archaeological team of Avigad. From an inscription on a lead weight which read "son of Kathros" Avigad concluded that the house belonged to a descendant of Kathros (High Priest in A.D. 44). The House was destroyed in A.D. 70. This is the area where many other large and lavishly decorated houses were found by Avigad including one mansion covering around 6000 square feet. Also in this neighborhood is the traditional location of Caiaphas's house.

A third social group within the elite class is the group of lay aristocrats. They are referred to as "elders," "first men," "notables," and "those first in rank and birth" (see e.g., Mark 6:21; 15:1; Josephus, *Ant* 20.123). These men were the non-priestly and non-royal members of the elite class who because of their wealth, influence, and achievements were leaders of their communities. Some of them were perhaps on the Sanhedrin in Jerusalem or a council in a smaller town (Mark 15:1; Josephus, *War* 2. 405) and some were local magistrates (Josephus, *Life* 134; *War* 2.237). These aristocrats apparently had to assist the tax collectors in collecting the taxes (Josephus, *Ant* 20.194). Most of these wealthy citizens in Jerusalem must have lived in the same high-classed quarter as the High Priests. The aristocrats not only left behind evidence of their wealth in Jerusalem in the remains of their luxurious mansions but also in extravagant tomb complexes (see Avigad).

These three groups, then, constituted the class of the elites or aristocrats, small in number — perhaps only 1% of the population — and socially and economically extremely elevated over the rest of the people.

The next class, termed by Lenski the retainers, stood between the elite and the peasants. Lenski maintains that most agrarian societies have employed retainers to mediate between the common people and the ruling class. The retainers administered the financial and political affairs of the upper class and enforced their goals. For this service they were rewarded economically and given power over the ordinary mass of people.

Tax collectors are the obvious first example of retainers. John the tax collector who resided at Caesarea (Josephus, *War* 2.287), Zacchaeus the chief tax collector who lived at Jericho (Luke 19:1-10) and Levi of Galilee (Luke 5:29) belonged to this class. The first two examples indicate that the retainers could become quite wealthy.

We should also expect the bailiffs or estate overseers to have played a very significant role in Palestinian society in the Herodian period. The office of bailiff was known all over the empire. These important officials are mentioned twice in Luke (12:42-48; 16:1-8). The second example in Luke, the parable of the dishonest bailiff, is especially revealing. Here we see the far-reaching authority the bailiff exercised over his master's economic affairs. Since bailiffs were often slaves or freedmen, the slaves referred to in Mark 12:2 and Matthew 24:45 are probably also to be understood as bailiffs.

The third type of retainer would be the judicial magistrate whom S. Freyne finds in Josephus, *War* 2.571 and Luke 12:58. Luke 18:2 may also refer to this official. The magistrates evidently judged legal disputes and served in nearly every town of any size.

With these officials we should also list soldiers, both Roman and Herodian. Also the lower officials of the royal court would be retainers.

The aristocrats and their retainers stood over the common people both in the city and the country. In the city were small merchants, artisans and day laborers whose standard of living could range from comfortable to very poor. Craftsmen could be quite well off but were always at any rate better off than the unskilled day laborers who often lived in poverty just above the level of beggars.

Peasants were rural agricultural workers. Some were quite comfortable economically but most lived on the edge of poverty. Upper level peasants owned enough acreage to feed their families and to live fairly comfortably. Lower level peasants received most of their living from their piece of land but had to supplement this income by working as a hired hand for a large landowner or by working as a craftsman. The tenants and rural day laborers owned little or no land and received most of their income from land owned by someone else. The tenant rented land and paid the landowner with a portion of his crop ($\frac{1}{3}$ to $\frac{1}{2}$ of the crop was standard). The day laborer worked for a daily wage, mostly at harvest time. There were also agricultural slaves.

Below the peasants in socio-economic standing were the unclean and degraded people. These consist of people called by Lenski "inferior to the masses of common people" due to occupation, heredity, or disease. The occupations which were scorned were prostitutes, dung collectors, donkey drivers, gamblers, sailors, tanners, peddlers, herdsmen and usurers among others (see Jeremias).

Those groups inferior to the common people due to heredity would have included mainly those born illegitimately. Mishnah Kiddushin 4:1 lists a hierarchy of births ranging from priests to the lowly four: bastards, Gibeonites, those that must be silent when reproached about their origins, and foundlings. The Hebrew word usually translated bastard was actually not quite the equivalent of the English word. He/she was the child of an adulterous or incestuous union (as defined by Lev 18 and 20). A bastard could not enter the congregation of the Lord (Deut 23:3). That is, he/she could not intermarry with Israelites. The Gibeonites were descendants of those people whom Joshua (Josh 9:27) made become temple slaves. The silent one must be silent when reproached about his heritage because he does not know who his father is (m. Kiddushin 4:2). The foundling is a child taken up from the street whose father and mother both are unknown (m. Kiddushin 4:2). Thus improper birth carried a great stigma. It has often been suggested that Jesus was being accused of being born in such a way and that John 8:41 alludes to this allegation. Jesus was of course born of the virgin Mary, but society may have branded him as one born illegitimately.

Finally, are those included in the unclean and degraded class due to disease. We should think here especially of the lepers who seem to have abounded in Palestine (Mark 1:40; 14:3; Luke 17:12). Such people were declared unclean by a priest (Lev 13:11, 25) and had to remain apart from everyone else crying out from a distance "Unclean!" (Lev 13:45f).

At the very bottom of the social structure, according to Lenski, were the "expendables." This group consisted of "criminals, beggars, and underemployed itinerant workers." Lenski estimates, based on statistics from Europe from the sixteenth to the eighteenth century, that most agrarian societies contained about five to ten percent of the population in this class.

We should list first of all the bandits as expendables. The ranks of bandits were swollen by runaway slaves, deserting soldiers and impoverished peasants. Josephus and the Gospels refer often to the plague of bandits in Palestine (Mark 14:48; Luke 10:30; John 10:1; Josephus, *War* 2.253, 4.135, 406).

Beggars also appear frequently in Palestine. They are lame (Acts 3:2; John 5:3; m. Shabbath 6:8) or blind (John 9:1; Matt 21:14; Mark 10:46) and sit along the roadside in the country (Mark 10:46) or along the streets and alleys in the city (Luke 14:21). A favorite place for beggars to station themselves was in the temple (Acts 3:2).

Palestinian society in Jesus' time was very class-oriented. Everyone knew his or her place on the socio-economic rung. What is interesting is that Jesus was more often found among the degraded and unclean classes than among the wealthy — although he ministered to the rich also. He emphasized ministry to the outcasts and sinners (Luke 15:1-2).

PEASANT HOME AND VILLAGE

Bibliography: H.K. Beebe, "Domestic Architecture and the New Testament" *BA* 38 (1975) 89-104; V. Corbo, *The House of St. Peter at Capernaum*; S. Dar, *Landscape and Pattern*; A. Edersheim, *Sketches of Jewish Social Life*; D.A. Fiensy, *The Social History of Palestine in the Herodian Period*; E.M. Meyers, *Jewish Ossuaries: Reburial and Rebirth*; J.F. Strange and H. Shanks, "Has the House Where Jesus Stayed in Capernaum Been Found?" *BAR* VIII:6 (1982) 26-37; Z. Yeivin, *Survey of Settlements in Galilee and the Golan from the Period of the Mishnah in Light of the Sources.*

Primary sources: Archaeology; Rabbinic literature.

The village house in Palestine in the first century A.D. was almost always one room attached to other one-room houses owned by extended family members or even by non-relatives and opening into a common courtyard. Courtyard houses according to S. Dar were built separate from each other at first but as villages grew and space became scarce the buildings began to touch each other. Thus families crowded into tiny one-room houses which adjoined other tiny one-room houses. The courtyard which was shared by three or four other families was where one went to do the wash, plant a small garden, eat (in hot weather), socialize and take care of other business necessary in life. Some courtyards were paved with flat stones but most were not.

Most houses were in first century Palestine made of stone, either the white limestone so abundant in much of Palestine or the black basalt found north of the Sea of Galilee. Sometimes the stone was hewn from a quarry and dressed — that is chiseled into rectangular blocks — but poorer peasants constructed houses of stones as they found them on the ground. The exception was in the coastal plain where houses were built of mud brick. Very poor peasants even in the hill country must also have had houses built entirely of perishable material (branches, straw and mud) so that no trace of them has survived. Ancient sources tell us that in extreme cases people had no houses at all, but merely wandered from place to place.

The artist's reconstruction shown here is from the group of houses in Capernaum claimed to contain the dwelling place of Peter. The houses (actually single rooms, one to a nuclear family) were constructed of crude basalt stones that were left undressed (not squared off) and without mortar. The largest house-room, the "venerated room" thought to be Peter's (here pictured without its roof), measured 7 x 6.5 meters.

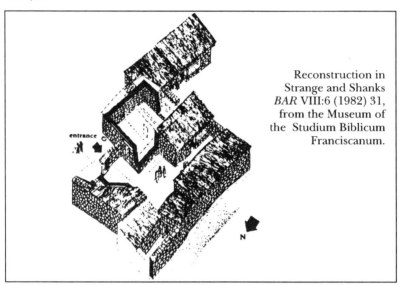

Reconstruction in Strange and Shanks *BAR* VIII:6 (1982) 31, from the Museum of the Studium Biblicum Franciscanum.

The roofs were often made of limestone slabs. Nevertheless, the poorer houses such as those at Capernaum must have had roofs of tree branches covered with mud and straw (cf. Mark 2:4) since the walls would have been too weak to support stone slabs. The roofs were flat and very often, when the walls were made strong enough to support it, an upper room stood on the roof, either the full size of the room below or only as a partial second story.

The individual house-room which held the nuclear family is the smallest social unit in the peasant village. Yeivin estimates that on average the typical peasant village room could house five people. Thus it is doubtful that anyone more than the nuclear family lived in a house under usual circumstances. Families with more than five people might be compelled to build a smaller upper room. Nevertheless, some evidence does exist that the extended families occasionally lived together in the same room (Mark 1:29). Dar notes that the Mishnah describes a small house as 4.48 x 3.36 meters and a large house as 4.48 x 5.6 meters (m. Baba Bathra 6:4). Dar found these same measurements commonly in his archaeological survey of Samaria and thus we could conclude they represented house sizes generally in Palestine in the Herodian period.

Villages were almost always supported by agriculture. Exceptions to this rule were the two villages in Galilee that were famous for their pottery production, and of course the fishing villages around the Sea of Galilee. Even the village craftsmen may have been farmers as well. Dar found that the individual farm plots (one for each nuclear family) were marked off by boundary stones in the fields surrounding the villages. The farmer did not reside on his farm plot but walked out to it from the village to work it. The average peasant lived in a crowded village ranging in size from a few hundred to one or two thousand.

The two main family and village rituals were weddings and funerals. Ordinarily a young man was expected to marry around sixteen or seventeen years of age but at least, says Edersheim, by age twenty. First a couple was engaged and from then on they were treated by others as already married. They could only separate by a divorce decree. Later a marriage contract was signed and the woman's father paid a dowry to the husband. If divorced, the dowry went back to the woman. The actual ceremony and festivities varied from location to location in Palestine. Sometimes the groom made a procession with groomsmen to the bride who awaited him at his house. Sometimes maidens awaited the groom with torches lit.

Funerals were the second main family ritual. Proper burial of the dead was considered a solemn obligation. The corpse was wrapped in linen, spices were burned at the burial site and sometimes coins and valuables would be left with the body. The body was carried on a bier to the burial site with mourners following. Burial was always outside the village. Both tombs (natural caves and hand-hewn tombs) and cist graves (or burial under the ground) were used. The well-to-do not only buried the deceased in a tomb but later returned to put the bones in a special bone coffin (ossuary) which was often ornately decorated. Cremation was considered a pagan practice and therefore not practiced by Jews.

TAXATION IN PALESTINE IN THE TIME OF JESUS

Bibliography: D.A. Fiensy, *The Social History of Palestine in the Herodian Period*; F.C. Grant, *The Economic Background of the Gospels*; W. Stenger, *Gebt dem Kaiser was des Kaisers ist*; J.E. Taylor, *Seleucid Rule in Palestine*; S.L. Wallace, *Taxation in Egypt.*

Primary sources: Josephus; Papyri from Egypt.

No discussion of the socio-economic life of Palestine would be complete without some indication of the tax burden for the average peasant freeholder (landowner). On average he would have possessed six acres of land and had five members in his household. He would, like almost all ancients, leave half of his land fallow each year to prevent soil exhaustion. He could usually expect a fivefold harvest. That is, he would reap five times as much as he planted. What did taxation then mean under such conditions?

The main direct tax for Palestine, as indeed for all the Roman empire, was the *tribulum soli* or tax on the soil. This tax implied that Rome actually owned all the land under its dominion. Therefore the peasant had to pay rent for its use. The rate of this tax was probably about 12% of the total crop. The Seleucid kings, Herod the Great, Herod's successors and Rome all enforced such a tax on Palestine. After the harvest the yearly tax would be paid in kind to the village granary and the peasant's name would be recorded. The wealthy owners of large estates, however, paid either no tax on the soil or a greatly reduced rate. Thus the main tax burden fell on the back of the small peasant.

The second direct tax which the Palestinian villagers paid was the *tribulum capitis* or poll-tax (tax on each individual). This tax was levied in Syria on every male between the ages of 14 and 65 and on females between 12 and 65 years old. In order to compile a list for this tax a periodic census was required. For the well-to-do the poll-tax was a tax on movable property (slaves, cattle, etc.). Thus the tax would vary from person to person. For the poor, however, who possessed little or nothing of value in movable property the tax was on his own body. Just as all land was considered as belonging ultimately to the Roman empire, and thus subject to taxation as a kind of rent, so also one's body belonged to Rome. As Stenger writes, "The poll-tax is none other than the payment for (one's body)." The average amount paid for the poll-tax by the poor villager in Palestine may have been one denarius per person per year (Mark 12:13-17).

The taxes were collected by τελῶναι (telōnai), probably small tax farmers, who could bid on the collection of the taxes of a district, of a city, or perhaps even of a village.

But the freeholding peasant had other obligations. There were the religious duties or tithes. F.C. Grant in his 1926 monograph on the economic life of first century Palestine listed no less than twelve different religious obligations which a landowner in Palestine would have had. Scholars have since that time, however, concluded that most of these tithes and offerings were not paid by the ordinary Jewish peasant.

Some peasants probably seldom paid the tithes. The rabbinic sources agree that they paid the "wave offerings," which were an unspecified percentage of the crops given to the priests to be eaten in ritual purity (Num 18:5, 11f, 21-32; Deut 18:4; Lev 22:10-14; m. Maaseroth 1:1). The rabbinical schools specified the amount as $\frac{1}{40}$ or $\frac{1}{30}$ of the harvest — $\frac{1}{50}$ if one were not generous — but the Old Testament left the amount unspecified. Beyond this offering it is difficult to say what the peasants contributed in religious dues. Surely some gave at least the "first tithe" to the priests and Levites when it was possible. But obviously some did not pay the tithe since the Mishnah speaks about the suspicion which always accompanied the produce of the "people of the land" (see m. Demai).

Thus the peasant paid around 12% of his harvest in land taxes, one denarius for every one of his household over 14 years old, and a wave offerings perhaps equalling $\frac{1}{40}$ of the harvest. We would estimate then, that the freeholder paid out at least 15% of his harvest each year. Since his land yielded usually five fold, then he had to keep back also 20% of the crop for seed for next year. Thus the peasant fed his family on 65% of his yearly harvest. If he paid the first tithe, then he had only 55% left.

CHAPTER 4

THE LIFE AND TEACHINGS OF JESUS

Bibliography: K. Bailey, *Poet and Peasant: A Literary and Cultural Approach to the Parables in Luke*; E. Bammel, *Jesus and the Politics of His Day*; C.K. Barrett, *NTB*; K. Beyer, *The Aramaic Language*; R.E. Brown, *The Birth of the Messiah*; F.F. Bruce, *The Hard Sayings of Jesus*; Idem, *The New Testament Documents: Are They Reliable?*; J.H. Charlesworth, *Jesus Within Judaism*; M. Connick, *Jesus, the Man, the Mission and the Message*; J.D. Crossan, *The Historical Jesus*; Idem, *The Parables*; R.D. Culvert, *The Life of Christ*; C.H. Dodd, *The Parables of the Kingdom*; A. Edersheim, *The Life and Times of Jesus the Messiah*; J. Finegan, *The Archeology of the New Testament*; R.C. Foster, *The Life of Christ*; S. Freyne, *Galilee Jesus and the Gospels*; D.P. Fuller, *Easter Faith and History*; G.R. Habermas, *Ancient Evidence for the Life of Jesus*; M. Hengel, *Crucifixion*; Idem, *The Charismatic Leader and His Followers*; Idem, *Was Jesus a Revolutionary?*; J. Jeremias, *New Testament Theology*; Idem, *The Parables of Jesus*; P.R. Jones, *The Teaching of the Parables*; J. Klausner, *Jesus of Nazareth*; G.E. Ladd, *A Theology of the New Testament*; W.R. Lane, *The Gospel According to Mark*; P. Lapide, *The Resurrection of Jesus*; E. Linnemann, *Jesus of the Parables*; J.G. Machen, *The Virgin Birth of Christ*; T.W. Manson, *The Teachings of Jesus*; I.H. Marshall, *I Believe in the Historical Jesus*; J.P. Meier, *A Marginal Jew*; E. Meyers and J. Strange, *Archaeology, the Rabbis, and Early Christianity*; C. Montefiore, *The Synoptic Gospels*; J. Riches, *Jesus and the Transformation of Judaism*; J. Robinson, *The New Quest of the Historical Jesus*; E.P. Sanders, *Jesus and Judaism*; S. Sandmel, *We Jews and Jesus*; H. Schonfield, *The Passover Plot*; A. Schweitzer, *The Quest of the Historical Jesus*; R.C. Trench, *Notes on the Miracles of Our Lord*; G. Vermes, *Jesus the Jew*; Idem, *The Dead Sea Scrolls*; M. Smith, *Jesus the Magician*; D. Strauss, *The Life of Jesus*.

THE QUEST FOR THE HISTORICAL JESUS

If the world stands another thousand years, how will future Christians judge our age? We can only hope they do not focus upon our understanding of the life of Jesus. No other religion has so intensely analyzed, criticized and variously interpreted the life and intentions of its founder as Christianity in the nineteenth and twentieth centuries. In the hundreds of books written about Jesus each author has pictured Jesus as he wished to see him, or perhaps, as he wished to see himself. To be fair, we must admit that many of these biographies of Jesus were written by people outside the church who sought to debunk Christianity. But a significant number of the works alluded to below have come from within the church.

Our starting point — the assumptions we bring with us to the task of Bible interpretation — determines our finishing point or conclusions. If we assume, for example, miracles cannot happen, we must picture Jesus in a way much different than he is portrayed in the Gospels. If we assume that Jesus could not have been the Son of God sent to die for the world, we must find some other motive for his ministry. If we are into social issues, Jesus must have been a social reformer, either violent or nonviolent. If we dislike the institutional church, we may want to picture Jesus as a simple Palestinian prophet, preaching love, but opposing religious hierarchies of all types. And so it goes.

The following is a list of the main schools of thought one finds in the biographies and other accounts of the "historical Jesus":

1) Jesus the revolutionary. This school of thought has seen Jesus as a Zealot who wanted a violent overthrow of Roman domination (e.g., Brandon).[1]

2) Jesus the conspirator. According to this view, Jesus plotted to trick the masses by performing bogus miracles and faking his own death (e.g., Schonfield).

3) Jesus the apocalyptic prophet. Jesus preached the end of the age and that suffering would come (e.g., Schweitzer).

---

[1]For a survey of this idea see Bammel. See also Hengel's refutation in *Was Jesus a Revolutionary?*

4) Jesus the Jewish rabbi. Jesus was thoroughly Jewish and taught about Jewish concerns, using Jewish methods. Adherents of this school of thought stress Jesus' similarities with Judaism and play down his differences (e.g., Montefiore).

5) Jesus the transformer of Judaism. These scholars stress Jesus' differences with the Judaism of his day (e.g., Riches). Most would deny, however, the ridiculous claim of W. Grundman[2] who said that since Jesus came from Galilee, he was never racially or religiously a Jew.

6) Jesus the charismatic. Jesus by his gifts of the Spirit and religious zeal commanded a following of devoted disciples (e.g., Hengel).

7) Jesus the magician. Jesus performed miracles, especially exorcisms, in the same way pagan magicians claimed to do so: by incantations and the use of black magic (e.g., Smith).

8) Jesus the mythological figure. Most of the Gospel material, say the proponents of this view, is myth or clothing religious ideas in historical or story form (e.g., Strauss).

9) Jesus the non-existent. Since B. Bauer in the nineteenth century, a few scholars have suggested that Jesus never existed at all but was entirely created by the imagination of the Christian community.[3] Apparently, Bauer never took seriously enough the question of where the Christian community came from if Jesus had never existed. Nowhere is the effect of presuppositions so evident as with Bauer. He was a radical Jew baiter and anti-semitist. The idea that the religion that had shaped western civilization could have been founded by a Jew was impossible for him to accept.

Most biographies of Jesus exhibit two methodological weaknesses. First, the authors rule out supernaturalism *a priori*. All events and actions must be explained by the natural order of cause and effect. Thus, Jesus cannot have had foreknowledge, cannot have performed miracles, and cannot literally have risen from the dead. This assumption then *begins* with the proposition that Jesus was not

---

[2]Cited in Freyne.

[3]See the summary of Bauer's thought in Schweitzer and Sandmel, and more recent reiterations of this idea listed in Charlesworth and Robinson. Charlesworth calls this notion ". . . a poison affecting our Western culture."

who the Gospels say he was. But such a reductionistic starting point can never understand a figure like Jesus. It will always produce a caricature.

Second, the authors will only use material from the Gospels which can be "proven" to be historical. But that dooms an accurate picture of Jesus to historical accident. One of the criteria for historicity of a saying of Jesus, for example, is dissimilarity. That means that authentic sayings in the Gospels are only sayings that are dissimilar from what the church later would have created or from what can be found in Judaism. Thus Jesus' statement, "Let the dead bury the dead" (Matt 8:22) would fit that criterion since it would shock both Jews and Christians alike. But the problem with such an approach is that one is left with only a "critical minimum." The minimalistic method can never understand Jesus either, because surely most of what Jesus said was used and proclaimed by the early church. If we rule out these sayings as inadmissable evidence we have eliminated the bulk of the Gospels' material. The better approach is to assume the historicity of the Gospels because some of the sayings and events can be proven to be historical. This assumption is just the opposite of the minimalistic starting point.

The presupposition that guides the present author is that Jesus was as the Gospel writers presented him. The Jesus of history and the Christ of faith are the same. If we allow that miracles are possible, that incarnation is possible, and that God wishes to reveal himself, nothing in the Gospels is historically improbable.

On the other hand to demand that the supernaturalist world view be entertained as a possibility does not mean that we have abandoned the "historical method." The Gospels, rather, exhibit the highest sort of historical accuracy when compared with other sources. Further, we will freely use ancient sources to place Jesus' message in its proper historical context.

Ancient Sources and the Four Gospels

If we did not possess the New Testament, we would still know that an extraordinary Jewish prophet had been executed during the

procuratorship of Pontius Pilate and that a large body of followers
hailed him as the Messiah.

A. Pagan Sources

Several writers living outside Palestine knew about Jesus and his
followers. Thallus, a Greek historian who wrote probably about
A.D. 52, referred to Jesus' death 22 years earlier and attempted to
explain rationalistically the darkness that fell on the land at the crucifixion. Mara Bar-Serapion, a Syrian philosopher who wrote sometime in the late first or second century A.D., also alluded to Jesus'
execution. Tacitus (early second century A.D.) one of Rome's greatest historians, who had access to the official government archives,
reported that "Christus" had been executed by Pontius Pilate when
Tiberius was emperor. Both Mara Bar-Serapion and Tacitus noted
that people still followed Jesus' teachings after his death. Pliny the
Younger wrote in A.D. 112, in a letter to Emperor Trajan, that
Christians in Asia Minor worshiped Christ as God.

These sources clearly indicate the historicity of Jesus of
Nazareth, that he was executed in Judea under Pilate, but that his
disciples continued to believe in him and worshiped him as God.
This testimony alone describes an extraordinary person. Why would
people continue to believe in and worship an executed man?

B. Jewish Sources

Jesus is referred to in the Jewish Talmud. Most of the references
are late and negative. J. Klausner, a Jewish scholar, has summarized
these statements: Jesus was a rabbi who beguiled Israel and mocked
the words of the wise. He expounded Scripture like the Pharisees
and gathered disciples. He practiced sorcery. He was finally hanged
(i.e., crucified) on the eve of the Passover, but his disciples continued to heal in his name.

These statements come from the Amoraic period of the Talmud
(A.D. 200-500) and so may be questionable as historical sources.
What we find in the Talmud, however, certainly supports the
Gospels. Beguiling Israel is a negative way of saying Jesus had a
large following. Mocking the words of the wise indicates Jesus had
strong and basic disagreements with the scribes. Practicing sorcery

is a negative way of reporting that Jesus performed miracles. The charge of sorcery was a strategy already attempted in Jesus' lifetime (Mark 3:22).

Even more significant is the report of Josephus, the Jewish historian of the first century A.D. His report is available in Greek, Slavonic and now, Arabic versions.[4] The Greek version — and to a lesser extent, the Slavonic — clearly contains later Christian interpolations. These versions mix a report about Jesus with a confession of him as the Christ. Since Josephus, as far as anybody knows, did not become a Christian, it seems unlikely that he would have hailed Jesus as the Messiah. It appears that a Christian has at some point inserted confessional phrases into Josephus's report about Jesus. Since the manuscripts of Josephus were preserved in Christian circles, this process of interpolation could have been easily done.

The recently discovered Arabic version, however, contains no apparent interpolations. This version agrees substantially with previous attempts to read the Greek version without interpolations. The Arabic version is as follows:

> At this time there was a wise man who was called Jesus. His conduct was good and (he) was known to be virtuous. And many people from among the Jews and other nations became his disciples. Pilate condemned him to be crucified and to die. But those who had become his disciples did not abandon his discipleship. They reported that he had appeared to them three days after his crucifixion, and that he was alive; accordingly he was perhaps the Messiah, concerning whom the prophets have recounted wonders.[5]

This remarkable text parallels the other non-biblical sources. Jesus was a teacher, had a large following and was crucified under Pilate. But what is only implicit in the other sources is here made explicit. The other sources note that Jesus' followers continued to believe in him after his death and even worshiped him as God. This source tells the reason for their continued allegiance: "They

---

[4]For the Greek version see any translation of Josephus. For the Slavonic see Barrett or Bruce. For the Arabic see Charlesworth.

[5]The translation is by S. Pines and is quoted from Charlesworth.

reported that he had appeared to them three days after his crucifixion, and that he was alive." Jesus' disciples continued to believe in him because of his resurrection from the dead. Indeed, no other event could adequately explain their allegiance.

C. The New Testament

One of the oldest documents witnessing to the life of Jesus is Paul's first letter to the Corinthians, written in A.D. 54. At two points in the letter Paul reminded the Corinthians what he had "delivered" to them (1 Cor 11:23-26; 15:3-11) namely, accounts of the Lord's Supper and Jesus' resurrection. The phrase "what I also delivered to you" (ὃ καί παρέδωκα ὑμῖν, *ho kai paredōka hymin*) refers specifically to transmitting teaching to students. Paul also said it was teaching he "received" (1 Cor 15:3) that is, from the earliest Christian community in Jerusalem and Galilee. Thus the terminology Paul used indicates these accounts came from eyewitnesses.

And what do the accounts indicate? They substantiate the narratives of the institution of the Lord's Supper in the Gospels (Matt 26:17-30; Mark 14:12-26; Luke 22:7-23). Paul says that Jesus instituted the Lord's Supper on the night he was betrayed and that he declared the emblems of the Passover (unleavened bread and wine) to be emblems now of his body and blood, signs of the new covenant. His body and blood are being given "for you." Jesus saw his death as something given for his disciples.

Paul's testimony about Jesus' post-resurrection appearances is also similar in character to those of the Gospels (Matt 28:1-10, 16-20; Luke 24:13-53; John 20:10-21:21). Paul says that Jesus also appeared to James, his brother, who was at that time an unbeliever (John 7:5). Jesus later appeared to Paul himself, who was also at the time an unbeliever. Highly significant is Paul's statement that Jesus had appeared to a group of over 500 brethren at one time, many of whom were still (i.e., in A.D. 54) alive and could verify the account.

Further evidence that the events of the life of Jesus were being carefully taught during the first century can be found in Luke's prologue to his Gospel (Luke 1:1-4). Luke called these teachers "eyewitnesses and ministers of the word" and wrote that he had carefully investigated their testimony. The presence of such teachers in the life and ministry of the church argues for a very high degree of authenticity and accuracy in the four Gospels.

The Epistle to the Hebrews also substantiates the Gospels. Probably writing sometime before A.D. 70, the author indicates that his witness to Christ was given him "by those who heard him (i.e., Christ)" (Heb 2:3). The author affirms on the basis of the eyewitness testimony he has received that Jesus lived as a man, endured temptations and suffering unto death, that he sought relief through "strong weeping" (a reference to Gethsemane), that he died by crucifixion "outside the gate" of Jerusalem, and that by all these trials he learned perfect obedience (Heb 2:10, 14, 18; 5:7, 8; 12:2; 13:12).

Likewise Peter, who was an "eyewitness" attests to the authenticity of Jesus' transfiguration (Matt 9:2-8) in his second letter (2 Pet 1:16-18).

Thus the nonbiblical sources, both pagan and Jewish, confirm the outline of what the four Gospels tell us about Jesus. Further, the New Testament indicates that eyewitnesses and reliable teachers and transmitters of the events of Jesus' ministry were taking great care to report these events accurately. The narratives in Paul's epistle to the Corinthians confirm those of the Gospels. Thus the Gospels should be accorded the highest respect as historical documents.

THE LIFE AND MINISTRY OF JESUS

Jesus' Birth

Jesus was born sometime before 4 B.C., the date of Herod the Great's death. Both Matthew (2:1) and Luke (1:5) indicate that Herod was still alive at Jesus' birth. Though Joseph and Mary were from Nazareth in Galilee, Jesus was born in Bethlehem, the ancient village of King David, their ancestor. The census of Quirinius,[6] proconsul of Syria, had made it necessary for Joseph and Mary to

---

[6]Space does not permit handling the historical problems relating to this census (Luke 2:1-3). See *SVM*, Brown, and A.N. Sherwin-White, *Roman Society and Roman Law in the New Testament*.

return to Bethlehem, their ancestral village. The purpose of their journey was to register for the poll tax or head tax.

Matthew informs us that sometime after Jesus' birth "wise men" (μάγοι, *magoi*) came to Palestine to find the new king. If the wise men are the *magoi* described by the Greek historian, Herodotus, they were a caste of priests from Persia.[7] That *magoi* would travel to hail a potentate is quite in line with similar happenings. Tiridates, for example, also a *magos*, traveled to Naples in Italy to see Nero.[8]

When Herod the Great heard about the birth of a new king, he was alarmed. He ordered all infants in Bethlehem under two years of age to be put to death. Such an action seems unthinkable in our society, but is quite in line with Herod's character. He had ordered the murder of his two sons and of his wife. His rule had in general been a reign of terror. On his deathbed he gave orders to execute many of the prominent Jewish leaders so there would be mourning in Israel.

God had warned Joseph in a dream to flee Bethlehem and so the infant Jesus escaped Herod's assassination attempt. Joseph took his family to Egypt, which had since the days of Jeremiah served as a place of refuge for Jews. By the first century A.D. a large population of Jews had settled throughout Egypt, especially in Alexandria. When Joseph heard that Herod had died he made his way back to his home village of Nazareth.

Jesus' Youth in Galilee

We know very little about Jesus' childhood. Luke says he grew and increased both physically and in wisdom and that the favor of God was upon him (Luke 2:40, 52). Luke also recounts the story of Jesus in the temple at Jerusalem confounding the teachers of the law (2:41-50). But apart from this meager information the four Gospels tell nothing. Their purpose was to narrate his ministry, especially his death and resurrection.

---

[7]See *TDNT* for other suggestions.
[8]Suetonius, *Nero* 13.

The apocryphal gospels of course tell many fanciful tales about the boyhood of Jesus. In these stories Jesus performs many destructive miracles and in general acts like a spoiled child who makes constant trouble for his parents. The nature of the stories and the late date of these texts demonstrate these gospels to be inauthentic.[9]

The rest of Jesus' childhood we must deduce. A knowledge of geography will help somewhat. Galilee is divided into two parts on a line from Capernaum to Ptolemais. The northern part, Upper Galilee, was less Hellenized and less in touch with outside influences than Lower Galilee. For example, archaeologists have found much less evidence that residents of Upper Galilee spoke Greek. For Lower Galilee, however, it seems clear that many people spoke Greek as well as their native Aramaic. Upper Galilee was further removed from cities and from important trade routes. Lower Galilee contained two significant cities, Tiberias and Sepphoris. The main trade route from the coastal plain turned east directly through the Plain of Esdraelon, along the western shore of the Sea of Galilee, and north toward Caesarea Philippi. Thus the trade route ran through the heart of Lower Galilee.

Nazareth is in Lower Galilee, only a few miles south of Sepphoris. Further, as one walks south out of Nazareth one quickly comes to the edge of the hills overlooking the Plain of Esdraelon. Thus Jesus came from the part of Galilee that was most progressive, economically and socially. He most likely learned Greek as a youth in addition to his mother tongue.

Because Nazareth was never mentioned in the Talmud or Josephus, some have in the past doubted that it ever actually existed. According to Finegan, however, scepticism regarding its actual existence in antiquity was laid to rest by two lines of archaeological evidence. First, archaeologists discovered clear evidence that beneath the present Palestinian town called Nazareth lies a Jewish village from the Roman period (the period in which Jesus lived).

---

[9]Three of the most entertaining of these apocryphal gospels are: The Protoevangelium of James; the Gospel of Thomas (the Greek text, not the Coptic sayings text); and the Arabic Gospel of the Childhood. See these and similar texts in Hennecke, Schneemelcher, and Wilson, *The New Testament Apocrypha*.

Second, a Hebrew inscription from Caesarea Maritima, dating from the late third to early fourth centuries A.D. mentions Nazareth. Clearly, then, archaeological evidence removes any reason to suspect that the Gospels created this village out of thin air. The village was not mentioned by other sources because it was small and economically insignificant.

The archaeological evidence indicates that Nazareth was an agricultural village. Finegan relates that there were storage silos for grain, cisterns, olive presses and millstones. Pottery was found from the Iron II period (900-600 B.C.) to the Byzantine period (A.D. 323-638) with a great deal of pottery from the Roman period (63 B.C.-A.D. 323). Numerous grottoes had been used for habitation in antiquity. Archaeologists found 23 tombs, most of which were in the typical Jewish style. From the location of the tombs, which would always have been outside the ancient village, one can get an idea of the size in area of the village. From the description of Meyers and Strange, it appears that the village had a population of around 500 people. It was then a typical village in Palestine in the first century.

Jesus was a carpenter and called the son of a carpenter (Mark 6:3; Matt 13:15). Since Joseph and Jesus had that title, we should think of them as deriving most of their living from their craft. Nevertheless, that did not in antiquity preclude ownership of a small plot of ground for raising grains and olives and a small vineyard. Since Sepphoris (three miles north of Nazareth) was built by Herod Antipas during Jesus' youth (or more precisely ornamented and built up) some have speculated that Joseph and his sons were employed there.

What sort of standard of living did Jesus enjoy as a youth? The life of a day laborer could be very grim. They worked hard and usually earned at the most one denarius per day. Historians seem to be reaching a consensus that a family must have struggled to survive on such an income. Yet a skilled craftsman could command more than one denarius a day. The evidence for the craftsmen that worked on the temple, for example, is that they earned as much as four times the ordinary day's wage.

Jesus, then, did not come from the poorest rung of society.

Joseph was apparently no aristocrat, but neither was he a pauper. His family was probably comfortable, but lived very simply. Still, Jesus' concern for the poor and his inclination to castigate the wealthy is not surprising (Matt 25:35-36; Mark 10:23-25; Luke 16:19-26; John 13:29). Historically, it is not usually the poorest people who lead in such denunciations, but those who are better off yet who have witnessed the cruel effects of poverty and have been moved with compassion.

Jesus' Baptism (Matt 3:13-17; Mark 1:9-11; Luke 3:21-22; John 1:29-34)

Several months or even years before Jesus began his ministry, John, called the Baptist or Baptizer, appeared in the desert[10] and began preaching a message of repentance and baptism for the remission of sins. John was a powerful speaker whose austere, prophetic clothing (cf. Mark 1:6 with 2 Kings 1:8 and Zech 13:4) and desert toughness must have made quite an impression on his audience. Both the Gospels (Mark 1:5; Luke 1:7) and Josephus (*Antiquities* 18.116-119) indicate that John was immensely popular. Hundreds flocked to the fords of the Jordan near Jericho to hear him preach and to submit to baptism. Josephus wrote, "they were greatly moved by hearing his words."

The symbolism of John's activity would have been obvious to many Jews and quickly learned by others. As Lane suggests, John's appearance in the desert and his quotation of Isaiah 40:3 was a call to all Israel to return to the time of the wilderness wandering, a time of intense trust in God. Demanding that all Jews be baptized, as Gentile proselytes would have been, meant that Jews were no longer truly a part of Israel. They must become proselytes. The radicalness of this message and the bluntness of his preaching (Matt 3:7-10) did nothing to dampen the enthusiasm of the crowds.

Some have maintained that John the Baptist grew up among the

---

[10]John also preached and baptized at Aenon near Salim (John 3:23). Finegan places this location some eight miles south of Scythopolis and near the Jordan river.

Essenes and was profoundly influenced by their theology and practice. It seems very likely that John knew the Essenes, for Qumran was only a few miles from the fords of the Jordan where he was baptizing. John emphasized a return to the desert as the return to trust in God as did the Essenes at Qumran. He also practiced a type of ritual bathing (baptism) which was obviously important at Qumran, judging by the literary evidence and the remains of *mikvaot* (ritual baths). Yet no Essene ever conducted the kind of prophetic campaign that John did. This difference is most striking. The Qumran covenanters went to the desert to withdraw from a corrupt society. John went to the desert to seek the repentance and salvation of all Israel. If John had known the Essenes he was not one of them.

At some point — probably in the year A.D. 28 — a young man, "about thirty years old" (Luke 3:23), also came to him for baptism. Since Jesus was without sin (Heb 4:15) why did he come for baptism? He said it was "to fulfill all righteousness" (Matt 3:15). In other words, it was to fulfill the requirements of relationship with God. He had come to the desert to reaffirm his devotion and obedience to God.

As Jesus arose from the waters of the Jordan, he saw the heavens open and the Holy Spirit descend on him softly like a dove (a common symbol of the Spirit) and he heard a voice saying, "You are my beloved Son, in you I am well pleased." The Holy Spirit was poured out on him (cf. 1 Sam 10:6; Ezek 2:2; Isa 63:1) and God called him to a ministry (cf. Isa 6:9-10; Jer 1:5; Ezek 2:3). His experience also fulfilled the word of the Lord to King David: "I will be his father and he will be my son" (2 Sam 7:14). God affirmed at Jesus' baptism that he was his Son and therefore he was the King of Israel, the Messiah. Thus Jesus' baptism was also his call to prophetic activity and to Messiahship (cf. Isa 42:1).

Jesus' Ministry in Galilee and Jerusalem

Except for brief visits to the villages of Nain, Cana, and his home village, Jesus confined most of his activity in Galilee to the Sea of Galilee basin. There he could sail around the sea, stopping to preach at different points. His home base was clearly Capernaum, a town of economic importance which was both a fishing community and stood at the border between the domains of Antipas and Philip. At Capernaum Jesus called his first disciples, taught in the synagogue, and performed many miracles.

The present synagogue ruins which date to A.D. 200 probably stand over the first century synagogue foundations. Finegan notes the distinct difference in the substance and style of the stone blocks. Thus Jesus probably stood on that foundation as he taught. Some archaeologists have also argued that they have found Peter's house where Jesus stayed and in which he often taught (Mark 1:29). It is a house made of crude basalt stones and must have had a stick and grass roof. One is hesitant to give much credence to such an identification, although the evidence is rather compelling.[11] At any rate, since virtually all the houses in Capernaum were of this type, Peter's house must have been similar.

Jesus was in the Decapolis area, Phoenicia, and Caesarea Philippi once each. All of these regions were Gentile, which confirms that, in spite of statements like Matt 15:24, Jesus contemplated a Gentile mission for his disciples during his lifetime.

In addition to the basin of Galilee, Jesus' main center for teaching and healing was Jerusalem. Although only the Gospel of John explicitly indicates that Jesus repeatedly went to Jerusalem,[12] the other Gospels imply that he did. As Connick points out, Jesus had friends in and near Jerusalem (Luke 10:38, cf. with John 11:1), his lament over Jerusalem (Matt 23:37 "how often would I have gathered you under my wings") indicates he had been there often, and opposition toward him in Jerusalem was already well advanced when he arrived there just before his crucifixion. Thus Jesus made at least six trips to Jerusalem, including his final journey.

Jesus as Teacher

Jesus was a master teacher. Not only was the content of his

---

[11]See Strange and Shanks, *BAR* 6 (1982).
[12]See John 2:13; 5:1; 7:10; 10:22; 12:12.

teaching innovative, his ethics demanding, but also his method made him a model teacher.

A. Jesus' Teaching Method

Jesus often used hyperbole. Hyperbole is an obvious exaggeration for emphasis which produces humor or surprise. Jesus said to those inclined to judge others: "Why do you see the speck in your brother's eye but do not perceive the wooden beam in your own eye?" (Matt 7:3); also "It is easier for a camel to go though a needle's eye than for a rich man to enter the Kingdom of God" (Mark 10:25). Both of these statements would have evoked laughter from Jesus' hearers. But they would not have forgotten his point. Jesus' admonition to remove offending body parts is an example of hyperbole which must have shocked his audience: "If your right hand causes you to stumble (i.e., to sin), cut it off and cast it from you" (Matt 5:30). The effects of sin are horrible and eternal life is more important than the physical body. Thus hyperbole makes vivid and emphatic Jesus' message.

Jesus also loved to use oxymoron or an apparent contradiction. By making statements that appear self-contradictory, he created spiritual riddles which drew the hearers to reflect. They could scarcely forget and disregard his message because they had to wrestle with it to understand it. Some Pharisees asked Jesus on one occasion when Jesus was speaking on spiritual blindness: "We are not blind too are we?" Jesus replied, "If you were blind you would have no sin. But now you say, 'We see' — your sin remains" (John 9:40-41). Also Jesus said, "But many that are first will be last, and the last first" (Mark 10:31). The hearer is left to ponder — in what way is Jesus using the terms blind and see and first and last? This technique draws the hearer into the message and compels him to think.

Jesus also used the beatitude/woe form.[13] This teaching method was employed by the psalmists (Ps 1:1; 85:5-6; 128:1) and the prophets (Isa 5:8-23). It emphasizes right conduct in the eyes of God by calling the result blessedness or happiness, and it discour-

---

[13]Our word "beatitude" comes from the Latin translation, *beatus*, of the Greek μακάριος (*makarios*, "blessed").

ages unethical life styles by labeling the result woe. Thus Jesus said, "Blessed are those who weep now for they will laugh," but "Woe to those who laugh now for they will mourn and weep" (Luke 6:21, 24). The beatitudes/woes are based on the final judgment. Those weeping now (i.e., who are in spite of their troubles righteous) will at judgment day laugh. Those laughing now (and ignoring God's call) will weep.

It is a characteristic of Hebrew poetry to place side by side contrasting statements.[14] Such a technique, besides appealing to the semitic tastes, rendered the statement memorable and emphatic. Manson and Jeremias believed that such statements were especially characteristic of Jesus. For example, "The Sabbath was made for man, and not man for the Sabbath" (Mark 2:27), and "When the eye is clear the whole body is illuminated, but when the eye is bad the body is in darkness" (Luke 11:34). Jeremias found no less than 108 instances of such statements in the Gospels. Thus Jesus also rendered his teaching vivid and memorable by using the technique of Hebrew poetry.

Finally, Jesus employed parables to explain his teaching. Parables are also fairly common in the Old Testament (2 Sam 12:1-4; 1 Kings 20:35-43) and very common in the Talmud and Midrashim (see *NTB* 165-167). Parables clarify and emphasize while at the same time drawing the hearer into the message. The stories themselves are so interesting that the hearer is entranced in the plot. But when the story has been told the listener (reader) begins to ask what it all means. The parable of the prodigal son is a good example of how parables work (Luke 15:11-31). We become so engrossed in the plot of the errant younger son, the compassionate and long-suffering father, and the unforgiving, jealous older brother that we are lost in the story. At the end of the story we begin to see Jesus' message. But one has to want to solve the riddle in order to understand the message. Those disinclined to accept that they are sinners will feel uncomfortable analyzing the older and younger sons. Thus Jesus said his parables also separate people, those whose hearts are hardened (Mark 4:10-12).

---

[14]Hebrew poetry also exhibits synonymous parallelism (e.g., Ps 19:2) and synthetic parallelism (Ps 90:2).

The following is a list of ten of Jesus' more important parables. Note that some of them are quite brief, but others are complete narratives. Jesus must have told these parables over and over again in the course of his ministry:

1. Pearl of Great Price (Matt 13:45-46)
2. The Unmerciful Servant (Matt 18:23-35)
3. The Light and Salt (Matt 5:13, 15)
4. The Sower and Soils (Mark 4:1-9)
5. The New Cloth and New Wine (Mark 2:21-22)
6. The Good Samaritan (Luke 10:30-37)
7. The Rich Fool (Luke 12:16-21)
8. The Great Supper (Luke 14:16-24)
9. The Prodigal Son (Luke 15:11-32)
10. The Vine and Branches (John 15:1-6)

In interpreting parables the hearer/reader must focus on the central point. Details within the story may or may not be significant. For example, in the parable of the Friend at Midnight (Luke 11:5-8) a man goes to a friend to ask for three loaves of bread. The friend is in bed and clearly does not want to get up in the cold and get the bread. Finally, after being pestered, however, the friend will get up and hand over the bread just to get rid of the borrower. The parable is supposed to illustrate persistence in prayer, but it would be a mistake to assume that God is like the friend who really does not want to be bothered by requests. Here the details are merely part of the scenery. Jesus' words after telling the parable (Luke 11:9-13) indicate what his point was.

B. The language of Jesus

Four languages played a major role in Palestine in the first century. Latin was the official language of the Roman government. Greek was the universal language of the eastern Roman empire and the language of trade and business. Hebrew was the academic language of the scribes and other scholars of the Old Testament, as most of the Dead Sea Scrolls and the Mishnah indicate. But Aramaic — specifically "Jewish Old Palestinian Aramaic" — was the mother tongue (Beyer).

Although it is very likely that Jesus could speak Greek as a second language and possible that he debated with the scribes in Hebrew, he seems to have done most of his teaching in Aramaic. In the first place, we still find Aramaic words in the Gospels such as *talitha koum* (Mark 5:41), *ephphatha* (Mark 7:34), or *Abba* (Mark 14:36). Second, there are definite Aramaisms or at least semiticisms still in the Greek text of the Gospels. That means that, although the words are in Greek, the syntax is Aramaic (or possibly in some cases Hebrew). For example, "the sons of the wedding hall" (Mark 2:19) is a semitic phrase meaning "the guests of the bridegroom." Also the use of the word "debt" meaning "sin" is Aramaic (Matt 6:12).[15]

C. Jesus' Theology

The central theme of Jesus' preaching was the kingdom of God. The kingdom of God[16] (Greek βασιλεία τοῦ θεοῦ, *basileia tou theou*; Aramaic אלהא ד מלכותא, *malkutha d'elaha*) as an expression and concept appeared in ancient Judaism as well, but not to the extent that Jesus used it.[17] Jesus' message is summarized in Mark (1:15): "Repent for the kingdom of God has come near." Matthew (4:23) and Luke (4:43) say he preached the "gospel of the kingdom." Many of the parables begin: "The kingdom is like . . ." (e.g., Mark 4:26, 30). Finally, the word kingdom appears in many sayings and teachings.

The Aramaic word *malkutha* did not, as Jeremias explained, mean the same to the oriental that kingdom means for the westerner. For westerners, kingdom denotes a territory or spatial area over which a king rules. But in the Old Testament and later Judaism[18] *malkut* (Hebrew, מלכות) or *malkutha* (Aramaic) meant the authority and power of the king which is always in process of being realized. Thus the concept is dynamic. That is, it describes action such as God's defending the poor or saving his people.

Jesus taught that God's reign was both present and would be manifested in the future in a final and all-encompassing way. Jesus

---

[15]For a more complete list of Aramaisms see Jeremias and Manson.

[16]In Matthew the term is always Kingdom of Heaven where "Heaven" is a circumlocution for "God." This was a customary usage for many pious Jews.

[17]Compare Jesus' frequent use of the title "Son of Man" which is also found rarely in Jewish sources.

[18]See Manson for texts concerning the kingdom in Jewish literature.

clearly indicated that the kingdom was already present when he said (Matt 11:12): "From the days of John the Baptist until now the kingdom of Heaven (= God's reign) has been making its way with triumphant force." Compare Luke 11:20, and especially Luke 17:21, "They will not say, 'Look here!' or 'There!' for the kingdom of God is within you (God is reigning in your midst)".

On the other hand Jesus also clearly taught that the kingdom was yet to come. Thus he says in his model prayer "May your kingdom come" (Matt 6:10). He is especially clear when in talking about his second coming and the consummation of the age he says, "There will be weeping and gnashing of teeth when you see Abraham, Isaac and Jacob in the kingdom of God (= in the sphere of God's reign) and you are cast outside" (Luke 13:28). Certainly if the three patriarchs are present, the general resurrection and the end of the age have come.

When did the present kingdom begin? Was it with John the Baptist (Matt 11:12)? Or was it with the beginning of Jesus' ministry (Matt 12:28)? Alexander Campbell, the nineteenth century reformer, correctly perceived that the kingdom began on Pentecost when the church was founded. Campbell's understanding of the nature of the kingdom is too western – he sees it more as territory – but his insight about the precise beginning of the kingdom remains nonetheless correct. Campbell saw John the Baptist and especially Jesus as the founders of the kingdom. The kingdom could not begin until the foundation (Jesus' death and resurrection) had been laid. Thus the logical starting point for the expression of God's rule was the beginning of the church (see *The Christian System*).

Entering the kingdom of God meant submitting to God's rule or entering the sphere of his rule. Jesus taught that nothing was more important in life than the kingdom. In the parables of the Pearl of Great Price (Matt 13:45-46) and the Treasure Hidden in the Field (Matt 13:44) Jesus explained that the kingdom is worth the most priceless treasure. In the Sermon on the Mount, Jesus admonished his disciples, "But seek first the kingdom and its righteousness" (Matt 6:33), that is, "Seek above all to submit to God's rule." Nothing must stand between one's commitment to the kingdom of God. That is why Jesus told the rich young ruler to sell all his pos-

sessions (Mark 10:17-22). We must be ready to give up everything —
even our own lives — if necessary for the kingdom (Luke 14:26).[19]

God in Jesus' teaching, then, is the king, the sovereign ruler of
the universe. But God is no remote potentate. As Ladd notes, God
seeks out sinners (Luke 15) and invites them to salvation, which
Jesus often pictures as a great banquet (e.g., Matt 22:1-14). It was
Jesus' mission to issue God's invitation to his banquet of joy and cel-
ebration. Thus God as king does not stand off in the universe and
demand that men and women submit to his rule, but he seeks them
out and invites them to know the joy of his rule.

But God is also the end-time judge. For those who reject his
loving invitation there awaits everlasting punishment (Matt 25:41).
Thus the decision one makes about the kingdom or rule of God
determines one's destiny.

Jesus as Healer

We said earlier that those who cannot accept the possibility of
miracles will try to find other explanations for Jesus' healings, exorcisms and the other supernatural actions. Such has been the case
with the rationalistic school of interpretation. This group of scholars was especially prominent in the nineteenth century, but obviously still has many representatives today. They sought to find a
rationalistic explanation for the supernatural. For example, the
voice of God heard at Jesus' baptism was really a meteor passing
overhead, according to one of the representatives of this school of
thought. Jesus' miracle of walking on water was really just a case of
walking in shallow water on the shore. The transfiguration in which
Jesus' glory was shown to Peter, James and John was just the sun in
their eyes. Healings and exorcisms were psychosomatic.[20] Many of
these absurd rationalizations require more faith to accept than to
believe in the miracle.

Another school of thought, led by Strauss and more recently
Bultmann, maintained that all miraculous elements were myth.

---

[19]Jesus' use of the word "hate" in this verse is, of course, hyperbole.
[20]See Schweitzer for a full description of this school of thought.

These stories, they maintained, were created by the Gospel writers and/or the early Christian community. They patterned the miracle stories on Old Testament stories and legends in Hellenistic and Jewish sources. But all four Gospels record miracles and the Christian community continued this practice.[21] The early Christian witness is strong and unanimous that Jesus did miracles. Thus it is historically improbable that these accounts were created.

More recently, Morton Smith has asserted that Jesus certainly did do miracles (though his definition of the term is unclear). The charge by the Pharisees that Jesus cast out demons because he himself was possessed by Beelzebub (Matt 12:22-29) is tantamount to an admission on their part that Jesus did miracles. The Pharisees never claimed he faked miracles. They accepted that he actually did them, but claimed he did them by the power of the devil. Unfortunately, Smith goes on to agree with the Pharisees that Jesus really was a practitioner of black magic. Apparently, Smith has not taken seriously enough Jesus' reply: "How can Satan cast out Satan?" (Mark 3:23). Why would Satan empower Jesus to exorcise demons and announce the ultimate downfall and destruction of Satan himself?

The best parallel for understanding Jesus' miracles is not the Greek magical papyri (as Smith maintains) but the Old Testament. The miracles of Elijah-Elisha and Moses were prototypes of Jesus' own miracles. But in Jesus was something greater than Moses and Elijah. God through Moses (Exod 14:15-31) overpowered the sea by dividing it so the Israelites could pass through. Jesus calmed the sea (Mark 4:35-41) during a raging storm and walked on the water (Mark 6:45-52). God fed the hungry through Moses (Exod 16:4), Elijah (1 Kings 17:7-26), and Elisha (2 Kings 4:1-7; 7:38-44). Jesus fed at least 5000 and later 4000 by multiplying a few small loaves (Mark 6:35-44; 8:1-9). Elisha healed a leper (2 Kings 5:1-14) but Jesus healed many lepers (Luke 17:11-19; Mark 1:40-45). Jesus also went beyond even the great Moses, Elijah, and Elisha. He performed many other healing miracles and even overcame demons, the emissaries of the Evil One (Mark 5:11-20). Jesus was a charismatic

---

[21]See the accounts in Acts (3:6-8; 8:7, etc.), the references in Paul's letters (1 Cor 12:7-11; Gal 3:5) and Hebrews 2:4.

healer and miracle worker like Moses, Elijah and Elisha, but he was far greater than they.

Jesus performed miracles because of his compassion for the suffering and needy. He healed diseases (Mark 1:41; 6:34; Luke 7:13), cast out demons (Mark 9:22) and miraculously fed the hungry (Mark 8:2) because he felt strong compassion (σπλαγχνίζομαι, *splangchnizomai*, from σπλάγχνα, *splangchna*) when he saw their plight. His mighty acts, therefore, were acts of mercy and love to help the unfortunate.

Jesus also performed miracles as "signs" (σημεῖα, *sēmeia*, John 2:11; 3:2) that the kingdom of God was breaking into history in his person. The kingdom of God brings about Satan's downfall and with it, his power to inflict suffering through demon possession. Thus Jesus' ministry was to "bind the strong man" (Satan) so that Jesus might plunder his house (i.e., release those held captive by demon possession, Matt 12:29). Jesus therefore affirmed, "But if it is by the Spirit of God that I cast out demons, then the kingdom of God has come upon you (= God now reigns in your midst; Matt 12:28). Jesus made a similar statement to John the Baptist when asked if he was the messiah (Matt 11:4-5). Jesus' miracles, therefore, were an integral part of his message and ministry.

THE FINAL WEEK OF JESUS' LIFE

Jesus had warned his disciples that he would be killed by the chief priests and scribes (Mark 8:31; see also 9:31; 10:33-34). Jesus knew that opposition on the part of the Jewish leadership had been growing against him for some time. On previous visits to Jerusalem the leadership had already determined to kill him when they had the chance (John 5:18; 10:31-33). In spite of the obvious hostility toward him, Jesus determined to go to Jerusalem for the Passover once more. Luke writes (9:51), "As the time came for Jesus to be delivered up, he fixed his face toward going to Jerusalem." This means he "set his jaw" with determination. He would not be deterred from making the journey, his journey of death. He said (Mark 10:45) he must die in order to make a "ransom payment" (λύτρον, *lytron*) for "many" (semitic for "everyone").

A. The Triumphal Entry (Matt 21:1-9; Mark 11:1-10; Luke 19:28-40; John 12:12-19)

A few days before the passover, Jesus arrived on the Mount of Olives, just east of Jerusalem. From the mount, he descended into the Kedron Valley and then up to the Temple Mount. Jesus had instructed his disciples to bring to him a donkey's colt for him to ride on from Bethany and Bethphage (two villages east of Jerusalem) to the temple. Obviously Jesus had a symbolic purpose for choosing to ride at this point after walking all the way from Galilee. The symbolism did not lie in the fact that he rode, but upon what he rode. He did not ride a war chariot, the means of conveyance for conquering generals in triumphal parades. He rode a donkey, the ordinary means of travel for poor people. Matthew and John point out that this action and its interpretation were predicted in Zechariah 9:9. The coming king (messiah) of Israel would be meek and lowly, a man of peace and not of earthly power and wealth.

It was also no accident that Jesus began his procession on the Mount of Olives. Zechariah had predicted that God himself would stand on the mount (14:4) on the Day of the Lord. Josephus noted that the Egyptian, a would-be prophet, had gathered his band of followers on the Mount of Olives where he promised to perform a great sign (*Antiquities* 20.168-171). Thus the mountain seems to have been the place where Jews expected God to do his work at the consummation.

As Jesus proceeded down the mount, then into the temple, many people spread their garments on the road, the greeting for royalty (2 Kings 9:13). Others carried palm branches, a symbol of rejoicing used both at feasts (Lev 23:40) and after a great victory (1 Maccabees 13:51). The crowd ran out of the city to meet Jesus and accompany him. This action was also a reception reserved for royalty (Josephus, *War* 7.100-102).

The crowd shouted "Hosanna," the Greek transliteration of the Hebrew הושיעה נא (*hoshi'ah-na*) which means "Save please!" The refrain comes from Psalm 118:25-26 and was recited or read at every major Jewish feast. It was a prayer beseeching God's help and salvation. Since here they are shouting the prayer to Jesus, the people are asking him to save them.

Clearly the crowd was acclaiming Jesus as the king, or messiah. They accepted him as a military messiah, like King David of old (they even hailed him as the "Son of David") as one who will deliver them from Roman occupation and domination by military conquests. Jesus responded to them not by denying he was the messiah, but by redefining messiahship. He rode an ordinary donkey, not a war chariot. He carried no weapons. Even so, the authorities were afraid of Jesus and determined to do whatever it took to stop him.

B. The Temple Cleansing (Matt 21:12-13; Mark 11:15-19; Luke 19:45-48)

Shortly after Jesus' entry into Jerusalem, he entered the temple and began to drive out those who bought and sold animals and the money changers. The Greek word for drive out (ἐκβάλλειν, *ekballein*) is a strong word, indicating physical expulsion. The animal sellers were those selling lambs, pigeons, etc. for sacrifices. The money changers were those who changed foreign coinage into the Tyrian shekel, the only coin allowed to pay the half-shekel tax (Exod 30:11-16).[22] Every free Israelite male over age 20 had to pay this yearly tax to the temple.

These two events, the Triumphal Entry and the Cleansing of the Temple, sealed Jesus' fate of death. The first event would have caused great concern on the part of Pontius Pilate. Here was someone hailed as a new king, a possible revolutionary leader — at least in the procurator's eyes. The second event pitted Jesus against the power base of the chief priests, who had long sought to remove Jesus from his ministry (John 5:18). The chief priests comprised one of the most influential and wealthiest groups within the aristocracy. Clearly the two — Pilate and the high priestly family — conspired together to have Jesus killed.

---

[22]See Mishnah Bekhoroth 8:9 and Shekalim 1:3. The reader must remember that Roman, Persian, Greek, Syrian, and Egyptian coins were current in Palestine. But the temple tax had to be paid (Exod 30:13) "according to the shekels of the sanctuary." Thus there had to be one standard coinage used for the temple.

Jesus and the Chief Priests

The chief priests (ἀρχιερεῖς, *archiereis*) were those members of the priestly caste that were directly related to the High Priest. Members of this clan formed an aristocratic group that held enormous political, economic, and religious power (see above Chapter 2). They were clearly affiliated with the Sadducees. At this time the High Priesthood was held by the house of Annas (Hebrew חנן, *Hannan*) one of only four great chief priestly clans in the first century. The current High Priest was Caiaphas, Annas's son-in-law.

It is clear that this group conspired with the Romans to have Jesus killed. Jesus had predicted that it would be they who killed him (Mark 10:33). They had sought to lay hands on Jesus to kill him after the temple cleansing (Matt 21:18) but could not. They subsequently met together to hatch a plot that would bring about his end (Mark 14:1). At the first opportunity they would seize him without upsetting the crowd — thus by night or secretly — quickly convict him, and pressure Pilate to enforce capital punishment.

The chief priests then were Jesus' main enemies within Judaism. They remained his enemies even after his death. It was they who first persecuted Christians, ordering them to cease preaching about Jesus, especially that Jesus had risen from the dead (Acts 4:1, 6; 5:17). The high priest continued his persecution later against Paul the apostle (Acts 23:2).

The chief priests wanted Jesus destroyed because he challenged the temple cultus, their base of power. He also castigated the wealthy, especially those who oppressed the poor. He further preached the doctrine of the resurrection of the dead, a doctrine unacceptable to Sadducees. Thus Jesus and his followers both before and after his death and resurrection appeared to this aristocratic caste as a dangerous sect which threatened their economic station.

Jesus and the Pharisees

We saw above (in Chapter 2) that the Pharisees were a religious-political sect within Palestinian Judaism that emphasized ritual purity and tithing. They — or more precisely, their scribes — had a body of oral interpretation of the Old Testament that they claimed began with Moses himself and was passed on in an unbroken chain until their day. Their religious aim was to learn and practice the law both written and oral. Their political aim was to make their oral law — their particular interpretation of the written law, which Jesus termed "the traditions of the elders" — the law of the land.

The Pharisees were certainly not legalistic in the sense of neglecting the inner spiritual life. They were not all covetous and hypocritical, though some of them were. Many of them were very pious men of faith and dedicated to God.

Jesus' own relationship with the Pharisees was complex. They criticized him, often severely, for eating with and receiving as disciples publicans and sinners (Luke 5:30; 15:2), for not fasting (Mark 2:18), for plucking grain on the Sabbath (Mark 2:24), for healing on the Sabbath (Mark 3:6), and for failing to wash his hands properly in order to maintain ritual purity (Mark 7:1). Jesus in turn accused the Pharisees and their scribes of abandoning the commandment of God in order to hold to the traditions of men (Mark 7:8) and of being hypocrites (Mark 7:6; Matt 23:13) and vainglorious (Mark 12:38-39). Indeed Jesus' denunciation of the scribes and Pharisees in Matthew 23 is about as scathing as one can find of any group in antiquity.

Yet Jesus had many things in common with the Pharisees. He taught that there would be a general resurrection of the dead. He preached the coming kingdom, a concept also found in the rabbinic (i.e., Pharisaic) writings. He was certainly fundamentally opposed to the Sadducees and chief priests as were the Pharisees.

Beyond these considerations are references in the Gospels to a more cordial — although perhaps always to a degree, disagreeable — relationship between Jesus and certain Pharisees. He was apparently often invited to eat a meal in a Pharisee's house (Luke 7:36; 14:1), something a Pharisee would never have done for just anyone, since they ate meals in a state of ritual purity. That Jesus was invited and accepted such invitations, means the relationship was not totally negative. One cannot imagine Jesus being invited to eat with the chief priests.

There is even one instance where some Pharisees may have tried to save Jesus' life. They warned him (Luke 13:31) that Herod Antipas wanted to kill him, probably for many of the same reasons he killed John the Baptist. Some historians mistrust the Pharisees' motives and suggest they were only trying to get Jesus out of Galilee, since when Herod later sees Jesus in Luke 23 there is no intent to kill him. A similar event happened later, after the church was established. The chief priests and Sadducees wanted to take harsh measures to destroy Christianity. Gamaliel, the Pharisee, however, advised against it. He cautioned that they could be found opposing God in such action. They should rather wait to see what would become of this new sect. Finally, there is the extraordinary exchange between Jesus and a scribe (Mark 12:32-34) — presumably a Pharisaic scribe — who commended Jesus for his perceptive answer and keen insight into Scripture, and Jesus responded to the scribe, "You are not far from the Kingdom of God."

Thus Jesus certainly had points of disagreement with the Pharisees and even on one occasion denounced some of them thoroughly and severely. But it is often true that the closer in theology two religious groups are, the more they argue and debate. It would have been fruitless, for example, for Jesus to have debated at length with the Sadducees, since they were not even in the right ballpark. Most Pharisees saw Jesus as impious because he ignored their traditions or oral law, but some were very interested in hearing his teaching and later became believers (Acts 15:5).

Jesus' Death (Matt 26:36-27:66; Mark 14:32-15:47; Luke 22:39-23:56; John 18:1-19:42)

The chief priests received unexpected good fortune. They had been worried about how and when to arrest Jesus in order to avoid a confrontation with the crowds (Mark 14:2). Then Judas Iscariot, one of his disciples, came forward and volunteered to betray Jesus. His motive for such action is now as obscure as what precisely he agreed to do. He apparently was disenchanted with Jesus and his "kingdom which is not of this world." When this disenchantment arose and why it turned to hatred we can only speculate. At any rate, one commonly held view — that Judas was only trying to help Jesus by forcing him to defend himself and thus bring on the kingdom — is very unlikely. Jesus represented Judas's actions as the work of Satan and Judas as the vessel of Satan (Mark 14:21; John 6:70) as did the Gospel writers (Luke 22:3; John 13:2).

The guards brought Jesus, after arresting him in Gethsemane, first to the house of Annas, the father-in-law of the High Priest. Next Jesus was taken to Caiaphas's house. The High Priest interviewed him and then ordered him taken to the Hall of Hewn Stones where the Sanhedrin met to judge court cases. The High Priest accused Jesus of blasphemy when Jesus responded affirmatively to his question, "Are you the messiah?" Therefore the Sanhedrin condemned Jesus to death and sent him to the praetorium, to Pontius Pilate, to be tried under Roman law. Jesus was subsequently executed by crucifixion in a place called in Aramaic, Golgotha.

The "trial" of Jesus was probably not a legal or valid trial. According to the Mishnah Sanhedrin (4:1-2) there should be no night trials; no capital cases should be deliberated on at night; and the verdict to a capital case must never come in the same day as the trial. Since the Mishnah was written down A.D. 200, it is possible that these exact rules of jurisprudence were not in effect at that time. But something similar to them must have been in effect, for they are the cautionary regulations of sober judgment. The "trial" then was done in haste, informally and unofficially, to expedite Jesus' condemnation and execution. There had to be no messy debate and lengthy deliberation. The conclusion was predetermined.

Nor was the charge of blasphemy convincing to anyone. According to the Mishnah (Sanhedrin 7:5) which is an interpretation of Leviticus 24:15-16, one committed blasphemy by using God's name "Yahweh" in a profane way. Claiming to be the messiah would not, strictly speaking, be blasphemy. Again, the Mishnaic rule probably became more precise later than it was in Jesus' time, but it cannot have changed that considerably. Jesus stood before the High Priest as a prisoner about to be executed, yet maintaining he was God's anointed. Caiaphas tried to charge that this was tantamount to blasphemy and pressed for a guilty verdict on that basis. It is extremely doubtful that the Sanhedrin would have condemned anyone as a blasphemer just because he was claiming to be the messiah, unless the verdict were already predetermined.

Pilate received Jesus with apparent uncertainty. He acted at times very weak and easily swayed by the chief priests and the mob. But Pilate himself must have worried about Jesus long before he finally met him. No Roman procurator could fail to worry about someone who was acclaimed king by his native folk. Nor would a Roman procurator release a dangerous revolutionary like Barabbas (Mark 15:11) in exchange for executing Jesus unless he really thought Jesus himself was even more dangerous. His actions, then, may be interpreted as only a feigned attempt to spare Jesus' life. A good politician tries to appear pressured into doing something that later might be unpopular.

That Jesus was condemned by Pilate as a revolutionary is clear not only from the accusation written on the cross (Mark 15:26, "King of the Jews"), but also from the type of execution Jesus suffered. Crucifixion was reserved in the main for rebels, violent criminals and robbers (Hengel). It was especially the punishment of rebellious slaves and subject peoples. In spite of Jesus' teaching about nonviolence and his refusal ever to entertain a worldly kingdom, Pilate had heard enough rumors — most recently about the Triumphal Entry — to determine to have him executed.

Jesus then was condemned by the chief priests and Pilate on the same charge. The chief priests said he was a blasphemer because he claimed to be the Messiah. Pilate condemned him for claiming to be a king. "King" is merely a secularized version of "messiah" (Lane).

Crucifixion was considered the worst form of execution in antiquity, even worse than execution by burning or by wild animals. Origen, the third century theologian, who was probably in a position to have witnessed a crucifixion, called it "the utterly vile death" (Hengel). Seneca, the pagan Roman philosopher of the first century A.D. described the horrors of crucifixion:

> . . . can anyone be found who would prefer wasting away in pain dying limb by limb, or letting out his life drop by drop

. . . can any man be found willing to be fastened to the accursed tree, long sickly, already deformed, swelling with ugly weals on shoulders and chest, and drawing breath of life amid long-drawn-out agony? (Hengel)

Josephus also described crucifixions which he witnessed:

(the Jewish fugitives) were first whipped and then tormented with all sorts of tortures before they died and were then crucified before the wall of the city . . . the soldiers . . . nailed those they caught, one after one way, and another after another, to the crosses, by way of jest . . . (Whiston)[23]

Jesus was first whipped with a *flagellum* (Greek φραγέλλιον, *phragellion*) or short whip during which he must have lost a considerable amount of blood. He was also mocked, an ancient form of emotional torture administered to the condemned,[24] then sent out to be

---

[23]For the quotations about crucifixion see Origen, *Commentary on Matthew* on 27:22ff; Seneca, *Epistle* 101; and Josephus, *War* 5.446-459.

[24]See Philo, *Flaccus* 36-39; Dio Cassius LXV.20f; and other reports in Lane.

crucified. They would have driven long nails through each wrist and through both heels together and so placed him on the cross in a twisted fashion that breathing required considerable effort (see illustration). The medical causes of his death are usually given as shock and exhaustion due to blood loss and inability to breathe freely while hanging on the cross.[25]

Jesus' Resurrection (Matt 28:1-20; Mark 16:1-8; Luke 24:1-53; John 20:1-21:25; Acts 1:6-11; 1 Cor 15:3-7)

P. Lapide, an orthodox Jewish scholar, wrote concerning the description of Jesus' death in the Gospels:

For only a sworn enemy of Jesus can describe the end of his life in such a brutal, concrete way — or men who are deeply convinced that this miserable dying of the Nazarene neither was nor is the last word of God — that his exit from this world became the entrance into blessedness.[26]

Modern Christian theologians both in Europe and in America would do well to listen to Lapide. For while many see the story of Jesus' resurrection as only a myth or a first-century metaphor which really means merely that "the cause of Jesus goes on" or some other nonsense, this Jewish historian has looked openly at the evidence and found it convincing. He argues that Jesus' resurrection was an authentic historical event and only this event can explain the beginning and growth of Christianity.

Jesus was buried in a tomb with a rolling-stone door. Most modern historians think Jesus' tomb is in the present Church of the Holy Sepulchre. Finegan suggests the tomb was of the archasolium type. Thus his body was placed in the tomb on a ledge under a

[25]See e.g., W.D. Edwards, W.J. Gabel, and F.E. Hosmer, "On the Physical Death of Jesus Christ" *Journal of the American Medical Association* 255 (1986) 1455-1463. See also the important archaeological find of the bones of a crucified man in Haas, *IEJ* 20 (1970) 38-59.

[26]*The Resurrection of Jesus*, p. 111. Translated from the German by W.C. Linss.

vaulted ceiling. The stone was rolled back over the door to keep wild animals and other intruders out.

The assertion made by some historians, that Jesus was not dead but only swooned on the cross and then was revived and refreshed from three days' rest in a cool tomb, is surely one of the absurdities of New Testament scholarship. If the Romans were competent in anything, it was in killing a man and in determining when he was dead. And even if they could have made such a mistake, could anyone so severely wounded roll back a heavy stone after three days without food and water and escape?

The evidence for the literal, historical resurrection of Jesus is of two types. First, the tomb was found empty three days after his death. Not only do all the Gospels attest to this fact, but Matthew records a story highly significant in this regard. When the chief priests heard that Jesus' body was missing they instructed the guards to tell others that his disciples stole his body (Matt 28:11-15). "This story," says Matthew, "is current among Jews to this day." In case one doubts the historicity of Matthew's account, we need only to point out that the disciples of Jesus would hardly create a story in which someone alleged they stole his body. Thus the account of the chief priests instructing the guards is historical. And if it is histori-cal, then it proves that the tomb was empty. Why would the chief priests invent such an excuse if Jesus' body were still in the tomb?

If the tomb was empty, how can we account for it? Some say the women who first discovered he had risen made a mistake and went to the wrong tomb. But surely not everyone of Jesus' followers could have been that muddle-headed. Others give credence to the story of the chief priests and allege that the disciples stole Jesus' body. But their willingness to suffer and die for their testimony about the risen Lord (e.g., Acts 5:27-32) rebuts any attempt to accuse them of lying or playing a hoax. Besides these considera-tions, one has to remember the Roman guard stationed at the tomb by Pilate. It is doubtful that a group of Galilean peasants, mostly unarmed and unskilled in the art of war, could overpower Roman legionaries.

Second, the disciples claimed to see Jesus after his death. He was seen by both men and women, at night and in the day time, in Judea and in Galilee, by believers and unbelievers (i.e., James his brother and later Paul) and by small groups and large crowds. Paul wrote that a crowd of over 500 had seen him alive (1 Cor 15:6). Again, these people obviously believed with all their might that they had actually seen him. Why else would they devote their lives to him in service, suffer hardships and even martyrdom? They were hardly lying and the frequency and variation of post-resurrection appearances would rule out hallucinations. A large group of people in various localities over many days does not share the same hallucination.

This evidence is very compelling and renders other explanations very forced. If one admits in the first place that God *can* raise people from the dead, the evidence is irrefutable.

Of course, ultimately, acceptance of Jesus as the Christ and risen Lord is a matter of faith. Cold reason and historical investigation do not alone call for commitment. Just as even those who actually saw these things had to embrace Jesus as Lord by faith, so must we. Then his resurrection becomes for us not just an historical marvel, but the event of salvation.

CHAPTER 5

THE GOSPELS

THE SYNOPTIC PROBLEM

Bibliography: K. Aland, *Synopsis of the Four Gospels*; W.R. Farmer, *The Synoptic Problem*; *FBK*; A.M. Farrer, "On Dispensing with Q" in D.E. Nineham, ed., *Studies in the Gospels*; R.C. Foster, *Introduction and Early Ministry*; B. Gerhardsson, *Memory and Manuscript*; Guthrie, *NTI*; H.C. Kee, "Synoptic Studies" in E.J. Epp and G.W. McRae, ed., *The New Testament and Its Modern Interpreters*; J.S. Kloppenborg, *The Formation of Q*; T.R.W. Longstaff, *Evidences of Conflation in Mark? A Study in the Synoptic Problem*; F. Neirynck, T. Hansen, and F. van Segbraeck, *The Minor Agreements of Matthew and Luke against Mark*; R. Riesner, *Jesus als Lehrer*; E.P. Sanders, *The Tendencies of the Synoptic Tradition*; B.H. Streeter, *The Four Gospels*; V. Taylor, *The Formation of the Gospel Tradition*; W.O. Walker, Jr., *The Relationship Among the Gospels*; J. Wenham, *Redating Matthew, Mark and Luke*.

The first three Gospels, Matthew, Mark, and Luke, are usually studied together because of their similarities. Hence they have come to be known as "synoptic" from the Greek word meaning "seen together." Scholars have asked themselves for centuries why the Synoptic Gospels are so much alike. They have many of the same stories and sayings. The order of these pericopes (sections or paragraphs) is usually identical in at least two of the Gospels and often in all three. Much of the vocabulary and phraseology is similar. Why are these similarities present in the Synoptics but not in John?

For the past 200 years scholars have proposed numerous theories basically under two categories: a non-interdependence among the Synoptics and a definite literary interdependence. That is, some scholars have believed that none of the authors had seen the other

Gospels before writing his own Gospel (a non-interdependence). Others concluded, however, that two of the authors of the Synoptics knew and copied from at least one other (a definite literary interdependence).

Hypotheses of Non-Interdependence (see FBK)

A. The Primitive Gospel Hypothesis. The Synoptics, according to this view, are varying copies and translations of one very old Aramaic Gospel, called the Gospel of the Nazarenes. The similarities among the Synoptics are because they copied or quoted from this primitive Gospel. The differences are due to translation differences, abridgments and editing on the part of the authors.

B. Fragment Hypothesis. The Gospels were compiled from notes and memoranda made by those who had been with Jesus. His disciples jotted down isolated sayings and deeds. These were later collected and used to compose the Gospels.

C. Tradition Hypothesis. There was a primitive oral Gospel transmitted at first in Aramaic and later in two different Greek translations.

Literary Interdependence Hypotheses

A. As early as Origen (A.D. 220) some declared that Matthew wrote his gospel first and in the Aramaic language, Mark wrote his Gospel second, and Luke third (see Eusebius, *H.E.* 6.25). Augustine (A.D. 400) also affirmed this order (see *The Harmony of the Gospels* 1.3). Each succeeding Gospel after Matthew knew and used the preceding one(s).

B. J.J. Griesbach in 1789 proposed the order as follows: Matthew, Luke, then Mark. Again each succeeding Gospel knew and utilized the preceding one(s). Griesbach's hypothesis has been given new life recently by W.R. Farmer and his school of followers (e.g., Longstaff).

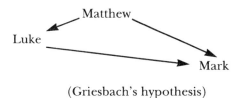

(Griesbach's hypothesis)

C. The Two-Source (and subsequently, Four-Source) Hypothesis was advanced in the nineteenth century. This hypothesis suggested that Mark wrote first. Matthew and Luke used Mark plus a second source containing mostly Jesus' sayings. This second source — which is purely hypothetical itself since no such source has been found — eventually came to be known as "Q", probably from the German word *Quelle* ("source").[1]

B.H. Streeter's Defense of the Two-Source (Four-Source) Hypothesis:

Although the Two-Source hypothesis was advanced in the early nineteenth century, its definitive statement was made by Streeter in 1924. By then this hypothesis had pretty well prevailed anyway and Streeter's well-written monograph seemed to settle the issue once and for all. He maintained that the priority of Mark was certain: "How anyone who has worked through those pages with a synopsis of the Greek text can retain the slightest doubt of the original and primitive character of Mark I am unable to comprehend" (p. 164).

Those who disagreed with Streeter were accused of having "eccentric views of what constitutes evidence."

Further, he believed the existence of the hypothetical document Q was almost certain. Streeter wrote that the assumption that there had been a Q and that it was used by Matthew and Luke: "though highly probable, falls just short of certainty" (p. 184). Thus, he left little room for nay-sayers to the Two-Source hypothesis.

---

[1]To find the alleged Q material in the Gospels, simply locate pericopes found only in Matthew and Luke. A good synopsis, such as Aland, makes this task easier. See e.g., Matt 6:24 = Luke 16:13 (Aland 224), or Matt 11:20 = Luke 10:12-15 (Aland 108). Q is usually considered this "double tradition."

Streeter's main arguments for the priority of Mark were as follows: (1) There is much common material between Mark and the other two. Matthew "reproduces" 90% of Mark and Luke reproduces over 50% of Mark. (2) There is a common order of events. Mark's order is always supported by either Matthew or Luke. (3) There is much common vocabulary between Mark and the other two. Matthew has 51% of the words of Mark; Luke less. But where the words and expressions are different, Matthew and/or Luke have often "improved" them. That is, they have used purer Greek. (For example, compare Mark 4:6 with Luke 8:6).

Streeter allowed that there were some "meagre" agreements between Matthew and Luke which are not in Mark. Compare, for example, the story of Jesus' cleansing of the temple. Matthew and Luke seem to say that Jesus cleansed it on the same day as his triumphal entry into Jerusalem. But Mark explicitly says he did so on the next day (see Matt 21:10-17; Mark 11:1-19; Luke 19:45-46). Now of course Matthew and Luke were compressing events in their narration. But the question is why did not at least one of them follow Mark's way of telling the story if they both indeed had used Mark as a source? Streeter said such arguments against Mark were of no consequence, but others are not so sure (for a complete list of these passages see Neirynck, Hansen and Segbraeck).

Streeter established the existence of Q as follows: (1) The narrative material common to Matthew and Luke (the double tradition) occurs in different contexts and different order. (2) The degree of resemblance between the parallel passages varies considerably.

There are three explanations for the above two observations. First, one of the Gospels might have used the other. Second, the authors might have shared an oral tradition. Third, the authors could have used a common written source. To accept the first explanation, wrote Streeter, one would have to believe that the author was a "crank" since he would have so radically rearranged the material of the other Gospel. The second solution Streeter considered more probable than the first. However, because there are such close verbal resemblances between Matthew and Luke, it must be more likely that the authors have used a written source, argued Streeter.

Streeter's line of argument raises some questions. Is it not a subjective conclusion that only a crank could rearrange the material of one Gospel to produce his own? Second, how dissimilar must the words of the common tradition be to allow for the probability of an oral source rather than a written one?

Streeter's version of the source hypothesis has become the most popular, and for all intents and purposes, the standard. Most graduate schools doing Gospels study operate under the assumption that the Two- (Four-) Source hypothesis is proven (the exception is the W.R. Farmer school, see below).

Streeter refined the hypothesis by adding two more main sources (and some other less important ones) to Mark and Q as the sources of Matthew and Luke. These two additional sources he called M (for the material found only in Matthew) and L (for the material found only in Luke). His source theory is as follows:

STREETER'S FOUR DOCUMENT HYPOTHESIS

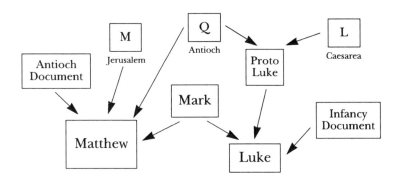

It should be noted that of the seven documents preceding Matthew and Luke, only one — the Gospel of Mark — is actually known to exist.

Farmer and His School

The most thorough criticism of the two-document hypothesis has been that of W.R. Farmer. Farmer not only attempted to discredit the existence of Q, but also the priority of Mark, reviving the Griesbach hypothesis. Griesbach had proposed the priority of Matthew and the subsequent use of both Matthew and Luke by Mark. Farmer's emphasis is that there were prior to Streeter — and there certainly have been since — valid reasons offered for doubting the Two-Source hypothesis. Yet, due to the prevailing intellectual climate, the Two-Source theory has gained supremacy. Marcan priority was accepted because Mark, more than any of the other Gospels, supported the philosophical presuppositions of the liberal theologians of the early twentieth century. With no birth narratives (and their stories of virginal conception), Mark was seen by many scholars as emphasizing the humanity of Jesus. Thus, it was desirable to have Mark as the earliest source of Christian teaching.

Regarding the Q hypothesis, Farmer maintained that since Luke has inserted his material common to Matthew in several large sections rather than dispersing it throughout his Gospel (as Streeter erroneously maintained), it is not incredible that Luke has used Matthew. Because Streeter's description of the arrangement of the "Q" material (i.e., the double tradition) in Luke was erroneous at this point, his conclusion that Luke had to have been a "crank" to use Matthew was also in error.

But Farmer's own solution to the Synoptic problem is not without its difficulties either. Farmer gives too little effort to discussing oral sources. He presumes that the data requires a literary relationship between Matthew, Mark, and Luke. Also, Farmer's solution has embarrassing inconsistencies, as he himself admitted. For example, Farmer argued that Matthew and Luke almost never agree in order against Mark, thus Mark probably wrote last and followed one or both of the other Gospels. But Farmer must admit that the apparent discrepancy between between Mark on the one hand and Matthew and Luke on the other concerning the day of the cleansing of the temple, is difficult to explain if Mark really did copy from both Matthew and Luke. One can understand the difference as merely Mark's way of telling the story if Mark was written independently. But it is hard to see why Mark would deliberately contradict both Matthew and Luke.

Recent Developments

A. The W.O. Walker Essays

In 1978 a group of New Testament scholars met to hear experts from other disciplines — oral literature, classics, rabbinics, and modern literature — discuss the Gospels. Their conclusions in general challenged the prevailing notions concerning both the literary relationship of the Gospels and the historicity of the Gospel material.

A.B. Lord — who had changed the course of Homeric studies by demonstrating that the *Iliad* and the *Odyssey* were originally oral poetry (see his *Singer of Tales*) — concluded that the Synoptics "have the appearance of three oral traditional variants of the same narrative and non-narrative materials" (p. 90 in Walker). By that statement, Lord — an expert in the study of oral literature — was indicating that he thought Matthew, Mark, and Luke had each written his Gospel from his own oral sources, not from copying from one another.

Even more fascinating was the conclusion of G. Kennedy, the classicist. Kennedy pointed to two phenomena in antiquity that most New Testament scholars seem unaware of. Gospel critics often assume that the materials in the four Gospels were passed on by word of mouth for decades and that these materials were often altered. Some even affirm that new materials were created by Christian communities so that much — some might even say most — of the Gospel narratives and sayings material is not authentically from Jesus.

But Kennedy pointed out that the ancients were wont to make notes on important people. Several of Socrates's followers went around taking notes on his sayings. This practice was followed, says Kennedy, not just by the intelligentsia, for a common cobbler also made notes of everything he could remember that Socrates said to him and he ended with 33 dialogues (p. 131 in Walker). Note taking was a very common practice in antiquity; thus we should expect that some of Jesus' disciples had notes of his sayings.

Furthermore, it was not uncommon for ancient people to display prodigious memories. Kennedy cites the example of the philosopher Seneca who memorized speeches he heard and years later wrote them down. Kennedy adds:

> It would have been a much less demanding task for regular hearers of Jesus or of the apostles to hold in memory a significant part of the teaching they had repeatedly heard and to recite it or write it down at any time there was reason to do so (p. 143 in Walker).

B. B. Gerhardsson

Gerhardsson published his work on the Gospels in 1961. His thesis was that just as the rabbis had transmitted their teaching about the Law orally — now preserved at least partially in the Mishnah — so Jesus transmitted his new Torah orally. Now the rabbis spent many years memorizing the oral Torah and later teaching it to students. They had a careful system to preserve the words of the sages. We should expect Jesus and his disciples to have done the same, maintained Gerhardsson. More recently, R. Riesner has argued similarly.

Although most New Testament scholars have not been convinced by all of Gerhardsson's arguments (see Kee), he did remind us of one important fact. Memorization of important teachings in Palestine was very commonplace. Therefore, it is highly probable that Jesus' words and deeds were carefully remembered and recited — and of course taught to others — until some decades later they were written down. Moreover, Jesus promised his apostles that the Holy Spirit would aid their memories (John 14:26), thus lending divine supervision and control to the process.

Conclusions Concerning the Synoptic Relationship

In reaching any conclusion in this area one must consider the evidence of the ancient Christian writer, Papias. Papias was bishop of Hierapolis in Asia Minor and wrote a treatise on the *Sayings of the Lord* in A.D. 133. Papias claimed to possess the oral teaching of Jesus' disciples and he was, according to the Christian historian, Eusebius (4th cent. A.D.), a hearer of John the elder, of Polycarp, and of one Aristion, all important late first century to early second century Christian leaders. Papias himself evidently did not know any of the twelve apostles but knew those who did. He wrote of his oral learning in one of the few fragments of his we have left:

> I will not hesitate to set down for you, along with my interpretations, everything I carefully learned then from the elders and carefully remembered, guaranteeing their truth. For unlike most people I did not enjoy those who have a great deal to say, but those who teach the truth. Nor did I enjoy those who recall someone else's commandments, but those who remember the commandments given by the Lord to the faith and proceeding from the truth itself. And if by chance someone who had been a follower of the elders should come my way, I inquired about the words of the elders — what Andrew or Peter said, or Philip, or Thomas or James, or John or Matthew or any other of the Lord's disciples, and whatever Aristion and the elder John, the Lord's disciples, were saying. For I did not think that information from books would profit me as much as information from a living and abiding voice (quoted in Eusebius, *H.E.* 3.39. Trans. in J.B. Lightfoot and J.R. Harmer, *The Apostolic Fathers*, p. 314).

Thus Papias sought out information about Jesus, the apostles and the "elders" from those who had known them. He valued living witnesses over written documents.

Papias describes the composition of the Gospels, Mark and Matthew, as follows:

> And (John) the Elder[2] used to say this: "Mark having become Peter's interpreter, wrote down accurately everything he remembered, though not in order, of the things either said or done by Christ. For he neither heard the Lord nor followed him, but afterward, as I said, followed Peter, who adapted his teachings as needed but had no intention of giving an ordered account of the Lord's sayings. Consequently Mark did nothing wrong in writing down some things as he remembered them, for he made it his own concern not to omit anything which he heard or to make any false statement in them. . . ."

---

[2]For the identity of John the Elder, see the discussion of John's Gospel, later in this chapter.

"So Matthew composed the oracles in the Hebrew language
and each person interpreted them as best he could" (quoted in
Eusebius *H.E.* 3.39. Trans. in Lightfoot and Harmer, *The
Apostolic Fathers*, p. 316).

Thus Papias indicates that Mark wrote from his memory of
Peter's eyewitness testimony concerning the events of Jesus' life.
This is much like the process described by Kennedy and the
Fragment and Oral Tradition hypotheses described above.

Matthew, according to Papias, wrote his "oracles" (λόγια, *logia*)
in the Hebrew (that is, probably Aramaic) language. Furthermore
Irenaeus (A.D. 180), Origen (A.D. 220), Clement of Alexandria
(A.D. 200), and Augustine (A.D. 400) wrote also that Matthew composed his gospel first in Aramaic.

Thus the testimony of the ancient Christian authors is that
Matthew wrote his gospel first and in the Aramaic language.
Further, Papias indicates — as do Irenaeus and Clement of
Alexandria — that Mark's Gospel is based on Peter's preaching.
Mark wrote down — either while Peter was yet alive (Clement) or
after his death (Irenaeus) — what Peter had taught and preached
about Jesus' life and deeds.

Luke, the author of the third Gospel, gives us some idea of his
own process in writing his work in the prologue (Luke 1:1-4):

Since many have taken it in hand to compose a narrative
about the events fulfilled among us, even as the eyewitnesses
and ministers of the word taught them to us orally from the
beginning, it seemed good to me also, most excellent
Theophilus, to write for you (an account) correctly and in
order since I have followed (these events) from the beginning.
That way you will know the certainty of the words you were
taught.

From Luke's statement we learn the following: First, there were
already several accounts of Jesus' deeds and words by the time Luke
wrote. Some of these accounts may have been nothing more than
the published notes of eyewitnesses, but it is equally possible that
Luke knew about Matthew. Second, Luke has gotten his materials

from the "eyewitnesses" and "ministers of the word" (possibly those who memorized and taught the sayings of Jesus) who taught these materials orally.[3] Third, Luke's purpose is to help his readers — and his patron, Theophilus — know with certainty that the words and deeds attributed to Jesus in his Gospel are accurate. Thus Luke was concerned to repeat only accurate descriptions of Jesus' life.

From such ancient evidence one should conclude that probably Matthew wrote his Gospel first. He published it in Aramaic and later in Greek.[4] Mark wrote his Gospel from his recollection of Peter's eyewitness testimony about Jesus. Luke wrote based on the testimony of numerous eyewitnesses and perhaps from others' notes. Luke (and Mark for that matter) may have known of, may even have read, Matthew. But a slavish copying of Matthew's Gospel seems out of the question.

J. Wenham's recent work probably best describes the process of Gospel composition. The Synoptics are three independently written documents, based on oral teaching and notes of eyewitnesses. But Mark probably was familiar with Matthew as was Luke. Mark and Luke were influenced by Matthew as far as the general outline of events but not much else. Wenham accepts the Augustinian order of composition (Matthew–Mark–Luke). But we will argue below for the Griesbach order. Thus we would adapt Wenham's diagram as follows:

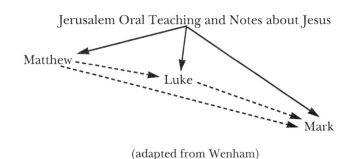

Jerusalem Oral Teaching and Notes about Jesus

Matthew

Luke

Mark

(adapted from Wenham)

---

[3]The Greek word παραδίδωμι (*paradidōmi*) in Luke 1:2 means to transmit information orally. Compare the Hebrew word מסר (*masar*) in m. Aboth 1:1.

[4]Compare Josephus's publication of the *Jewish War* which was written in Aramaic and later translated into Greek with the help of certain Greek stylists.

FORM CRITICISM

Bibliography: R. Bultmann, *History of the Synoptic Tradition*; M. Dibelius, *From Tradition to Gospel*; E.V. McKnight, *What is Form Criticism?*; V. Taylor, *The Formation of the Gospel Tradition*.

Form criticism (German: *Formgeschichte* "history of the forms") is the name given to the study of the oral transmission of the Gospel material. The assumption is that the sayings and narratives of Jesus were transmitted orally using certain fixed forms. The pioneers in the discipline were M. Dibelius and R. Bultmann.

Dibelius's Analysis of Narrative Forms

A. Paradigms. These are stories about Jesus, wrote Dibelius, which the early church used for sermon illustrations. These illustrations reach a high point at the end of the story; they are brief and simple; they are thoroughly religious in tone; and they usually conclude with a memorable saying of Jesus. Mark 2:1-12, the healing of a paralytic and 9:38-40, the teaching about the unknown exorcist, are examples of this form.

B. Tales. These are stories of Jesus told with color and art, according to Dibelius. They were not used by the church in preaching but told for the pleasure of the story itself. They possess lively realism and deal with Jesus as a wonder worker but they have no didactic (or teaching) purpose. Details are usually presented about an illness, the technique of healing, and the success of the miracle. These Tales, alleged Dibelius, are less historical than the Paradigms because they are imitative of Hellenistic religions. Some examples of this form are Mark 1:40-45, the healing of the leper and 8:22-26, the healing of the blind man.

C. Legends. This form was also popular in the literature of the surrounding world. Legends tell why a saint or great man was so revered. Luke 2:41-49, Jesus' talking with the elders, is a story also told of Buddha, Josephus, and Rabbi Eleazar ben Hyrcanus (where a young lad is seen as precocious). These forms are not historically authentic, according to Dibelius.

D. Myths. These forms, allege the form critics, describe interaction with non-human persons and are not historical. Such are Jesus' baptism (Mark 1:9-11), the temptation (Mark 1:12-13), and the transfiguration (Mark 9:28).

Bultmann's Analysis

Bultmann's conclusions were similar to Dibelius.[5] but he devoted much more space to the sayings of Jesus, whereas Dibelius had concentrated mostly on the narratives. Bultmann classified the sayings as:

A. Wisdom sayings or proverbs (e.g., Matt 12:34b).

B. Prophetic sayings (e.g., Luke 6:24-26).

C. Legal sayings (e.g., Matt 6:2-4).

D. Parables (e.g., Mark 4:3-8).

Bultmann, like Dibelius, was sceptical that very many of the narratives in the Gospels were historical. Bultmann was also reluctant to conclude that the sayings were historical. All of them, he wrote, have been adapted, shaped, and modified by the needs of the early church. Many of them were created outright by the church. The wisdom sayings are too similar to Jewish wisdom and so have the least claim to authenticity. Many of the prophetic sayings contain ideas which are typically Jewish and are thus probably not authentic, maintained Bultmann (e.g., Matt 24:37-41; Luke 6:24-36). The same can be said for the legal sayings. The "I" sayings are especially suspect: "I have come not to abolish the law and the prophets but to fulfill them" (Matt 5:17).

Thus Dibelius and Bultmann emphasized the church's role in transmitting the oral Gospel material. The church did not, they alleged, simply pass on the narratives and sayings. The church modified them and even added to them. They were therefore very hesitant to affirm that much material in the Synoptics was authentic.

It is important to note at this point that the way form critics

---

[5]Bultmann's terms were apothphegms (=Paradigms), Miracles Stories (=Tales), Historical Stories and Legends (=Legends and Myths). Bultmann, as did Dibelius, dismissed most of the Gospel material as unhistorical.

handle oral literature is quite different from the way an expert in oral literature such as A. Lord (in Walker) analyzes it. Lord affirms that it is a fallacy to conclude that a narrative or saying is unhistorical simply because one can find parallels to it in content or in form in other traditions or literature. Events or sayings may be recounted in certain customary ways or forms but that hardly means that the event or saying is unhistorical. Dibelius and Bultmann assumed the opposite but they did not prove it.

Further, the assumption of form critics — that the church freely changed and created Gospel material — ignores the possibility that at least some did not. If even one person proceeded along the lines suggested reasonably by Kennedy (see above) then many of the unhistorical and inaccurate narratives and sayings would have been exposed. What were the eyewitnesses of Jesus' life doing while this process of changing history was going on?

Finally, Dibelius and Bultmann beg the question in their conclusions about Tales, Legends and Myths. The real problem for them — as they would have admitted — was the presence of the miraculous. They did not believe in miracles; thus any story with a miraculous element was unhistorical. But this assumes the very point one must prove.

Since most of the work done by form critics has been based on the above named fallacies, it is in the main useless in any investigation of the history of the Synoptic tradition. It does, however, underline the importance of the oral transmission of Gospel material.

REDACTION CRITICISM

Bibliography: G. Bornkamm, *End-Expectation and Church in Matthew*; H. Conzelmann, *Theology of St. Luke*; W. Marxsen, *Mark the Evangelist*; N. Perrin, *What is Redaction Criticism?*; J. Rohde, *Rediscovering the Teaching of the Evangelists*.

Redaction criticism (German: *Redaktionsgeschichte* or "history of the editorial activity") focuses not on what the early church did to the oral Gospel material (as form criticism does) but on what the authors of the Gospels have done with it. The conclusion of many of these scholars is that the "evangelists" (i.e., the authors) edited, shaped, and even created Gospel material to make their Gospel relevant to the situation of their congregation.

We will examine below the theological emphases of the Gospel writers. Certainly they did seek to make the life and teachings of Jesus relevant to their environment. But the assumption common to many redaction critics — that the events of the Gospels are in general unhistorical — must be rejected.

Marxsen affirmed, for example, that Mark has inserted references to Galilee throughout his Gospel out of theological reasons. Mark is said to have written his Gospel in Galilee among the Galilean Christians and thus it was important to Mark for Galilee to be the place for Jesus' activity. But why cannot one conclude that Mark has all the references to Galilee in his gospel because Jesus *was* mostly in Galilee?

Surely the Gospel writers did interpret events of Jesus' life. They were, it is true, theologians, not just collectors of information. But it is one thing to interpret and explain the actual words and deeds of Jesus by the way they are presented and highlighted, and quite another proposal to say that the Gospel authors created material to fit their theological needs. Redaction critics have made a contribution to our understanding of the Gospels but their works must be used cautiously and critically.

THE AUTHORSHIP, DATE, PURPOSE, AND CONTENT OF THE SYNOPTICS

THE GOSPEL OF MATTHEW

Bibliography: B.W. Bacon, *Studies in Matthew*; W.D. Davies, *The Setting of the Sermon on the Mount*; W.D. Davies and D. Allison, *The Gospel According to Matthew*; *FBK*; Guthrie, *NTI*; J. Jeremias, *The Sermon on the Mount*; J.A.T. Robinson, *Redating the New Testament*; K. Stendahl, *The School of St. Matthew*; M.J. Suggs, *Wisdom, Christology and Law in Matthew's Gospel*; J. Wenham, *Redating Matthew, Mark and Luke*.

Authorship

Four ancient authors mentioned that Matthew the apostle of Jesus wrote a Gospel: Papias (A.D. 140), Irenaeus (A.D. 180), Pantaenus (A.D. 180), and Origen (A.D. 220).[6] In addition, the title of the Gospel in all the oldest manuscripts is "According to Matthew" (see Guthrie). Thus ancient tradition affirms that Matthew authored a Gospel and that our first Gospel was that one. Any denial of the tradition must show why this cannot be so. We have taken the position that one should accept the tradition unless it can be shown conclusively that one cannot.

The reasons for doubting the Matthean authorship have to do mostly with the belief in the priority of Mark. Would Matthew, an apostle and eyewitness, have used Mark? But we have concluded that Matthew's Gospel was written first. (Even if, however, Mark were prior to the other two, it is only an unproven assumption that Matthew would not have used it.)

---

[6]Papias (in Eusebius *H.E.* 3.39) calls it Matthew's "oracles (*logia*) of the Lord." Irenaeus's reference is in *Adversus Haereseis* 3.1. Pantaenus's statement is in Eusebius, *H.E.* 5.10. Origen's affirmation is also in Eusebius, *H.E,* 6.25.

Date

The most commonly assigned date today is somewhere between A.D. 80 and 100 (see *FBK* and Davies). This conclusion is based on two assumptions. First, scholars assume it has been proven that Mark was written first (c. 70) and that Matthew utilized Mark. Second, scholars assume that Jesus could not have predicted the Jewish war and the destruction of Jerusalem (see Matt 22:7). But both of these assumptions must be questioned. Gospel critics too often form hypotheses which rashly assume that miracles are impossible. Thus the structure for dating Matthew late crumbles when examined.

J. Wenham may be taken as a representative of those who date Matthew early (see also J.A.T. Robinson). Wenham dates Mark at A.D. 45 and Matthew before it, at around A.D. 40.

There is really not a good indication of the date in the Gospel itself and no strong external testimony about when it was written either — as Wenham also admits. Therefore we would date it somewhere between A.D. 50 and 55 for the following reasons: First, Matthew probably preceded Luke and Wenham's argument that Luke was written before A.D. 62 seems valid. Second, a date of 50 to 55 gives at least 20 years — from the crucifixion and resurrection of Jesus — for Matthew to have written a rough draft or partial draft of his Gospel in Aramaic and then a final version in Greek. The apostles may have been too preoccupied preaching in the earlier years to have attempted such an enterprise. Yet we must admit that a date any time between A.D. 40 and 60 is possible.

Occasion

The various purposes suggested for the writing of this Gospel are:

1. To produce a church manual of conduct for church leaders.
2. To produce a catechism for those about to be baptized.
3. To appeal to Jews to accept Jesus as the Christ.

Each of these suggestions has merit but of course the most obvious purpose for this Gospel was to record and preserve the words and deeds of Jesus.

Content

B.W. Bacon observed that Matthew contains five great discourses:

Chapters 5-7	The Sermon on the Mount
Chapter 10	Sending out the Twelve Apostles
Chapter 13	Parables of the Kingdom
Chapter 18	Community Life
Chapters 24-25	Teaching on the End of the Age

Bacon's hypothesis, however, that Matthew wished with these five large collections of Jesus' teaching to present Jesus as a new Moses, giving a new Pentateuch, is tempting but not compelling. One can say with certainty that Matthew focused as much on Jesus' words as on his deeds. Jesus as teacher is of primary importance to the author.

Second, Matthew demonstrates a definite interest in Judaism. Only in Matthew are Jesus' words: "I have not come to destroy the law (of Moses) but to fulfill it" (5:17). Only Matthew records Jesus' statement to the Canaanite woman: "I was sent only to the lost sheep of Israel" (15:24), indicating Jesus' commitment to preach his message of the kingdom first to Jews. Only Matthew tells us that Jesus said in his discourse on the destruction of the temple and the end of the age, "Pray that your flight will not take place in winter or on the Sabbath" (since Jews could only legally travel 2000 cubits on the Sabbath; Matt 24:20). Because of these and other similar passages, many scholars have rightly concluded that Matthew's Gospel was written to speak to Jews. This conclusion fits well with the two facts attested by ancient Christian authors: Matthew wrote his Gospel first and he wrote in Aramaic. If Matthew wrote his Greek Gospel in the early fifties as we have postulated then his Aramaic version must have been written in the forties, before the Gentile mission was in full bloom. It is reasonable that he should have appealed to Jews to accept Jesus as the Christ and therefore that he would write in his native Palestinian Aramaic. Later, he wished to appeal to Greek-speaking Jews and so (like Josephus the historian) had his Gospel translated — and perhaps expanded — probably with the help of Greek-speaking Jewish Christians. This conclusion leads us to a third observation about Matthew.

Third, Matthew appeals to his readers to accept Jesus as the long-awaited Jewish Messiah, foretold in the Old Testament. Matthew quotes numerous Messianic prophecies (e.g., 1:23; 2:6, 15; 4:15-16; 8:17) to demonstrate that Jesus fulfilled Old Testament predictions. He is the Messiah as the Bible foretold and thus Israel should accept him.

Because Matthew was written in some form of Aramaic first and appealed to Jews, and because his Gospel is first quoted by Ignatius of Syrian Antioch (A.D. 110) and the Didache (c. 120-140) also of Syria, most historians conclude that it was written in Syria or Palestine.

THE GOSPEL OF MARK

Bibliography: M. Hengel, *Studies in the Gospel of Mark*; H.C. Kee, *Community of the New Age; Studies in Mark's Gospel*; W. Lane, *The Gospel According to Mark*; N. Perrin, *What is Redaction Criticism?*; J.A.T. Robinson, *Redating the New Testament*; V. Taylor, *The Gospel According to Mark*; E. Trocmé, *The Formation of the Gospel According to Mark*; E. Schweitzer, *The Good News According to Mark*; J, Wenham, *Redating Matthew, Mark and Luke*.

Authorship and Place of Writing

The ancient testimony is strong that a person named Mark wrote the second Gospel in Rome as a compendium of the apostle Peter's preaching. Papias of Asia Minor (A.D. 140), Irenaeus of Gaul (A.D. 180), Clement of Alexandria (A.D. 200), Origen of Alexandria and Caesarea (A.D. 220) and Jerome of Palestine (A.D. 400) all attest to Mark's authorship. Three statements in particular are important for us: those of Papias, Irenaeus and Clement.

The statement of Papias (quoted above) informs us that Mark was Peter's interpreter or Greek translator. He evidently spoke fluent Greek and Aramaic and so traveled with Peter — who probably spoke at least a little Greek himself — to assist in speaking to Greek audiences. Papias indicates that Mark wrote down from memory — thus Peter was dead by then? — what Peter had taught about the words and deeds of Jesus (see above).

Irenaeus's statement is as follows:

> Matthew published a Gospel in writing also, among the Hebrews in their own language, while Peter and Paul were preaching the Gospel and founding the church in Rome. But after their decease Mark, the disciple and interpreter of Peter — he also transmitted to us in writing the things which Peter used to preach (*Adv. Haer.* 3.1; trans. in Robinson, p. 110).

Thus Irenaeus adds to Papias's testimony that Mark wrote after Peter's death (somewhere around A.D. 65).

Another brief text, the so-called Anti-Marcionite Prologue found in some manuscripts of Mark (A.D. 180 or later)[7] confirms Irenaeus: "(Mark) was the interpreter of Peter. After the death of Peter himself, he wrote down this same Gospel in the regions of Italy" (Trans. in Robinson, p. 110).

On the other hand, Clement of Alexandria (A.D. 200) and Eusebius (A.D. 330) indicate that Peter was still alive when Mark wrote. Clement maintained that the following tradition was from "the oldest presbyters" in Alexandria:

> When Peter had proclaimed the word publicly at Rome, and declared the gospel under the influence of the spirit; as there was a great number present, they requested Mark, who had followed him from afar, and remembered well what he had said, to reduce these things to writing, and that after composing the gospel he gave it to those who requested it of him. Which, when Peter understood, he directly neither hindered nor encouraged it (*H.E.* 6.14; trans. in Cruse, *Eusebius*, p. 234).

At any rate the ancient testimony is very strong that a person named Mark, who was in the company of Peter, wrote our second Gospel. Although it is true that the Latin praenomen, Marcus, was very common, we should probably conclude that this Mark was the same as the one often appearing in the New Testament. He was sometimes designated John Mark (Acts 12:12, 25; 15:37) but usually just Mark (Acts 15:39; Col 4:10; 1 Pet 5:13; Phlm 24; 2 Tim 4:11). From these verses we learn that Mark's mother owned a house in Jerusalem which was evidently a habitual meeting place for the Christian community. Mark was Barnabas's cousin and thus also had roots among the Greek-speaking Jews of Cyprus (Acts 4:36) as well as in Jerusalem. He therefore would have been, like Paul and Barnabas, ideal for missionary service outside of Palestine — since he was undoubtedly fluent in Greek — and thus the perfect interpreter for Peter. Mark was later in Rome in company of Paul and Peter, as these texts indicate.

---

[7]See the notes on this and other alleged Anti-Marcionite Prologues in Haenchen, *Acts*, p. 10 and W.T. Howard's article in *Expository Times* 47 (1935-36) 534-38.

Thus we should conclude that the Mark referred to in the New Testament composed his Gospel in Rome. That Mark is first quoted in the epistle of Clement of Rome (A.D. 96) and the Shepherd of Hermas, also written in Rome (A.D. 148), also supports this conclusion.

Date, Purpose, and Content

Did Mark write his Gospel before Peter's death — as Clement of Alexandria and Eusebius maintained — or after his death — as Irenaeus maintained? To settle the issue we can only turn to the content and purpose of Mark itself.

N. Perrin has argued persuasively that Mark's Gospel is primarily the Passion Narrative (i.e., the story of Jesus' death) in chapters 14 and 15 with an extended introduction. Further Perrin has shown that chapters 8-10 explain and interpret what Jesus' death meant. Mark has narrated three episodes in the life of Jesus using the following pattern:

	Mark 8	Mark 9	Mark 10
1. Jesus predicts his death	8:31	9:31	10:33-34
2. The disciples misunderstand	8:32f	9:32-34	10:35-41
3. Jesus teaches them	8:34-38	9:35-37	10:42-45

Jesus' death means that the servant of all gave his life as a ransom price for the sin of the world (10:45). Disciples of Jesus must also learn humility and commitment even to the point of taking up the cross (8:34).

Perrin believed that Mark so emphasized Jesus' death and the call to his disciples to be ready to die because he wrote his Gospel just after the persecution of Nero (thus sometime after A.D. 64/65). Therefore, the Gospel of Mark would have been written around 66 or 67, after Peter's death. It was meant both to record the life of Jesus and to show how Jesus' life should be imitated by his followers.

This date agrees roughly with the date most scholars have assigned to Mark. But Robinson and Wenham date Mark much earlier, to A.D. 45.

Such a setting and purpose help explain three other characteristics of Mark. First, Mark stressed action, not discourse (contrast with Matthew). When teaching is included, as Guthrie observes, it nearly always is in a setting of some narrative. Mark is a quickly moving drama heading toward the crucifixion as the narrative climax. It is more the actions of Jesus, the suffering servant, that are crucial for Mark's situation.

Second, Mark has no Jewish coloring such as we find in Matthew. In fact, he finds it necessary to explain Jewish customs such as handwashing (7:3) and he always translates Aramaic phrases (e.g., 5:41; 7:11). Mark wrote for a Gentile-Christian audience in Rome.

Third, Mark is careful to point out the weaknesses of the disciples of Jesus (4:13; 6:52; 8:17, 21; 9:10, 32). They are selfish, slow to understand, and worldly-minded. The author noted these characteristics to give encouragement to Roman Christians. Not everyone acts entirely unselfishly and nobly during a persecution. Mark wanted to give his readers hope of forgiveness and renewal by the example of Jesus' disciples.

THE GOSPEL OF LUKE

Bibliography: H. Conzelmann, *The Theology of Luke*; F. Danker, *Luke*; E. Ellis, *The Gospel of Luke*; J. Fitzmyer, *The Gospel of Luke*; I.H. Marshall, *Commentary on Luke*; N. Peterson, *Literary Criticism for New Testament Critics*.

Authorship and Date

The questions of the authorship and date of the Gospel of Luke are in the main handled below in Chapter 6 on Acts. The same evidence that indicates Luke wrote Acts also demonstrates that he wrote the third Gospel, for the two works were clearly — as the prologues show — written by the same person.

Since we conclude that Acts was written sometime between A.D. 62 and 64 (see Chapter 6), we should place Luke before 62, perhaps between 58 and 60 when Paul was imprisoned in Caesarea Maritima. Luke would have been close there to Palestinian oral sources on the life and words of Jesus and he would have had the leisure to undertake such a project.

Content

The outline of Luke is as follows:
1. Introduction — 1:1-4:13
2. Jesus in Galilee — 4:14-9:50
3. Journey to Jerusalem — 9:51-19:27
4. Jesus in Jerusalem — 19:28-24:53

The really distinctive material in Luke — apart from the birth narratives in the first section — is found in section three. Luke's travel narrative is longer than that of other Gospels and it contains material not found anywhere else. Here, for example, we find the parables of the Good Samaritan (10:25-37) and the Prodigal Son (15:11-32). Here are the narratives of Jesus' dining at a Pharisee's house (14:1-14) and at Zacchaeus's home (19:1-10).

Luke's Gospel is distinguished from the others by the following features: First, Luke is careful to preserve Jesus' words about the poor (6:20; 7:22) especially in the parables (see the Rich Man and Lazarus 16:19-31). In general the poor are elevated as especially protected by God (1:53) while the selfish wealthy are struck down (1:51-52; 12:13-21).

Second, Luke refers more than any other Gospel to the women disciples of Jesus. He mentions thirteen women not referred to by other Gospels (e.g., 23:27; 7:12, 37).

Third, Jesus' prayers are noted more often in Luke (3:21; 5:15-16; 6:12; 9:18-22, 29; 10:17-21; 11:1; 22:39-46; 23:34, 46).

Fourth, as in Acts, the Holy Spirit is an important participant in Jesus' life, especially at the beginning of his ministry. He receives the Spirit at his baptism (3:22) and is full of the Spirit when he is tempted (4:1). He begins his ministry in Galilee in the power of the Holy Spirit (4:14). Jesus' empowerment at the beginning of his ministry corresponds to the empowerment of the church in its beginning (see Acts 1:1-2:47).

THE GOSPEL OF JOHN

Bibliography: C.K. Barrett, *The Gospel According to St. John*; R. Brown, *The Community of the Beloved Disciple*; Idem, *The Gospel According to John*; R. Bultmann, *The Gospel of John*; D.A. Carson, D. Moo, and L. Morris, *An Introduction to the New Testament*; C.H. Dodd, *The Interpretation of the Fourth Gospel*; E.E. Ellis, *The World of St. John*; R. Fortna, *The Gospel of Signs*; M. Hengel, *The Johannine Question*; E. Kaesemann, *The Testament of Jesus*; G. McRae, *Invitation to John*; L. Martyn, *History and Theology in the Fourth Gospel*; D.M. Smith, *Johannine Christianity*; B.F. Westcott, *The Gospel According to St. John*.

The Author

A. Bultmann's View

R. Bultmann has been so influential that we must begin by summarizing his view concerning the author of the Gospel of John. Bultmann postulated three sources for the Gospel: (1) a sign source, (2) a discourse source, and (3) a passion source.

The sign source is found dispersed throughout John 1-12. Originally it simply enumerated Jesus' signs (miracles) and briefly described each one (e.g., 2:11; 4:54; 12:37). There are seven signs or miracles in John. Since Bultmann did not believe in miracles, he found very little historical value in the sign source.

According to Bultmann, the discourse source was originally a Gnostic (that is, pre-Christian Gnostic) text in Aramaic. In other words the long sermons of Jesus (e.g., John 6:26-59; 14:1-17:26) were not uttered by him, maintained Bultmann, but were Gnostic texts that were put in his mouth in the Gospel of John.

The passion source (about Jesus' suffering and death; John 18-19) is more historical and is rather similar to that of the Synoptics.

Bultmann alleged that an editor/author — himself a convert from Gnosticism to Christianity — had molded these three sources into something approximating our present Gospel of John. Later, another editor rearranged the Gospel — causing some things to be out of place, cf. 14:31 which is yet followed, wrote Bultmann, by three more chapters of discourse — and also "cleaned up the theology" a bit, adding references to the sacraments (3:5; 6:51-58) and eschatology or the end-time (5:28f; 12:48).

R. Brown has rightly criticized Bultmann's analysis. Bultmann said that the author did not believe in the sacraments or in eschatology so a later editor must have added them. But this begs the question. Bultmann first decided what he wanted the author to believe, then gave the rest to the editor. The most obvious conclusion is that since these verses are in the Gospel of John, the author wrote them and believed them.

Brown also criticizes Bultmann's source hypothesis. Often the signs and discourses are so closely woven together it is hard to see two sources. The sermon on the bread of life, for example (John 6:26-59), flows naturally out of Jesus' miracle of multiplying the loaves to feed the five thousand (John 6:1-25). Second, Brown notes that many of the sayings in John were very similar to those of the Synoptics,[8] thus ruling out the idea that the author in a rather empty-headed moment simply took a Gnostic sayings-source and attributed it all to Jesus.

B. Brown's View

Brown himself posits five stages in the composition of the Gospel:

1. An oral tradition independent from the Synoptics but parallel to them. This stage lasted from A.D. 40 to 60.

2. A Community which molded and preached this tradition headed by one outstanding evangelist. This phase was from A.D. 60 to 75.

3. After a time, the evangelist collected the materials and published

---

[8]For examples of the many similarities of Jesus' sayings in the Synoptics and John see R. Brown, *John*, Vol. II, p. 694. Some of the similarities cited are:

John	Matthew	Mark
15:18	10:22	
15:20	10:23, 24	
16:1	24:10	
16:2		13:9

See also Aland's *Synopsis* for many other examples.

them (sometime between 75 and 85).

4. Later the evangelist re-edited the Gospel — perhaps several times — to speak to a new situation (85-95).

5. A member of the evangelist's community about A.D. 100 collected and inserted all material from stage 2 not already in the Gospel.

Originally Brown concluded that stage one was based on the eyewitness testimony of John the apostle, who was also the Beloved Disciple. Brown has lately changed his mind, however, on the identity of the Beloved Disciple.

The advantages of Brown's hypothesis are he is much more sensitive to the historicity of John than Bultmann and he is less dependent on unproven assumptions such as the existence of a document like the signs-source or a pre-Christian Gnostic discourse-source. The problem with Brown's hypothesis is he gives too little weight to the external testimony on the identity of the author of John.

C. Hengel's View

M. Hengel's construction of the author's background is as follows: Behind the Johannine literature — the Gospel, Letters, and Revelation — stands a Palestinian Jew who founded a school in Asia Minor sometime between A.D. 60 and 70. The school existed until around 100 to 110. This teacher, named John, was "the beloved disciple" of Jesus (John 13:23; 19:26-27; 20:2-9; 21:24), but is not the apostle John. He lived to an advanced age in Asia Minor and was there known as "the elder." Hengel supports his hypothesis by an exhaustive analysis of the ancient sources. One of the most important of these sources was Papias (see above, p. 131):

> And if anyone chanced to come who had actually been a follower of the elders, I would enquire as to the discourses of the elders, what Andrew or what Peter said, or what Philip, or what Thomas or James, or what John or Matthew or any other of the Lord's disciples; and things which Aristion and John the elder, disciples of the Lord, say (*H.E.* 3.39.4-5).

The striking thing is that in this list there are two people named John: John — obviously the apostle — and John the Elder. From this statement Eusebius (A.D. 320) argued that there were two great teachers named John in Asia Minor. He also pointed to two tombs in Ephesus which supposedly contained a person named John (*H.E.* III.39). The same argument was advanced by Dionysius of Alexandria (A.D. 240; in Eusebius, *H.E.* VII.25).

D. Evidence for the Identity of the Beloved Disciple

The place to begin in examining the evidence for the authorship is with the references to the Beloved Disciple. There are two types of references in John to an anonymous disciple. He is called the "other disciple" in at least one passage, possibly two (John 20:2-10 and maybe 18:15-16) and the "Beloved Disciple" in six places (John 13:23-26; 19:25-27; 20:2-10; 21:7, 20-23, 24). That the two are the same is clear at least in John 20:2 where he is called "the other disciple whom Jesus loved."

The Beloved Disciple was a close and valued disciple of Jesus. He was seated closest to Jesus at the last supper (John 13:23) and it was to him that Jesus committed the care of his mother (19:25-27). He is closely associated with the apostle Peter in the fishing trade in Galilee (21:1-14, 20-23) and it was he and Peter that ran first to the empty tomb of Jesus (20:2-10).

The statement in 18:15 has caused much debate. There we read that "another disciple" who accompanied Peter to the courtyard of the High Priest to see how Jesus' trial was proceeding was "known to the High Priest." In other words this anonymous disciple in John 18:15 was a friend of the High Priest. Historians ask how a disciple of Jesus could have been also a friend or even a friendly acquaintance of the High Priest for surely he would have therefore been recognized as Jesus' disciple and arrested (as Peter evidently feared he himself would). Thus some have suggested that this "other disciple" was not the Beloved Disciple but Nicodemus (see John 3:1-4; 7:45-52; 19:38-40) a secret disciple. Others have suggested that the "other disciple" was Judas Iscariot. Either of these suggestions is possible since the other references to the "other disciple" in John 20:2 has the definite article — "*the* other disciple whom Jesus loved" — but in John 18:15 there is no definite article — "another disciple."

Furthermore, the Beloved Disciple is clearly the eyewitness

behind the Gospel of John. In 19:35, after narrating the death of Jesus and the piercing of his side with the soldier's lance, the author writes, "And he who has seen has testified and his testimony is true and he knows that he speaks the truth that you may believe." Thus either the author or the witness behind the author was present at Jesus' crucifixion. He was probably then a disciple of Jesus.

This conclusion is even firmer with respect to 21:24-25. Here the text clearly says that the Beloved Disciple, the one who was present at the last supper (13:23-26), ". . . is the disciple testifying concerning these things and writing them." Thus the material in the Gospel of John comes from the Beloved Disciple.

Who was the Beloved Disciple? The following have been suggested:

1. Lazarus. John 11:3, 5, 11, and 36 say Jesus loved him.

2. John Mark. This is more a guess than a conclusion based on evidence.

3. An unknown disciple.

4. The apostle John, son of Zebedee. He was clearly one of the elite three disciples (i.e., Peter, James, and John) in the Synoptics and he is often associated with Peter in both the Gospels and Acts. Further, John was a Galilean fisherman as was the Beloved Disciple. Therefore, John, the son of Zebedee, is the best choice. It is best to conclude, therefore, that the witness to the life and words of Jesus comes from the apostle John.

We conclude that the composition of the Johannine literature parallels that of the writing of the Gospel of Mark. John is the apostolic eyewitness who stands behind the Gospel tradition in the Gospel of John — as did Peter for the Gospel of Mark — but John the Elder was the actual writer. Such a conclusion may explain all the evidence, both internal and external. Since the elder signed his name to 2 and 3 John and the style and content is virtually the same also in 1 John and the Gospel, we could conclude that he wrote all four documents, giving them his distinctive vocabulary and theological style. But since an eyewitness, called the Beloved Disciple, stands behind the Gospel accounts, we should also conclude that John the apostle is the source of the Gospel material narrated by John the Elder.

Date and Place of Writing

The tradition is strong that John the apostle and John the Elder lived in Ephesus. Irenaeus, Clement of Alexandria (A.D. 200), Eusebius (A.D. 320), Jerome (A.D. 400; see Westcott) all report this tradition. Almost as strong is the tradition that John the apostle lived into the reign of Trajan and wrote (or as we conclude, gave testimony for) his Gospel last of all the Gospels (Clement of Alexandria in Eusebius, *H.E.* VI.14; Muratorian Fragment). The dates commonly advanced for the composition of the Gospel of John are:

1. The 60s A.D. (Robinson)
2. c. A.D. 90-100
3. c. A.D. 170

The third suggestion is no longer tenable since the discovery of the Rylands fragment (P52) which dates about 125-140. This is a fragment of the Gospel of John, found in Egypt. Thus the Gospel must have been written long enough before this date to allow for its spread to Egypt. It is possible that the Gospel was written as early as Robinson wanted to date it but the church tradition seems to place it later. We are inclined toward A.D. 90 as the date.

Occasion of Writing

A. The Docetic problem

The Gospel in 1:14 emphasizes that Jesus really lived on earth in the flesh: "The Word became flesh and lived among us." In 19:34-35 the author states emphatically that Jesus really died on the cross. John the apostle saw it and we know his testimony is true. In the first epistle, the problem is made clearer: "Every spirit that confesses that Jesus Christ has come in the flesh is of God" (1 John 4:2; 2 John 7).

Thus the Gospel and first and second epistles of John deal with a group that did not accept that Christ actually lived in the flesh. This error was called in antiquity "docetism" (Greek: δοκεῖν, *dokein* "to seem," i.e., only to seem to be in the flesh). There were many such sects roughly affiliated with early Christianity. The most likely sect, however, which John dealt with is the sect founded by Cerinthus. Consider the following quotation from Irenaeus (*Adv. Haer.* 1.26):

> Cerinthus, again, a man who was educated in the wisdom of the Egyptians, taught that the world was not made by the primary God, but by a certain power far separated from him, and at a distance from that Authority who is supreme over the universe, and ignorant of the God who is above all. . . . Moreover, after his baptism, Christ descended upon him in the form of a dove from the Supreme Ruler, and that then he proclaimed the unknown Father, and performed miracles. But at last Christ departed from Jesus, and that then Jesus suffered and rose again, while Christ remained impassible, inasmuch as he was a spiritual being (trans. in Stevenson, *A New Eusebius*).

Cerinthus's theology has a Gnostic ring to it. The concept of the creator as different from the primary God and far separated from him is certainly one of the main tenets of most Gnostic groups. Cerinthus's teaching about Jesus was that he was just a man until his baptism when the eternal Christ descended upon him. Then at his crucifixion — or just before it — the eternal Christ departed and the human Jesus was crucified, not the eternal one. Thus the Gospel and epistles emphasized to the contrary that Christ really suffered and died in the flesh.

That John the apostle knew Cerinthus is made clear in the following also from Irenaeus (2.3):

> There are also those who heard from (Polycarp) that John, the disciple of the Lord, going to bathe at Ephesus, and perceiving Cerinthus within, rushed out of the bath-house without bathing, exclaiming, "Let us fly, lest even the bath-house fall down, because Cerinthus, the enemy of the truth, is within" (trans. in Stevenson, *A New Eusebius*).

Therefore, one of the main purposes behind the composition of the Gospel and the epistles — besides imparting information about Jesus (John 20:31) — was to oppose the docetic heresy.[9]

---

[9]Surprisingly, there was a presbyter of Rome, Gaius (A.D. 200) who tried to argue that Cerinthus was actually the author of all the Johannine litera-

B. The Problem with John the Baptist's Followers

Acts 19:1-7 records an encounter in Ephesus Paul had with some individuals that had only a knowledge of the baptism of John the Baptist. Several scholars have found hints in the Gospel of John that there was still a problem in Asia Minor with these groups in the latter part of the century (cf. John 1:8-9, 20, 30; 3:28; 5:33-36; 10:41).

Content

The most convenient way to organize the Gospel of John is around the six Jewish feasts referred to: (1) 2:23 Passover, (2) 5:1 Purim (?), (3) 6:4 Passover, (4) 7:2 Tabernacles, (5) 10:22 Dedication (or Hanukkah), (6) 13:1 Passover. At each of these feasts there is a discourse section tied — sometimes loosely — to the theme of the feast and usually Jesus is presented as the replacement of the feast or an element connected with the feast.

At the first feast Jesus speaks of his body as the new temple (2:19-22) which will be raised anew. Then he discourses to Nicodemus about spiritual, new birth (3:1-21). At the second feast Jesus seems to have made himself the replacement for the Old Testament Law. The scriptures really testify of him (5:39, 46). At the third feast Jesus declares that he, not the bread of Passover, is the Bread of Life (6:35) and then discourses on the necessity of consuming this bread. At the fourth feast, in which both light and water were major themes, Jesus said, "If anyone is thirsty let him come to me and drink" (7:37); and later, "I am the light of the world. He that follows me will not walk in darkness" (8:12). At the fifth feast Jesus says that he is the one sanctified or dedicated (10:36), not the temple. Finally at the sixth feast Jesus is crucified and is clearly presented by the author as the substitute for the Passover lamb (19:36) because he quotes Exodus 12:46 on the bones of the Passover lamb with reference to Jesus.

---

ture. But Gaius did so mainly because he so intensely disliked the book of Revelation and sought to discredit it by attributing it to a heretic.

The message therefore of the Gospel of John is much like that of the epistle to the Hebrews. Jesus is the new temple, the new feasts, the new Passover Lamb, and the new Law. He has superseded Judaism and its institutions.

John and the Synoptics

Finally, we must consider the similarities and differences between the Gospel of John and the Synoptics on the one hand and the Gospel of John and the epistles of John on the other hand. Scholars have noted for centuries that John stands apart from the Synoptics. It is true that John has basically the same narrative structure as the Synoptics. We have the ministry of John the Baptist, the calling of the disciples, the early abundance of miracles, Jesus' teaching and debate with the Jews, his arrest, trial, death, and resurrection. There are also many of the same stories in John that are in the Synoptics such as the cleansing of the temple, feeding of the five thousand with five loaves, calming the storm, the anointing of Jesus before his death, the triumphal entry, and of course the passion narrative (from the arrest of Jesus through his death). There are even numerous similarities to Jesus' sayings in the Synoptics (see note 8). These similarities must not be taken lightly or underemphasized. Clearly John and the Synoptics are based on the same history about Jesus. One has merely to compare the Synoptics with any of the apocryphal Gospels to see how really similar John is to the former.

On the other hand, the differences are striking too. First, the style, vocabulary, and theology of Jesus in the Gospel of John are more like the Johannine epistles than the Synoptics. The vocabulary in the Gospel and epistles is very plain with very few different words. Any first year Greek student knows how easy it is to read the Gospel and letters of John compared with the rest of the New Testament. The Greek is very grammatical but also very simple. Furthermore, everybody's vocabulary — Jesus', John the Baptist's, the author's — sounds the same. In chapter 3 of the Gospel, for example, Jesus speaks (vv. 5-15), the author comments on Jesus' discourse (vv. 16-21), then John the Baptist speaks (vv. 27-30? or 27-

36?). But all three use the typical Johannine vocabulary: love, truth, life, light, witness, believe. These are terms used over and over in the Gospel and epistles.

Second, many of the literary forms commonly used by Jesus in the Synoptics are absent from John. Jesus utters no proverbs in John and almost no parables.

Third, many themes which are common in the Synoptics — such as the Kingdom of God — are rare in John (only at 3:3 and 18:36).

Fourth, many events in John are not in the Synoptics (e.g., changing the water into wine, the story of Nicodemus, the story of the Samaritan woman at the well, the raising of Lazarus). The converse is also true. Much material in the Synoptics is absent from John. There are no demon exorcisms in John, no infancy narratives, no account of the transfiguration, and no account of the Lord's Supper.

How do we account for these facts? First, the author has recast many of the words of Jesus and John the Baptist into his own vocabulary. One can in relating a story — especially if one is also giving the story in a language (Greek) different from the language (Aramaic) originally used by the characters in the story — put the events and even discourses in one's own words. Thus the words of the author, in John 1:1-14 e.g., sound very much like the words of Jesus, as do the epistles of John. They are still Jesus' words but put in Johannine vocabulary.

Second, the author was obviously trying not to repeat what was in the Synoptics. We should assume he had some knowledge of at least one or two of the Synoptics and that he is writing to supplement them, both in terms of new events and discourses and also in terms of theological interpretation. This conclusion is very much like what Clement of Alexandria (A.D. 200) wrote:

> But John, last of all, perceiving that what had reference to the body in the gospel of our Saviour, was sufficiently detailed, and being encouraged by his familiar friends, and urged by the spirit, he wrote a spiritual gospel (Eusebius, *H.E.* VI.14; trans. in Cruse, *Eusebius*).

CHAPTER 6

THE BOOK OF ACTS AND THE EARLY CHURCH

AUTHORSHIP, DATE, HISTORICITY AND CONTENT OF ACTS

Bibliography: F.F. Bruce, *The Acts of the Apostles*; H.J. Cadbury, *The Book of Acts in History*; Idem, *The Making of Luke-Acts*; M. Dibelius, *Studies in the Acts of the Apostles*; J.D.G. Dunn, *Jesus and the Spirit*; *FBK*; F.J. Foakes-Jackson and K. Lake, eds., *The Beginning of Christianity*; D. Gaertner, *Acts*; W.W. Gasque, *A History of the Criticism of the Acts of the Apostles*; Guthrie, *NTI*; E. Haenchen, *The Acts of the Apostles*; M. Hengel, *Acts and the History of Earliest Christianity*; Idem, *Between Jesus and Paul*; L.E. Keck and J.L. Martyn, eds., *Studies in Luke-Acts*; S.J. Kistemaker, *Acts*; J.W. McGarvey, *Commentary on Acts*; I.H. Marshall, *Acts*; W. Neil, *The Acts of the Apostles*; J. Neyrey, ed., *The Social World of Luke-Acts*; W.M. Ramsay, *The Bearing of Recent Discovery on the Trustworthiness of the New Testament*; Idem, *St. Paul the Traveller and the Roman Citizen*; A.N. Sherwin-White, *Roman Society and Roman Law in the New Testament*; J. Smith, *The Voyage and Shipwreck of Paul*; C.C. Torrey, *The Composition and Date of Acts*; J. Weiss, *Earliest Christianity*; M. Wilcox, *The Semitisms of Acts*.

Authorship

As Cadbury[1] pointed out, "The tradition of Christian writers since the second century has been that the Third Gospel and the Acts were written by Luke the Physician. . . ." The New Testament refers to Luke at least three times and possibly five times. Paul

---

[1]See Foakes-Jackson and Lake, Vol. II, p. 209.

called Luke (Λουκᾶς, *Loukas*) the "beloved physician" in Colossians 4:14 and his "fellow worker" in Philemon 24. In 2 Timothy 4:11 as Paul's death approached he wrote that "only Luke is with me." (If the Lucius of Acts 13:1 and Romans 16:21, spelled Λούκιος (*Loukios*), is the same person as in the above three references, then Luke would be from Cyrene originally and one of the five great Christian prophets of Antioch.)

The external testimony (or testimony outside of Acts) linking this New Testament person with the author of the Gospel of Luke and the Acts begins with the Muratorian Canon of A.D. 180 and includes Irenaeus (A.D. 180), Clement of Alexandria (A.D. 200) and Eusebius (A.D. 320).

The internal evidence focuses mainly on the so-called "we" passages of Acts or passages in which the author uses the first person plural to indicate that he was present when the events happened. These sections are: Acts 16:10-17; 20:5-15; 21:1-18; 27:1-28:16. Since Luke the Physician was a fellow worker with Paul, he would certainly be a good candidate for the author of Acts.

Further, the author of Acts is almost certainly the author of the third Gospel as well, as the prologues (Luke 1:1-4; Acts 1:1-2) indicate by: (a) addressing both works to Theophilus and (b) referring in Acts 1:1 to the "former treatise." This author had made, he writes, an "accurate investigation" into the life and teachings of Jesus (Luke 1:3) and was thus in touch with the "eyewitnesses" (Luke 1:2). Again Luke the fellow worker and associate of Paul would certainly have been in a position to make such an investigation.

Though the internal evidence is not conclusive, it supports well the external evidence. Thus we can see no good reason to doubt the tradition concerning the authorship of Acts, even though some have done so.[2]

Date

Three principal dates have been proposed for Acts: (1) between A.D. 62 and 64, (2) between A.D. 70 and 80, and (3) sometime in

---

[2]See e.g., H. Windisch in Foakes-Jackson and Lake, Vol. II, p. 298.

the early second century.

The first date (Guthrie) commends itself because the story of Acts ends around A.D. 62. There is no reference to the fall of Jerusalem in A.D. 70, to Nero's persecution of Christians in Rome in A.D. 64 and most importantly, there is no reference to Paul's death.

The second date has been suggested because Acts obviously was written after the Gospel of Luke. Many modern exegetes have concluded that the author of the third Gospel used Mark (to which they assign a date of A.D. 66). Thus Luke would have been written sometime after Mark (probably after A.D. 70, they argue) and Acts was written after Luke (see Chapter 5).

The third date was suggested by F.C. Baur and the school of interpreters he led in Tübingen, Germany in the nineteenth century.[3] Baur believed that the author of Acts was attempting to reconcile two warring factions within the church: the Petrine and Pauline factions, or Jewish Christian and Gentile Christian factions. These two hostile groups came together in the second century due to efforts at "Cathologizing" or making everything uniform. The book of Acts was written then to make the early church appear to have been more uniform and harmonious than it really was, maintained Baur.

The first date is the obvious best choice. The middle date, between A.D. 70 and 80, is chosen if one assumes that Mark wrote his Gospel first and Luke used Mark. But in Chapter 5 we argued otherwise. The late date is dependent on Baur's very suspect reconstruction of early church history. The marks of the second century — problems with Gnosticism and Montanism — are absent from the book of Acts. The early date explains the facts without appeal to other hypotheses such as Marcan priority or Baur's historical revisionism.

Historicity

The historicity of Acts was challenged in the last century especially by F.C. Baur (1792-1860) and the Tübingen school.[4] Baur

---

[3]See H. Harris, *The Tübingen School.*

employed a method of historical investigation which he called Tendency Criticism (German: *Tendenzkritik*). He believed that early Christianity was characterized by two warring factions: Jewish and Gentile. Every early Christian writing supported one of these two factions, he alleged. Later in the second century, writers began to seek peace and to play down the earlier differences. Since Baur saw Acts as a second century product written with the intention of glossing over tensions between Jewish Christians and Gentile Christians, he could easily assign it a place alongside some of the other mostly fictional histories of antiquity.

M. Dibelius (1883-1947) and his followers challenged the historicity of Acts on a different basis. He examined each pericope or section in light of his method called Style Criticism. Dibelius determined there were thirteen small literary units (e.g., Acts 3:1-10 the healing of the lame man and 9:36-42 the story of Tabitha) which were based on traditional stories that circulated by word of mouth. Most of these have been highly embellished by the author of Acts, wrote Dibelius, so that they combine history with fiction. Second, Dibelius identified an "itinerary document" which narrates Paul's missionary travels. This document allegedly stands behind much of Acts 13:1-14:28 and 15:35-21:16. Luke, however, has inserted into this framework material of his own composition, especially the speeches, maintained Dibelius. The rest of the material in Acts is mostly Luke's own free composition and is completely fictional, he asserted. Thus Acts was for Dibelius and those who used his method mostly non-historical.

But not all German scholars have questioned the basic historical reliability of Acts. A. Harnack (1851-1930) is one of the most noteworthy exceptions. He tried to demonstrate by a careful comparison of Acts and Paul's epistles that Luke has accurately presented the story of Paul. His conclusion contrasts sharply with many other German New Testament scholars: "From almost every possible angle of historical criticism (Acts) is a solid, respectable, and in many respects, an extraordinary work" (see Gasque, p. 334).

The Anglo-American world has seldom been as sceptical regard-

---

[4]For this entire section on historicity see W.W. Gasque.

ing the historicity of Acts as German scholarship has. An older work by J. Smith, for example, demonstrated that the author of Acts had actually been on a sea voyage in a storm. The accurate description of what happens in such cases shows that the account is surely by an eyewitness.

W.M. Ramsay (1851-1939) also became a champion of the reliability of Acts. He began his study of Acts convinced that the Tübingen school was correct in its conclusion about Acts, but years of research in epigraphy (the study of inscriptions on stones) in Asia Minor and Greece changed his mind. Luke invariably used the proper terminology for the different political officials encountered in each city of Paul's journeys. Even if such accuracy does not necessarily prove that Luke was there with Paul — though it strongly suggests he was — it does show that Luke was meticulous about getting his facts correct. Thus Ramsay developed a very high estimation of the historical accuracy of Acts.

The work of a classical scholar, A.N. Sherwin-White, has also confirmed the historical reliability of Acts. He evaluates the trials of Paul before Gallio, Felix, and Festus (Acts 18:12-16; 24:1-22; 25:1-12) and Paul's status as a Roman citizen. Based on his knowledge of Roman law, he pronounced Acts very accurate even on fine points of detail. Sherwin-White wrote (p. 189): "For Acts the confirmation of historicity is overwhelming . . . any attempt to reject its basic historicity even in matters of detail must now appear absurd. Roman historians have long taken it for granted."

Other British scholars such as F.F. Bruce, I.H. Marshall and W. Neil have accepted these conclusions, as well as a more recent member of the Tübingen faculty, M. Hengel. Thus where we can check the historicity of Acts we find a striking reliability. There is therefore every good reason to accept the whole as historically reliable.

Content

Why was the book of Acts written? There are two important suggestions for the purpose of Acts. The first one we will consider is actually a rather recent hypothesis but it has had a great influence in Europe and North America. H. Conzelmann proposed that the main motive for Luke's two-volume work, the Gospel of Luke and Acts, was to explain the delay of the *parousia* (Greek word παρουσία meaning "presence") or the second coming of Christ. The earliest Christians, he contends, expected the parousia within their lifetime and the failure of this to happen left many of them confused and weakened. Luke must therefore interpret for them the importance of waiting for the parousia and participating in history. The book of the Acts of the Apostles then narrates the unfolding of God's purpose in history and thus alleviates confusion and impatience in waiting for the parousia.

Conzelmann surely is correct that one of Luke's goals was to demonstrate God's work in history. An historical account presupposes such a goal. But there is little reason to tie this goal with a crisis in the ancient church over the delay of the parousia. Documents such as the New Testament book of Revelation (A.D. 90), Clement of Rome's letter (A.D. 95) and Papias's writings (A.D. 125), to name a few, demonstrate no crisis or confusion over the delay of the parousia.

Another suggestion as to Luke's purpose in writing Acts is that he was writing a defense or apology (ἀπολογία, *apologia* = "defense").[5] Some have argued that what Luke is defending is Christianity as a whole against hostile pagans. There is some merit to this suggestion since Luke takes pains to report that Roman officials repeatedly pronounce the innocence of Christians, especially of Paul (Acts 16:39; 18:15f; 19:37; 23:29; 25:25; 26:32). Surely Luke hoped that interested pagans would read his Acts and be impressed at the verdict of these Roman political figures. But while Christianity as a whole is extolled and explained in Acts, there can be little doubt that the hero of the story is Paul. From his conversion in Acts 9 through the end of the book Paul dominates the narrative. His conversion is narrated three times; his missionary journeys are described in some detail; his trials and imprisonment, and finally, his voyage to Rome are presented in dramatic fashion. While the

---

[5]See *FBK* for a list of scholars embracing this view.

twelve apostles, especially Peter, are referred to in the earlier part of Acts, they play a decreasingly important role after Paul's conversion and after Acts 15 they do not appear in the narrative at all.

Yet the reader should not suppose that Acts is a romance novel about a great man named Paul. Luke's interest in Paul is mainly in defense of Paul's gospel; that is, salvation by grace through faith apart from works of law, a salvation open to Gentiles as well as Jews. The Acts of the Apostles is the Lucan equivalent, then, of Paul's letter to the Romans. Both defend and explain Paul's gospel, one by narrative, the other by epistle. Luke explains and defends Paul's gospel by narrating how the Holy Spirit guided the early church, especially Paul, to admit Gentiles and even to undertake a mission among them.

Acts falls easily into three parts. Part I (Acts 1 through 6:7) relates the life of the primitive Jerusalem church. This community waited in Jerusalem for the promised baptism of the Holy Spirit (1:4-5) which came on the Day of Pentecost (2:1-4). Life in the Holy Spirit characterized the primitive community (4:31).

Part II (Acts 6:8 through chapter 12), the transition section, is — as far as the narrative purpose goes — the most important part. The church passes from a provincial and nonpluralistic community to a movement encompassing all of Syria and embracing all races and social classes. This transition begins with Stephen, one of the Hellenist Christians (Greek-speaking Christians) who was chosen to be among the Seven, a group of church officials serving as aides to the apostles. Stephen saw clearly by the power of the Spirit that the Old Testament ritual was abrogated by Jesus and his teaching such things brought about his martyrdom (6:8-8:1).

The persecution which resulted from Stephen's death — a persecution in which Paul actively participated — caused many of the Christians to flee. Acts 8 shows that some of the old barriers in Judaism began to fall after this. First, Samaritans were admitted to the church. Those racial and religious enemies of the Jews (see Chapter 2) were now brothers in Christ and God showed his approval by sending the Holy Spirit on them (Acts 8:17). Next Philip — one of the Seven also — baptized the Ethiopian eunuch who because of his physical impairment could not be accepted as a full member of the Jewish community (Deut 23:1). Thus the half-Jewish Samaritans and the outcast eunuch were accepted into the church.

Acts 9 (and also Acts 22 and 26) narrates the conversion of one who would become the great apostle to the Gentiles, Saul of Tarsus also called Paul. He sees the risen and exalted Christ who has chosen him to preach to Gentiles (9:15). From this point on the direction of the church takes a decisive turn. Peter is once more at the center of the story in Acts 10 and 11 but only to set the stage for Paul. For in these chapters is told how Peter was miraculously led by God to a Gentile named Cornelius to whom he preached the gospel. While Peter was preaching, the Holy Spirit fell upon all who heard the message (10:44-46) and they spoke in tongues as the apostles had on the Day of Pentecost. This event then was a second pentecostal experience, a Gentile Pentecost. God had shown his acceptance of Gentiles by pouring on them the same Spirit that he had given to Jews. God is no respecter of persons (Acts 10:34); all stand before him on equal footing.

The last part of Acts 11 (verses 19-30) discloses the developments in Antioch of Syria where the Christian faith has made many Gentile converts. Paul eventually settles there along with Barnabas. It appears that Antioch has now superseded Jerusalem as the center of Christian missions. The church is beginning to become a Gentile church.

Part III (Acts 13 through 28) mostly has to do with the movements of Paul. He is a prophet ministering in Antioch when he and Barnabas are called by the Holy Spirit (13:2) to become missionaries to Asia Minor. Paul and Barnabas have great success and, after the Jerusalem council (Acts 15) places its stamp of approval on Paul's offering the gospel to Gentiles, Paul is off again on another missionary trip.

Paul intends to continue preaching in Asia Minor but the Holy Spirit (16:6-7) leads him to Troas where he has a vision in the night calling him to do missionary work in Macedonia and Greece. At every step the Holy Spirit guides his ministry.

Finally, Paul is compelled by the Spirit (20:22) to go to Jerusalem. He is warned repeatedly by the Holy Spirit (20:23) that prison and hardship await him but he is determined to be obedient and "finish the race" (20:24). He is imprisoned and ultimately taken to Rome, the largest city of the ancient world, the Gentile capital of the Roman empire. Luke leaves the story there with Paul proclaiming that the gospel is for the Gentiles as well as Jews (28:28). In reaching Rome Christianity has made the transition complete from a Jewish to a Gentile church. The transition was largely the work of Paul, who was led at every step by the Holy Spirit.

THE NATURE OF THE EARLY PALESTINIAN CHURCH
A.D. 30-32

The Members

The core of the earliest Christian community was the Twelve Apostles. These men had been with Jesus from his baptism to his resurrection (Acts 1:22) and had benefitted from his teaching and his exemplary life. They now became — after Jesus' ascension and the coming of the Holy Spirit (Acts 1:9; 2:4) — the interpreters of Jesus' message and of the message about Jesus, the risen Lord. Their ministry was one of prayer and preaching both to convert unbelievers and to build up believers (Acts 6:4).

Next to the Twelve in significance stood the 120 (Acts 1:15) which included those other disciples of Jesus that had followed Jesus in his ministry. Many of these were women (Acts 1:14; Mark 15:40-41) who had been involved for some time in ministering with Jesus' group. From this group Matthias, the replacement for Judas, was chosen.

The earliest church was not entirely homogeneous culturally. Acts 6 indicates that almost from the beginning two groups existed: the Hebrews and the Hellenists. Most scholars conclude that the Hebrews were primarily Aramaic-speaking Jews and native Palestinian in dress, manners, and customs. The Hellenists were on the other hand Jews that had — perhaps for several generations — adopted Greek as their language as well as Greek dress and customs.[6] The latter were still loyal Jews at the time of their conversion but would have worshiped in the Greek language, while the former would have worshiped in Aramaic.

From the Hellenists were chosen the Seven. Congregations composed of two ethnic groups can easily have difficulties. Eventually they arose in the primitive church. The Hellenists claimed their widows were being neglected. Thus the church as a whole selected seven prominent men from the Hellenists to oversee the works of charity (Acts 6:5). But clearly these Seven were not merely administrators of the church dole. They were also great preachers in their own right and soon began to be used in extraordinary ways by the Lord (Acts 6:8-10; 8:4-7).

The first venture out of strictly Jewish circles came in the Samaritan mission. One of the Seven, Philip, preached to them and converted many. Shortly thereafter, Peter and John came to Samaria to confer the miraculous gifts of the Holy Spirit on them (Acts 8:4-7, 14-17). The despised Samaritans had now joined the Hebrews and Hellenists in the primitive church.

Early Church Practice

A. Baptism

Bibliography: K. Barth, *The Teachings of the Church Regarding Baptism*; G.R. Beasley-Murray, *Baptism in the New Testament*; A. Campbell and N.L. Rice, *The Campbell-Rice Debate*; O. Cullmann, *Baptism in the New Testament*; J. Cottrell, *Baptism: A Biblical Study*; E. Ferguson, *Early Christians Speak*; W.S. LaSor, "Discovering What Jewish Miqvaot Can Tell Us About Christian Baptism" *BAR* 13.1 (1987) 52-59.

The early church continued the practice of baptism begun by John the Baptist and Jesus. On the day the church began, 3000 people were baptized (Acts 2:41). Later in many cases where a

---

[6]The suggestions that the Hellenists were Essenes or Gentiles have very little to commend them and indeed have found very few supporters.

conversion takes place, it is explicitly recorded that the converted one was baptized (e.g., Acts 8:38; 9:18; 10:48; 16:15, 33; 18:8; 19:5). In the other cases where baptism is not mentioned, we may presume that Luke is only giving a quick summary of the conversions (e.g., 8:6). Thus clearly baptism formed an essential part of the process of conversion in the early church.

The background for Christian baptism is surely to be found in the Old Testament practices of ritual cleansing. One became unclean, according to the Old Testament Law, by nocturnal emission (Deut 23:10-11), by sexual intercourse (Lev 15:16-18), by contact with a corpse (Num 5:2-3), by being leprous (Lev 13:1-7) and women were unclean during their menstrual period (Lev 15:19-30). To become clean again — that is able once more to go into the temple or have an offering made for oneself — always involved ritual bathing or immersion.

By the New Testament period this ritual bathing took a precise form. The Mishnaic tractate *Mikvaot* ("baths")[7] gives the instructions for proper cleansing, indicating that the Pharisees practiced ritual bathing scrupulously. In addition there were several other Jewish sects such as the Essenes (see Chapter 2) that practiced ritual immersion. Some of the groups required immersion occasionally and others required it every day.

Even more informative is the archaeological evidence. Actual *mikvaot* or ritual bathing places have been found at Masada, Herodium, Qumran, and Jericho. They were especially plentiful in Jerusalem, both near the main entrance to the temple — so worshippers could cleanse themselves before entering the temple — and even in many private houses. Archaeologists have discovered thus far, for instance, 48 *mikvaot* near the entrance of the temple (LaSor).

There can be no doubt that in ritual baths a person completely immersed himself or herself. This was a rabbinical requirement in the first place and the size of the *mikvaot* also indicate it. Each *mikveh* had to be four and one-half feet deep so a person, by bending his knees, could completely go under the water. This

---

[7]The singular form is מִקְוֶה, *mikveh*, "bath."

argues strongly that Christian baptism did the same as LaSor states: "But the archaeological and Mishnaic evidence seems to support the argument for immersion. That is clearly what occurred in the contemporaneous Jewish *miqvaot*, so that is probably what happened in early Jewish-Christian baptism" (p. 58). This conclusion harmonizes well with the meaning of the Greek word βαπτίζω (*baptizō*). The definition given for *baptizō* is always "dip, immerse" (see *BAGD*).

Ritual bathing was very common in first century A.D. Palestine and bears many similarities to John's baptism but it has important differences. Ritual bathing was done often and to render one clean for temple worship. Baptism was done once to initiate one into new life in Christ. John clearly associated his baptism with repentance and the remission of sins (Mark 1:4) as it was also by the early church and therefore obviously by Jesus (Acts 2:38). But ritual bathing was not connected with these things.[8]

Thus John's baptism was based on Old Testament ritual washing but it was not identical to it. Christian baptism was something new with its own meaning, especially union with Christ and the reception of the Holy Spirit. Baptism, like faith and repentance, is our response to the grace of God through the gospel of Jesus Christ.

B. The Lord's Supper

Bibliography: R. Brown, *The Gospel According to John*; J.D.G. Dunn, *Unity and Diversity in the New Testament*; A.J.B. Higgins, *The Lord's Supper in the New Testament*; J. Jeremias, *The Eucharistic Words of Jesus*; I.H. Marshall, *Last Supper and Lord's Supper*; Ed. Schweizer, *The Lord's Supper According to the New Testament*; G. Vermes, *The Dead Sea Scrolls in English*.

The Lord's Supper was an important part of the earliest

---

[8]Many have suggested that Jewish proselyte baptism was the forerunner of Christian baptism. When a Gentile became a Jew he was circumcised, he made an offering in the temple, and he was immersed in water. But Jewish proselyte baptism is never mentioned in the Old Testament, the Apocrypha, or Josephus. References to it first occur in the Stoic philosopher, Epictetus (A.D. 50-120) and the Mishnah (written down in A.D. 200). Thus the references to proselyte baptism postdate the rise of Christianity by many years and it is doubtful that Jewish proselyte baptism existed before Christianity arose.

Christian worship. Acts 2:42 reads, after describing the first converts to Christianity on the day of Pentecost: "And they continued in the teaching of the apostles, in sharing, in breaking the loaf, and in prayers." Since the word "loaf" or "bread" (Greek ἄρτος, *artos*) has the definite article, "the loaf," we are safe in assuming that the reference is to the Lord's Supper (contrast Acts 2:46 where the definite article is not used). Therefore the Lord's Supper was one of those four basic and essential practices of the early church.

As with baptism, the Lord's Supper finds its background in the Old Testament in Passover meals, in the covenant establishment, and in meals anticipating the Messianic banquet. Jesus clearly instituted the Supper during the season of Passover. Further, the two physical emblems of the Lord's Supper are taken directly from the Passover meal: the unleavened bread and wine.[9] Jesus himself was to become the Passover lamb as the Gospel of John clarifies.[10] The symbolism is thus obvious. Jesus as our Passover lamb by his own blood protects us from the consequences of our sin. Passover commemorates God's deliverance from Egypt by the death of the lambs.

Second, the Lord's Supper is rooted in the Old Testament idea of the covenant sacrifice. In Exodus 24 when Israel entered into the covenant (or treaty) with Yahweh, they offered up burnt offerings and peace offerings. Moses caught in basins the blood of the slaughtered animals. Half of the blood, which he called "the blood of the covenant," he sprinkled on the altar and the other half he sprinkled on the people in a solemn ritual to implant in their minds the importance of their pledge to serve Yahweh. Jesus also called the cup of wine the symbol of "my blood of the covenant" (Mark 14:24). Just as the blood of oxen and other animal victims sealed the covenant relationship between Yahweh and his people, so Jesus' own blood makes possible the new covenant.

---

[9]The Old Testament (Exod 12) did not require wine at Passover but by the time of Jesus four cups of wine were considered necessary. See m. Pesahim.

[10]See John 19:29 where the hyssop branch is mentioned. The blood of the lamb had to be smeared on the doorposts by a hyssop branch. Also see John 19:36, a quotation about the Passover lamb in Exod 12:46 which is applied to Jesus. Compare also 1 Cor 5:7 where Paul explicitly identifies Christ with the lamb.

Third, the Lord's Supper is rooted in the Old Testament Messianic banquet. Isaiah 25:6 predicts that "on this mountain" (i.e., Mt. Zion) God will make a feast of "wine and fat things" (cf. Isa 65:13). The Old Testament prediction of a great feast when the Messiah comes stirred the imagination of many Jewish writers. The Pseudepigraphical book, 1 Enoch, speaks of the righteous and elect eating with the Messiah (1 Enoch 62:14). The Essenes at Qumran looked forward to the day the Messiah would come and sit at a common meal with them (1QSa 2:11-22). Jesus also predicted that at his second coming there would be a great banquet (Luke 22:30; Matt 8:11-12). The Lord's Supper is therefore partly an anticipation of this banquet. Jesus said at its institution: "Truly I say to all of you that I will in no way again drink of the fruit of the vine until that day when I drink it anew in the kingdom of God" (Mark 14:25). Thus Jesus ate and drank with his disciples as the earthly Jesus for the last time on that night and looked forward to the renewed fellowship in heaven. In the meantime, the Lord's Supper is a banquet in anticipation of this heavenly one.

Community of Property in the Jerusalem Church

Bibliography: S. Applebaum, "Economic Life in Palestine" in S. Safrai and M. Stern, *Judaism in the First Century*; R. Batey, *Jesus and the Poor*; H.L. Boles, *A Commentary on Acts of the Apostles*; E. Haenchen, *The Acts of the Apostles*; M. Hengel, *Property and Riches in the Early Church*; J. Jeremias, *Jerusalem in the Time of Jesus*; S.E. Johnson, "The Dead Sea Manual of Discipline and the Jerusalem Church" *Zeitschrift für die alttestamentliche Wissenschaft* 66 (1954) 106-120; K. Lake, "The Communism of Acts II and IV-VI and the Appointment of the Seven" in H.J. Foakes-Jackson and K. Lake, *The Beginnings of Christianity*; E. Troeltsch, *The Social Teaching of the Christian Churches*.

The practice regarding personal property and wealth is one of the most striking and controversial aspects of the primitive church. By these events a lot is demonstrated about the Jerusalem church's attitude toward the words of Jesus, toward the poor, and toward the future heavenly kingdom. Thus a correct understanding of the earliest church in this regard is very important. The main text — but compare also Acts 2:44-45 — is found in Acts 4:32-34. The church in this period of time demonstrated a unity of purpose and a sense of love and community that stand as models for the modern church. That period was one of exceptional self-sacrifice and sharing on the part of many of the wealthier disciples in order to care for the needy. Everyone so focused on the risen Christ that material possessions seemed unimportant.

Let us here answer two questions: What was the problem that required drastic economic action? What exactly did the Jerusalem church do?

The problem the early church faced has been variously explained:

1. Some maintain that it was an emergency situation brought about by the conversion of so many Jewish pilgrims who had been present for the feast of Pentecost (Acts 2:1, 9-11). Around 3000 people were baptized during the feast (Acts 2:41), most of which were probably pilgrims who had remained in Jerusalem without any means of financial support (see Boles).

2. Others maintain that many elderly people came to Jerusalem to wait for their death, thinking it to be preferable to die in the holy city. These people were almost always quite poor, it is alleged (see Batey).

3. Finally it is asserted that most of Jesus' disciples, who became the core of the Jerusalem church, were from Galilee, and they had sold everything in order to follow Jesus (Mark 10:28-30). Thus the Galileans were now impoverished (see Haenchen).

The first explanation probably has some validity since converted pilgrims to the feasts did no doubt contribute to the financial burden of the early church. But it is questionable that this was the main or sole problem. The second explanation is also problematic because this practice — of coming to Jerusalem to die — is not well attested in the ancient sources. The last explanation listed above has difficulties also. The text given (Mark 10:28) does not say that the Galileans have in every case sold their possessions to follow Jesus but that they have only left everything. The property may have still been in their possession.

The best way to understand the problem which the Jerusalem church solved by its amazing generosity is to view the situation in terms of its broader social and economic context. In other words, we see no reason to appeal to special circumstances or an emergency as is usually done. The situation is quite understandable in light of the ongoing problem in Jerusalem with poverty.

We discussed the broad picture of Palestinian society in Chapter 3. The wealthy elite class, most of whom owned large landed estates, in the main lived in Jerusalem in the high-classed quarter where archaeologists have found the ruins of so many expensive first century houses. On the other hand many small peasant farmers had lost their land and had fled to Jerusalem to find economic refuge (see Applebaum, Hengel). The landless poor who fled to Jerusalem formed an urban proletariat that lived by an endless series of hard jobs and inadequate wages. One might work as a bathhouse attendant, a cook, a messenger, a manure gatherer, a thorn gatherer, a watchman over children or over the sick, and a burden bearer. The wages paid for such work could vary considerably. The common assertion that the day's wage was usually one denarius (Matt 20:2) must be accepted cautiously. That wage was perhaps only average. In general a skilled laborer received several denarii per day. An unskilled burden bearer would receive less. There are even examples of workers being paid only $1/24$ denarius a day (m. Shebiit 8:4; see Jeremias).

Not only were there poor day laborers in Jerusalem but many were reduced to begging, either out of physical handicap or mere poverty. Indeed Jerusalem was the center in Palestine for beggars to come. They stationed themselves at holy places in the city, especially at the temple gates. So numerous were the beggars around the temple that the Septuagint translation of the Old Testament (at 2 Samuel 5:8) contains a prohibition against beggars' entering the temple area (see Jeremias). It would be surprising if the Jerusalem church — which contained 5000 members at this time (Acts 4:4) — did not have a large group of both poor day laborers and beggars.

How did the church seek to meet the needs of these poor people? That too is debated:

1. E. Troeltsch in 1911 popularized the communistic explanation when he termed the church's activity in Acts 4:32-34, "communism of love." This view has received a revival of support since the discovery of the Dead Sea Scrolls. The Essenes according to both the Scrolls (1QS 1:12, 6:16-20) and Josephus (*War* 2.122-123) practiced a form of communism in which the novice retained possession of his private property until his final vows, at which time he turned over everything he owned to the community. Some scholars maintain, then, that the Jerusalem church practiced an Essene-type of communism or mandatory communism (S.E. Johnson).

2. Others maintain that the church modeled its actions in caring for the poor on the Jewish village charity called the *quppah* (קופּה) or "basket" and the *tamhui* (תמחוי) or "tray" (Lake). The former was a weekly collection and the latter a daily collection for the poor. Village collectors went from house to house requesting funds for the indigent. The donations were made both in money and food.

We should not however, conclude that either the Essene communism or the village charity was the model for the church's practice. In the first place communism was clearly mandatory for membership in the Essenes but for the Jerusalem church one was not required to give away all his possessions. Acts 5:4 indicates that contributions in the early church were entirely voluntary. Further, Acts 12:12 demonstrates that some Christians did not sell their houses. Finally there is no evidence that other churches practiced communism either. The Antioch church for example (Acts 11:27-30), took up a collection for the poor which implies private property ownership. Thus ownership of private property was certainly an option for the early church members. The practice of village charity also seems an unlikely model for the Jerusalem church. The sources indicate that the village residents contributed occasionally a few coins or a small quantity of grain but never that anyone sold his house or other possessions to give the proceeds to the poor.

The obvious place to find the model for the church's action is in the life and ministry of Jesus. Jesus' message to the wealthy was essentially as follows: "Do not lay up for yourselves treasures on earth where moth and rust consume and where thieves break in and steal, but lay up for yourselves treasures in heaven" (Matt 6:19-20).

How this message translated into life seems to have varied. Usually this principle meant that one was to give alms generously to the poor (Mark 12:41-44; Matt 6:2-4; 25:31-46; Luke 19:8). But Jesus also advised a potential disciple on one occasion to sell all his possessions and give the proceeds to the poor (Mark 10:17-25). In Luke 13:33, moreover, Jesus said, "So therefore, whoever of you does not renounce all that he has cannot be my disciple." Jesus does not here explicitly say this meant selling one's property but he could have meant that. Further, in Luke 12:33 Jesus commanded, "Sell your possessions and give alms." Thus Jesus' message to the rich was that wealth could make one unfit for the kingdom of God. The remedy for this condition is to lay up treasures in heaven by giving away at least part of one's wealth in alms.

Yet Jesus did not always or even usually tell disciples to give away all their possessions. Zacchaeus the tax collector gave away only a portion of his possessions (Luke 19:8) although much of his wealth may have been dishonestly acquired. Other wealthy friends of Jesus seem to have kept their possessions (houses) also (Luke 10:38-42). Thus there was not just one appropriate response to the message of the kingdom as far as the handling of one's possessions was concerned, but several responses.

Jesus' ministry to the poor was just that, a ministry. He never tried to bring down the wealthy by force or demanded that his followers do so. He preached his message of the kingdom to the wealthy and poor alike and waited for God to bring about the end-time judgment and reversal (Matt 13:47-50). The ministry to the poor by Jesus and the early church was not a program, then, which had as its goal the creation of a utopian society but the affirmation of belief in and solidarity with the kingdom of God and God's ultimate overthrow of injustice. As Troeltsch wrote: "It is therefore clear that the message of Jesus is not a program of social reform. It is rather the summons to prepare for the coming of the Kingdom of God" (p. 61).

CHAPTER 7

THE GRECO-ROMAN WORLD IN THE NEW TESTAMENT PERIOD

At Acts 9 we leave the story of the Jerusalem church and begin the story of the church as a worldwide movement, for in that chapter is narrated the conversion of Paul the Apostle to the Gentiles. From now on the early church is less oriental, less Jewish, and less regional. It moves out into the arena of paganism, of philosophy, and of world history, the world where two great cultures were meeting. This was the Greco-Roman world.

HISTORY OF ROME, 146 B.C. TO A.D. 135

Bibliography: E.M. Blaiklock, *The Century of the New Testament*; J. Buchan, *Augustus*; *CAH* Vols. VIII, X, XI; M. Carey, *History of Rome*; J. Carporino, *Daily Life in Ancient Rome*; E. Ferguson, *Backgrounds of Early Christianity*; A. Garzetti, *From Tiberius to the Antonines*; M.T. Griffin, *Nero*; H. Mattingly, *Roman Imperial Civilization*; M.C. Tenney, *New Testament Times*.

Primary sources: Livy, *From the Founding of Rome*; Suetonius, *Lives of the Twelve Caesars*; Tacitus, *Annals* and *Histories*; Dio Cassius, *Roman History*; *NTB* 1-19.

Roman political developments came quickly in the second and first centuries B.C. By 146 B.C. the three Punic Wars (against Carthage) and the three Macedonian Wars had been fought and Rome controlled most of the Mediterranean world. These territories were organized into provinces which paid Rome taxes in money and produce. The city of Rome had now mastery of an empire.

But the empire brought wealth only to a few people. There were the Optimates, the "old money" of Rome (the Senatorial class) with both nobility and wealth; the Equites, the "new money" who possessed only wealth; and the Populares, the lowest class which often had become completely dispossessed from land ownership. In 133 B.C. an altruistic Senator, named Gracchus, tried to redistribute government land to the urban poor but was assassinated by a group of Senators. Ten years later his brother tried to install a welfare system for the poor but was eventually driven to suicide by his enemies. Marius, a political and military leader of Equestrian rank also tried reforms for the poor but failed and resigned from office in 99 B.C. There clearly was a class struggle developing with the Populares and Equites — and a few altruistic Optimates — on one side and the noble aristocracy on the other.

A civil war was brewing and needed only an incident to boil over. When Sulla, the consul — the highest political leader — left Rome to lead an army into battle in Asia Minor (85 B.C.), a man from the Populares was elected to replace him. When Sulla returned to Rome, the first civil war began with Sulla and his allies victorious. After the war was over the victors effected a terrible vendetta with thousands of people murdered and families disenfranchised from their wealth.

In 62 B.C. Pompey, a former lieutenant of Sulla (and the conqueror of Palestine in 63 B.C.) made a pact with Caesar, a relative of Marius. Together with another important man, Crassus, the wealthiest man in Rome, they formed the first Triumvirate ("rule of the three"). The alliance was actually illegal according to Roman republican law but it was hoped it would prevent another civil war. It kept the lid on the boiling pot for only a short time. In 50 B.C. a second civil war began between Pompey and Caesar.

In 46 B.C. Caesar was victorious over Pompey and was elected dictator for ten years. At last, many thought, peace and stability have arrived. Caesar reinstated the programs of helping the poor. But once more the world was convulsed when Caesar was assassinated in 44 by allies of Pompey, by some of his own disgruntled friends, and by republican purists who lamented the deterioration of their system of government.

The two ringleaders of the coup d'état, Brutus and Cassius, were in turn defeated by the next Triumvirate: Mark Antony, Octavian (later called Augustus) and Lepidus. Antony and Octavian, when the dust had settled, divided up the empire. Antony received the east (Greece, Asia Minor, Syria, and Egypt) and Octavian the west (Italy, Africa, Spain, and Gaul). This division would become ingrained in the ancient mind so that centuries later when the church had its first great schism, the domain that had been Antony's went with the Eastern Orthodox Church and the area that had belonged to Octavian became the Roman Catholic Church.

As with the first Triumvirate, the second one broke down and once again civil war ensued. Octavian was the ultimate victor in 31 B.C. and subsequently his unrivaled rule of the empire began an era of peace and stability. From this point on historians dub the single leader of Rome the emperor[1] although the Romans themselves called him the *princeps* or "first citizen."

Thus Octavian became the first emperor of Rome. He was also given the name Augustus ("consecrated"), a title of divinity, and indeed in the east he was worshiped in temples while he was yet alive. Only much later would emperor worship be practiced in the west. Augustus was a powerful political figure from the beginning, but his power increased as more and more of the responsibilities of the government — and with them, the authority — fell to him. By the end of his reign he was an absolute despot and the Roman system of government was forever changed.

The Roman Emperors

Julio-Claudians   (year of the four emperors)
Augustus 31 B.C.-A.D. 14   Galba A.D. 69
Tiberius A.D. 14-37   Otho A.D. 69
Gaius Caligula A.D. 37-41   Vitellius A.D. 69
Claudius A.D. 41-54
Nero A.D. 54-68

---

[1]The Latin word *imperator* meant a military conqueror. The emperors were also given that title but it did not carry with it the same meaning as our "emperor."

Flavians	*Antonines*
Vespasian A.D. 70-79	Nerva A.D. 96-98
Titus A.D. 79-81	Trajan A.D. 98-117
Domitian A.D. 81-96	Hadrian A.D. 117-138

None of the rest of the Julio-Claudian emperors — all of whom were related either to Augustus or to his wife, Livia — possessed Augustus' political savvy. His immediate successor, Tiberius, however, was quite competent as was Claudius. The former is referred to in Luke 3:1 and the latter in Acts 18:2. Gaius Caligula and Nero, on the other hand, are synonymous with madness and debauchery. They knew no moral restraint and possessed no respect for human life. Caligula almost touched off a Jewish war when he ordered (in A.D. 38) his statue to be erected in the Holy of Holies in Jerusalem. Nero ordered the first Christian persecution (A.D. 64) executing hundreds (perhaps thousands) of believers in the cruelest of fashions, among them Peter and Paul (see Chapter 8).

Nero's downfall brought chaos to the government. Four different emperors (including Nero) ruled within one year. Finally, Vespasian, the founder of the next dynasty, brought order. Vespasian was conducting the Roman attack on the Jews in Palestine when he was proclaimed emperor. As emperor he was above average in competence and he brought a new stability to the empire.

Vespasian's son, Titus, had the misfortune of being emperor when Mount Vesuvius erupted, burying the cities of Pompeii and Herculaneum (near Neapolis in Italy) under ash. The event killed thousands and stunned the rest of Italy. Titus also was the one who took over the prosecution of the Jewish war when Vespasian left Palestine for Rome. He captured Jerusalem and was given a triumphal parade in Rome. Domitian, also Vespasian's son, was a second Nero. He demanded his titles include *dominus et deus* ("lord and god") and thus he both searched constantly for any discontents in Rome and zealously pressed the cult of emperor worship. Under Domitian a second Christian persecution arose, this one spreading well beyond the city of Rome into the eastern provinces. The book of Revelation was written during this time.

At Domitian's death the Roman Senate erased his name from

monuments and voted his memory forever cursed, so strong was their hatred of him. They chose as his replacement, Nerva, thus beginning a new dynasty. Since Nerva was at that time well over 60 years of age, he early on named as his successor — and adopted as his son — Trajan, his ablest general.

Trajan, being of Spanish descent, was the first non-Italian emperor. He pushed the borders of the empire well beyond those of the first century A.D. to include Dacia, Arabia Petraea, Armenia, and Babylon.

Hadrian — Trajan's cousin — succeeded him and continued to expand the borders of the empire. He also built the famous wall in northern Britain which was to keep the barbarians out of the southern part of the island. In A.D. 132 he found it necessary to suppress the second Jewish revolt in Palestine.

Rome's dominance led to three important results for the spread of Christianity: First, finally under Augustus peace and stability were established. The *pax Romana* ("Roman peace") made it possible for Christian missionaries to travel without fear of war. Even the highway robbers and pirates at sea were controlled to some extent. Second, Rome quickly set about building good roads to ensure effective communication with its far flung empire. But these roads meant easier travel for Christian travelers as well and thus the gospel could spread more quickly and easily. Most of the earliest churches were started in towns along these Roman roads. Third, the imperial period witnessed the rise of the emperor cult which always stood in opposition to Christianity. In a sense, then, the same empire and system that finally resulted in peace under Augustus and enabled the early spread of Christianity would soon try to kill it off.

THE SOCIAL LIFE IN THE CITIES
OF THE ROMAN EMPIRE

Bibliography: G. Alfoeldy, *The Social History of Rome*; S. Benko, *The Catacombs and the Colosseum*; H.J. Cadbury, *The Book of Acts in History*; R. MacMullen, *Roman Social Relations*; M. Rostovtzeff, *Social and Economic History of the Roman Empire*; G. Sjoberg, *The Preindustrial City*.

Although only about 10% of the population lived in cities, most of the activity of early Christianity centered there. Outside of Palestine Christianity was a very urban movement. Further, most of the church's success was not among the wealthy urbanites but the other urban classes: the craftsmen, slaves and beggars. They were the "foolish of the world . . . the weak of the world . . . the lowly and despised of the world . . ." (1 Cor 1:26-28) to which Paul referred.

The two largest cities in the empire, according to MacMullen, were Rome and Alexandria, each with over a half million inhabitants. But Carthage and Antioch were close to that size and there were yet others only somewhat smaller (Corinth, Ephesus, and Pergamum, e.g.). The other cities were much smaller with only tens of thousands in population.

Most of these cities contained not only the theaters, amphitheaters, baths, temples, basilicas, ornamental fountains and porticoes well known from modern guidebooks on art and architecture, but also the narrow streets, very crowded conditions and severe sanitation problems that are not so well known to moderns studying the ancient city.

The vast majority of the lower class urban dwellers spent most of their time out of doors in public places such as those named above. Houses were very small and conditions too dirty to afford the kind of stay-at-home life that many moderns practice. Some residents lived in tiny apartments two or three stories high; others lived in hovels on back alleys. They returned home mostly to sleep and perhaps to eat but otherwise they could be seen daily in the various places of work or leisure. The market places especially were jammed with gossipers and gawkers as well as peddlers and shoppers. The exceptions to this rule were those craftsmen that worked in their places of residence. In this case the residence doubled as a private dwelling and a place of business.

One chose the precise location of his residence in the city based on one of three factors: ethnic identity, occupation, or wealth (or a combination of these). Whole sections of cities could be inhabited by members of a local tribe or clan. Or immigrants from a foreign region might settle together. Jews almost always did this, forming Jewish ghettoes which were often even allowed to adjudicate their own civil court cases.

Within the broader, ethnic region — if it existed for one's ethnic background — divisions were made according to occupation. Those with similar occupations usually lived on the same street. Some of the streets even took their names from the occupation of their inhabitants. Thus whole streets could be taken up by, for example, cobblers, dyers, barbers, perfumers, jewelers, smiths, or vintners, each of whom worked their craft in their home. If one asked where a certain person lived, the response would be, "Among the barbers," or "among the smiths." That is why Barnabas could find Paul so easily in Tarsus (Acts 11:25-26) and that is why Paul quickly met Aquila and Priscilla when he came to Corinth (Acts 18:1-3). Barnabas knew Paul would be living among the tentmakers. Likewise, Paul found Aquila and Priscilla on the tentmakers' street for they had the same craft as Paul.

The wealthiest class lived in the center of town. The farther away one lived from the center, the poorer the individual and the lower on the social scale one stood (just the opposite from modern society). Those on the fringes of the city were also on the fringes of society.

There was no middle class in this ancient urban society, only upper and lower classes. The lower classes consisted of those born free, the freedmen (or former slaves), the slaves and the outcasts. Virtually all made their living engaged in a craft and had little education beyond the apprenticeship in their trade. The freedmen or former slaves enjoyed less social standing among the lower classes than those born into freedom. Yet they might be just as well off financially. The outcasts would include those doing jobs considered offensive (e.g., burying the dead) and beggars. The evidence indicates the craftsmen labored hard and long hours, barely able to make ends meet. Their economic standing was probably no better than the rural agricultural worker.

Many lower class urbanites belonged to a guild or club of a sort, called a *collegium*. The clubs were ostensibly burial clubs, designed to insure that every member received a decent burial. But they developed also into opportunities for socializing. The clubs were organized according to occupation. Each craft had its own club and offered its members a sense of comradeship and belonging in an otherwise grim existence. R.W. Wilken observes (in Benko, *Catacombs*): "The collegia gave men a sense of identity and comradeship, a social unit larger than the family and smaller than the state where they could meet together with friends, eat and drink, worship, play, and share common experiences."

GRECO-ROMAN RELIGION AND PHILOSOPHY

Bibliography: A.H. Armstrong, *Ancient Philosophy*; S. Benko, ed., *The Catacombs and the Colosseum*; E. Bevan, *Later Greek Religion*; F.F. Bruce, *The Spreading Flame*; F. Copleston, *A History of Philosophy*; Vol. I; F. Cumont, *After Life in Roman Paganism*; Idem, *Oriental Religions in Roman Paganism*; E.R. Dodds, *The Greeks and the Irrational*; E. Ferguson, *Backgrounds of Early Christianity*; J. Ferguson, *Greek and Roman Religion*; W.H.C. Frend, *The Rise of Christianity*; R.L. Fox, *Pagans and Christians*; E.R. Goodenough, *Philo Judaeus*; R.M. Grant, *Gods and the One God*; S. Jellicoe, *The Septuagint and Modern Study*; H. Jonas, *Gnosticism*; H.C. Kee, *Medicine, Miracle and Magic in the Roman World*; G. Machen, *The Origin of Paul's Religion*; R. MacMullen, *Christianizing the Roman Empire*; L.M. Martin, *Hellenistic Religions*; W. Meeks, *The First Urban Christians*; G. Murray, *Five Stages of Greek Religion*; R. Nash, *Christianity and the Hellenistic World*; M.P. Nilsson, *Greek Piety*; K. Rudolf, *Gnosis*; S. Sandmel, *Judaism and Christian Beginnings*; Idem, *Philo*; M. Tenney, *New Testament Times*; B.Z. Wacholder, *Eupolemus*; H.R. Willoughby, *Pagan Regeneration*; R. Wilken, *The Christians as the Romans Saw Them*; H.R. Wolfson, *Philo*.

Primary Sources: Apuleius, *The Metamorphoses*; Euripides, *Bacchae*; *Greek Magical Papyri* (translated by H.D. Betz); Lucian, *The Syrian Goddess*; Philostratus, *Life of Apollonius*; Seneca, *Moral Essays*; NTB 26-31, 58-115, 225-237.

As Paul and Barnabas traveled on their missionary journey in Cyprus, they encountered a sorcerer (Acts 13:8) who opposed their preaching. Later, at Lystra on the mainland of Asia Minor the misguided villagers jumped to the conclusion that Barnabas was really the Greek god Zeus and Paul was Hermes (14:12). On Paul's second missionary journey, with Silas as his partner, he encountered a girl who had a spirit of divination (16:16) or the "spirit of the python" which means she was supposedly possessed by the god Apollo. As Paul was preaching in Athens, he encountered the Stoic and Epicurean philosophers (17:18). Finally, in Ephesus a mob rioted, yelling, "Great is Artemis!" because Christianity was causing devotion to that pagan deity to diminish (19:23-41).

Clearly we are no longer in the Jewish world of Pharisees and Sadducees but we have entered a new culture with many strange religions. What were these Greco-Roman religions, many of which seem very bizarre or extreme, and who belonged to them? We will begin by describing the Pantheon deities of classical Greece — and later Roman counterparts — and then trace the development of religion in the Hellenistic age.

Pagan Religious Practices

A. The Pantheon Deities

The twelve Pantheon deities in Greek and Roman mythology were as follows:

Greek	Roman
Zeus	Jupiter
Hera	Juno
Poseidon	Neptune
Athena	Minerva
Aphrodite	Venus
Ares	Mars
Apollo	Apollo
Artemis	Diana
Hermes	Mercury
Hestia	Vesta
Demeter	Ceres
Hephaestus	Vulcan

Each city-state had its special protecting deity. For example, Athens had Athena; Corinth had Apollo; Ephesus had Artemis. Although many other deities were also worshiped in each city-state, the protecting deity was especially honored. Worship of this god or goddess was both a civic and religious duty.

But the prominence of the city-state religion collapsed when so many of the city-states were conquered repeatedly from the time of Alexander the Great until the coming of the Romans. The political chaos that prevailed in this period (300 B.C. to A.D. 200, called the Hellenistic and Roman periods) resulted also in a religious chaos so that people lost faith in the protection of the old Pantheon deities. They turned to other deities that had already been known to them but had never been as prominent as they would become, and they also imported esoteric religions from afar, especially from the orient (Egypt, Syria, Persia, and Asia Minor).

The political chaos in the eastern half of the Mediterranean, followed by Rome's own political convulsions led to a spiritual weakening that G. Murray has termed a "failure of nerve." It was a loss of confidence, and a loss of hope in this life. Mankind longed for revelation from God and was rather indifferent about the welfare of the state or society. Emphasis was on personal conversion of the soul to God and pardon for unworthiness. The world was no good and seemed to them to have become very old. They must find meaning somehow by faith in something, by contempt for the world, by ecstatic experiences, and by suffering.

B. Worship of Fate and Fortune

Murray writes that the religious life in the Greek-speaking world in the period from around 300 B.C. to A.D. 200 resulted in three new tendencies. The first was the worship of Fate and Fortune as goddesses. They could no longer believe that the gods rewarded the pious and the just because so many whimsical despots had conquered the Greek cities. All one could do was placate the capricious powers of Fate or Fortune. Fate emphasized the idea of predestination and Fortune the idea of chance. Either everything was predetermined or everything happened by a mere roll of the dice but either way the state and society had seemed to lose power to change the course of events. Individuals would then have to make their peace with these inscrutable forces. By the first century B.C., Fortune — regarded as a kind, beneficent force — had lost popularity. Now it was Fate, a cruel and implacable tyrant, that was regarded by most as the force ruling the universe.

C. Protective Worship

The second tendency was worship that was seen as a way of predicting, manipulating or circumventing one's Fate.

1. Astrology. Astrology began in Mesopotamia but spread to all parts of the Greco-Roman world in the Hellenistic and Roman eras. It taught that the stars were deities that controlled one's destiny or fate. There is, said astrologers, a sympathy or harmony between things on earth and the heavenly bodies so that the movements of the stars affect what will happen on earth.

Astrologers thus became greatly admired in this age and astrology was considered by many ancients to be the queen of the sciences. Emperor Tiberius, for example, consulted an astrologer often to learn about his horoscope. If one could not stop Fate, at least one could have some warning.

2. Magic. Magic was essentially the attempt to manipulate demons, deities, or Fate. In this manipulation of the unseen powers, sorcerers used various methods: philtres, the Evil Eye, amulets, magic wheels, magical symbols, conjurations and magical papyrus documents (called Ephesian letters). Special objects were used in these processes such as parts of animals, herbs, precious stones and fluids of the human body (e.g., saliva). Amulets made of precious stones with magical poems carved on them were special favorites. These could be for protection or love amulets.

The main object of these magical techniques was the demonic world. Demons increased in religious importance in the Hellenistic and Roman periods. They were believed to be intermediate beings, either good or evil, between the gods and humans. The practitioners of magic, as the surviving texts show, thought the air was positively swimming in demons. They caused illness and misfortune as well as health or success. They could protect you from humans who wished to harm you or they could harm you themselves. They could cause someone to fall in love with you or put a jinx on you. Demons were believed to be everywhere and must therefore be controlled and manipulated.

A good example of a magical text or "Ephesian letter"[2] soliciting the help of a demon in romance is given by Kee: "I adjure you, demon of death, cause to pine away Sarapeion out of love for Dioskorus, whom Tikoi bore: burn his heart, let it melt and let his blood dry up through love, longing and pain over me until Sarapeion, whom Psametra bore, comes to Dioskorus . . ." (PGM XVI, translated by Kee).

The practice of magic is referred to several times in the book of Acts. Simon the Samaritan was a magician (8:9-13) as was Elymas of Cyprus (13:6-8). The residents of Ephesus were deeply involved in the practice of magic (19:19). The abundance of magical papyrus texts discovered in Egypt also makes it clear that the practice of magic was quite popular in the ancient world.

3. The Mystery Religions. The mystery religions lifted one above the sphere of Fate. The stars might work their will on the body but the soul was beyond Fate's reach and would one day, if one adhered to a mystery cult, go to the sphere of the gods. The four most popular mystery cults, which spread throughout the entire empire by the first century B.C., were the cults of Dionysus, Isis, the Great Mother, and Mithra.

a. Dionysus. This cult existed in Greece and in the Greek colonies (on the coast of Asia Minor) long before the Hellenistic period. But with Rome's dominance of the Mediterranean, this cult soon spread west to Italy.

The Greek god, Dionysus (the Roman name was Bacchus) was the god of wine. He was worshiped first and foremost by physical intoxication. The experience, when done in the context of the religious cult, was viewed as an experience of ecstasy, for the wine was believed to have the divine power of Dionysus. Sexual immorality was also common at these drunken feasts.

Another important ritual for this cult was the feast of the raw

---

[2]The magical texts were commonly nicknamed "Ephesian letters" because magic was so popular in Ephesus. See Acts 19:19.

flesh. Originally they had in a frenzied state torn apart a living human being to eat his quivering flesh. Later the victim became an animal — goat, fawn, or bull — either still alive or killed only shortly before they ate it raw. They believed that they were in this ritual somehow in direct communion with the deity because Dionysus was temporarily in the sacred victim. He was the quivering flesh and the warm blood and thus they were united or joined with him in eating.

The third ritual of this cult was the frenzied dance. Participants whirled around and tossed their heads back until vertigo set in. They dressed like Dionysus as he was pictured commonly, carrying a wand tipped with a pine cone and entwined with ivy, bearing snakes in his hair and wearing a fawn skin. The dance typically took place at night to the accompaniment of flutes, tambourines, and their own shouts. When they were sufficiently dizzied and frenzied by the dancer they believed they were in communion with the spirit of Dionysus. In this way they had a foretaste of the happy existence in the future life when at death the soul is joined with the deities.

b. Isis. This cult originated in Egypt long before the Hellenistic period but was revived and made the state Egyptian religion under the Ptolemies. By the first century B.C., it had made its way to Rome, carried there by sailors, for the religion was very popular among them. Women in general were also very much attracted to the cult of Isis.

The religion centered on the cycle of the Nile river which floods each spring, bringing once again fertility to the river valley. The myth of the cult parallels the cycle of the seasons. Osiris, the brother and consort of Isis, is killed by Set and dismembered. Isis retrieves Osiris's dismembered body and restores it to life.

This myth was reenacted each fall in a public ritual of the greatest lamentation (at Osiris's death) then the wildest jubilation in the streets (at his restoration to life). The practice of immorality along with such festivities was common.

There were also private rituals associated with this cult, especially the ritual of initiation. As in practically every mystery religion, the initiate went through a ceremony to identify him with the god. The initiate in the cult of Isis first went through an immersion in water which was symbolic of the life-giving powers of the sacred

Nile river. After the immersion, one abstained from meat, wine and sex for ten days. On the tenth day a priest took the initiate into the most sacred part of a temple of Isis. There a ritual death took place in which the initiate probably played the role of Osiris and went into the underworld. The next morning the initiate was given a new robe and carried a torch. He stood in front of the statue of Isis. He was Osiris; he had been deified and was now immortal. Finally, the process ended with a banquet.

c. The Great Mother. The Great Mother was a fertility goddess worshiped in Syria and Asia Minor. She was called Cybele in Asia Minor and commonly called Atargatis in Syria. The worship of Atargatis seems to have involved the elements from the old Syrian religion: sacred prostitution — sexual union with a temple prostitute as an act of symbolic union with the goddess — and a human sacrifice — especially of children. Even in the Roman period as the cult spread through the empire there were clandestine rites in which children were sacrificed.

The cult of Cybele in Asia Minor was a wild and frenzied religion. The most important public rites took place in the spring when the trees and flowers bloomed once more.

According to the myths, Cybele's consort, Attis, had either killed himself by mutilation or been killed by Cybele's father. This death symbolized winter time and the death of vegetation. The members of the cult would mourn Attis's death during the winter. But Cybele is believed to have revived the fallen Attis. Thus in the spring takes place the festival celebrating the return to life of Attis and of all vegetation.

The spring rite involved first a vegetable fast for a few days during which time meat could be eaten but no cereals or vegetables. Then came the day of blood, a day of frenzied dancing to cymbals and flutes during which the celebrants could cut themselves as Attis did. Some male fanatics might even go to the extreme of emasculating themselves.[3] This rite — the orgiastic dancing and the wounding of oneself — was believed to unite the participant with Cybele. Even

---

[3]The Apostle Paul probably alludes to this cult in Gal 5:12 (as J.B. Lightfoot, *Galatians* maintained). Living in Asia Minor, the Galatian Christians would have been very familiar with the cult of Cybele. Paul sarcastically compares Jewish circumcision with the emasculation of Cybele.

more gruesome is the consecration rite for a priest in the cult of the Great Mother. This consecration rite, called the *taurobolium* ("bull slaughter") involved the bathing of one's entire body in the blood of a bull. The priest was placed in a pit with a lattice-work covering over it. Next the bull was slaughtered over the pit so that its blood would flow down over the priest below. The priest caught the flow of spurting blood on his head and the rest of his body insuring that even his ears, lips, nostrils, eyes, and inside his mouth were covered with the gore. Next the priest emerged from the pit to receive worship from the rest of the cult because he was believed to have been washed clean by the blood of the bull (see *NTB* 109).

d. Mithra. The final mystery cult we will consider came from Persia. It stood apart from the other cults in that it was a religion for men only (mostly soldiers) and it demanded a much stricter lifestyle than the others.

In Persian mythology Mithra was both a god of beneficent light and the wrathful foe of all evil. He is usually represented as coming from a cave and as slaying the sacred bull. Therefore the cult-centers (called Mithreums) were caves or underground grottoes instead of temples.

There were seven grades (from the seven planets identified by the ancients) of membership in the cult: the Raven, the Occult, the Soldier, the Lion, the Persian, the Courier of the Sun, and finally, the Father. For each initiation the participant wore a mask appropriate to his level and acted the part he would become (e.g., crowing for the Raven). The level of Soldier seems to have been especially important since the initiate received a mark of sealing (a sign burned on his forehead).[4] Apparently at each level of initiation there were also tortures applied — whippings, punishments by water, fire, frost, hunger, thirst, and long journeys — all arranged with increasing severity.

There were also at these initiations water ablutions by sprinkling or by total immersion. In at least two levels honey would be put on the tongue and the hands of the initiate (as was customary to put

---

[4]Is this practice behind the reference in Rev 13:16 to the mark of the Beast?

into the mouth of a newborn infant). Finally a meal would be eaten of bread and wine which, they believed, would give them power to combat evil spirits.

Mithraism was characterized by strict morality, even asceticism. They resisted sexual immorality and engaged in rigorous fasting. Mithra stood for truth and holiness and thus, it was believed, would not tolerate laxity of morals.

They believed that when one died he ascended through the seven levels of heaven, each of which was presided over by one of the seven planets. Because the cult member had learned the right formulas (like passwords) by his initiation into the seven levels of the cult, he could pass through each of these levels after death and be joined to the gods.

The mystery religions, then, offered their members an escape (after death) from the grim clutches of Fate. The members of these cults believed they would rise to the level of the gods and be divinized themselves. Fate might control them now but their souls were free. The mysteries were then a way of liberation, it was believed, and even salvation from the uncertain and grim existence that so many people experienced.

4. Gnosticism. Another means of escape from the harshness of this life and from Fate and the stars was one of the various groups now known as Gnostics. Not every group sharing the common features listed below called itself "Gnostic" but the term has become standard for historians and it does describe one of the main doctrines of all these groups. That is, adherents of this religion believed they would be saved — rise above the stars after death — by *gnosis* ("knowledge").

The great Gnostic thinkers whom we know by name lived in the second century A.D. and maintained some connection to Christianity (at least they claimed to be Christians). Nevertheless, Gnosticism as a religious movement surely began before the advent of Christianity and was a widespread pagan belief. Not only do we have the description of the beliefs of the "Christian" Gnostics[5] but

---

[5]These descriptions are found in the orthodox Christian writers such as Irenaeus (A.D. 180), Clement of Alexandria (A.D. 200) and Hippolytus of

we have the so-called Hermetic literature (see *NTB* 84-90) which is a corpus of texts of pagan and Jewish origin. In addition to these texts, the sands of Egypt have given us important ancient documents. These new Gnostic texts from Nag Hammadi in Egypt have provided a much clearer picture of the ancient religion.[6] Clearly Gnosticism could attach itself to Judaism, paganism, or later to Christianity.

Although each Gnostic sect had its own set of beliefs, common themes run through all the sects. These common themes as presented by H. Jonas are set out below:

a. God. God is absolutely transmundane and completely alien to the universe. God did not create the world and does not govern it. He is even opposed to it. The physical universe is the work of lowly spiritual powers that do not know the true God.

b. The universe. The universe is a vast prison whose innermost dungeon is the earth. Lower spiritual powers, called *archons*, rule over the world in the form of Fate. They enslave mankind by laws and they bar passage of the souls of dead persons that seek to ascend to the true God after death.

c. Humanity. Man's origin is both mundane and extra-mundane. The *archons* shaped both the body and the soul of man and gave him his appetites for food, drink and sex. Man's body and soul therefore are part of the world and subject to Fate. But the spirit (or spark) in some persons is a divine substance. It has come from beyond this universe and has somehow (different Gnostic sects explained it variously) fallen into this world. In its unredeemed state the spirit is enclosed in the soul and body and is unconscious of itself and its other-worldly origin. It is "asleep" or "drunk" or "ignorant." But not every person has this divine spark, only the elect.

d. Death. As God is alien to this world so is the spiritual self. One must therefore release the inner man — the spark — from the bonds of this world and return it to its natural realm of light, that is, to the transmundane God. But to do this the spirit must know

---

Rome (A.D. 200). For a convenient summary of these works see B. Leyton, *The Gnostic Scriptures*.

[6]For an English translation of these texts (which are in the Coptic language) see J. Robinson, et al., *The Nag Hammadi Library*.

about the transmundane God, who cannot be discovered in this world. Thus a messenger comes from the world of light with this revelation. With this revelation or knowledge (γνῶσις, *gnōsis*) the spirit or spark can at death travel upward, leaving behind at each sphere or level the psychical "vestment" that was contributed by it. (This process is similar to that envisioned in Mithraism.)

e. The spiritual ones. Those possessing *gnōsis* set themselves apart from others. They are hostile and contemptuous of all earthly ties. "The world is no good." With that statement all Gnostics would have agreed. But what are the ethical implications of this statement? How did Gnostics behave since they believed the world was no good? Different groups interpreted these words to lead them to avoid contact with the world and even perhaps to punish their own flesh. After all, if the world is no good (and therefore their own flesh is no good), one should deprive it and punish it. But others went just the opposite direction. If the world is no good, then all the commandments and laws of the world are also no good. Therefore one should oppose the *archons* by breaking every commandment even if it means indulging in the worst sort of moral debauchery. Thus some groups were ascetics and some were the worst libertines.

D. Other Pagan Religious Practices

1. Healing Cults. Asclepius was the most widely venerated healing deity.[7] His temples were scattered around the eastern half of the Mediterranean and were frequented by religious pilgrims who suffered from various illnesses and impairments. Each year hundreds of sick were allegedly healed at these temples either while praying in the temple, at night in a dream-vision, or while receiving a hot bath or other treatment. Inscriptions made by the healed patients as well as by clay copies of the diseased body parts that were left behind testify that people were healed of blindness, withered limbs and other diseases. But apparently many that visited the temples were not healed and the temples were as much "clinics for the ailing" (Kee) as places of healing.

---

[7]But numerous healings are also alleged to have taken place while worshiping Isis.

2. Holy Men and Hoaxes. Philostratus has left us an interesting biography of a philosopher and healer named Apollonius of Tyana (first century A.D.). Apollonius traveled widely through Asia Minor, Persia, India, Egypt and Rome teaching his doctrine of ascetic moralism. He is also supposed to have healed the sick and cast out demons. His life was threatened both by Emperor Nero and later by Emperor Domitian. Philostratus's account, written over a hundred years after Apollonius's death, is full of exaggerations and legendary material. But the general outlines of Apollonius's life are probably accurate. He was one of many itinerant holy men — philosophers combining moralistic teaching with wonder working.

Alexander of Abonoteichus, who attempted to be like Apollonius, was a charlatan. Alexander (second century A.D.) practiced his quackery for many years until he perfected the ultimate scam. He planted some bronze tablets in a temple of Apollo at Chalcedon. On the tablets was inscribed a message to the effect that the god, Asclepius, would soon appear at the town of Abonoteichus. Alexander then showed up at that town (in Asia Minor) and pretended to go into a frenzy as if he were a cult member of the religion of Cybele. Pagans were always very impressed with such carryings-on. He then ran to a preplanned site and recovered a blown goose egg in which he had inserted a small snake. He broke the egg to reveal what he claimed was the animal form of the god Asclepius. Days later he announced that the deity would receive visitors. By now he had caught a larger snake (the naive crowds were amazed at how quickly Asclepius had grown) and he attached a dummy's head to the tail of the snake, hiding the snake's own head. He had rigged it by horse hair controls so that he could work the mouth of the dummy's head. Thus it was that the snake-god would deliver oracles to the ignorant visitors and every oracle was of course interpreted by Asclepius's special prophet, Alexander. Alexander became enormously famous throughout the Roman Empire for this hoax.

3. Emperor Worship. Alexander the Great and his successors had allowed themselves in the east to be worshiped as people had worshiped kings in Egypt and Mesopotamia for millennia. Augustus was also hailed as "savior" (a divine term) in the eastern provinces and was upon his death pronounced a god by the Roman senate.

The mad Caligula tried to take the title of "divine" while he was yet alive but he was not taken seriously. Not until Emperor Domitian, toward the end of the first century A.D., does emperor worship become entrenched in the Greco-Roman world. From then on until Constantine, it would usually be required of everyone (except Jews) to sacrifice to the emperor, and during this period Christians would be horribly persecuted for their refusal to participate.

Hellenistic Philosophy

Philosophy in the Hellenistic and Roman periods must be considered in the category of religion. Like the other pagan Hellenistic religions, philosophy sought to offer salvation and liberation from Fate, from man's grim existence, and from death. Two overarching influences shaped Hellenistic philosophy: the figure of Socrates and the collapse of the city-states. In one way or another most philosophic minds reflected a strain of Socrates's thought (the Sceptics and Epicureans were exceptions). Second, the collapse of the city-states and the consequent instability of life led to the psychological defense mechanism of denial of both desire and fear. G. Murray has compared the situation to that of two men fighting a battle. After the battle, the winner says the goal in life is success but the loser says winning is not everything. Classical philosophy was rooted in success, in winning, but Hellenistic philosophy was rooted in defeat.

The most famous student of Socrates was Plato and Plato's most famous student was Aristotle. But normally the life and thought of these two luminaries are discussed under classical philosophy. Therefore we shall simply note that Plato founded the Academy in Athens and Aristotle founded the Lyceum there. Both of these schools were still very active in the New Testament period.

A. The Cyrenaics

Aristippus (born in Cyrene, 435-356 B.C.) was a student of Socrates and later founded his own school called the Cyrenaic School. He disdained the study of logic and metaphysics and concentrated exclusively on ethics. His central doctrine was that pleasure alone constitutes the happiness of man. Pleasure is the only good. He was then a genuine Hedonist. But Aristippus and his followers did not pursue bodily pleasure exclusively (though primarily). They also wanted to develop, to some extent, mental enjoyments.

B. The Cynics

Antisthenes (born in Athens, 444-365 B.C.) was also a student of Socrates. As with most of the other students of Socrates that began their own philosophical schools, Antisthenes exaggerated what Socrates had taught. Socrates taught that virtue was the *highest* good. Antisthenes taught that virtue was the *only* good and that vice is the only evil. Everything else — riches, honors, freedom, health, life, poverty, shame, slavery, sickness, and even death — is a matter of indifference. Antisthenes rejected completely Aristippus's Hedonism. The worst error is to believe that pleasure is good.

The essence of virtue is self-control or absolute freedom from all material needs. Thus the Cynics renounced the basic joys of life: pleasure, comfort, family, society and religion. They lived a very ascetic life, wandering as beggars, going barefoot and wearing a simple rough garment. Antisthenes, himself, dressed as the poorest of men and accepted as students only those willing to endure such hardships. He often drove new-comers away with a stick.

Since the Cynics renounced society as a matter of indifference, they tried to ignore social custom and convention and live life "according to nature." Thus they developed an immodest behavior that flouted all standards of decency, earning their nickname "Cynics" ("dog-men") because, like dogs, they were apt to perform any bodily function in public. Indeed the Cynics believed it their duty to do so.

One of the best known Cynics was Diogenes of Sinope (400-325 B.C.) who was perhaps a student of Antisthenes. Next to Alexander the Great he was the most famous person in all of Greece in his day. Diogenes in true Cynic fashion maintained that every convention of the world was false. Every title, every claim to wisdom, greatness and happiness was false. Only virtue was worthwhile. He rejected religion, civil life, marriage, wealth, and reputation. He allegedly carried a lantern, wandering about in the daytime "looking for a man," (looking for a real man of virtue).

Diogenes was true to his own teaching. He lived in an old urn and when he was once chided for carrying a drinking cup — as possessing too luxurious an item — he threw it aside. Alexander the Great once met Diogenes and, standing over him and casting his shadow on him, asked the famous philosopher, "May I grant you a favor?" Whereupon Diogenes replied, "You can get out of my light." As he lay dying, Diogenes requested that his body be fed to the wolves and dogs so he could thereby "serve his brothers."

Cynicism was a very unusual and extremist philosophical school in a very stressful era. It sought to offer relief to those troubled in soul and mind by urging them to stop worrying about "man-made" conventions and honors. If one can just live according to nature, they taught, the stresses of life will vanish.

C. The Stoics

The founder of the Stoic school, Zeno (336-264 B.C.), was himself a student for a time of the Cynic philosopher, Crates. Stoicism therefore, bore a strong resemblance in many ways to Cynicism. Zeno was born in Cyprus and made his way to Athens after a shipwreck destroyed his wealth. There he studied philosophy, no doubt searching for answers to the sort of questions one asks after suffering such a reversal of fortune. After studying with Crates the Cynic and a few other teachers, he founded his own school. His tendency to lecture in the Painted Porch (Greek στοά, stoa), a public art gallery in Athens, earned his followers the name Stoics.

A later head of the school, named Chrysippus (head of the school from 232 to 204 B.C.) came from Tarsus in Cilicia, the apostle Paul's hometown. Three other notable Stoic teachers came from Cilicia, indicating perhaps the influence of Stoicism in that city.

Stoicism eventually made its way to Rome where it was rather popular among the upper classes. The greatest Roman Stoics were Seneca (A.D. 3-65), the personal tutor of Emperor Nero; Epictetus, the philosopher-slave (fl. A.D. 90); and Emperor Marcus Aurelius (A.D. 121-180). All of these great Roman philosophers have left philosophical writings.

The Stoics taught that everything is predetermined. God pervades, controls, and determines all things. One must understand this and accept it, they maintained, to be content. If it is accepted, many of life's problems are eliminated. Chrysippus illustrated life as follows: Picture a dog tied to an ox cart. When the cart moves forward the dog must also move. He can walk behind the cart voluntarily or he can be dragged, fighting, but either way he must follow the cart. We are that dog. Everything is predetermined by God. We may cheerfully accept our role and play it or we may be dragged through it. The latter course will, however, bring much unhappiness.

Stoic ethics concerned the absolute conformity with the Divine Reason that controls and determines all things. To live according to Divine Reason (God), who is also in us, means to negate and renounce the passions and emotions. The goal was to achieve *apathia* (ἀπάθεια, "apathy") or freedom from all passion, emotion or affections. Thus the Stoic (like the Cynic) was indifferent about all external things such as health, riches, beauty, and pleasure or their opposites (sickness, poverty, ugliness, and pain). They also tried to live without any trace of affection for family and friends. They avoided hurt and suffering by avoiding affection.

Since life and death were also matters of indifference to the Stoics, when certain circumstances arose that indicated death would be better, the Stoic would leave life by committing suicide. Zeno is said to have committed suicide as did at least three other notable Stoic masters.

Since the soul is material, it will not exist after death in a separate state, maintained the Stoics. But they did believe in a kind of reincarnation (as did the Pythagoreans and Platonists). Everything moves in a cycle. Some day the cosmos will be destroyed by a great fire, then the cycle will begin again. We will be born again in this new world. And so the story will continue endlessly as a continuous cycle.

Paul encountered Stoics at Athens (Acts 17:18) and they disputed with him about his gospel and about Jesus' resurrection from the dead. But he surely must have met them in nearly every city he preached in, for they were very common in the cities of Asia Minor, even in Paul's own home city, Tarsus.

D. The Peripatetics

These are the followers of Aristotle. Although they were active during this period (300 B.C.-A.D. 200) they were never very popular. They were always too much like the classical philosophy of old Hellenism. Aristotle's wide interest in botany and zoology and his love of metaphysics was an oddity in this age of defeat and of feeling that the world was no good or at least inadequate. One man wrote that he in one evening went from a Peripatetic lecture to hear Chrysippus, the Stoic, speak. He claimed it was like turning from listening to a man to listening to the gods.

E. The Sceptics

The founder of the Sceptical School, Pyrrho of Elis (360-270 B.C.), left no writings behind. Yet his basic thought can be determined from later sources. His philosophy can be summarized as follows. We can only know how things appear to us, not how they really are. Since we cannot know how things really are, we should withhold judgment and accept that inquiry is futile. If we withhold judgment, we will find *ataraxia* (ἀταραξία, a state of not being disturbed) in which human happiness consists.

Thus the Sceptics found their refuge from the instability in which they lived by renouncing any claim on knowledge. They thought that if one admitted that nothing can be known for sure, one would find peace of mind. Thus peace of mind comes by doubting everything.

F. The Platonists

Plato's academy in Athens continued to flourish long after his death. The history of the academy is usually divided into three periods: the Old Academy (347-250 B.C.), the Middle Academy (250-129 B.C.), and the New Academy (129 B.C.-A.D. 529). The academy only imperfectly preserved Plato's thought. The teachers mixed in ideas from Pythagoras and even from the Sceptics. Platonism exerted very little influence on New Testament Christianity but later Christian thinkers such as Origen (A.D. 185-254) and Augustine (A.D. 354-430) were strongly influenced by Plato.

G. Epicureanism

Epicurus (341-270 B.C.) founded his own school in a garden in Athens after first teaching in Mitylene, then Lampsacus. He too sought relief from the instability of his age and found it in a concoction all his own. His metaphysics or physics was based on that of Democritus, who had suggested the theory of atoms. This theory is correct, taught Epicurus. Everything consists of small particles called *atomoi* (ἄτομοι, "unsplittables"). These atoms while falling through space, swerve at random and for no apparent reason, bumping into each other and causing clusters. These clusters form the various material objects of our world. Humans are also the result of clusters.

From this basis, Epicurus thought he could save mankind from anxiety over Fate and death. His solution was the Fourfold Remedy:

1. Meditate on the blessedness of the gods. The gods do exist but have little to do with humans. They are immortal and therefore if we think about their existence, it will give us a certain peace of mind.

2. Overcome the fear of death. Epicurus taught that there was no life of any kind after death. Only the gods are immortal. Thus there should be no fear of death. One will not be punished in the underworld. One will cease to exist, cease to know, cease to be conscious. Thus the Epicureans laughed at Paul when he preached the resurrection (Acts 17:18).

3. Interpret the true meaning of pleasure and pursue it. Epicurus and his school were more interested in mental pleasure than the Cyrenaics. They also strongly sought the pleasure of friendships. The various pleasures of life (bodily and sensual too, but especially mental) made life bearable and friendship was especially helpful.

4. Avoid pain. One should not live foolishly so as to bring pain to oneself. Therefore we must obey civil law and control our appetites to some degree. Otherwise pain and discomfort may result. Epicurus did not believe in Fate and determinism. We are absolutely free to choose our own way, he taught. Neither the gods nor some blind force has any control over our affairs or any interest in them for that matter. Epicurus sought, above all, *ataraxia* as the Sceptics did. His Fourfold Remedy, he believed, was the way of

liberation from the anxieties of his age. Fear should play no role in one's life because death and Fate have been debunked. Hellenistic philosophy was rooted in anxiety and defeat, or in what G. Murray termed "the failure of nerve." Most of these schools of thought sought relief from fear of death, political upheaval, and personal tragedy. The remedies varied from the drop-out philosophy of the Cynics, to the apathy of the Stoics and the life of doubt of the Sceptics, to the life of pleasure of the Cyrenaics and Epicureans. Whatever the method, the motive remained the same: to get relief and peace of mind.

Diaspora Judaism

Whenever Paul and his companions went to a new city to preach the gospel, they invariably started in the local Jewish synagogue (e.g., Acts 13:5, 14; 14:1). Most towns of any size in Asia Minor, Greece, and Syria had a population of Jews and thus a synagogue. Even Rome had a large number of Jews. The largest number of Jews outside of Palestine lived in Egypt. In the entire Roman empire at the time of Augustus there were perhaps five million Diaspora Jews in addition to about one to one and a half million Jews living in Palestine. Thus most Jews lived in the "Diaspora" (dispersion). Furthermore, in any given city of good size from 10% to 15% of the residents were Jews (see Meeks).

The reasons the Jews left Palestine were numerous. Many had remained in Babylon after the exile. Others were traveling merchants who settled for business reasons in a foreign land. Some may have been slaves or former slaves. But most Jews left the tiny country of Palestine for economic reasons. There was simply not enough land (using ancient farming techniques) to support many more than the one and one-half million Jews plus the Samaritans and Gentiles that lived in the land.

The Diaspora Jews learned to speak good Greek. In their synagogues they read the Old Testament in a Greek translation (but probably someone also read it in the Hebrew original). In many cases they could speak nothing else but Greek. They took Greek names and sometimes even adopted Greek philosophical thought. Some of them even left their Jewish faith and became totally assimilated into the pagan environment. Most, however, remained Jews, albeit Jews with a decidedly Greek accent.

The Greek translation of Scripture began with the Septuagint ("seventy" translation), so-called because allegedly seventy scholars worked on it. The Septuagint was commissioned by King Ptolemy Philadelphus of Egypt in the third century B.C. The Pentateuch — the first five books of the Old Testament — was completed within a relatively brief period. Much later (by the mid-second century B.C.) the Prophets and Writings were translated. This important translation became not only the Bible of Diaspora Jews but of early Christians as well. It is often quoted in the New Testament.

By the second century A.D., Jews felt that they needed a new translation of the Old Testament into Greek. Christians had by now appropriated the Septuagint as their own. Thus there followed in quick succession translations by Aquila, Theodotion, and Symmachus. Today we have only fragments left of these versions.

In addition to the Greek versions of the Old Testament, Diaspora Judaism produced several notable authors[8] such as Cleodemus, Eupolemus, Artapanus, and Aristobulus. All of these works were written in Greek and most of them were propagandistic. That is, they sought to impress the Greek readership — both Jews and non-Jews — with the antiquity and wisdom of Judaism. Thus Artapanus claimed that Abraham in his trip to Egypt instructed Pharaoh in astrology and Moses invented music. Cleodemus made the absurd claim that the Greek hero Hercules married Abraham's granddaughter. Aristobulus wrote equally absurdly that the philosophers Pythagoras, Socrates, and Plato had used parts of the Old Testament in constructing their philosophical systems.

The most important of these Judeo-Greek authors — aside from Josephus who also published in Greek — was Philo of Alexandria (c. 10 B.C.-A.D. 50).[9] Because of his great learning — not only in the

---

[8]Their works are extant only in fragments and can be found in *OTP*, Vol. II.

[9]Philo's many works can be found conveniently translated in the *LCL*.

Old Testament but in Plato and Stoicism — and because of the massive productivity of his pen, Philo stands as the giant of Jewish writers in the Diaspora. Philo's works demonstrate great versatility but he is best known for his commentaries on the Old Testament.

Greco-Jewish Literature

I. Bible Translations
1. Septuagint (abbreviated LXX)
   Pentateuch finished in 3rd century B.C.
   Prophets and writings finished by 132 B.C.
   "barbarous Greek"
2. Aquila — translated O.T. in A.D. 138, very literal
3. Theodotion — translated O.T. A.D. 180–192. More a revision of the LXX.
4. Symmachus — translated O.T. at the end of 2nd century A.D. Periphrastic style.

II. History, chronography (many of the following are quoted in Alexander Polyhistor)
1. Demetrius — Alexandrian, 3rd century B.C. Chronology from 722 B.C. to his day.
2. Eupolemus — lived around 158 B.C. Work on the kings of Judea.
3. Philo the epic poet — wrote on Jerusalem in epic meter
4. Josephus — 1st century A.D.

III. Ezekiel the tragedian — wrote a tragedy on the Exodus

IV. Propaganda
1. Artapanus — Abraham, he wrote, instructed Pharaoh in astrology, Joseph taught the Egyptians proper agriculture, and Moses invented culture (music, poetry)
2. Cleodemus Malchus — claimed that the sons of Abraham knew Hercules. Hercules married Abraham's granddaughter.
3. III Maccabees — the story of an attempt at persecuting Jews in Egypt.

V. Philosophy
1. Aristobulus — second century B.C. He found Greek philosophy in the O.T. and claimed the O.T. was used by Pythagoras, Socrates, and Plato.
2. IV Maccabees — says that Jewish ethics of the Torah are equal to the "right reason" of the Greeks.
3. Philo of Alexandria — 1st century A.D.

VI. Apology
1. Josephus — *Against Apion*
2. Philo of Alexandria — several works of apology

Philo found the greatest ideas of Plato and the Stoics in the Old Testament. Like Aristobulus, Philo alleged that the philosophers had received originally many of their truths from the Hebrew Bible. Of course most other readers fail to see these philosophical "truths" in the Old Testament Torah and Philo even admitted they were not obvious. To see them there one had to allegorize the Bible. That is, one must not pay attention to the literal meaning of Scripture but see a figurative or allegorical meaning. For example, the four rivers flowing from the garden of Eden (Gen 2:10) represent the four cardinal virtues of Plato's thought (i.e., prudence, temperance, courage, and justice). Likewise, the garden from which the four rivers flowed represents virtue. Philo was also influenced to some extent by the mystery religions. He interpreted the lives of Abraham, Isaac, Jacob and especially Moses in terms of the mysteries. In most of the pagan mystery religions the initiate went through a course of rituals until he or she became divinized or became a god or goddess (so they believed). In Philo's view, the patriarchs also traveled a kind of mystic road. Moses especially on Mt. Sinai went closer than any man to God. He became a listener to the divine music of the cosmos. Moses' soul became a lyre which produced the most beautiful music. The patriarchs did not become divinized (Philo's monotheism did not allow that idea) but they did come closer to God than non-mystics. Clearly Philo thought more happened on Mt. Sinai than the giving of a few commandments. The Law of Moses or the Torah is therefore both a law code for the duller masses and the path to a mystical experience of God for those who are ready to travel the mystic road.

The influences of Platonism, Stoicism, and the mysteries make Philo's writings on the Old Testament an interesting blend of Yahwism and Hellenism. Whether Philo went too far in importing pagan ideas is debated. Certainly he was not orthodox in the strict sense. Yet he never abandoned his Jewishness. Historians often compare Philo to his contemporary, another Diaspora Jew, Paul of Tarsus. Philo remained loyal to the Torah, to circumcision, and to monotheism, but allowed himself to be deeply influenced by pagan philosophy and religion. Paul did not allow the influences of paganism into his thought but he renounced the Torah (as the means of salvation) and circumcision — though certainly not monotheism. Yet Paul maintained consistently that what he was preaching was very

Jewish because Christians are now the true Israel (Rom 3:21f; 9:8). Philo viewed the Old Testament through the spectacles of Greek thought; Paul viewed it through the spectacles of his vision of the risen Lord.

Jewish life in the Diaspora could be very pleasant. They were often allowed to adjudicate their own court cases. They usually lived together in their own section of the city making it easier to remain Jewish. They often excelled in business and some received citizenship in their city or even Roman citizenship. They could enjoy the best of city life and benefit from Greek learning.

But the life of a Diaspora Jew could also be uncomfortable, even painful. Anti-Semitism was rather common among pagans and therefore many false allegations were made against Jews. Some maintained that the Hebrews at the time of Moses had actually been expelled from Egypt because they were lepers. Jews worshiped, it was alleged, a golden donkey-head which stood in the temple in Jerusalem. Even worse calumnies were spread about them. Pagans asserted that Jews had taken secret oaths of hatred toward the Greeks. And some ignorant pagans believed the slander that Jews annually kidnapped a Greek, fattened him up, then ate him.

One can easily see why such rumors and silly accusations started. Although some Jews assimilated and became Greek, most remained Jews and thus held themselves aloof from pagan society. Jews would not eat with Gentiles or marry them. They refused to participate in worship of any deity except Yahweh, something pagans found very strange, even "atheistic," since most pagans belonged to several cults and worshiped several gods.

The ill-will between Gentiles and Jews often resulted in violence. There were riots in Alexandria and Caesarea. Jews were several times expelled from Rome.

To answer these charges and to explain Judaism, some Jewish authors engaged in apologetics (from the Greek word ἀπολογία, *apologia*, "defense"). Josephus, the historian, who lived in Rome after the Jewish war, answered such charges and attacked the writers that made them. He even occasionally poured scorn on the Greeks — he was careful never to criticize Rome — even though he clearly admired much of Greek culture. He used freely the ideas of the older Jewish propagandists — that much of Greek wisdom came originally from the Old Testament — and he challenged the historical conclusions of the antagonists of Judaism. Josephus's apologetic writing became a prototype for Christians who would only forty years later engage in their own defense against slander.

Diaspora Judaism was very important to early Christianity. Many of the great missionaries came from its ranks: Paul, Barnabas, Silas, Apollos, and Timothy. Further, the core of most early churches outside of Palestine probably consisted of Diaspora Jews. Finally, its literature — both the Septuagint version of the Old Testament and Jewish apologetic literature — had a very significant influence in the early church.

Christianity

The final religion in the Greco-Roman world we will consider is Christianity. The Christian church quickly spread throughout the Mediterranean world in the first century, winning converts from among Jews and pagans alike. There were wealthy and powerful politicians in its ranks (Rom 16:24) as well as the very poor and powerless (1 Cor 1:28). Some had black skin and some white skin (Acts 13:1). Some were formerly pious Jews (Acts 16:13-15); others formerly lived in unspeakable immorality (1 Cor 6:9-10). They came from all social classes and all ethnic backgrounds. One of the main reasons for this remarkably quick spread of the faith was the missionary activity of the Apostle Paul and the missionary vision of the church at Antioch, Paul's sponsor. Paul made three missionary tours that are recorded in Acts. Beginning in Antioch he and Barnabas traveled to Cyprus then northward into the towns of Pamphylia, Pisidia and Galatia establishing churches in almost every location. Paul's second missionary journey — made without Barnabas — began again in Antioch and continued overland through Cilicia, Galatia, Asia and, crossing the Aegean Sea, into Macedonia and southward into Achaia (or Greece). His third journey began again in Antioch and proceeded overland to Ephesus in Asia. After a lengthy stay in Ephesus, he crossed the sea again to

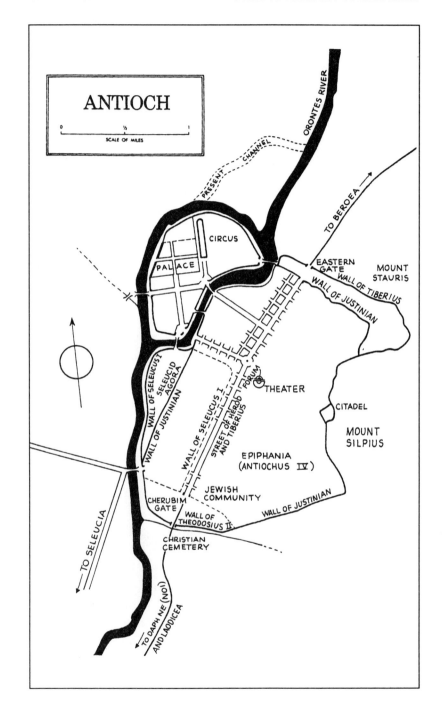

Macedonia and on to Greece. Some of Paul's most important letters were written in Ephesus (the Corinthian letters) and Greece (Romans) while on his third missionary journey.

Finally, Paul made it to Rome, though as a prisoner. There in Rome he was greeted by a significant group of Christians. The church had already been established for some time when Paul arrived there and he had many personal acquaintances there (see Rom 16).

Obviously Paul and his companions were not the only missionaries. Barnabas continued to travel and preach after his break with Paul (1 Cor 9:6). Two other missionaries much like Paul were Peter (Gal 2:11-12; 1 Cor 9:5) and Apollos (Acts 18:24-26; 1 Cor 1:12) who traveled at least to Antioch and Corinth and preached both to Jews and Gentiles. There is also a strong — and credible — tradition that Peter preached in Rome (see Chapters 8 and 10) as did the John Mark of Acts 13:5, according to the early Christian writer Papias (see Chapter 5). Such missionaries as these — and probably many others whose names we do not now know — accounted for the rapid growth of the faith in Jesus the Christ.

But the rapid growth did not take place without a price. Thousands of Christians gave their lives as martyrs to enable the faith to spread. Even in the earliest history of the church there were martyrs. Stephen (Acts 7) and James the Apostle (Acts 12:2) were executed because of their commitment to Jesus Christ. But the first severe persecution happened under Nero in A.D. 64 — and perhaps lasted as long as two years — as a result of Nero's attempt to find a scapegoat for the great fire of Rome. Hundreds of Christians were killed in the most inhumane of fashions. Among those martyred were Peter and Paul (see Chapter 8). Peter may have written his epistle shortly before his death in which he praises those who suffer "as a Christian" (1 Pet 4:16). After this, it may have become illegal just to be a Christian. Emperor Domitian's reign produced a severe persecution in Asia Minor which is referred to in the book of Revelation. By the time the author wrote this book several believers had already been martyred because they would not worship "the Beast" (i.e., the Emperor of Rome, see Rev 7:14; 13:11-18). Later in A.D. 112, Pliny the Younger, the governor of Bithynia, wrote to

Emperor Trajan to ask about executing Christians. It was clearly illegal, a capital crime, just to be a Christian. Trajan agreed that Christians should be punished but ordered Pliny not actively to pursue them. Only if someone accused a person of being a Christian, should that person be investigated.

Not only did the Roman government hate Christianity; many of the citizens did as well. Suetonius the historian claimed that Christianity was a new and evil superstition (*Nero* 16) and Tacitus, also an historian, alleged that Christians were guilty of hatred of the human race (*Annals* 15.44). Not only men of letters disliked Christians; many of the common folk did as well. Tacitus wrote in the above cited passage that his view of Christianity was the common one. It is further a generally held conclusion that Nero could only have successfully blamed the fire of Rome on Christians because they were held in such contempt by the lower classes.

Why did pagans dislike Christians so intensely? They did so for many of the same reasons they disliked Jews. Christians were also aloof from others. They did not worship other gods and did not participate in the wild goings-on of the festivals and banquets. They were "clannish," always taking care of one another. Moreover, they claimed only Christ as absolute authority, not the Emperor. In addition to these similarities to Judaism, Christians had other problems in the eyes of pagans. They predicted that the world would soon be destroyed by fire — which seemed to pagan minds a hateful prophecy — and they lashed out against the moral vices of paganism. Also we must not forget that Jesus himself was executed by a Roman official, Pontius Pilate. If a Roman official condemned him to death, most Romans would be suspicious of his religion.

Thus being a Christian brought one into danger. The believer would be slandered by pagans and could be arrested and executed. In the following centuries — until Constantine — thousands would be martyred in bloody persecutions aimed at either wiping out the church or making its members bow down to the Emperor.

Aside from ducking the Roman authorities, what was it like to be a Christian in the first century? Christian fellowship used family terminology. God is the father and the believers are brothers and sisters. The church is the household of God. The members call each other beloved (1 Thess 1:4, 6) and the senior members call the new converts "children" (Gal 4:19; Phlm 10).

All this familial language and sentiment indicate that the churches formed a cohesive and intimate group. This sense of belonging not only applied to members of the local Christian house-churches but to the universal brotherhood of believers. Thus hospitality was an important Christian virtue (Rom 12:13; Heb 13:2). Christians, though total strangers, would be accepted into a household and given shelter.

In addition to hospitality, care for one another in sickness or in prison characterized the Christian community. Jesus' admonition in his parable of the sheep and goats (Matt 25:31-46) made a profound impression on the believers. An account found in the second century A.D. writer, Lucian of Samosata, about a man named Peregrinus illustrates this fact well. Peregrinus (A.D. 100-165) traveled to Palestine and there became a Christian. For his activities as a Christian, he was imprisoned. There, wrote Lucian, he enjoyed the utmost attention and care from fellow members of the church.

Brotherly love also led believers to take up collections for the poor. The collection for the Jerusalem disciples often alluded to in Paul's letters (1 Cor 16:1-4; 2 Cor 8, 9; Rom 15:25-27) is a clear example. There were also earlier collections made (Acts 4:32-36; 11:29-30).

The early Christian communities were, then, islands of warmth and caring in a dark sea of instability and anxiety. Outside was violence, social class snobbery, and the "failure of nerve." Inside was an accepting, loving family. The family, the household of God, would feed you, visit you in prison, tend to you if you were sick, and give you shelter. And they would only ask you if you believed that Jesus was Lord. Small wonder then that in spite of the anti-Christian slander that came from pagans and in spite of the actual danger in professing to be Christian, more and more residents of these ancient cities were drawn to consider the truth claims of Christianity.

CHAPTER 8

PAUL OF TARSUS

Bibliography: F.C. Baur, *Paul*; E. Best, *Paul and His Converts*; H.D. Betz, *Galatians*; W. Boussett, *Kyrios Christos*; R. Bultmann, *Theology of the New Testament*; C. Beker, *Paul the Apostle*; F.F. Bruce, *Paul, Apostle of the Heart Set Free*; Idem, *The Acts of the Apostles*; W.J. Conybeare and J.S. Howson, *The Life and Epistles of St. Paul*; E.E. Ellis, *Paul and His Recent Interpreters*; D. Georgi, *The Opponents of Paul in 2 Corinthians*; T.R. Glover, *Paul of Tarsus*; E.J. Goodspeed, *Paul*; R.M. Grant, *Gnosticism and Early Christianity*; J.J. Gunther, *St. Paul's Opponents and Their Background*; A. Hengel, *Between Jesus and Paul*; Idem, *The Pre-Christian Paul*; R. Hock, *The Social Context of Paul's Ministry*; B. Holmberg, *Paul and Power*; F.J.A. Hort, *Judaistic Christianity*; R. Jewett, *A Chronology of Paul's Life*; S. Kim, *The Origin of Paul's Gospel*; J. Klausner, *From Jesus to Paul*; J. Knox, *Chapters in the Life of Paul*; G.E. Ladd, *A Theology of the New Testament*; G. Machen, *The Origin of Paul's Religion*; A. Malherbe, *Paul and the Popular Philosophers*; W. Meeks, *The First Urban Christians*; Idem, *The Writings of St. Paul*; J. Munck, *Paul and the Salvation of Mankind*; A.D. Nock, *Conversion*; W.M. Ramsay, *The Cities of St. Paul*; R.L. Rubenstein, *My Brother Paul*; S. Sandmel, *The Genius of Paul*; E.P. Sanders, *Paul and Palestinian Judaism*; W. Schmithals, *Paul and the Gnostics*; Idem, *Gnosticism at Corinth*; H.J. Schoeps, *Paul*; A. Schweitzer, *Paul and His Interpreters*; Idem, *The Mysticism of Paul the Apostle*; J. Stewart, *A Man in Christ*; G. Theissen, *The Social Setting of Pauline Christianity*; G. van Groningen, *First Century Gnosticism: Its Origin and Motifs*; W.C. van Unnik, *Tarsus or Jerusalem?*; S. Weserholm, *Israel's Law and the Church's Faith*; R. McL. Wilson, *Gnosis and the New Testament*; E. Yamauchi, *Pre-Christian Gnosticism*.

PAUL AND HIS INTERPRETERS

Like Jesus, Paul the missionary, the man, and the theologian has been variously interpreted. The following are the main views, both ancient and modern, of Paul's life and thought:

1. Paul was the messenger of Satan (Paul's Judaizing opponents in the ancient world).

2. Paul was the only true apostle (Marcion, second century A.D.)

3. Paul was the second founder of Christianity (Harnack).

4. Paul was anti-Semitic (Nietzsche).

5. Paul was a perverter of Jesus' teachings (George Bernard Shaw).

6. Paul was a perverter of Judaism (Schoeps, Buber).[1]

7. Paul did not exist. As with his analysis of Jesus' life (see Chapter 4), so B. Bauer doubted that Paul had ever lived (see a summary in Schweitzer).

8. Paul was the opponent of Peter and the Jerusalem apostles (F.C. Baur).

9. Paul was the apostle to the Gentiles but remained within the fellowship of the Jerusalem church (Munck).

10. Paul was the Christian apostle to the Gentiles but remained essentially Jewish/rabbinic (Davies).

11. Paul was a mystic (Schweitzer).

12. Paul was a Hellenist (Boussett, Bultmann).

13. Paul was an eschatological (or end-time) prophet (Beker).

Such extreme diversity in opinion indicates that Paul was both controversial and complex. To some — whom Paul called "Judaizers" — Paul's casting off the Law was a terrible offense. On the other hand, others more recently, who were inclined toward anti-Semitism anyway, have mistakenly seen in Paul a justification for their prejudice. Paul evokes strong emotions.

Yet he was much more complex than any one of the above mentioned descriptions. Indeed, some of them are so simplistic as to be caricatures. Who was this man then who planted Christianity in the eastern Roman empire, who roused the anger of Jews, and who was

---

[1]For a summary of interpretations 1 through 6 see Meeks, *Writings*.

sent to Rome in shackles? To a great extent that question can only be answered in the detailed analysis of his letters in Chapter 8. We can, however, begin our explanation with a biographical sketch.

PAUL'S PRECONVERSION LIFE

Paul said he was born in Tarsus and was a citizen of that city (Acts 22:3; cf. 9:11; 21:39). That means that Paul was a city boy from the start and thus it is not surprising that he later ministered primarily in urban areas. Tarsus was a large and prosperous city in Paul's day. It had probably a population of several hundred thousand and flourished from trade and from the fertile valley in which it was situated. A respected university was located in Tarsus and one of its leading scholars, Athenodorus the Stoic philosopher, had been the personal tutor of Emperor Augustus.

Although Paul gained at some point some acquaintance with Greek literature, it is unlikely that he ever studied at the university of Tarsus. He quotes Greek poets on occasion (Acts 17:28; 1 Cor 15:33; Titus 1:12) and writes fluent — occasionally eloquent — Greek. He also employs diatribe, that manner of teaching which the Stoic and Cynic philosophers employed.[2] He used terms peculiar to the Stoics such as συνείδησις (syneidēsis), "conscience."[3] As Malherbe has shown, Paul can use typically Cynic or Stoic metaphors such as calling himself "gentle as a nurse" (1 Thess 2:1-12), and can use athletic metaphors (1 Cor 9:24-27) or medical imagery (1 Tim 1:10). Clearly Paul was familiar with the world of Gentile popular philosophers, but unlike his contemporary Philo, he was not unduly influenced by them.

That Paul was a citizen of Tarsus (Acts 21:39) — not everyone in antiquity had citizen status in their city — indicates his family was

---

[2]For a good description of diatribe see S.K. Stowers, *The Diatribe and Paul's Letter to the Romans*; and M.S. Enslin, *The Ethics of Paul.* Enslin lists the characteristics of diatribe as: a series of short questions (Rom 3:1,3,9); direct address often with harsh tone (Gal 3:1; Rom 2:1); assuming the position of the opposition (Gal 3:19, 21).

[3]See W.D. Davies, "Conscience" in *IDB* and J.N. Sevenster, *Paul and Seneca.*

possessed of some financial means. To be enrolled as a citizen in that city one had to own at least 500 drachmas. Furthermore, Paul had been born a Roman citizen (Acts 16:37; 22:28). The city of Rome sometimes conferred citizenship on certain honored people even if they did not reside in Rome. Since he was born a Roman citizen, his father and perhaps grandfather had also had Roman citizenship before him. Only those who had done some special service to Rome — or had purchased it at great cost — were granted such citizenship. The dual citizenship that Paul's family possessed indicates that it was a family of social distinction and had at least a modest level, if not more, of economic comfort.

Though Paul's family was honored in pagan circles of Tarsus, it did not assimilate, or become like Gentiles. Paul wrote that he was an Israelite, of the tribe of Benjamin, a Pharisee and a son of a Pharisee, and a "Hebrew of Hebrews" (Phil 3:5; Acts 23:6; 26:5). His father had reared him to know and keep the Law according to the strict interpretation of that sect (see Chapter 2).

That Paul was a Hebrew of Hebrews meant evidently that his family was culturally and linguistically Palestinian or Aramaic (the word "Hebrew" often meant in the first century "Semitic" or "Aramaic," see *TDNT*). His family in immigrating from Palestine had maintained its culture and language. Thus Paul could speak Aramaic (Acts 21:40; 22:2).

A third evidence of the refusal of Paul's family to assimilate is his other name, Saul. He evidently had a Jewish name (after Saul, the first king of Israel) and a Gentile name. Ramsay speculated reasonably that Paul's complete Latin name was Gaius Julius Paulus. Acts 13:9 ("Saul who is also called Paul") indicates that Paul always possessed dual names. His associate, Silas, also had a Latin name, Silvanus (Acts 15:40; cf. 1 Thess 1:1) and another apostle, Thomas, had a Greek name, Didymus (John 11:16). Dual names for Jews, one in Aramaic and one in Greek or Latin, were quite common.

At some point in Paul's young life his family moved back to Jerusalem. Van Unnick has shown, largely from the Greek word ἀνατεθραμμένος, *anatethrammenos* ("brought up" in this city) in Acts 22:3, that Paul must have been rather young when this happened. He was perhaps no older than ten years. That the entire family moved back is seen in that Paul's sister and nephew also lived in Jerusalem (Acts 23:16).

In Jerusalem Paul received his formative education studying finally under the great sage, Rabban Gamaliel I (Acts 22:3). Gamaliel was truly one of the luminaries of his day. His title "Rabban," which appears in the Mishnah, means "our Master" and was considered more honorific than "Rabbi" ("my Master"). He lived and taught from the last part of the first century B.C. to the first half of the first century A.D. His opinions and teachings are widely scattered throughout the Mishnah (and Tosephta) indicating his authority and prestige. Of Gamaliel was said, "When Rabban Gamaliel the Elder died the glory of the Law ceased and purity and abstinence died" (m. Sotah 9:15; trans. in Danby, *The Mishnah*).

Under Gamaliel Paul would have learned Torah, that is both the written Old Testament and the *halacah* or traditional, oral Law. Much of this oral law is now found in the Mishnah. Paul would have learned rabbinic hermeneutics and midrash and would have been skilled in debate and argumentation. Paul clearly excelled in his studies. He wrote, "I advanced in Judaism beyond many of my contemporaries since I was so very zealous for the traditions of my fathers" (Gal 1:14).

Though Paul excelled as a student of Torah, by all accounts he was not physically impressive nor particularly talented as an orator. His critics at Corinth said of him, "The presence of his body is weak and his speaking ability is worthless" (2 Cor 10:10). Paul admitted that he was "unskilled" (ἰδιώτης, *idiōtēs*) at speaking (2 Cor 11:6) and that he had been present at Corinth "in weakness" (1 Cor 2:3).

In addition to the above, there is a remarkable description of Paul's physical appearance which has the ring of accuracy. It is found in the apocryphal Acts of Paul and reads as follows: "Paul . . . small of stature, with a bald head and crooked legs, in a good state of body, with eyebrows meeting and nose somewhat hooked, full of friendliness . . . ."[4]

Though the above quote comes from a text written around 100 years after Paul's death, the description seems to have been based

---

[4]Translation in *NTA*.

on an actual remembrance of Paul's appearance. The main reason for this conclusion is that the description is not very flattering. If one were to invent a description of Paul, who became a hero in most Christian circles of the second century, one would probably make him more Apollo-like.

Thus Paul, though possessed of superior intellectual faculties, was not a commanding presence and this "weakness" was seized upon by his opponents after his conversion. Further, he was untrained in classical rhetoric and so unable to impress people by his public speaking.

PAUL'S CONVERSION

In spite of Gamaliel's caution that moderation and tolerance should be exercised in dealing with the new Christian faith (Acts 5:34-39), Paul found himself at some point actively persecuting it. Luke notes that Paul or Saul was present at Stephen's stoning (Acts 7:58; 8:1). He could hardly have been merely a bystander, but rather must have been in league with those who stoned Stephen. Three other references to Paul as persecutor are found in Acts (9:1-2; 22:4; 26:9-11). These references, two of which are on the lips of Paul himself, indicate a zealous rage against the Christians which led him to imprison some, coerce some into blasphemy, and sentence others to death. (See also Gal 1:13; 1 Cor 15:9; Phil 3:6.)

It was Stephen's preaching that so alarmed Paul. Stephen did not just preach a messianized Judaism but that the temple and the Law were now abrogated (Acts 6:13). Paul now saw the clear implications of Christianity and determined it must be stopped. As Bruce wrote, "If Stephen saw the logic of the situation more clearly than the apostles, Paul saw it more clearly than Gamaliel" (p. 70).

How long this persecution lasted we do not know. Paul was not content merely to gather up all those in Jerusalem; he would carry his pogrom also to the Diaspora, beginning in Damascus. It was on his way to Damascus that Paul's life-changing experience happened.

Luke writes that Paul saw a bright light and heard a voice that said "Saul, Saul, why do you persecute me?" (Acts 9:4; 22:6-7; 26:13-14). When Paul asked whose the voice was, the response was, "I am

Jesus whom you are persecuting" (Acts 9:5; 22:8; 26:15). In Paul's letters he writes, "But when the one who had set me apart from my mother's womb and called me through his grace was pleased to reveal to me his Son so that I might preach his gospel to the Gentiles . . ." (Gal 1:15-16). Thus Paul describes his experience in terms reminiscent of Jeremiah's call to be a prophet (Jer 1:5). In 1 Cor 15:8 Paul writes, "Last of all as to one untimely born, (Christ) appeared to me also." Paul here presents his experience on the road to Damascus as identical to that of the other apostles who saw Jesus after his resurrection. Thus in 1 Cor 9:1 he can write, "Am I not an apostle? Have I not seen Jesus our Lord?"

The picture we get from the Scripture texts is quite different from the psychoanalyzing efforts of many commentators. Paul maintained that this was an objective appearance of the risen Christ — the same as the appearances to the other apostles — and that Christ called him in this appearance into service as a prophet to the Gentiles. Further, the commonly accepted scenarios of this experience — Paul the broken and anguished man is converted and becomes strong and psychologically integrated — is the opposite of that presented in the text. Paul left for Damascus a proud Pharisee, blameless in the Law (Phil 3:6), burning with angry zeal, and arrived there a broken and humiliated man. He was blinded, unable to eat, and in shock (Acts 9:9). The last thing he ever expected to see was what he saw. He was called to give up everything to follow Christ (Phil 3:7).

Thus Paul's experience was hardly a mere "flash of insight," personality integration, or resolution of inner conflict. His experience was unexpected and life-changing. Naturalistic explanations will hardly suffice. His experience is a powerful testimony of the resurrection of Jesus. One simply does not hallucinate or imagine such a totally unexpected experience. Paul began his journey to Damascus fully confident that he was correct to persecute followers of Jesus. He completed his journey having become a follower — no, even more than that — an apostle, of Jesus. As George Lyttleton wrote in his *Observations on the Conversion of St. Paul*: "The conversion and apostleship of St. Paul alone, duly considered, was of itself a demonstration to prove Christianity to be a divine revelation."[5]

---

[5]Quoted in Bruce, *Acts*.

PAUL'S OPPONENTS WITHIN THE CHURCH

Great men, men who move their world into change, seldom go unopposed. Paul certainly knew the sting of sharp criticism, the danger of enemies who plotted to harm him, and the stress of looking over his shoulder to protect the churches he had founded from those who would "slip in secretly." This much is clear from his letters and from Acts.

Paul was opposed in almost every city in which he preached. Often the opposition was from unbelievers (e.g., Acts 13:45; 16:19-20) both Jewish and pagan. But Paul's letters indicate he also faced opposition from within the church and this source of opposition was far more potentially damaging.

Who were these opponents? Were they the same people or representatives of the same beliefs in every case? F.C. Baur said the opponents in every case were Jerusalem emissaries, Judaizing Christians, who followed Paul from city to city trying to undo his work of grace. W. Schmithals on the other hand has maintained that the opponents in every case were Gnostics. Many scholars would be inclined to see a different set of opponents in just about every one of Paul's letters. Actually, though, many of these suggestions are quite similar and one can group most of the suggested opponents into three groups: Judaizing Christians, Gnostic Christians, and Propagandistic Christians.

Judaizing Christians

Both Acts and Paul's letters make it clear that some element within the early church wanted Gentile converts to Christianity to keep the Old Testament Torah or, in short, become a Jew as well as a Christian. Some people said, according to Acts, "Unless you are circumcised by the custom of Moses you cannot be saved" (Acts 15:1). And also certain of the Pharisaic sect who had become Christians maintained, "It is necessary to circumcise (the Gentiles) and to admonish them to keep the Law of Moses" (Acts 15:5). Clearly, such a claim was being made among the Galatian churches (Gal 2:21;

3:10; 5:2) by a group similar to those referred to in Acts. Likewise, in Philippi they tried to press the Gentile Christians to be circumcised (Phil 3:2-3) and boasted of their Jewish heritage (Phil 3:4).

These Judaizing Christians were almost certainly Jews and not (as Munck maintained) Gentile Judaizers. References in Acts 15 indicate a Palestinian origin for this group. Further, Philippians indicates that these people were proud of their Hebrew (or Aramaic language) origins.

The second century successors to Paul's Judaistic opponents seem also to have been Christians of Hebrew origin (see Hort). Justin Martyr, who came originally from Samaria, wrote that in his era (A.D. 140) there were two kinds of Jewish Christians. One group kept the Mosaic law but did not demand that Gentiles do so. With them Justin and other Gentiles could have fellowship. The other group of Jewish Christians did demand that Gentiles keep the Law in order to be saved. These Justin did not accept as brothers (*Dialogue with Trypho* 47.1-4).

The Judaizing Christians believed Paul was apostate from the Law and therefore would not be saved. That such a group dogged his ministry to some extent seems clear from the letters of Paul and Acts. To them it was necessary to correct Paul's apostate theology. Paul's response was: "You who are justified by the Law have been cut off from Christ, you have fallen from grace" (Gal 5:4).

Proto-Gnostics

As we saw above in Chapter 7, defining Gnosticism is difficult since there were so many sects sharing certain Gnostic traits but quite different in other respects. Thus the task of identifying Gnostic opponents in Paul's churches is much more difficult than in identifying Judaizing opponents. Nevertheless, since the late nineteenth century, a large group of scholars has favored the view that some form of Gnosticism influenced the opponents of Paul in some churches.[6] Most would accept that proto-Gnosticism or incipient

---

[6]For a survey of the studies on Gnosticism and the New Testament, see Yamauchi and Georgi.

Gnosticism existed before the New Testament. Thus, some form of what became classical Gnosticism in the second century A.D. could well stand behind some of the problems alluded to in Paul's letters.

W. Schmithals has written most extensively on the Gnostic background of Paul's opponents. He has suggested that every group of Paul's critics was in some way influenced by Gnosticism. His works have met with stiff criticism, however. Most scholars would agree that the Colossian heresy was Gnostic in some way and nearly all would find such a background to the problem in the Pastoral Epistles.[7] Perhaps the opponents — or some of the problems at least — in 1 Corinthians were akin to what later became Gnosticism. But beyond these conclusions, the debate rages.

The Propagandists

We will examine this group more completely when we discuss 2 Corinthians. For now we will offer only a very brief sketch. D. Georgi, led by the earlier works of K. Lake and H. Windisch,[8] determined that the opponents in 2 Corinthians were different from those in 1 Corinthians. The opponents in 2 Corinthians were Christian missionaries who had modeled themselves on Hellenistic-Jewish wandering prophets, magicians, saviors, and philosophers. They believed that they were God's special envoys and sought to exalt themselves by revelations and miracles. They were very competitive with others of their kind. They thought it necessary to compete with Paul and to make comparisons with him. They thus called his qualifications into question and alleged that he was not a true "pneumatic" or wonder worker. They thrived on putting on regal airs and doing signs to legitimate themselves and thus Paul, who wanted nothing of such boasting, was judged by them inadequate.

Georgi's historical construction may undergo some revision in

---

[7]Even Yamauchi, who argues strongly against pre-Christian Gnosticism, thinks the problem reflected in the Pastorals springs from incipient Gnosticism.

[8]Lake, *The Earlier Epistles of St Paul*; Windisch, *2 Korintherbrief.*

the future, but he has certainly convinced many scholars to look beyond Gnosticism at least to understand the opponents of 2 Corinthians.

Paul then was opposed at every turn by some group or other who found his gospel either a stumbling block, folly, or weakness. The difficulty of dealing with groups as different as Judaizers and Gnostics must have been enormous. Small wonder Paul wrote that the worry over the churches weighed heavily on him each day (2 Cor 11:28). The difference in opponents helps to account for the difference in content and vocabulary in his letters. None of these letters are the reflective products of a man at leisure; none are "ivory tower" theology. Rather they always address burning issues and dangerous opponents, opponents that threatened to undermine the very essence of the gospel.

PAUL'S MARTYRDOM

Three different dates are usually suggested for Paul's death: 62, 64/65, or 68. The first date (Jewett) would mean that Paul's court case before Nero had gone against him and that Paul was executed at the end of his two year waiting period in Rome (Acts 28:30). This date would also make it difficult to fit the Pastoral Epistles into Paul's life but numerous scholars do not accept that Paul wrote the Pastoral Epistles (see Pastoral Epistles in Chapter 9, The Epistles of Paul).

The third date (Conybeare and Howson) pushes Paul's death back to allow time for him to have written the Pastoral Epistles and to have traveled to the places indicated in them. But one wonders what prompted Nero to arrest Paul in A.D. 68 and have him executed.

The second date (Bruce) seems best. It is still late enough for Paul to have been released from prison in A.D. 62, to have traveled to Crete and Ephesus as the Pastorals allude, and even possibly to have traveled to Spain as Paul wrote that he hoped to do (Rom 15:24). Also this date explains why Paul was executed: as a result of the fire in Rome and subsequent persecution of Christians. Third, this date accords well with later testimony and tradition.

In A.D. 64 a great fire erupted in Rome between the Palatine and Caelian hills, in the poorer section of the city. Winds and the very flammable buildings spread the fire far and quickly, resulting in great loss of life. Nero, whether rightly or wrongly, was blamed by the populace for the fire. To escape criticism, he tried to implicate Christians for starting the fire and therefore a great persecution resulted. Tacitus, the Roman historian, described the events which followed (*Annals* 15.44):

> Those who confessed to being Christians were at once arrested, but on their testimony a great crowd of people were convicted, not so much on the charge of arson, but of hatred of the entire human race. They were put to death amid every kind of mockery. Dressed in the skins of wild beasts, they were torn to pieces by dogs, or were crucified, or burned to death: when night came, they served as human torches to provide lights. Nero threw open his gardens for this entertainment, and provided games in the Circus, mingling with the crowd in a charioteer's dress, or else standing in the car. These Christians were guilty, and well deserved their fate, but a sort of compassion for them arose, because they were being destroyed to glut the cruelty of a single man and for no public end.[9]

It seems the best choice to conclude that Paul (and Peter) died in this persecution. Clement, one of the bishops of Rome, who wrote about thirty years after the persecution, indicated that Paul and Peter had died in Rome, evidently due to a persecution (1 Clement 5:1-7), though he does not say specifically when they died. Dionysius, a bishop in Corinth (A.D. 180), attested that both were martyred at the same time in Rome (quoted in Eusebius *H.E.* 11.25). Tertullian (A.D. 200), the Christian writer of Carthage, indicated that Paul was martyred by a death "like John's" (i.e., John the Baptist) and Peter was crucified in Italy (*de Praescriptione Haereticorum* 36).

Eusebius of Caesarea, the eminent church historian (A.D. 325),

---

[9]Translation in D.R. Dudley, *The Annals of Tacitus.*

stated explicitly that Paul and Peter had been martyred in the Neronian persecution (*H.E.* 2.25) and that Peter had been crucified but Paul was beheaded. Finally, Sulpicius Severus (A.D. 400), the church historian of Gaul, wrote that Paul and Peter were martyred, by beheading and crucifixion respectively, during the Neronian persecution (*Chronicle* 2.29). The testimony, therefore, seems strong, though late, that Paul died in Rome during the Neronian persecution that began in A.D. 64 and lasted perhaps a year or even longer.

Paul's life those final weeks must have been pretty horrible. According to tradition, he was held in the public prison — now called Mamartine Prison — until his execution (see *WHG*). This place was a chamber of horrors. The Roman historian, Sallust, described it as follows: "Its filthy condition, darkness, and foul smell gave it a loathsome and terrifying air" (*Conspiracy of Catiline* 55; trans. by S.A. Handford). Yet in spite of his unpleasant circumstances, he felt joy in thinking of his future heavenly abode, as he testified in 2 Timothy 4:6-8.

Paul was led out along the Ostian Way (also called Via Triumphalis) and there beheaded. The present basilica, which is built over one erected by Constantine, may well be where Paul was buried. A Christian presbyter from Rome, Gaius, testified in A.D. 200 that there was a grave marker for Peter's grave in the Vatican and to Paul's grave on the Ostian Way. Gaius wrote: "But I can show the trophies (i.e., grave markers) of the apostles. For if you will go to the Vatican or to the Ostian road, you will find the trophies of those who have laid the foundation of this church."[10] Eusebius, who quotes this testimony from Gaius, indicates that the grave stones with the names of Peter and Paul on them were still standing in his day (early fourth century). That Paul would have been buried beside the road and close to his place of execution is not unusual. Many people were buried by the roadside in antiquity.

The present Church of St. Paul's Outside the Walls, located a little over a mile from the ancient walls, stands over the ancient church built by Constantine. In doing remodeling work around the altar of the modern church, workmen found a Latin inscription

---

[10]Translation in C.F. Cruse, *Eusebius' Ecclesiastical History.*

from Constantine's church which read: "To Paul, Apostle and Martyr" (see Finegan). The type of lettering was that used in the age of Constantine. Surely, then, argues Finegan, the old Constantinian church, erected in the fourth century A.D., was built over the "trophy" grave marker of Paul.

About a mile farther down the old Ostian Way stands the fifth century Church of St. Paul of the Three Fountains where, according to tradition, the actual beheading took place.

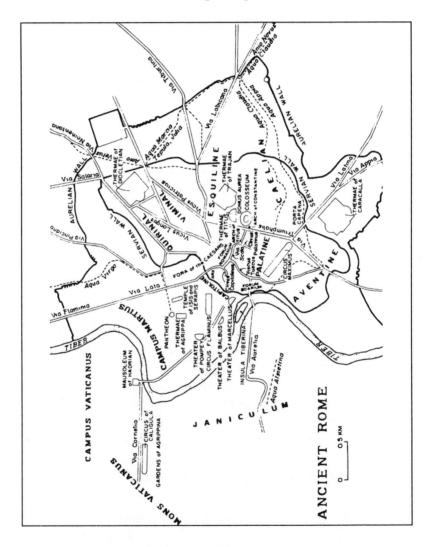

CHAPTER 9

THE PAULINE EPISTLES

THE EPISTLE TO THE ROMANS

Bibliography: C.K. Barrett, *The Letter to the Romans*; K. Barth, *The Epistle to the Romans*; C. Beker, *Paul the Apostle*; M. Black, *Romans*; R. Bultmann, *Theology of the New Testament*; C.E.B. Cranfield, *Romans*; W.D. Davies, *Paul and Rabbinic Judaism*; C.H. Dodd, *The Epistle to the Romans*; K.P. Donfried, editor, *The Romans Debate*; J.D.G. Dunn, *Romans*; J. Fitzmyer, "Romans" in *Jerome Biblical Commentary*; V.P. Furnish, *Theology and Ethics of Paul*; E.F. Harrison, "Romans" *The Expositor's Bible Commentary*; D. Hill, *Greek Words with Hebrew Meanings*; E. Käsemann, *Romans*; J. Knox, "Romans" in *Interpreter's Bible*; M.E. Lard, *Romans*, J.W. McGarvey, *Romans*; J. Munck, *Paul and the Salvation of Mankind*; A. Nygren, *Romans*; J. Piper, *The Justification of God*; W. Sanday and A.C. Headlam, *The Epistle of Paul to the Romans*; E.P. Sanders, *Paul and Palestinian Judaism*; H.J. Schoeps, *Paul*; A. Schweitzer, *The Mysticism of Paul the Apostle*; R. Scroggs, *The Last Adam*; H.J. Shires, *The Eschatology of Paul*; P. Stuhlmacher, *Der Brief an die Römer*.

The City of Rome

Rome was the largest and most powerful city in all the Mediterranean world in the era of the New Testament. With a population of about 500,000 and the palaces of the emperors located there, it was clearly the political hub. According to tradition it was founded in 753 B.C. but archaeologists have found evidence of settlements at least 100 years earlier. By Paul's day the city was full of marble temples and giant basilicas (shopping and business malls).

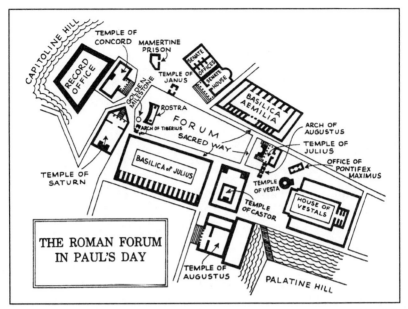

THE ROMAN FORUM
IN PAUL'S DAY

Emperor Augustus boasted that he had found Rome a city of brick
and had left it a city of marble. The forum alone was an impressive
display of architecture but added to that were the circuses (for
chariot races), the baths, and the temples.

Jews were present in Rome well before 139 B.C., when they were
expelled for the first time. But less than a century later they had
returned and made up a sizeable portion of the population of the
city. Again in A.D. 19 Jews were expelled from Rome (along with
members of the cult of Isis) and yet again in A.D. 49. These expul-
sions were probably for several reasons but one of these, as Wiefel
(in Donfried) argues, was surely anti-Semitism.

Several synagogues existed during the New Testament era. One
was founded by former slaves of Augustus; one was named in honor
of the Herods; some were named after the districts or cities from
which the members had immigrated; still others were named "synagogue of the Hebrews" or "synagogue of the Vernaculi" indicating
that in the former Aramaic was spoken but in the latter Greek was
used (see Wiefel in Donfried).[1]

---

[1]Even in Rome, the capital of the Latin language, many people spoke
Greek, especially immigrants.

Thus the reader should be aware that the Jewish community in Rome was pluralistic. Jews emphasized different languages and banded together according to their place of birth or social standing (e.g., slaves or former slaves). We should expect then that Jews accepting Jesus as the Messiah would be of varied backgrounds and biases.

Second, the reader should remember the rather strong anti-Semitism prevalent in ancient Rome. This prejudice inevitably was felt to some extent in the early church as the letter to Romans attests (see below).

Christianity in Rome

How Christianity began in Rome is unclear. There were Jews from Rome present when the church began on the day of Pentecost (Acts 2:10). But surely — in light of the way people tended to immigrate to Rome — we should conclude that some Christians came from parts of the east. At any rate neither Paul nor Peter founded the church in Rome, though both of them labored there later.

Regardless of the origin of Christianity in Rome, by the time Paul wrote his letter (A.D. 57) to Rome the membership had changed dramatically. Only eight years before in A.D. 49 all or most

The Christians of Romans 16

Non-Oriental				Oriental Origins			
Julia	S	W		Junia	S	J	W
Hermes				Aquila	H	J	
Rufus				Andronicus		J	
Prisca		W		Philologus	H		
Maria	S	W		Appeles			
Urbanus				Stachys			
Ampliatus	S			Phlegon			
Tryphaena	S	W		Persis	S		W
Tryphosa	S	W		Hermas	S		
Nereus	S			Epaenetus			
				Asynkritos	H		
				Olympas			
				Patrobus			
				Herodion	S	J	

Key
S   Slaves or former slaves
H   House churches
J   Jews
W   Women

Jews were expelled from Rome. Suetonius the historian wrote: "Because the Jews at Rome caused continuous disturbances at the instigation of Chrestus, (Emperor Claudius) expelled them from the city" (Suetonius, *Claudius* 25, translated by R. Graves). The "Chrestus" he refers to is undoubtedly Christ. Suetonius mistakenly believed that Christ himself was stirring up Jews in Rome. What was actually happening was that Jewish Christians were preaching about Christ in the synagogues and this activity caused riots. Such response in synagogues is also well known from the accounts given in the book of Acts (Acts 13:45; 15:19-20; 17:5, 13; 18:12-13). Thus the Jews and Jewish Christians were expelled from Rome — and therefore from the Roman church — several years before Paul wrote the letter to the Romans. By A.D. 57 a few Jews had begun to trickle back into the city — for example Aquila and Prisca — but the percentage of Jews in the church was still rather low.

P. Lampe (in Donfried) has given us a composite of the Christian community in Rome based on a comparison of the 26 names of Romans 16 and numerous inscriptions (see Table, p. 229). If his results are accurate[2] then there were at the time of Paul about seven house churches with 15% of the members being Jews and over half being immigrants. Lampe can identify fairly positively ten slaves or former slaves but speculates that several others were as well. Thus he maintains that roughly two-thirds of the Christians in Rome were of servile origin. This figure may be a bit high but surely there were many Christians of the servile ranks, just as probably one-half the population of the city of Rome was servile.

---

[2]Some scholars (e.g., T.W. Manson) maintain that Romans 15 and 16 were not originally a part of the Roman letter but part of a letter sent to Ephesus. The reason is that Marcion, the Gnostic, had only 14 chapters in his version of Romans, as did the oldest copies of the Vulgate, a fourth century Latin translation of the Bible. In addition some Greek manuscripts place the doxology (Rom 16:25-27) after chapter 14 (a few others place it after chapter 15), perhaps indicating, according to these scholars, that the letter originally ended there.

But we must point out that no extant Greek manuscript omits chapters 15 and 16 from Romans, though a few do put the doxology in a different place. Therefore, assertions that chapters 15 and 16 were not originally part of Romans are only speculation. Donfried indicates that most scholars now accept the authenticity of Romans 15 and 16.

The Purpose of Romans

Even the casual reader notices a difference in the tone and structure of Romans from that of, for example, 1 Corinthians. Romans is both loftier in tone and much more complex in argument. Is Romans then really a letter sent to a specific group of Christians in order to address real problems? In the main, three different answers are given to this question today:

1. Some maintain that Romans is not really a letter for the Roman believers but a "Last Will and Testament" (see G. Bornkamm in Donfried). Paul wrote this document toward the end of his life to summarize his theology and to defend his life's work.

2. Others have alleged that the epistle to the Romans was really written with Jerusalem in mind (Jervel in Donfried). Even as Paul wrote the letter, he was preparing to travel to Jerusalem (Rom 15:25-27) bearing the monetary contribution for the poor which the churches in Macedonia and Achaia had given. That he was worried about Jewish opponents in Jerusalem is clear (Rom 15:30-32) because he asks the Romans to pray for him. Thus while the letter was also sent to Rome, its contents are really for Jerusalem. He wants the letter to be a defense of his gospel.

The above conclusion is supported somewhat by the evidence we have that some copies of Romans may not have had the sixteenth chapter (see footnote 2). Some manuscripts have the closing benediction or doxology (Rom 16:25-27) after chapter 14 or 15 as if the letter originally ended there. Yet we must consider that virtually every manuscript contains chapter 16 in spite of where the benediction is placed.

3. Still others maintain that the epistle was written specifically to the Romans to address real problems within the Roman church (Stuhlmacher). By the time the letter was written, some Jews had returned to Rome. Many of these — both Jews and Jewish Christians — were opponents of Paul's preaching just as they similarly opposed him in Galatia and Philippi. They taught that Paul was preaching "cheap grace," that he allowed Christian Gentiles to live lawless and immoral lives. Paul answered this charge in his letter and referred to these attacks on his gospel (see Rom 3:8, 31; 6:7; 7:7, 12, 14).

Paul wants to defend his gospel to as many Roman Christians as possible because he hopes to bear some fruit in Rome as an apostle (Rom 1:11-15) and then to be sent on by them to do mission work in Spain (Rom 15:15-24).

The third view is less speculative than the others and seeks to understand Romans for what it claims to be, namely a letter sent to a specific community. Therefore, it is to be preferred. Nevertheless, there is probably some truth in all of these views. Paul may well have viewed the epistle as a summation of his theology and may have carried a copy of it with him to Jerusalem.

The Content of Romans

Most of Romans is a carefully argued document. One is often hard pressed to understand a passage in the epistle without delving profoundly into the context of that passage. It thus resists a summary treatment in which one only hits the highlights.

Romans may be divided into three parts: Chapters 1-8 contain the exposition of Paul's gospel; 9-11 explain Israel's role in salvation history; 12-15 are ethical exhortations based on the truths of the gospel.

A. The thesis of chapters 1-8 — indeed of the entire epistle — is stated in 1:17 and repeated in expanded form in 3:21-26: "For in [the gospel] a righteousness of God is being revealed, from faith unto faith . . ." (1:17).

The key to this verse and to understanding Romans is the meaning of the phrase "righteousness of God" (rendered "from God" in the NIV). Theologians have labored with this concept for centuries. Three views about its meaning predominate:

1. The righteousness is that human righteousness which counts in God's eyes.

2. The righteousness is a gift from God to mankind.

3. The righteousness is God's own activity in saving humanity.

These are three seemingly very different conceptions. Which one is correct? Based on the Old Testament usage one would have

to say the third one is correct. As D. Hill has shown, the righteousness of God in the Old Testament is subjective. In other words it
describes what God does. Thus, for example, in Judges 5:11; 1
Samuel 12:7 and Micah 6:5 the righteousness of God — translated
"righteous acts of God" in the NIV — refers to God's saving activity.
God's righteousness is his self-consistency, his acting in conformity
with his nature and his word. His nature and word involve judgment and salvation. But in the cross both were satisfied. The righteousness of God includes his holy demand that sin be punished; the
cross fulfills this demand and at the same time allows God to save
his people (see J. Cottrell, *God the Redeemer*).

Therefore, Romans 1:17 should be understood as an explanation of verse 16. Paul is not ashamed of the gospel — that is he confesses the truth of the gospel — because in the gospel he can see
God's saving action for humanity. Since God has acted to save
humanity, God is clearly faithful to his promises made in the Old
Testament. God has not lied but he has kept his word (3:4).

Romans is then a theodicy or defense of God in light of the
Jewish-Gentile problem in the church. If God has cast off the Jews,
whom he promised always to love, maybe God is not righteous (i.e.,
faithful in saving). Paul's answer is first to show that God's righteousness is manifested in the gospel. It was always God's intention
to do so.

God always intended that people would be justified — or
declared righteous by him — by faith apart from the law (3:21, 28).
Having such faith means believing that the power of God was at
work in Jesus Christ and submitting to it. Abraham, the forefather
of the Jews, was justified also by faith (Rom 4:1-3) and this happened before he had been circumcised (4:10). Thus he is the spiritual forefather of Gentiles who have faith in Christ even as he is the
physical forefather of Jews (4:16). God therefore has not changed
his plans toward Israel but is carrying out his plans for all humanity.

B. Romans 9-11 is for some scholars only an afterthought, tacked on
to the main part of the letter, chapters 1-8. For others it is the
center and heart of the letter and chapters 1-8 are only preparatory.
Perhaps the best conclusion is that chapters 9-11 are a necessary

continuation and development of chapters 1-8.

The main problem with these chapters is the apparent contradiction between 9:6-13 and 11:25-29. In the former Paul says that the promise of salvation was not made to all Israel according to the flesh but to the remnant of believers. Thus God is not unfair or unrighteous for casting off Israel. But in the latter Paul seems to say that all of historical, physical Israel will be saved *because* it is Israel according to the flesh.

We do not have the space here to survey all the thinking on these important texts[3] but we can indicate the conclusions we have reached. The text in Romans 9 is speaking mainly to Jews. A Gentile might have wondered about the Jewish question (Why are the Jews now cast off?) but to a Jewish Christian it was a tragic, heartbreaking situation. Paul's line of argument seems calculated to refute the current Jewish notions of Israel's eternal relationship to God providing individual salvation. God has not forgotten his promises to Israel but Jews must realize that election was always unmerited, based on God's love and responded to by faith.

When we get to Romans 11, we have a different problem. There is the danger of the Gentile Christians' feeling superior to the Jews. The Gentiles seem to be in danger of the same chauvinism that the Jews were often guilty of. As we noted above, there were strong anti-Jewish feelings in Rome especially after the expulsion of the Jews in A.D. 49. Therefore Paul indicates that Gentiles as branches of the tree (11:17-24) can be broken off just as Jews have been. Also, Jews can be once more ingrafted if they believe. But the main point is that Israel is the root of the tree from which Gentiles receive their strength.

The Jews had to bear in mind that they were not saved by ethnic origin; the Gentiles had to keep in mind that Israel was still God's precious elect.

C. Paul at last comes in Romans 12-15 to the parenetic section of the letter, the section dealing with ethical exhortation and practical application. After general admonitions to change or transform

---

[3]See the excellent works of Munck and Piper on Romans 9-11.

one's character because of the grace of God (12:1-2), Paul reiterates themes reminiscent of his first letter to Corinth. He teaches about the necessity of solidarity for the body of Christ (12:3-8; cf. 1 Cor 12:4-26) and of love (12:9-21; 13:8-16; cf. 1 Cor 13). After other considerations such as obedience to governmental authorities, Paul takes up what must have been the major issue in the Roman church.

In 14:1-15:13 Paul discusses the disagreement between the "strong" and the "weak" (again reminiscent of the language of 1 Corinthians but not with exactly the same meaning). The weak did not believe that Christians should eat meat at all (14:2), taught that Christians should observe certain special holy days (14:5) and perhaps required Christians to abstain from wine (14:17,21). The strong believed one could eat anything and that no one had to observe any special days.

What was the origin of this disagreement? The weak were obviously acting out of their cultural or private convictions. But what sort of convictions? This problem seems not to have had anything to do with meat offered to idols — which was the problem at Corinth — because the word "idol-meat" is never used. Most scholars would find the background of this dispute in one of the following:

1. The influence of pagan ascetic philosophy which sometimes taught against eating any kind of animal flesh.

2. A Gnostic ascetic group like that alluded to in 1 Timothy 4:3 and 5:23. These two passages of Scripture seem to allude to a group that forbade eating meat — at least some kinds of meat — and drinking wine.

3. A Jewish group which abstained from meat altogether since there were no kosher butchers. Romans was probably written shortly after Jews began returning to Rome after the expulsion of A.D. 49. The Jewish population would still be small and it could very well have been the case that a lack of kosher meat caused some Jewish Christians to forego meat entirely and judge the Gentile Christians who ate it.

We would incline toward the last suggestion because the known historical background furnishes a very plausible explanation. On the other hand, we have no other indications in the letter to the Romans that there was a Gnostic problem or a sect influenced by pagan philosophical asceticism in the Roman church.

Paul's admonition to the weak is to stop judging the strong (14:3). They have no right to pass judgment on someone else's servant. The master (= God) of the servant alone has that right (14:4). To the strong Paul commands not to despise the weak (14:3) and not to cause him to stumble (14:13-15). The strong are correct; every food is clean (14:20). But they must be careful of the conscience of the weak (14:20-21). Paul's admonition is similar to that in 1 Cor 10:23-30 except here in Romans he also admonishes the weak, an element lacking in 1 Corinthians.

The entire letter to the Romans is thus permeated with Jew-Gentile issues, from the means of salvation, the defense of God's righteousness, the ultimate destiny of God's people the Jews, and the eating of unkosher food. The letter was written at a time when Jews were only recently returning to Rome and anti-Jewish feelings among Gentiles were high. These feelings also were somewhat prevalent in the church.

Paul's letter masterfully addressed these local issues while also offering his defense of his ministry. Romans is then partly a theological compendium and partly Paul's last will and testament. But he presents these ideas in the context of the historical situation in Rome.

1 CORINTHIANS

Bibliography: C.K. Barrett, *I Corinthians*; Idem, "Things Sacrificed to Idols" *NTS* 11 (1964) 138-153; S. Bartchy, *Mallon Chresai: First Century Slavery and the Interpretation of 1 Corinthians*; G. Bornkamm, *Paul*; O. Broneer, "The Apostle Paul and the Isthmian Games" *BA* 25 (1962) 1-31; F.F. Bruce, *1 and 2 Corinthians*; R. Bultmann, *Theology of the New Testament*; T. Callan, "Prophecy and Ecstasy in Greco-Roman Religion" *Novum Testamentum* 27 (1985) 125-140; H. Conzelmann, *I Corinthians*; W.D. Davies, *Paul and Rabbinic Judaism*; E.R. Dodds, *The Greeks and the Irrational*; G. Fee, *1 Corinthians*; J. Fitzmyer, "A Feature of Qumran Angelology and the Angels of 1 Cor 11:10" in J. Murphy-O'Connor, ed. *Paul and Qumran*; J. Hering, *First Epistle of Paul to the Corinthians*; R. Hock, *The Social Context of Paul's Ministry*; G. Hodge, *First Corinthians*; B. Leyton, *The Gnostic Scriptures*; W.H. Mare, "1 Corinthians" *The Expositor's Bible Commentary*; J. Munck, *Paul and the Salvation of Mankind*; J. Murphy-O'Connor, *St. Paul's Corinth*; Idem, "The Corinth that Saint Paul Saw" *BA* 47 (1984) 147-159; Idem, "Sex and Logic in 1 Corinthians 11:2-16" *Catholic Biblical Quarterly* 42 (1980) 482-499; N. Papahatzis, *Ancient Corinth*; A. Robertson and A. Plummer, *First Epistle of St. Paul to the Corinthians*; W. Schmithals, *Gnosticism in Corinth*; R. Scroggs, *The Last Adam*; G. Theissen, *The Social Setting of Pauline Christianity*; W.L. Willis, *Idol Meat in Corinth*.

History and Archaeology of Corinth

The ancient city of Corinth, which flourished from the sixth century B.C. on, was destroyed in 145 B.C. by the Roman general Mummius and its inhabitants were either killed or sold into slavery. The harsh treatment was Corinth's punishment for heading the Achaean League which opposed Rome.

In 44 B.C. Julius Caesar refounded the city on the same spot and made it the capital of the province of Achaia. The new city as a Roman colony assumed more Roman characteristics. Thus to the architecture of the city, in addition to the old Greek stoas and the

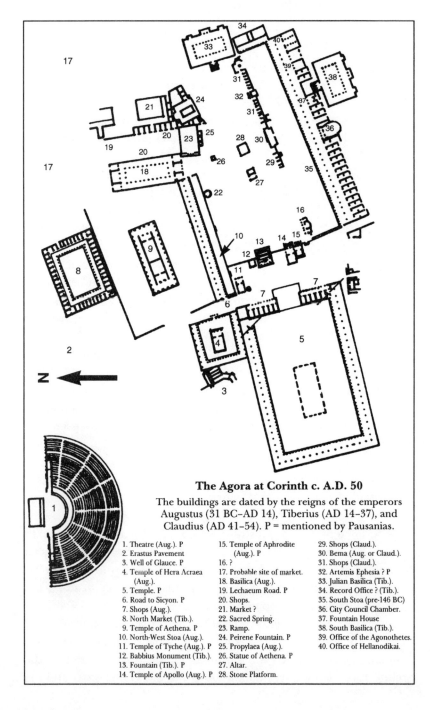

The Agora at Corinth c. A.D. 50

The buildings are dated by the reigns of the emperors
Augustus (31 BC–AD 14), Tiberius (AD 14–37), and
Claudius (AD 41–54). P = mentioned by Pausanias.

1. Theatre (Aug.). P
2. Erastus Pavement
3. Well of Glauce. P
4. Temple of Hera Acraea (Aug.).
5. Temple. P
6. Road to Sicyon. P
7. Shops (Aug.).
8. North Market (Tib.).
9. Temple of Aethena. P
10. North-West Stoa (Aug.).
11. Temple of Tyche (Aug.). P
12. Babbius Monument (Tib.).
13. Fountain (Tib.). P
14. Temple of Apollo (Aug.). P
15. Temple of Aphrodite (Aug.). P
16. ?
17. Probable site of market.
18. Basilica (Aug.).
19. Lechaeum Road. P
20. Shops.
21. Market ?
22. Sacred Spring.
23. Ramp.
24. Peirene Fountain. P
25. Propylaea (Aug.).
26. Statue of Aethena. P
27. Altar.
28. Stone Platform.
29. Shops (Claud.).
30. Bema (Aug. or Claud.).
31. Shops (Claud.).
32. Artemis Ephesia ? P
33. Julian Basilica (Tib.).
34. Record Office ? (Tib.).
35. South Stoa (pre-146 BC)
36. City Council Chamber.
37. Fountain House
38. South Basilica (Tib.).
39. Office of the Agonothetes.
40. Office of Hellanodikai.

Greek theatre they added Roman style basilicas, Roman baths, an *odeion* (music hall), and farther east toward Cenchreai, a Roman amphitheater for gladiatorial contests.

Pausanias writes, "Not one of the Corinthians of antiquity still lives in Corinth; instead there are colonists sent from Rome."[4] Even the language of the city changed. Most of the inscriptions from the first century A.D. found in Corinth are in Latin. Naturally, one would expect, living in the middle of Achaia, that the residents knew Greek — Paul wrote his letters to them in Greek — but the official language was Latin and probably for many if not most of the upper level citizens Latin was their mother tongue.

Corinth was large — with a population of probably around 200,000 — and economically very important. It had harbors on two seas, and trade routes by land from central Greece to southern Greece (called the Peloponnesus). Finally, it administered the nearby Isthmian games which occurred every four years. These were athletic contests — similar to the more famous Olympic games of antiquity — which brought visitors from all over the Mediterranean world. Thus Corinth was a trading/business center.

The Founding of the Church in Corinth

Paul founded the church at Corinth on his second missionary journey. After leaving Thessalonica, he moved south to Berea, on to Athens and finally arrived in Corinth. There, true to his pattern, he first began preaching in the Jewish synagogue on Sabbaths while working as a tentmaker with two other new arrivals in Corinth named Priscilla and Aquila. They were a Jewish couple which had recently been expelled from Rome by emperor Claudius (Acts 18:2). It is not clear if they were already Christians before they met Paul in Corinth or if Paul converted them. At any rate, they worked with Paul at Corinth and became important Christian leaders (Rom 16:3-4; Acts 18:26).

---

[4]Pausanias lived in the latter part of the second century A.D. and wrote a *Guide to Greece* in several books. The translation is by P. Levi.

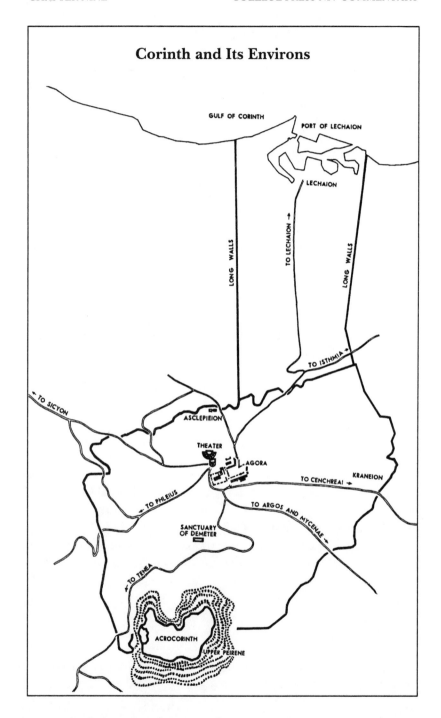

Corinth and Its Environs

The same result ensued at Corinth as at Thessalonica. Soon many of the Jews had turned against Paul and his associates and Paul subsequently left the synagogue to preach solely to Gentiles. Some significant conversions were made in the synagogue, however, especially Crispus the leader of the synagogue (Acts 18:8; 1 Cor 1:14). Paul also converted and lodged with Gaius Titius Justus who lived next door to the synagogue (Acts 18:7; 1 Cor 1:14; Rom 16:23).

Paul remained and preached in Corinth for one and one-half years (Acts 18:11), and toward the end of his stay an event happened which helps to date his time in Corinth. Some Jews brought Paul before the newly arrived proconsul of Achaia, Gallio,[5] and accused him of teaching people to worship God contrary to the civil law of Corinth. Gallio dismissed the case summarily as only a religious dispute between Jews (Acts 18:12-17). But the significant point is that Gallio's name was mentioned. Since we know from a Greek inscription (see *NTB* 46) that Gallio was proconsul in early A.D. 52 we can conclude that Paul arrived in Corinth in late A.D. 50 and left in 52.

After Paul left, a man named Apollos entered Corinth. He was an Alexandrian Jew, well educated both in Greek learning and in the Old Testament, perhaps much like Philo of Alexandria. He was evidently a disciple of Jesus in some sense but had inadequate information. After he was taught in Ephesus by Priscilla and Aquila he was encouraged by the churches there to come to Corinth (Acts 18:24-28).

Apollos made quite a splash in Corinth. His ability at debate was impressive and his knowledge was obvious. He was able to refute antagonists in debate with ease and to argue effectively from the Old Testament that Jesus was the Messiah.

At this point, probably in late A.D. 52, Paul began his third missionary journey. He set out overland from Antioch, moved through southern Galatia and came to Ephesus. There he remained two years and three months. During this time, from early A.D. 53 to 55, there was constant communication from Corinth (just across the Aegean Sea). First someone reported to Paul that some of the

---

[5]Gallio was the brother of Seneca, the Roman Stoic philosopher and tutor of Nero.

Corinthian believers were still too closely allied with worldly practices. Paul therefore wrote a letter — now lost[6] — that urged them
not to make company with sexually immoral people (1 Cor 5:9).

Sometime after writing this first letter, reports came to Paul
from "Chloe's people" (1 Cor 1:11) that there were divisions among
the churches, that one man was committing incest (1 Cor 5:1), that
believers were taking their Christian brothers to court (1 Cor 6:1)
and that some were still participating in prostitution (perhaps
temple prostitution).

In addition to the oral reports from Chloe's household, Paul
received a letter from the Corinthian believers. This letter asked
questions about several important issues that were dividing the
churches in Corinth. One issue was about the Christian's attitude
toward and practice of marriage (1 Cor 7:1), one was about the
eating of meat sacrificed to idols (1 Cor 8:1) and the third question
was about spiritual gifts (1 Cor 12:1). Two other issues, improprieties in the worship service (11:3-34) and the resurrection (15:12),
were perhaps learned also from Chloe's people or from the bearer
of the letter to Paul.

Thus the letter we refer to as "First" Corinthians — actually the
second letter Paul wrote to them — was a response both to the oral
reports from Chloe's people and to the letter from the churches
asking three questions. Paul wrote this letter in about the year A.D.
53 or early 54.

Content of the Letter

A. The first four chapters deal with the problem of divisions at
Corinth. Some people were saying "I follow Paul," some, "I follow
Apollos," some, "I follow Cephas," and still others, "I follow Christ"
(1:12). These divisions into a Paul-sect, an Apollos-sect, a Peter-sect
and perhaps even a Christ-sect seem to have had something to do
with: (1) who baptized the members (1:13), (2) the employment by
the sect members of worldly wisdom (1:18-2:16), (3) the denigration

---

[6]Speculation that this letter was later imbedded in 2 Cor 6:14-7:1 is probably incorrect. That passage makes perfect sense where it is.

of the preaching of the cross (1:23-24; 2:1-2) and (4) the members' improper elevation of their respective sect leaders. The sect leaders do not seem to have been willing participants in these divisions. Paul certainly did not wish to be followed as a cult leader (1:13) and we would have to conclude, with no evidence to the contrary, that Peter and Apollos did not either.

J. Munck has most clearly summarized the Corinthian problem as seen in 1 Corinthians 1-4. The Corinthian believers had three misunderstandings:

1. They believed the gospel was wisdom in the secular sense, and claimed they received the gospel from a wisdom teacher or from a philosopher. Since in their culture a philosopher — or orator or sophist[7] — is most popular when he can captivate an audience by his learning and eloquence, the outward form — the appearance and style — of the wisdom teacher is all important.

2. They believed that Christian leaders were like secular wisdom teachers. They valued them, says Munck, both too highly and too lowly. They valued them too highly in that they failed to take into account the Christian leaders' position as servants of Christ; they valued them too lowly in that they subjected the leaders to their (the Corinthians) own judgment of greatness.

3. The Corinthians misunderstood their own position. They regarded themselves as wise and boasted of their wisdom received from their great teachers. They also boasted about themselves and regarded themselves as already possessing resurrection and life.

So much is clear. But what was the nature of this secular wisdom? In the main two answers are given to this question. Some scholars say the wisdom was Gnosticism or proto-Gnosticism (Schmithals). Others maintain the wisdom was simply a popular mixture of Greek philosophy (Scroggs). The two positions are not really that different, however. If Gnostic ideas were beginning to be prevalent in the first century, these ideas would have formed at least a part of any such mixture of Greek philosophy.

---

[7]A sophist could argue any proposition without regard for truth, relying on his own cleverness. Many would go to any length to attract attention, to gain wealth because of their learning, to become famous and to get a following.

What is important to bear in mind about this wisdom, whatever its precise content or origin, is that it denigrated preaching of the cross. In an ideological system that praised wealth and success, death by crucifixion — the vilest and most shameful of executions — hardly recommended someone. Thus the Corinthians, or at least some of them, played down the crucifixion and played up the "wisdom" they had received in the gospel.

Paul responded to these three misunderstandings as follows. First, the gospel is not wisdom to the secular world but folly. The world looks at the cross and sees a man who was defeated, who lost. In the world's value system to follow such a person is foolishness. Thus God has stood the world's values upside down. As Isaiah predicted (29:14 quoted in 1 Cor 1:19) God has destroyed the wisdom of the wise according to the values of the world. The gospel is not wisdom to those who are perishing (1:18), but folly and an offense. But to those who apprehend it in faith, it becomes God's wisdom and power (1:21-25).

Second, Christian leaders are not wisdom teachers but God's servants. God is everything. His missionaries and apostles are only the vessels through whom he works (4:1-2; 3:21-23).

Third, instead of judging some Christian leaders as inadequate, they should realize that God will judge us all. He will decide who is adequate as a teacher or leader (4:5).

B. Paul also found it necessary to address issues of sexuality. One of the issues — immorality with prostitutes — he discusses based on a report from Chloe's household, and the second issue — sexual abstinence in marriage — he was asked specifically to clarify in the letter from the Corinthian congregation.

It is clear that some Corinthian believers were frequenting prostitutes (6:15,18). Furthermore, those engaging in such activity justified it on the basis of freedom in Christ. They extended the slogan about freedom to eat what they wanted ("Everything is permissible" 6:12) to apply also to sexual practices. They said about eating, "Food for the stomach and the stomach for food" (6:13a). Paul hints that they were also saying something similar about sexuality ("Sex is for the body and the body is for sex"; contrast 6:13b).

Such ideas are not surprising coming from former pagans, especially those from Corinth. The city was notorious in antiquity as a trap for one's sexual morals. The ancients coined a word, "to Corinthianize" (κορινθιάζεσθαι, *korinthiazesthai*), meaning to practice sexual immorality. The phrase "Corinthian girl" (κορινθία κόρη, *korinthia korē*) came to mean a prostitute.[8] Sexual morals were very lax in pagan Greece and Rome anyway (see for example the evidence uncovered in the ruins of Pompeii and Herculaneum in Italy) but Corinth as a seaport was even more given to immorality. Where sailors took their rest and relaxation, prostitution always abounded.

Beyond these general considerations is the well known quote from Strabo[9] the geographer about the temple of Aphrodite located on the Acrocorinth:

> The temple of Aphrodite was so rich that it owned more than a thousand temple-slaves, prostitutes whom both men and women had dedicated to the goddess. And therefore it was also on account of these women that the city was crowded with people and grew rich. For instance, the ship-captains freely squandered their money, and hence the proverb, "Not for every man is the voyage to Corinth" (trans. in Murphy-O'Connor, *St Paul's Corinth*).

Murphy-O'Connor believes Strabo is confused about what was in the city of Corinth in this passage and he doubts that such things went on in the temple of Aphrodite. But we must urge caution in dismissing this text. Strabo visited Corinth in 29 B.C. — after the founding of the Roman city — and thus certainly knew what was there. He has possibly exaggerated the details but it is not likely he was so confused as to describe something he had not seen at all. That the oriental practice of sacred prostitution (see the mystery cult of the Great Mother in Chapter 7) has entered Roman Corinth is not surprising since this practice had by this time spread through-

---

[8]These terms are found in literature which predates the Roman city of Corinth founded in 44 B.C. Thus they are referring to the old Greek city. We cannot think, however, that conditions in a large seaport would have changed considerably in the later period.

[9]Strabo came from Pontus in northern Asia Minor and, after traveling about, settled in Alexandria. His geography was completed in 7 B.C.

out the empire. In sacred prostitution the act of sexual union with the temple slave was believed to be an act of symbolic union with the deity, in this case the goddess Aphrodite.

Such an idea seems to be behind the practice of some of the Corinthian Christians. They thought their freedom in Christ — with respect to food regulations — also allowed complete sexual freedom. But Paul counters with an argument about Lordship. He accepts the slogan — if rightfully understood — "Everything is permissible" (6:12). But when you join yourself to a prostitute, especially a sacred prostitute, you accept a different Lord. This prostitute unites you, it is believed, with the pagan goddess. But you belong to Christ so such a union is a repudiation of your Lord, Jesus Christ. Such an argument is implied in 6:15-17.

Paul further argues that the body is not a matter of indifference. It is not something that can be abused and then cast aside as one would cast the husk from the wheat. The body of a Christian is a temple of the true God (6:19). The temple of God should glorify God, not dishonor him.

Thus everything in Paul's refutation of their misconception is based on Lordship. Paul does not cite commandments against immorality here as he does elsewhere (e.g., just above in 6:9) but argues on the basis of who is Lord. "Who is your Lord? You should act accordingly." It is a very effective argument in this situation.

But the problem in chapter 7 is just the opposite. Another group has concluded that one should abstain from sexuality regardless of the context, even if one is married. Here one is led to conclude that some kind of Gnostic belief has affected the group of abstainers. The early second century A.D. Gnostic, Satorninus, wrote that marriage and sexuality should be rejected: "And (Satorninus) says that marriage and the engendering of offspring are from Satan" (trans. in Leyton, *The Gnostic Scriptures*). Other Gnostic texts teach similarly (e.g., the Apocryphon of John, the Acts of Peter and the Acts of Andrew) as did the second century archheretic, Marcion. A Gnostic sect called the Encratites (from the Greek meaning "continence") abstained from sex even in marriage: ". . . from Satorninus and Marcion those who are called Encratites preached celibacy, setting at naught the primitive creation of God, and tacitly censuring Him who made male and female for the generation of mankind . . . and (one of their number) Tatian . . . proclaimed marriage to be corruption and fornication . . ."[10]

A story in the third century A.D. Gnostic work, the Acts of Thomas, is especially enlightening. In this collection of tales, Thomas, the apostle, allegedly attended the wedding of a king's daughter and taught the couple to think on spiritual marriage and not physical. Later, in the bridal chamber, Jesus is supposed to have appeared to the newlyweds and said:

> ". . . if you abandon this filthy (sexual) intercourse you become holy temples, pure and free from afflictions and pains both manifest and hidden, and you will not be girt about with cares for life and for children, the end of which is destruction. . . ." When the young people heard this, they believed the Lord and gave themselves entirely to him, and refrained from the filthy passion (trans. in *NTA*, p. 449).

In this text, the giving of oneself entirely to the Lord was understood by the author to involve celibacy.

Thus this peculiar belief about celibacy for all Christians, even married ones, would seem to have originated in a Gnostic or proto-Gnostic ideological environment. Naturally we do not suggest that these particular texts influenced the Corinthians since the texts postdate the first century A.D. But the same ideas that later became so important to the main Gnostic leaders and sects were already swirling around in a syncretistic city like Corinth.

Paul responds to this problem much as he did to the previous one. He begins by agreeing in part with their slogan: "It is good for a man not to marry ('to touch a woman')" (7:1). He admits the wisdom of this statement but not the reason behind it. He never agrees that sexuality *per se* is immoral or from Satan. His reason for the statement is purely pragmatic. An unmarried man or woman can devote his or her full energy and time to the Lord (7:32-34). Thus Paul wishes that everyone could live celibately, as he lives (7:7), and so devote himself or herself completely to the Lord's work.

---

[10]See the translation in J. Stevenson, *A New Eusebius*.

But Paul understands that not all men and women can do that. If one cannot live celibately, he or she should find a spouse. "It is better to marry than to burn with passion" (7:9). Each person has his own gift (7:7). Some have the gift of celibacy and some do not. But it is certainly no sin to marry (7:36).

If someone was already married when he or she became a Christian, then that person should remain married. Nor should the marriage become platonic. Rather each should understand that in Christian marriage his body belongs to the spouse just as it belongs to the Lord. Paul here uses language reminiscent of his earlier statements about one's body belonging to the Lord (6:13). That means "the wife does not have authority over her own body, but her husband has authority over it. Similarly the husband does not have authority over his own body, but the wife" (7:4). Both spouses live for the Lord but also for each other in their sexuality as well as in their love and commitment. Thus Paul's argument is just the opposite of that in the passage of the Acts of Thomas quoted above.[11]

C. The next question Paul answers is about eating εἰδωλόθυτον (*eidolothyton*) or ἱερόθυτον (*hierothyton*)[12] that is, meat dedicated to pagan gods or idols (1 Cor chapters 8-10). First, Paul handles the problem in a general way (chapter 8). Next, he explains the principle behind his instruction by referring to his own apostleship (and defending it; chapter 9). Finally, Paul returns again to the problem of meat offered to idols but this time from another perspective.

This pagan sacred meat was a problem for two reasons. First (see 10:25) it was sold in the meat market (*macellum*, Gk. μάκελλον). Much of the meat sold in a Greco-Roman meat market would have

---

[11]Paul's instruction here is reminiscent of that in the Mishnah, Eduyoth 4:10: "If a man vowed to have no intercourse with his wife the School of Shammai say (She may consent) for two weeks. And the School of Hillel say: For one week (only)." Translation in Danby. In general the rabbis prohibited sexual abstinence in marriage (m. Yebamoth 6:6; m. Ketuboth 5:6).

[12]The Greek word *hierothyton* was the normal designation for this meat and meant "sacred meat." The Jews, however, refused to call the meat "sacred" and thus designated it "idol meat." Paul uses the second term usually, only employing the first term when quoting what a pagan or former pagan might say (1 Cor 10:28).

been dedicated to a pagan deity. Should a Christian buy such meat or now buy only Jewish kosher meat?

Second, the pagan sacred meat was a problem because some of the Corinthian Christians — especially the wealthier ones — would be invited to eat such meat at banquets in pagan temples (note the abundance of temples in Corinth; see 8:10). During such a banquet the meat was divided into three parts. Certain of the entrails were burned upon the altar of the pagan temple, other parts were given to the worshipers to eat and a third portion (says W.L. Willis) was placed on a special "table of the pagan god." This latter meat would be the sacred meat. In theory the meat was for the god but in practice the worshippers ended up eating this portion of meat as well.

The question is, how did the worshippers regard eating the sacred meat? Many have claimed (e.g., E.R. Dodds) that they believed, in consuming the sacred meat, they were consuming the god. "If you want to be like god you must eat god," wrote Dodds (p. 277). He was speaking of the practice in the cult of Dionysus (see Chapter 7) but many New Testament scholars have concluded that the idea was current in paganism in general. Willis denies that the above concept was in vogue in the first century A.D. and maintains instead that these banquets were mostly social gatherings with only minimal attention paid to the religious or numinous ideas about the sacred meat. The idea may not in the first century have been as strong as Dodds thought but some of the Corinthian pagans who became Christians saw a link between the meat and the idol. That much is clear (cf. 8:7).

G. Theissen is careful to point out that the social and economic classes present in the Corinthian church may have contributed to the problem. As Paul indicates in the first chapter of his letter (1:26-28) many of the church members have come from lowly origins. But there were also wealthy members, maintains Theissen. Gaius, Paul's host, evidently had a rather large house since he also hosted house church meetings (Rom 16:23).[13] Crispus, the former synagogue ruler, as well as Stephanus (1 Cor 1:15-16; Acts 18:8) were probably wealthy since they were specially mentioned by Paul. One member, Erastus, is

---

[13]Much of the information in Romans 16 illumines the Corinthian situation since Paul was in Corinth when he wrote Romans.

called a city administrator by Paul in Romans 16:23 (see also 2 Tim
4:20) and a later inscription found at Corinth indicates his subsequent elevation to the position of aedile, the director of public works.
Such high office almost required a man of at least some wealth.

Now suppose, write Theissen and Murphy-O'Connor, a person
of high social standing is invited to a banquet in a temple such as
the temple of Asclepius. This temple had three dining rooms and a
swimming pool and was rather like a country club. During the
banquet it would almost be certain that meat sacred to Asclepius
would be served. For a man like Erastus to decline such invitations
would be politically very unwise. Could a Christian then not be
involved in politics or in secular society at all?

Theissen and Murphy-O'Connor maintain that for these wealthier Christians, eating the "sacred" meat meant nothing. They understood that the pagan gods did not really exist. They were the strong
Christians. But the poorer Christians could not see that. The
"sacred" meat still held for them a numinous quality. In some sense
they still believed that the idols were real. Thus when they learned
that a few of the Christian brothers were eating the "sacred" meat
they were shocked and offended. These shocked and offended
Christians were the weaker brothers (8:7, 11).[14]

But consideration of social class alone — though very helpful —
cannot entirely account for these differences. Some have cited theological differences. For example, Jews who kept kosher would never
eat meat sacred to a pagan deity and the apostolic council in
Jerusalem (Acts 15:20, 29) also requested that Gentile Christians
refrain from eating it. On the other hand, Schmithals has reminded
us that Gnostic Christians in the second century made a point of
eating the idol meat. Irenaeus reported about them: ". . . they eat . . .
at every festival of the heathen and in every banquet in honor of the
idols" (trans. in Schmithals). The Gnostics were not just indifferent to
these banquets in honor of pagan deities but made it a point deliberately and willfully to participate in them as a sign of their freedom.[15]

---

[14]Compare Rev 2:14, 20; Didache 6:3; Justin, *Dialogue with Trypho* 34
where eating meat offered to idols is strictly forbidden.

[15]For the same reason Gnostics participated in sexual immorality and
gladiatorial spectacles.

Therefore, one is tempted to conclude that Gnostic — or proto-Gnostic — ideas have played a role in this dispute as well as Jewish ideas. Thus the "stronger brothers" exhibit the Gnostic attitude and many of them may have been the wealthier Christians. The weaker brothers were probably the poorer Christians converted from paganism and may have included some converts from Judaism.

The stronger brothers believe they are sophisticated, liberated and superior Christians. They regard the weaker brothers as lacking in knowledge and as subject to the superstitions of the ignorant. The weaker brothers view the stronger ones as worldly compromisers who have not completely yielded to the Christian way of life.

Paul will position himself between these two groups and thus will disagree with them both. Throughout this section (chapters 8-10) Paul speaks almost exclusively to the strong brothers. He speaks about the weak but not to them. Paul agrees in principle that the idols are nothing (8:4-6). There is only one God, the Father, and one Lord, Jesus Christ. The pagan gods do not really exist. The strong are correct about this. They really do have knowledge (8:1).

Yet Paul does not agree that they should therefore eat the "sacred" meat or idol meat. In the first place, they may in doing so give offense to a weaker brother. The weaker brother — for whom paganism still has power — might imitate the stronger brother in eating the meat but subsequently feel that he had sinned terribly (8:7,10). Paul hints that the weaker brother might even be lured back into paganism in such a fashion (8:11). Thus the first reason that the strong and liberated should refrain from eating the meat is to protect the weak. Christians have responsibility to the entire body of Christ (i.e., to the Christian community). No one lives only for himself (10:24).

Second, Paul warns about intentional participation in paganism. The strong, who have knowledge (8:1), may think their liberated and sophisticated status will make them immune to the dangers of paganism — as the Gnostics thought — but they are wrong. The pagan gods do not exist but paganism is demonic (10:20). Demons possess the people that exhibit the kind of orgiastic behavior common in the cult of Dionysus, for example. Thus the Corinthian Christian cognoscenti may be getting in over their heads when they knowingly and willfully eat the "sacred" meat in a pagan temple.

Paul applies the same theological principle in this case as above for 6:12-20 (sexual immorality). The strong used the same slogan regarding the "sacred" meat as in the passage in chapter 6: "All things are lawful" (in both 6:12 and 10:23). Again Paul argues on the basis of Lordship and participation in Christ rather than on a specific commandment (commandments would not work very effectively on these people). To eat such meat willfully and knowingly is to participate in or have fellowship with demons (10:20) and to partake of the cup and table of demons (10:21). But they already, in the Lord's Supper, have fellowship with Christ and partake of his cup and table. They can have only one Lord.

Further, the Corinthians should beware. They too can fall from grace. The Israelites had many great spiritual experiences too — the parting of the Red Sea, the manna, the water from the rock — but they still lapsed into idolatry and worshiped the golden calf (10:1-7). Thus the strong at Corinth can do the same.

Paul concludes this section with three hypothetical cases. First, if one shops in the meat market, he should buy whatever is there without investigating its origin and without asking whether it is idol meat (10:25). Second, if one is at a party in a temple or private house, he should eat whatever is put before him again without investigating it (10:27). Thus Christians do not have to withdraw from pagan society. They can still go to the "country clubs" in temples and can still be active in public life. Third, if a person, however, explicitly informs the Christian that, "This is sacred meat," then the Christian should not eat it. Thus the strong must not in theory eat idol meat. Paul then adhered to the apostolic council's decision (Acts 15:29).

Sandwiched between Paul's teaching on meat offered to idols in 1 Corinthians 8 and 10 is a long section — something of an interruption — on the fact that Paul accepted no money from the Corinthians. Chapter 9 to be sure is supporting Paul's exhortation about the strong refraining from idol meat to keep from offending the weak. But it is also doing more than that. This chapter defends Paul's status as an apostle.

The problem was that Paul worked for a living. Ancient philosophers — Paul would have been considered as such by pagans —
could live one of four ways as R. Hock has shown. 1) They could
charge fees for their lessons like the sophists. But such people were
often considered flimflam men. 2) They could find a rich patron to
support them. These philosophers usually found themselves more
solicitous about flattering their patrons than teaching. 3) They
could beg like the Cynics. The famous Diogenes for example
(described in Chapter 7) lived in the Kraneion area of Corinth in
his large urn some 400 years before Paul. But begging might identify one with the weird practices of the Cynics and so hinder the
receptiveness of the audience. 4) They could work at a trade. Paul
chose the last lifestyle.

Murphy-O'Connor has suggested that Paul rented a shop in the
Agora. The shops there were about 12 x 9 feet with only a door for
light. Paul as a tentmaker or leatherworker (Acts 18:3) would have
made not only tents but also leather thongs, wineskins, harnesses,
saddles and shields. Murphy-O'Connor suggests that Paul taught the
gospel — his "philosophy" — while working or perhaps during a lull
he could have stood in the door of the shop and taught.

O. Broneer argues effectively that Paul also must have sold his
tents and other wares at the Isthmian sporting games. There athletic
contests dedicated to the god Poseidon would have occurred during
Paul's stay in Corinth from A.D. 50-52. Tents were needed by the
visitors to shelter them from the chilly and rainy spring nights. The
games at nearby Isthmia would have been too good an opportunity
to preach the gospel, maintains Broneer, for Paul to have ignored
them. Paul even refers to the athletic contests in his letter (1 Cor
9:24-27). Thus, Paul and his associates — Silas, Timothy, Luke,
Priscilla and Aquila — probably hawked their tents to the thousands
of visitors from all over the Mediterranean world and at the same
time introduced them to the gospel of Jesus Christ.

The problem to the worldly-minded Corinthians was Paul
appeared very weak and unsuccessful in this lifestyle. The philosopher, Micylus, a poor shoemaker, was laughed to scorn by another
philosopher, Lucian, of more affluent means (see Hock). If some of
the Corinthian Christians had that same attitude perhaps they chal-

lenged Paul's apostleship. Paul could not be a true apostle, so they might have said, because he lived as a penniless tentmaker.

Paul answers this charge and reinforces his argument of chapter 8 in one stroke. He is an apostle; he has seen the risen Lord (9:1). But a true apostle is a servant that is willing to give up rights for the sake of the gospel, rights such as monetary donations, marriage and certain kinds of food and drink (9:3-6). Paul has the right to ask them for money. He can prove his right from the Old Testament (9:8-10). But he has given up this right to keep from hindering the gospel (9:12, 15). Now the strong need to learn as well how to give up rights for the sake of the gospel.

D. Paul next moves to the topic of improprieties in the worship service. One of these topics, spiritual gifts, was obviously asked about in the letter the Corinthians wrote Paul (see 12:1)[16] The other two topics, covering the head in worship and the Lord's Supper, evidently were not asked about in the letter but Paul has somehow heard of the problems.

The first problem Paul addresses (11:2-16) provokes many hermeneutical and historical questions in the modern interpreter. To explore these[17] would require more space than we have here. Suffice it to say that Paul's teaching is that one should not offend the ordinary sense of propriety by the way one dresses in the worship service.

The second issue (11:17-34) concerns divisions in the congregation during the Lord's Supper.[18] While some have a party, others go hungry. Paul responds to the problem by quoting the story of Jesus' institution of the Lord's Supper. In light of the holy significance of this ordinance, how can some treat it like a trivial party time and insult their Christian brothers?

The third question the Corinthians asked about in their letter to Paul concerned spiritual gifts. Paul answers their question in chapters 12 and 14 and sandwiches between them the chapter on love

---

[16]One can conclude this because in 12:1 the same preposition (περί, *peri*) introduces the topic as in 7:1 and 8:1.

[17]The author recommends here the stimulating essays of J. Fitzmyer and J. Murphy-O'Connor.

[18]See especially Theissen and Murphy-O'Connor.

(using the same literary technique as in chapters 8-10). Clearly spiritual gifts were as big a problem at Corinth as divisions or idol meat.
Paul gives the greatest amount of space to these three issues. Like
the other two problems, the problem of spiritual gifts is rooted in
the Corinthians' pagan background.

To understand the issues involved in chapters 12-14 we must
recall the characteristics of pagan religion, some of which we discussed in Chapter 7. There was a strain in Greek religion — which
has been very well described by E.R. Dodds — which called for the
participant to lose control of his or her faculties. This was true of
that famous Greek institution, the Delphic Oracle. To Delphi in
northern Achaia people came from all parts of the Greek world to
consult the prophecies of the god Apollo. There a woman, called the
Pythia, would go into a frenzy — by some means not now known —
indicating she was possessed by Apollo and utter oracles probably
sounding like babbling to the onlookers. A male prophet would
interpret her oracle and put it into poetry (see W.K.C. Guthrie
"Delphic Oracle" in *OCD*). T. Callan notes that Plato (fourth century
B.C.) called the prophetess' inspiration at Delphi a "madness"
(Greek μανία, *mania*, see *Phaedrus* 244 A-B) and Lucan (first century
A.D.) said Apollo entered her and expelled her mind (*de Bello Civili*
5.167-9). Dodds comments also concerning the Delphic oracle that
the ancients believed, "the god (Apollo) entered into her (the Pythia)
and used her vocal organs as if they were his own, exactly as the so-
called 'control' does in modern spirit-mediumship" (p. 70).

Plato, in a classic text on pagan prophecy, also describes this loss
of reason in frenzy: "No one . . . in control of his faculties is seized
by inspired and true prophecy, but his power of reason is taken
away and he is changed either by a dream, by disease, or by a
certain inspiration (ἐνθουσιασμός, *enthousiasmos*, literally, "infusing
of a god"). (Plato, *Timaeus* 71e, Author's translation; text quoted in
J. Behm, "Γλῶσσα" *TDNT*).

Philo of Alexandria's view of Old Testament prophecy was apparently influenced by the pagan notion as he expressed in the following passage: "For no pronouncement of a prophet is ever his own;
he is an interpreter prompted by Another in all his utterances, when
knowing not what he does he is filled with inspiration (ἐνθουσία,

enthousia) as the reason withdraws and surrenders . . ." (*de Specialibus Legibus* 4.49; trans. by F.G. Colson in *LCL*).

Thus Plato and Philo emphasize the loss of reason and the possession by the one who is inspiring the prophet. This loss of reason usually was equal to a frenzy or madness (called *mania* in Greek and *furor* in Latin).

The loss of the faculties of reason through frenzy was also a common feature in some of the Mystery cults, namely the cults of Cybele and Dionysus (see Chapter 7). Through whirling dances or wine, the participants entered an ecstatic state in which they believed they were possessed by the god. Sometimes the celebrants of the Dionysiac Mystery would also utter prophecies: "Men, apparently out of their wits, would utter prophecies with frenzied bodily convulsions" (Livy 39.13; trans. in M.W. Meyer, *The Ancient Mysteries*). But whether or not they uttered prophecies, the worshippers believed the frenzied state indicated possession by the deity.

With the above background in mind, the problem at Corinth becomes clearer. The Corinthians, or at least some of them, valued tongue speaking too highly. Tongue speaking had been a part of the church from the beginning. On the first Pentecost after Jesus' resurrection it had been a sign of the latter days predicted by Joel (Acts 2:4, 13, 16-21). When Cornelius and his household were baptized, they spoke in tongues (Acts 10:44-46). The phenomenon of tongues ("languages") was seen in the Jewish environment as a sign of salvation history. God was consecrating and approving the event by the outpouring of his Spirit.

But in pagan culture speaking in tongues was inevitably regarded as an act of frenzied possession such as those described above. It was considered more a personal and individual experience and one that the Greeks highly prized. Thus the more one spoke in tongues in public — or, to put it in the Greek way, was possessed — the more one could boast and feel especially favored.

Paul gives four responses to this attitude. First, the real sign of the Holy Spirit is not tongues but the believer's confession (12:2-3). Second, there are many spiritual gifts and no one of them is better than the other (12:4-30). Third, the mark of a mature Christian is love, the eternal virtue (13:1-13). Fourth, practically speaking, prophecy is more helpful to the church as a whole than tongue speaking (14:1-40).

Paul begins this section by warning the Corinthians that their problem lies in their past experiences in paganism. "When you were pagans . . . you were influenced and led astray to mute idols" (12:2). The Greek word for "led astray" (ἀπάγω, apagō) can mean "carried away in frenzy" as it probably means here. The Corinthians must beware not to interpret their new experience in Christ in pagan terms. Paul writes that the real sign of God's Spirit in someone's life is that he or she (sincerely) says "Jesus is Lord" (12:3). Spiritual gifts of a miraculous nature need not be present in order for one to be a Christian.

Nor is there reason overly to value tongue speaking. God has given so many other gifts: wisdom, knowledge, miraculous faith, healing, wonder working, prophecy, discernment of spirits, interpretation of tongues (12:8-10).[19] To focus on just one gift is like wanting only one body part in the physical body or excluding a part. One does not cut off his foot because it is not a hand, does he (12:14-26)? The church is Christ's body. Each individual is a member of his body and has value and importance regardless of his or her particular gift (12:27-31).

In chapter 14 Paul gives more specific instructions even as he did in chapter 10 on the idol meat controversy. What is of tantamount importance, writes Paul, is the good of the congregation as a whole. Therefore, prophecy, because it is understandable to the audience, is more beneficial than tongue speaking (14:5-12). But if one really wants to speak in tongues in the worship service, he must have an interpreter to explain the message of the tongue speaker to the audience (14:13-19). If there is no interpreter available, then the tongue speaker should keep silent and speak in the tongue later to God alone (14:28). If one is prophesying and someone else has a message he wants to give, the first one should then sit down. They should prophesy one by one (14:30). There should be no confusion, no frenzied outbursts, no individual

---

[19]Compare other lists of spiritual gifts in Rom 12:6-8 and Eph 4:11.

demonstrations of how much one is possessed by the Holy Spirit (14:32-33, 40)[20]

Paul used the same literary pattern in chapters 12-14 as in 8-10. He began with general principles (chapters 8,12) moved to a discussion of a topic which seems at first unrelated to the issues — giving up one's rights in chapter 9 and love in chapter 13 — then gave specific instructions (chapters 10, 14). Thus Paul's sandwiching the love chapter between two chapters on tongue speaking was a favorite and effective technique to emphasize its importance.

Chapter 13 was almost certainly not composed impromptu. It reads almost poetically. It has a certain rhythm and lofty language. Thus some have suggested that Paul wrote it previously and that perhaps it was even intended originally to be sung as a hymn.

The chapter on Christian love (ἀγάπη, agapē) can easily be divided into three parts: verses 1-3 state that love alone is important; verses 4-7 indicate that love alone is ethically normative; verses 8-13 say that love alone endures.

As with chapter 9 this chapter seems at first to have little to do with its context. But on closer examination one can detect that it is fundamental and essential in properly solving the problem. The point is: however we evaluate the spiritual gifts love is the standard to test them. Without agapē love, no spiritual gift has value.

---

[20]Chapter 14:33-36, "Let women be silent . . ." has been problematic for centuries. Paul states in 11:2 that women can pray and prophesy in the worship if they wear a veil. Therefore what does he mean here? (a) Some say this is an interpolation, that is, that some editor, years after Paul wrote the letter, composed this section. But that solution assumes there is no other explanation and sounds too much like a modern prejudice. (b) Others say Paul refers here only to speaking in tongues. Women cannot speak in tongues in the worship but may pray and prophesy. But verse 35 does not seem to have anything to do with tongue speaking. (c) Still others suggest that this command is only for the Corinthian women because they were the ones most disruptive in the worship. But verse 33 would seem to say that this practice was adhered to in all the churches. (d) Finally some have maintained that the Greek word for "silent" (σιγάω, sigaō) in verse 34 has the double meaning of "quiet," that is, that it can refer to not speaking or also not causing a disturbance. Paul also admonishes tongue speakers to be quiet (verse 28) if there is no interpreter.

E. In 15:12 Paul writes, "How can some among you say that there is no resurrection from the dead?" Some Corinthian Christians denied then that there would be a general resurrection of the dead at Jesus' second coming. But why did they deny it?

Davies, Robertson and Plummer are surely correct that the errorists were Gentile Christians who had found it difficult to believe in *bodily* resurrection. They did not deny afterlife or the immortality of the soul but rejected the resurrection and glorification of the body.

Many Greek thinkers in general tended to regard the physical body as at least inadequate and some regarded it as evil. Plato repudiated the body as a detriment to wisdom and a hindrance to the immortal soul. In the dialogue called *Phaedo* for example, Socrates states that purification is "separation of the soul from the chains of the body." True philosophers, says Socrates, are "enemies of the body and want to be alone with the soul . . . and to be rid of the company of their enemy" (trans. in B. Jowett, *Dialogues of Plato*).

The sentiment expressed above became radicalized in Gnosticism where the body is believed to be vile and evil in itself. It is only to be despised. Thus the Hermetic Gnostic literature states, speaking figuratively about the body:

> You must (through thought) tear off the tunic (or the body) that you are wearing . . . the bond of corruption, the dark enclosure, the living death, the perceptible corpse, the portable grave, the resident brigand, who acts in hatred through what he loves and with his instruments of hatred causes corruption. Such is the tunic, the enemy that you have put on which strangles you and pulls you down toward itself (trans. in B. Leyton, *The Gnostic Scriptures*, p. 462).

It is thus in such a cultural environment that Paul has taught the doctrine of the resurrection from the dead.

Paul counters their error with two arguments: In 15:1-34 he argues for the bodily resurrection of all believers because Jesus was raised from the dead (as the eyewitnesses can testify) and because of our solidarity with Christ. In 15:35-58 Paul clarifies the nature of the resurrection body. It will be a glorified and incorruptible body, thus not exactly like our present physical bodies but also not just a disembodied soul.

The Corinthian church was full of problems. This church should serve as a warning above all to discipline ourselves against cultural bias in understanding our faith. Naturally no one can get outside of his skin to view the Bible completely without the perspective of his own culture. But we can be conscious of our bias and we can certainly never allow it to contravene the principles of our faith or ethics as the Corinthians did.

2 CORINTHIANS

Bibliography: C.K. Barrett, *The Second Epistle to the Corinthians*; H.D. Betz, *2 Corinthians 8 and 9*; F.F. Bruce, *1 and 2 Corinthians*; R. Bultmann, *2 Corinthians*; V.P. Furnish, *II Corinthians*; D. Georgi, *The Opponents of Paul in Second Corinthians*; J. Gnilka, "2 Cor 6:14-7:2 in Light of the Qumran Texts and the Testaments of the Twelve Patriarchs" in J. Murphy-O'Connor, ed., *Paul and Qumran*; M.J. Harris, "2 Corinthians" *The Expositor's Bible Commentary*; J. Hering, *The Second Epistle of St. Paul to the Corinthians*; C. Hodge, *The Second Epistle to the Corinthians*; C. Holladay, *Theios Aner*; P.E. Hughes, *Paul's Second Epistle to the Corinthians*; R.P. Martin, *2 Corinthians*; A. Plummer, *Second Corinthians*; J. Price, *Interpreting the New Testament*; W. Schmithals, *Gnosticism in Corinth*; J.L. Sumey, *Identifying Paul's Opponents*; M.E. Thrall, "The Problem of II Cor. VI.14-VII.1 in Some Recent Discussion" *NTS* 24 (1977) 132-148.

The Events Behind 2 Corinthians

Paul wrote at least four letters to the Corinthians, possibly five. We saw in the above section on 1 Corinthians that Paul had written an earlier epistle to them — mentioned in 1 Corinthians 5:9 — and that our 1 Corinthians was actually Paul's second letter to that church.[21] After that letter was written, Paul wrote a third letter which he called the severe letter or sorrowful letter (2 Cor 2:4, 7:8). (The older view of Hodge and others is that this "sorrowful letter" was 1 Corinthians. However, the language Paul used to describe the sorrowful letter does not fit 1 Corinthians.) Fourth, Paul wrote our 2 Corinthians, or at least part of it (i.e., 2 Cor 1-9).

---

[21]Some scholars have argued that in 1 Cor 5:9 Paul was actually referring to 1 Cor itself. He "wrote" the letter (in the past) in the sense that by the time the Corinthians received it, the writing would be in the past. Such a usage of the past tense (called aorist tense in Greek) in letter writing was not unheard of in antiquity. The problem with this view is it does not fit the context. Paul's brief description of his Letter A to the Corinthians in 1 Cor 5:9 cannot easily refer to anything in the rest of 1 Cor (e.g., the incestuous man of 5:1-5). Thus another letter, now lost, must be posited.

Further, Paul made a visit to Corinth that was not recorded in the book of Acts. He writes in 2 Corinthians 12:14 and 13:1 that he is about to visit them a third time but Acts indicates only two visits. Thus there was a visit between the second and third missionary journeys. Paul would have sailed directly across the Aegean Sea from Ephesus for a quick check on the situation in Corinth. Evidently this quick trip, unmentioned in Acts, was a very painful one (2 Cor 2:1) during which time someone in Corinth caused Paul "grief" (2 Cor 2:5), perhaps by a verbal attack on him. Paul wrote the sorrowful letter after his painful visit. Paul then left Ephesus to travel north to Macedonia and then south to Achaia — retracing his second missionary journey. In Macedonia Paul met Titus who had sailed directly to Corinth with the sorrowful letter. Titus reported that the Corinthian church had turned back to Paul's favor and had punished the offender. Paul, relieved and happy at the news, wrote his thankful letter (2 Cor 2:12-14; 7:13-15).

The third fact that we need to know is that 2 Corinthians in some places seems to change its tone abruptly. This is especially true of 2 Corinthians 10-13. The feeling of this section seems more sarcastic and hotter than chapters 1-9, which are in the main thankful and positive. Many scholars have therefore concluded, since 1870 when it was first suggested, that chapters 10-13 are actually a different letter from chapters 1-9. Some scholars believe 10-13 were the sorrowful letter originally and that it has been later attached to Paul's fourth letter. Other scholars view chapters 10-13 as yet a fifth letter (thus the sorrowful letter is lost).

The sequence of events in connection with the Pauline correspondence to Corinth is then as follows (cf. Price):

Corinthian letters and background	*Present state of the letter*
LETTER A: Paul while in Ephesus writes a letter urging the Corinthian believers to withdraw from sexually immoral people (A.D. 53; see 1 Cor 5:9).	Now lost. A few scholars say the letter is preserved in 2 Cor 6:14-7:1. Older scholars maintained that 1 Cor 5:9 (by an epistolary aorist) was referring to 1 Cor itself.
LETTER B: Some of the Corinthians — Chloe's people — visit Paul in Ephesus and	1 Corinthians

report on certain problems. Paul also receives a letter asking questions (1 Cor 1:11; 7:1; 16:17). Paul writes his second letter to address these problems and questions (early A.D. 54).

LETTER C:
Paul hears of further developments in Corinth and makes a quick trip across the Aegean — the painful visit — to assess the situation. He is confronted and attacked by one of the believers. He returns and writes the sorrowful letter (2 Cor 2:1-4; 7:8, 12; late A.D. 54).

Some say 2 Cor 10-13 contain this letter (e.g., Plummer, Price). Others say this letter is lost. Still other older scholars (Hodge) maintained that 1 Cor was the severe letter.

LETTER D:
Paul leaves Ephesus and meets Titus in Macedonia with news from Corinth (2 Cor 2:13; 7:13). The news is that Paul is supported in Corinth and the offender has been punished. Paul writes the thankful letter (2 Cor 1:11; 2:14; 8:16; 9:12, 15; A.D. 55).

2 Cor 1-9 (but many older commentators believed chapters 1-13 were a unit and explained the mood change between chapters 9 and 10 by the reception of new information while Paul was writing 2 Cor).

LETTER E (?):
Some scholars suggest that Paul got further information while he tarried in Macedonia and wrote another strong letter.[22]

2 Cor 10-13 (according to Barrett, Furnish, Martin, Bruce; thus they would conclude that letter C, the severe letter, is lost).

Thus Paul wrote at least four letters, at most five.[23] At least one of these letters — perhaps two — is lost. All of the letters, however, were written within the space of two years, A.D. 53-55. Three of the

---

[22]The present author thinks it unlikely that there was a fifth letter.

[23]Some scholars have not stopped here. Schmithals has posited six letters. Others see either 2 Cor 8 or 2 Cor 9 as separate letters (Betz). Still others insist that 2 Cor 2:14-7:4 is an interpolation from a previous Pauline letter to the Corinthians (Georgi). Finally, some argue that 2 Cor 6:14-7:1 is an interpolation — perhaps written by Paul, perhaps not — that was inserted into another interpolation, 2 Cor 2:14-7:4. (For a discussion of this see Thrall and Gnilka.) The partition and interpolation theories regarding 2 Cor are seemingly endless.

letters were written in Ephesus and one — two if Paul wrote five letters in all — was written in Macedonia. One thing should be pointed out in this regard. The majority of contemporary scholars, conservative ones included (see Plummer, Martin, Bruce), view 2 Cor 10-13 as a letter separate from 2 Cor 1-9. This requires us to believe, however, that 2 Cor 1-9 lost its conclusion and 2 Cor 10-13 lost its salutation and thanksgiving, before the two were combined.

We will assume that Paul wrote only four letters. There is no need to posit a fifth letter and to do so only complicates the picture further. Nevertheless, since this conclusion is by no means certain, we should leave open the possibility that 10-13 are letter E or a fifth letter.

Paul's New Opponents in Corinth

Both parts of 2 Corinthians indicate different conditions than that in 1 Corinthians. The congregational situation is no longer that of residual problems with paganism. Now Paul has a unified group of opponents which has recently entered Corinth and now is challenging Paul's authority and qualifications as an apostle. Paul wrote chapters 10-13, and to some extent chapters 1-9, as a rebuttal and corrective of this group.

The group of opponents clearly regarded themselves as apostles. Paul calls them — sarcastically — "super apostles" (11:5; 12:11) as if they regarded themselves as such. Once he gives his own blunt assessment of them. They are really "false apostles, workers of deceit making themselves out to be apostles of Christ" (11:13). In so doing they imitate Satan who pretends to be an angel of light (11:14).

Clearly the opponents boasted about their rhetorical ability. They took pride in their impressive bodily appearance and their eloquent speech and belittled Paul for lacking both (10:2, 10). They chided Paul for being ἰδιώτης (idiōtēs), "untrained" in speech (11:6). Thus these opponents were people who had benefitted from the rhetorical learning of ancient Greece and, since Paul did not, they judged him inadequate as an apostle.

Second, the opponents must have boasted about their Jewish racial background. Paul writes in 11:22: "Are they Hebrews? So am I. Are they Israelites? So am I. Are they Abraham's descendants? So am I." Thus we should view the opponents as Hellenistic Jews who have, like Philo of Alexandria, merged their Jewish heritage with considerable learning in Greek rhetoric and perhaps Greek philosophy.

Third, the opponents probably boasted about having visions. Otherwise, Paul's account of a vision he had had fourteen years earlier and his refusal to boast about it are irrelevant in this context (12:15). The opponents sought to qualify themselves as apostles then by the criteria of worldly erudition, racial correctness, and pneumatic experiences.

The opponents were, fourth, in the habit of both recommending themselves — by listing the impressive credentials noted above — and by carrying letters of recommendation from others (3:1; 10:12, 18). The self-commendation is equal to their boasting that Paul so often alludes to (10:13; 11:18, 30; 12:5).

Finally, it is clear that these opponents regarded themselves as Christians, even superior Christians. They not only boasted of Hebraic origins but of being servants of Christ (11:23, cf. 10:7) and apostles of Christ (11:13). These were traveling Christian missionaries like Paul, Barnabas, Peter, and Apollos.

Paul on the other hand does not accept them as true apostles of Christ or even as true Christians. They are intruders who have brought in "a different Jesus . . . a different Spirit . . . a different gospel" (11:4; cf. the words in Gal 1:6). They are hawking the gospel for money (2:17). They have deceived and seduced the Corinthian Christians in the same way that Satan, masquerading as the serpent, deceived Eve in the garden of Eden (11:3). They are messengers of Satan, pretending to be angels of light (11:13-14). Thus Paul's evaluation of his opponents in Corinth is the hottest polemic of any of Paul's letters except for Galatians.

Paul's answer to these opponents who glory in their outward appearances (10:7) and value the standards of the world (10:2-3) is to turn their values upside down. Although the opponents boast of their learning and Hebrew heritage, Paul boasts about his suffering.

He has often been in prison, he has been flogged five times and beaten with rods three times, he has been stoned and shipwrecked and he has labored at his trade night and day to support his ministry (11:23-29). Further, even though Paul can cite his own visions and revelations (12:1-5) he chooses not to boast about these (12:5-6) but to boast about his "thorn in the flesh." This thorn — some kind of disease?[24] — came from a messenger of Satan to torment Paul. Even though Paul prayed three times to have the thorn removed, it was not. Instead, "He (i.e., Christ) said to me, 'My grace is enough for you. For my power is complete in (human) weakness' " (12:9). Then comes the classic Pauline rebuttal of these opponents: "For when I am weak (humanly), then I am powerful (in Christ)" (12:10b). Thus when one boasts of his own weakness, he glories in the power of God. But when one boasts of his own strength, he ignores the power of God.

The Subsequent History of the Corinthian Church

The later history of the Corinthian church is reflected in the first epistle of Clement of Rome, written in the mid-nineties A.D. (hence forty years after 2 Cor). In this letter Clement, a bishop in Rome, writes to the Corinthian church to correct a problem. Some of the members were refusing to honor the elders of the congregation and this was causing divisions. Clement exhorts them to remember Paul's letters in which he also admonished them to cease their factiousness. Thus the congregation remembered Paul with respect but they continued to have problems with divisions.

---

[24]What disease did Paul have? In the main three suggestions have been made: an eye disease, epilepsy or a speech impediment. Some have also opined that Paul suffered from severe emotional stress, others that Paul battled a strong temptation to hate certain individuals. Most of these ideas are ludicrous but the eye disease may have some evidence (Gal 4:15; 6:11).

THE EPISTLE TO THE GALATIANS

Bibliography: H.D. Betz, *Galatians*; J.M. Boice, "Galatians" in *The Expositor's Bible Commentary*; K. Boles, *Galatians-Ephesians*; F.F. Bruce, *Galatians*; R. Bultmann, *New Testament Theology*; E.D. Burton, *The Epistle to the Galatians*; G.S. Duncan, *The Epistle of Paul to the Galatians*; *FBK*; J. Finegan, *The Archaeology of the New Testament*; F.J. Foakes-Jackson and K. Lake, *The Acts of the Apostles*; Guthrie, *NTI*; J. Klausner, *Between Jesus and Paul*; J.B. Lightfoot, *St. Paul's Epistle to the Galatians*; R.N. Longenecker, *Galatians*; J. Moffatt, *An Introduction to the Literature of the New Testament*; J. Munck, *Paul and the Salvation of Mankind*; W.M. Ramsay, *A Historical Commentary on St. Paul's Epistles to the Galatians*; H.N. Ridderbos, *The Epistle to the Churches in Galatia*; E.P. Sanders, *Paul and Palestinian Judaism*; W. Schmithals, *Paul and the Gnostics*; A. Schweitzer, *The Mysticism of Paul the Apostle*; T. Smith, "The Recognitions of Clement" in *The Ante-Nicene Fathers*; A. Wickenhauser, *New Testament Introduction*; T. Zahn, *Introduction to the New Testament*.

The Destination of the Letter

In 279 B.C. a large body of migrating Celts or Galatians left the Danube valley and crossed into Asia Minor, ravaging as they went. They finally settled in the north central part of the country, the three tribes, Tolistobogioi, Tektosages, and Troknoi being centered around three cities: Pessinus, Ankyra, and Tavium. They dominated the whole area until 189 B.C. when Rome subdued them. In 25 B.C. the area of the Celts along with parts of Phrygia, Pisidia, Lycaonia and Isauria to the south were made into a Roman province called Galatia.

The problem involved in the epistle to the Galatians is whether or not Paul sent his epistle to old ethnic Galatia (which would mean the northern part of the Roman province) or to the Roman province of Galatia (thus including the southern part of the province as well). If the epistle was addressed to the Roman province, it probably was meant primarily for the churches listed in

Acts 13 and 14 (Antioch, Iconium, Lystra, and Derbe), in other words southern Galatia. The different conclusions about the destination of the letter affect both the conclusion about the date the letter was written and to some extent the understanding of the letter.

The early or ancient interpreters believed the epistle was sent to old Galatia or northern Galatia. The south Galatian view was first proposed by the German scholar J.J. Schmidt in 1748. The position was widely assailed at first but gradually gained the support of certain other German scholars (e.g., T. Zahn) and especially of the British historian, W.M. Ramsay. The original view was stoutly defended, however, by such luminaries as J.B. Lightfoot and J. Moffatt.

A. The North Galatian Hypothesis

The evidence for the northern view is as follows:

1. Lightfoot argued that the ethnic meaning of Galatia was still used in Paul's day and he gave citations from Acts (18:13, 14; 14:6) to show that Luke used the old geographical terminology when he wrote of Pamphylia, Pisidia and Lycaonia.

2. Luke may have recorded that Paul preached in northern Galatia in Acts 16:6 and 18:23. It is hotly disputed whether "Phrygia and the Galatian region" means the old territory or the part of Phrygia in the southern area of the Galatian province. But Moffatt contended that these verses must be referring to northern Galatia (or the old ethnic region of Galatia) because Luke did not use the terms "*the* Galatia" or "*the* province of Galatia." Moffatt further maintained that the Greek verb "they passed through" (διῆλθον, *diēlthon*) in Acts 16:6 implies that Paul also went throughout the province preaching.

3. Third, Lightfoot argued from the similarities of the characteristics of the people in the epistle with the Celts of north Galatia. That the recipients of the letter so quickly abandoned their commitment to Christ (Gal 1:6) is typical of this race of people, maintained Lightfoot: "Fickleness is the term used to express their temperament. This instability of character was the great difficulty against which Caesar had to contend in his dealings with the Gaul. . . ."

Proponents of the south Galatian view answer the above arguments as follows. In regard to the first point they would say that it does not matter what usage Luke employed. Paul wrote the epistle to the Galatians and addressed it. Paul usually (but not always) used the provincial designation for a church. Since Paul writes that the recipients of the letter are the churches in Galatia (1:2), that argues strongly for the south Galatian view regardless of Luke's terms.

Second, that Paul passed through north Galatia — if indeed Acts 16:6 and 18:23 refer to north Galatia! — does not mean still that he sent his epistle there. The argument that Paul preached in north Galatia, which Moffatt proposes, is not compelling.

Third, it is very difficult to characterize a whole ethnic group by such terms as "fickleness." Were all Galatians fickle? Ramsay, on the other hand, argued that the Galatians were stubborn and traditional, just the opposite from Lightfoot. It is doubtful if any argument can be made in either direction from the ethnic and cultural characteristics of the Celtic people.

B. The South Galatian Hypothesis

The evidence for the southern view is as follows:

1. Because of the lack of information in Acts concerning north Galatian churches and the abundance of information concerning the southern churches, it is evident that Paul's epistle is sent to the south because Luke probably would discuss churches to whom Paul had sent letters.

2. Ramsay, followed by Bruce, pointed out that Paul usually followed the main roads and preached in the major metropolitan centers. That practice would lead Paul exactly where Luke places him in Acts 13 and 14. Thus, historical geography would indicate southern Galatia was the only part of Galatia Paul was ever in and thus Acts 16:6 and 18:23 do not refer to northern Galatia.

3. Some of the details of the epistle are presented as evidence in favor of the southern view. The mention of Barnabas (Gal 2:1, 9, 13) implies the readers knew him. Barnabas was certainly in south Galatia with Paul but we have no evidence he was in north Galatia. Further, there are no representatives to the Jerusalem church from north Galatia bearing the offering to Jerusalem but there are some

from the southern area (Gaius from Derbe and Timothy from Lystra; Acts 20:4-5). In Galatians 4:14 Paul calls himself "the messenger of God" which may refer to the incident (Acts 14:12) at Lystra where Paul was mistakenly taken by the ignorant natives for Hermes, the messenger god. Galatians 6:17, "the marks of the Lord Jesus" is often interpreted to mean Paul's scars from the stoning he received (Acts 14:19) at Lystra.

The evidence for either side is somewhat subjective. It is possible that Paul did establish churches in north Galatia but we have no clear evidence that he did and even so that does not mean the epistle was sent there. The fact that Paul tends to use the provincial designation most often would lead one toward the southern view. We shall tentatively accept south Galatia — thus the churches in Acts 13 and 14 — as the recipient of the letter.

Date

One's view regarding the destination of the letter — whether north or south Galatia — affects in turn one's view of the date. If the south of Galatia is accepted as the destination, an earlier date is required than if the north of Galatia were the destination.

It is probable from the evidence within the letter (4:13) that Paul had made two visits when he wrote his epistle: "You know that in sickness I preached the gospel to you the first time." The Greek term πρότερον (*proteron*, "first time") may imply Paul has been among the churches twice. The first visit — if we accept the southern view — is recorded in Acts 13:13-14:20. The second visit was either when Paul and Barnabas retraced their steps in the first missionary journey back through the cities just visited (Acts 14:21) or it was when Paul and Silas visited these cities in the second missionary journey (Acts 16:1-6).

Bruce argues that two lines of evidence indicate the second visit of Galatians 4:13 refers to the retracing of steps in the first missionary journey. First, Paul wrote in Galatians 1:6 that he was amazed that the Galatians could so "quickly" turn from their convictions. Although "quickly" could refer to a time a year or two after their conversion, it perhaps fits better with only a few weeks or months having passed. Thus one could conclude that Paul wrote the epistle only a few months after the Galatian Christians accepted the gospel.

Second, there are difficulties in assuming that the epistle was written after the Jerusalem Conference (Acts 15) which would be the case if the second visit is that recorded in Acts 16:16.[25] The decision of the council was clearly to reject the contention of Judaizers that a Gentile had to be circumcised and keep the law to be saved (Acts 15:24-29). Paul could have cited this decision in his letter, if he had written after the council, for surely such a decision from Peter, James (Acts 15:7, 13) and the apostles would have carried a lot of weight with the Galatian Christians. Therefore, Galatians may be Paul's first epistle — as early as A.D. 48 — and the oldest book of the New Testament.

The Occasion of the Letter

J. Munck was correct when he observed that the Galatian Christians had fallen under three misconceptions. First, they had mistakenly come to believe since Paul's visits that one had to be circumcised and keep at least part of the law. Second, they became convinced that Paul was not an apostle sent out by a revelation of the risen Lord but merely an emissary of the Jerusalem Twelve Apostles. Paul, in an effort to please men, had, the Galatians believed, changed the message the Jerusalem apostles gave him originally. He had watered down the gospel making it no longer necessary to keep the law. The third misconception was that the Jerusalem church and the Twelve Apostles preached circumcision and the observance of at least part of the law. Paul's letter was written then to refute these three errors.

---

[25]Some scholars, however, question the historicity of the events of Acts 15. See E. Haenchen, *Acts*.

Paul's Opponents

But how did the Galatian Christians reach these mistaken notions after Paul had been in their churches? Clearly a group of people — how large a group we cannot tell — has entered the scene in Galatia teaching the above listed errors. Paul refers to "certain people who are troubling (the Galatian churches) and wanting to alter the gospel of Christ" (1:7; cf. 5:10, 12). The hold these new people have on the Galatians is almost like a spell, a bewitching (3:1). These troublers are zealous to win over the Galatians but their zeal is not for the good of the churches but for their own good (4:17). They want to "shut off" the Galatian Christians — evidently from Paul (4:17). The newcomers are "wanting to make a good impression in the flesh" only to coax the Galatians into being circumcised (6:12). Paul alleges that the errorists hope to avoid persecution because of the cross by leading the new Christians in Galatia to circumcision (6:12). The troublemakers themselves do not keep the entire law, says Paul, but wish to shackle the Galatians with it in order that they may boast about their victories (6:13). Finally, the opponents of Paul in Galatia evidently put the Jerusalem apostles, especially Peter and James the brother of Jesus, on a pedestal (1:18; 2:7, 9, 11-12) and compared Paul unfavorably with them.

What sort of group would do such a thing? At least four identifications have been suggested:

1. The errorists or opponents of Paul were local Jews trying to win Gentile converts to the synagogue (see Lake).

2. The opponents, according to Munck, were Gentile Judaizers. Some Gentiles who have become Christians have also, by reading the Old Testament, decided that they must keep the law.

3. Schmithals affirms that the opponents were Gnostics. Galatians 4:8-10 sounds Gnostic, he noticed, and thus the opponents must have been influenced from that quarter.

4. The most commonly held view (e.g., Bruce, Betz) is that the opponents were Jewish Christians similar to — perhaps even identical with — those in Acts 15:1 who taught "unless you are circumcised according to the custom of Moses, you cannot be saved." Whether this group was the same or somewhat different from the

group of Pharisaic Christians referred to in Acts 15:5, is not clear but any differences must have been slight.

The first suggestion has some merit to it but one wonders why Diaspora Jews, who accept Gentile God-fearers (uncircumcised) into their synagogues, would object to Gentiles becoming Christians without circumcision. The second suggestion is also an interesting possibility but we have no good evidence that such a phenomenon ever occurred in the early church. The prime movers behind Judaizing — i.e., pressing others to be circumcised and keep the law — were in all other cases Jewish Christians. The identity of the opponents offered by Schmithals is extremely problematic. Would Gnostics want people to keep the O.T. law?

Thus the fourth explanation remains the best. We have ample evidence that such a group existed (see Chapter 8). It was present in the New Testament period (Acts 15) and later (e.g., the Ebionites). In city after city it tried to force the O.T. law on Paul's converts.

The Argument of the Epistle to the Galatians

H.D. Betz has suggested that the epistle follows a rhetorical outline or the kind of outline a good orator would have used in antiquity for a formal speech. Betz's suggested outline is as follows:

> (1:1-5 Epistolary Prescript)
> I.   1:6-11 Introduction (*Exordium*)
> II.   1:12-2:14 Statement of the Facts (*Narratio*)
> III. 2:15-21 Proposition (*Propositio*)
> IV.   3:1-3:31 Proof (*Probatio*)
> V.   4:1-6:10 Exhortation (*Exhortatio*)
> (6:11-18 Epistolary Postscript)

Although this rhetorical outline does not perfectly fit Galatians as some have noted,[26] still it gives a fairly good summary of the content of the letter.

The reader will recall that Munck isolated three allegations on the part of Paul's opponents. Two of these allegations — that Paul

---

[26]G. Jeremias (Tübingen lectures, 1989) has pointed out that in a normal rhetorical defense speech there is no *exhortatio*.

was not really an apostle called by a revelation of the risen Lord and that the Twelve preached circumcision and keeping the law — are handled in section I, the Narratio. The facts do not support the opponents' claims. Paul was an independent apostle from the beginning and the Jerusalem leaders do not preach circumcision.

In chapter 3 of Galatians Paul begins his argument against the claim that Christians must be circumcised and keep the law.[27] Paul establishes that the gospel was older than the law. Undoubtedly, Jews had challenged the truth of Christianity because it was so new. Paul shows that the gospel came — i.e., was announced in seminal form — 430 years before the law. First he maintains that God's promise to Abraham — "All the nations will be blessed in you" (Gal 3:8, quoting Gen 12:3) — was the gospel in summary. The blessing that all the nations or Gentiles receive in Abraham was the Messiah, Jesus Christ, Abraham's descendant. If that is true, then two conclusions are obvious: First, those that live by faith in Christ — as opposed to those that are loyal to law — are the true sons of Abraham (3:7). Second, the law which came 430 years later by Moses cannot annul the earlier promise (the gospel) given to Abraham, just as in secular Greek life someone cannot later annul or add to a person's last will and testament. Once ratified, the will cannot be touched. Those who want to add circumcision and keeping the law to faith in Christ as the means of being saved, are like people trying illegally to add a codicil to someone's will (3:15-18).

Paul next uses another comparison from Greek (or is it Roman?) secular life: the legal guardianship of a child (4:1-7). A child under age — especially a wealthy child — was under the oversight of guardians and trustees. He was legally no better than a slave. But at the time appointed by his father for his coming of age he would be legally a free adult, able to conduct his own business and able to have full command of his wealth. This practice, writes Paul, is like salvation history. Thus:

---

[27]Paul's circumcision of Timothy (Acts 16:3) was for two reasons: Timothy was considered Jewish (because his mother was Jewish) and Paul wished to avoid trouble where possible with Jews. It was one thing to demand that Gentiles be circumcised in order to be saved but another to do it to render one more suitable as a missionary.

The youth under age	=	all men and women
The period of being under age	=	the era before Christ
The appointed time of reaching adulthood	=	Christ's coming in the fullness of time (4:4)
The guardians and trustees	=	the law
The father	=	God

The Old Testament law was then only temporary, for an immature age. But now we are mature — in terms of salvation history —
and free from the law.

Finally, Paul offers an allegory (4:21-31) as evidence that the law
has ceased to play a role in God's plan of redemption. Paul shows
that the well-known story of Hagar, Abraham's slave, and Sarah,
Abraham's wife, represents the situation of Judaizers and non-
Judaizers (i.e., free). Paul contrasts Hagar (= the law) with Sarah
(= the gospel or promise), Ishmael (the slave son of Hagar = Judaizers) with Isaac (Sarah's freeborn son = non-Judaizing Christians).
The climax of the story comes in Galatians 4:30 where Paul quotes
Genesis 21:10 "Cast out the slave woman and her son. . . ." Thus the
law, represented by Hagar in the allegory, must be cast out or dis-
carded.

It is important for the reader here to understand the significance, even radicalness, of Paul's arguments. To argue that the law
was a late-comer in the history of salvation, that it was for an immature age, and that it should be "cast out" would have sounded
shocking, even blasphemous, to most Jews (and perhaps to many
Jewish Christians).

If salvation is not through the law then why did God give the
law? Paul gives three reasons: to highlight transgressions, to protect
us, and to bring us to Christ. Thus in Galatians 3:19 Paul answers
the question, "Why then the law (if we cannot be saved by it?)" by
the words "because of transgressions." After law was given, we
understood how sinful we were because we — as the human race —
saw we could not keep the law. Thus the purpose of law was to highlight transgressions or demonstrate to us how exceedingly sinful we
are.

The second function of the law was to "hold us in custody after we had been delivered over to prison" (Gal 3:23) until faith in Christ should come. Is the custody for our protection as some maintain or for our punishment as others claim? Probably the former since that meaning fits the context of the following verse. Thus the law guards us or protects us until we can come to faith. Its commandments, though we do not keep them perfectly, give us moral direction until we can, in coming to Christ, receive the Holy Spirit and the transforming power of the gospel in which we desire to live only for God and love him above all else; thus we need no commandment.

Finally, the law, writes Paul, is the παιδαγωγός (*paidagōgos*) who brings us to Christ (Gal 3:24). The translation "tutor" or "schoolmaster" of the older versions is incorrect. The *paidagōgos* was not a teacher but a slave entrusted with accompanying a boy to school and everywhere else. He was often responsible for the boy's discipline and sometimes could be quite harsh. The terms "baby sitter" or possibly "nanny" come closer to the meaning of *paidagōgos*. Thus the law is what brings us to Christ who is the Teacher. It disciplines us — its commandments may even be a little harsh — and leads us to Christ.

The law then was not given with no purpose. Its functions are holy and good but it cannot save us. The law prepares us to be saved through faith in Christ.

Galatians may well have been Paul's earliest letter but we should not think of it as an immature effort. He wrote it at least sixteen years after his conversion, after years of preaching, teaching and interacting with Jews and Gentiles and after years of study under Gamaliel before that. The arguments in this letter are the product of these many years of maturing. They were written by a man of genius in his late forties or early fifties as he was led by the Spirit of God.

THE PRISON EPISTLES: GENERAL
INTRODUCTION

Paul's letters to the Philippians, Ephesians, Colossians, and Philemon are called his Prison Epistles because throughout these letters he refers to his imprisonment (Eph 3:1, 4:1, 6:20; Phil 1:7, 13, 14, 17; Col 4:3, 18; Phlm 1, 23). The question is, where was Paul imprisoned when he wrote these letters? We should not necessarily assume that Paul wrote all of them, of course, while imprisoned in the same place. Paul states that he was imprisoned several times (2 Cor 11:23) and a later author, Clement of Rome (A.D. 96), maintained that Paul was imprisoned seven times (1 Clement 5:6). We know from the book of Acts that he was imprisoned for lengthy periods twice: once in Caesarea (Acts 23:23-26:32) for two years and later in Rome (Acts 28:11-31) also for two years. For reasons given below, we will consider Philippians alone and then the other three together.

Some scholars posit that Paul was imprisoned during his two year stay in Ephesus (Acts 19:10). Indeed, 1 Corinthians, which was written at Ephesus, does indicate some persecution (1 Cor 15:32). But nowhere in 1 Corinthians does he indicate he was in prison nor does Acts indicate it. Thus the Ephesian hypothesis seems unlikely.

Second, other scholars are inclined to point to Caesarea as the place where Paul was imprisoned while writing Philippians. This is a very good possibility and if Paul has written to the Philippians from Caesarea, then the date of the epistle would be A.D. 57-59.

Most scholars, however, regard Rome as Paul's place of captivity when writing Philippians. The reference to the Praetorian Guard (Phil 1:13), while not impossible for a location outside of Rome, most easily points to Rome. The same is true of the allusion to Caesar's household (Phil 4:22). Thus we consider it more likely that Paul wrote Philippians in Rome and therefore some time between A.D. 61 and 62.

The other three letters can be considered together because Tychicus carried them all and Onesimus accompanied him (Eph 6:21; Col 4:7, 9; Phlm 10-12). Thus they were all sent at the same time and, of course, to destinations quite close together. The same three imprisonment sites are commonly suggested for these letters as for Philippians. We may again quickly dismiss Ephesus as Paul's place of imprisonment since we have no explicit evidence that he was ever imprisoned there. Once again, however, Caesarea must be seen as a good possibility as the place where Paul wrote the three letters to western Asia Minor. But Rome is more likely the place of writing. The background of the letter to Philemon is that the slave, Onesimus, has run away and somehow found Paul. But would a runaway slave flee to Caesarea, a rather small seaport, or to Rome, a giant metropolis where he could easily melt into the background? Thus we would conclude that these three letters as well were written in Rome, again sometime between A.D. 61 and 62.

EPHESIANS

Bibliography: T.K. Abbott, *A Critical and Exegetical Commentary on the Epistle to the Ephesians and to the Colossians*; M. Barth, *Ephesians*; K. Boles, *Galatians-Ephesians*; J. Crouch, *The Colossian Haustafel*; F.V. Filson, "Ephesus and the New Testament" *BA* 8 (1945) 73-80; F. Foulkes, *The Epistle of Paul to the Ephesians*; E.J. Goodspeed, *The Key to Ephesians*; R.M. Grant, *A Historical Introduction to the New Testament*; Guthrie, *NTI*; J.L. Houlden, *Paul's Letters from Prison*; K.G. Kuhn, "The Epistle to the Ephesians in Light of the Qumran Texts" in J. Murphy-O'Connor, ed., *Paul and Qumran*; A.T. Lincoln, *Ephesians*; C.L. Mitten, *Ephesians*; F. Mussner, "Qumran and Ephesians" in J. Murphy-O'Connor, ed., *Paul and Qumran*; P.T. O'Brien, "Ephesians I: an Unusual Introduction to a New Testament Letter" *NTS* 25 (1978) 504-516; R. Oster, "Numismatic Windows into the Social World of Early Christianity: A Methodological Inquiry" *JBL* 101 (1982) 195-223; M.M. Parvis, "Ephesus in the Early Christian Era" *BA* 8 (1945) 61-73.

The City of Ephesus

Greek colonists from Athens first settled in Ephesus in 1044 B.C. They gradually accepted the local Anatolian deity, a fertility goddess, although they gave her the name of a Greek goddess, Artemis.[28] Eventually the residents of the city were divided into three tribes: the native people, the colonists from Athens and Greek colonists from other cities. Later two more tribes were added. In 133 B.C. Ephesus became part of the Roman province of Asia.

Ephesus was a large and prosperous city. Filson thought the population of the city in Paul's day was well over 225,000 people. It was prosperous for two reasons. First, it was well located, with a seaport to serve as a trading center. Second, its temple of Artemis was one of the seven wonders of the ancient world. People came from all over in March-April for the festival of Artemis. They not only

---

[28]The Roman goddess, Diana, was roughly the equivalent to the Greek Artemis. The King James Version uses the name Diana in Acts 19.

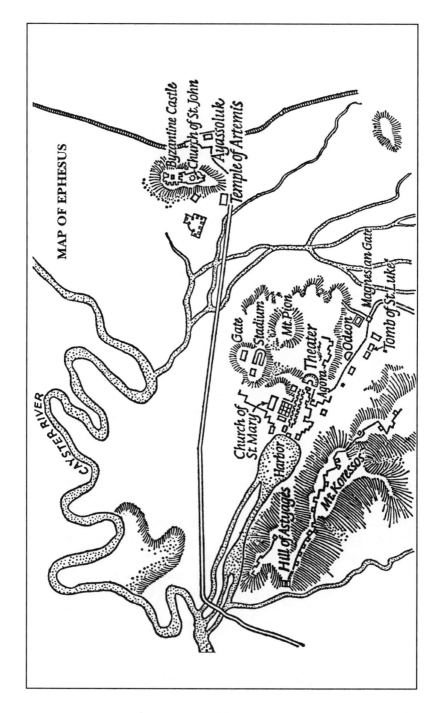

MAP OF EPHESUS

worshiped the goddess; they also deposited large sums of money in her temple for safe keeping. Thus the temple of Artemis became the largest bank in Asia (see Filson).

Other features in the city were the large theatre which could hold 25,000 people. It was into this theatre that the rioting mob ran when they protested the rise of Christianity and the neglect of the worship of Artemis (Acts 19:29). In front of the theatre was the main business street of the city, called the Arkadiane. Here were numerous shops and it is thus possible that Paul had a tentmaking shop here (Acts 20:34), though he was also free to teach and debate daily in the hall of Tyrannus (Acts 19:9).

The story of the founding of the church in Ephesus is somewhat confusing (Acts 18:19). Paul encountered some "disciples" when he later returned there but they had not received the Holy Spirit and were not baptized into Jesus (Acts 19:1-7). Had these ill-informed disciples helped found the church? If so, Paul surely greatly fostered its growth. Both 1 Corinthians 16:9 and Acts 19:26 indicate the great success of Paul's evangelistic efforts. The church was then evidently quite large by the end of Paul's stay in the city of Ephesus (Acts 19:10).

Authorship

There are four dominant views regarding the authorship of this epistle:
1. The letter is a genuine epistle from Paul (e.g., Barth).
2. The letter is the result of a dual authorship.
   a. Paul wrote the outline of the letter and a later editor fleshed out the rest of the letter.
   b. Or Paul's secretary or amanuensis wrote a draft which Paul edited, adding his particular theological emphasis (like a presidential speech today).
   c. Or an associate of Paul or an editor put together a collection of prayers and other fragments written by Paul.
3. The letter is non-Pauline (e.g., Goodspeed).
   a. Onesimus (see the letter to Philemon) wrote the letter as an introduction to a collection of Paul's letters. He summarized and quoted from Paul's letters.

    b. Or the letter was written by an unknown student and admirer of Paul.

  4. It is impossible to decide with certainty who the author is so one should suspend judgment.

The arguments against the Pauline authorship of the letter are as follows :

1. The language and style are un-Pauline. There are 91 words in Ephesians not in other Pauline letters and the writing style is uncharacteristically complicated.

But the reader should beware of placing too much emphasis on writing style. Good writers can change their style (see below on Colossians). As Grant (p. 201) observes, "Paul was never a slave to a dictionary."

2. This letter has borrowed from Colossians (e.g., Eph 4:15 = Col 2:19). Paul would not borrow from his own letter.

But how do we know he would not borrow from his own letter? Since the letters were written about the same time, it is not at all improbable that Paul would repeat himself somewhat or use similar phrases.

3. Ephesians 2:14f mentions the tearing down of the "wall of partition" which sounds like a reference to the destruction of the temple in A.D 70. Therefore Paul — who died in A.D. 64/65 — could not have written the letter.

But the author does not say the wall of partition is in the temple. It may well be only a logical illustration to indicate that Jews and Gentiles are now one in Christ.

4. There are certain theological emphases that are in tension with other Pauline letters.

    a. Ephesians 4:11 lists different gifts than in Romans 12. But the gifts in Romans and 1 Corinthians are also not identical.

    b. There is no doctrine of dying and rising with Christ in Ephesians but it is in Romans 6, Galatians 2, 2 Corinthians 4 and 5, and Colossians 3. But this doctrine does not appear in Philippians either. The absence of a doctrine cannot prove inauthenticity.

    c. The view of marriage in 1 Corinthians 7 (remain unmarried if you can) is different from Ephesians 5. But

Ephesians does not command marriage. Rather it extols it and explains marital obligations. Likewise 1 Corinthians 7 does not denigrate marriage but counsels that persecution associated with the Christian faith may make it better not to marry if one has the gift of celibacy.

d. Ephesians 1:9 and 3:1 use the term "mystery" (μυστήριον, *mystērion*) in a way different from the earlier Pauline letters (e.g., 1 Cor 15:51). But surely Paul was capable of using words in many different ways. Even within Ephesians the term is used differently (cf. 5:32 with the references above).

None of these arguments is really compelling. This letter clearly claims to have been written by Paul (1:1; 3:1). The second century witnesses — manuscripts, translations, writers both orthodox and heretical — maintained that Paul wrote the letter. One needs much stronger evidence than that presented above to deny the Pauline authorship of Ephesians.

Furthermore, every scholar admits that there are many similarities between Ephesians and the other Pauline letters. There are many vocabulary similarities — in spite of the fact that there are also some words here otherwise rare in the Pauline letters. The theology is certainly essentially Pauline — in spite of some alleged tensions. The letter is written in typical Pauline form (greeting, thanksgiving, doctrinal exposition, ethical admonitions, salutations, benediction).

Therefore, the burden of proof must certainly lie with those disputing the Pauline authorship. Since they have by no means proven their case, we must go with the tradition, as M. Barth and R.M. Grant write, and accept Ephesians as a genuine Pauline letter.

Destination

The words "in Ephesus" (Eph 1:1) are absent in some manuscripts. Papyrus 46 from A.D. 200 and the two best parchment manuscripts, Sinaiticus and Vaticanus, from the fourth century A.D. are among the manuscripts omitting these words. If they are correct, then the destination of the letter is unknown. Or perhaps there was more than one destination and therefore, the destination was omitted in the original letter.[29] Thus the letter we now call Ephesians may have been a circular letter originally, especially since it includes no personal greetings.

While the above suggestions are possible, there are many other manuscripts which have the words "in Ephesus." Therefore, the number and weight of these manuscripts tilt in favor of Ephesus as the destination though it is possible Paul sent out two editions of the letter: one for Ephesus and one as a circular epistle.

Content of the Epistle

The religious, social and even economic life of Ephesus centered around the great temple of Artemis. This structure, completed in 334 B.C., was 180 feet wide and 377 feet long. It was decorated with white, blue, red and yellow marble and with gold. Within the temple was an altar 20 feet square, behind which stood a statue of Artemis, the many-breasted goddess. This statue was possibly carved from a meteorite (Acts 19:35).[30] The coins from Ephesus which picture this temple show an opening or doorway in the base of the temple which was believed by the pagans to be the "door of heaven" (see Oster). Here they thought the goddess herself would appear miraculously.

Paul evidently referred to this belief in the epistle in three verses. He alludes to our being in Christ "in the heavenly realms" (ἐν τοῖς ἐπουρανίοις, *en tois epouraniois*; 1:3; 2:6; 6:12). The emotional attachment to this large temple and its myths must have been strong for new converts to Christianity. Paul reminds them that the real heavenly places are not in that temple but in the Christian community, the church. Christians live now in the power of heaven and with heavenly blessings.

The goddess, Artemis, was to the Ephesians a mother goddess who nourished heaven and earth. She was referred to as the "nurse" or the "protectoress" (Acts 19:35) of the Ephesians (see Oster). Paul

---

[29]In Marcion's text, the heading indicated the letter was sent to Laodicea.
[30]See *WHG* and Parvis.

is surely countering this conception in Ephesians 3:14-15: "For this reason I kneel before the Father, from whom his whole family in heaven and on earth derives its name." Thus God is the true father and all the people of the earth and the creatures of heaven are his children (*WHG*).

The references to immorality may also be allusions to the fertility cult, for there was a multitude of priestesses that served as temple prostitutes in the temple of Artemis at Ephesus. Thus Paul writes about the former life of the recipients of the letter: "All of us also lived among them at one time, gratifying the cravings of our sinful nature and following its desires and thoughts" (2:3). Paul refers to the lifestyle of Gentiles (or pagans) who "have given themselves over to sensuality" (4:19). Finally the apostle urges against sexual immorality (5:3) and warns that "no sexually immoral person . . . has any inheritance in the kingdom of Christ and God" (5:5). Therefore, the life of immorality, which the cult of Artemis invited, must be rejected for the new life of holiness in Christ.

But the Artemis cult was not the only strong pagan influence in Ephesus. In addition to numerous other gods and religions — for pagans would follow and revere many gods at the same time — the belief in black magic was especially pronounced. So important was Ephesus as a center for the practice of the magical arts that the Greek term in antiquity for magic text or magical formula was "Ephesian letters" (ἐφέσια γράμματα, *ephesia grammata*).[31]

The strong appeal which magic had for the Ephesians is confirmed by the book of Acts. Because of the great success of the Christian mission, many of those practicing these demonic arts were converted and brought their magic texts to burn them. The value of the texts burned was 50,000 pieces of silver (Acts 19:17-20).

At one time many of the Ephesians were under the domination of superstition and demonic powers and were thus "dead in your trespasses and sins" (2:1). But even in such a horrible state God was full of mercy and love (2:4) so that he made them alive in Christ (2:5).

Here we meet with one of the recurring themes in this letter: "by grace you have been saved" (2:5). Surely the Ephesian believers did

---

[31]See the Greek lexicon of *LSJ*.

nothing to deserve or earn such love from God, living as they did
under the power of Satan and his hosts. God's election of these
Christians and his granting of forgiveness, new life, and power was
entirely God's own doing, his own achievement. Thus Paul can
emphasize: "For it is by grace you have been saved — and this not
from yourselves, it is the gift of God — not by works, so that no one
can boast" (2:8-9).

There is a possible reference to the magical arts of Ephesus in
6:12: "For our struggle is not against flesh and blood but against the
rulers, against the authorities, against the powers of this dark world,
against the spiritual forces of evil in the heavenly realms."[32] As
Christians, the recipients of Paul's letter are locked in a spiritual
warfare against the very forces of evil they once served. Such
warfare requires the protection of God — against evil spells? — and
so one must arm himself.

Paul presents his classic metaphor of the soldier's armor in his
admonition (6:13-17). This metaphor, which Paul used once before
(1 Thess 5:8), was taken and expanded from Isaiah 59:17. In the
passage in Isaiah, Yahweh puts on armor — "righteousness as a
breastplate and the helmet of salvation" — in order to do battle
against injustice. Paul urges Christians to put on the same armor
that God used to do battle against Satan. In general he writes that
the protection against these spiritual powers is faith in the gospel of
Christ. In Christ there is victory over every spiritual or demonic
power because Christ in his resurrection has conquered all the
forces of evil (Eph 1:19-22).

Another of the great themes of this letter is unity. This is the
underlying idea in 2:11-22 and in 4:1-16. Christ has brought all
humanity together by the work of the cross. All humanity is viewed
as Jews and Gentiles. Since Christ has abolished the law by his death
(2:15), the wall of separation between Jews and Gentiles is now gone
(2:14). Thus Christ has united all people under him.

Since the above is true, we must live accordingly. Therefore we
must give every effort to keep the unity which comes from the Holy

---

[32]Notice Paul here combines the practice of magic with the cult of
Artemis. See just above for the phrase "heavenly realms."

Spirit (4:3), understanding that all Christians are one ecclesiastically, charismatically, confessionally and sacramentally (4:4-6). Our differences never outweigh our commonality if we have truly accepted Jesus as our Lord. We will have various duties and gifts (4:11-13) but all of these gifts are from the same triumphant and glorified Lord, Jesus Christ (4:9-10).

The letter to the Ephesians can easily be divided into two parts: Chapters 1-3 contain doctrinal teaching and chapters 4-6 contain the corresponding ethical admonitions. In light of what is true in chapters 1-3, one should live in a certain way (chapters 4-6).

One special kind of ethical teaching in Ephesians was termed by Martin Luther "Haustafeln" or household instructions. Household instructions, found in Ephesians 5:21-6:9, are paralleled in Colossians 3:18-4:1 and in 1 Peter 2:13-3:7. Paul admonishes virtually every member of the house — husbands, wives, children and slaves — to treat others in a way fitting with their new status in Christ.

Scholars have noted that lists of household duties have also been found in the writings of Stoic philosophers (e.g., Epictetus 2:14 and Seneca *Epistles* 94; see Crouch). Some Jewish writers also have such admonitions (ben Sirah 7:18-36).

But although one can find parallels to the practice of giving admonitions to members of the household, these passages in the New Testament are genuinely Christian. Paul begins the Haustafeln section in Ephesians with the general admonition to "be subject to each other in reverence for Christ" (5:21). The basis for such submission is our commitment to Christ. There follows the instruction for wives to submit to husbands even as the church is subject to Christ (5:22-24). Husbands should love their wives as Christ loved the church and gave himself for it. Thus one's relationship to Christ becomes the foundational ethical principle of marriage. Slaves also should obey their masters as if they were obeying Christ (6:5) even as masters must realize that the Master in heaven is Lord over both slaves and slave owners. Masters must not be cruel and threatening (6:9). Christ, then, has become the defining influence in household relationships.

Later History of the Ephesian Church

It may be interesting, finally, to track the subsequent history of the Ephesian church as we did above for the Corinthian church. We next are informed about this congregation when we read in the first letter to Timothy (A.D. 63) that he must beware of false teachers in Ephesus that have entered the congregation of late. These teachers are clearly teaching a form of Gnosticism which Timothy must oppose partly by ordaining faithful bishops (1 Tim 3:1-7; 4:3).

Next the church is referred to in the book of Revelation, written around A.D. 95. In Revelation 2:1-7 John wrote a brief letter to the Ephesians. He commended them for rejecting false teachers, especially the Nicolaitans[33] — evidently Timothy's campaign was a success — and for their perseverance in persecution. In spite of this glowing commendation, John rebuked the Ephesians for leaving "their first love." (Rev 2:4). Evidently John found their present level of Christian commitment lower than they previously demonstrated.

Finally, we get a glimpse of this congregation in A.D. 110 in the writing of Ignatius, bishop of Antioch. Ignatius wrote a letter to the Ephesian Christians commending them for turning away false teachers (*Epistle to Ephesians* 6:1; 8:1) although there were still clearly some false teachers around trying to influence the church (7:1; 9:1; 16:1-2). Ignatius urged them to continue in their faithfulness and to adhere closely to what their bishop, Onesimus,[34] instructed them (1:3; 6:1-2). Thus the congregation seems to have been about the same in A.D. 110 as in A.D. 95.

---

[33]The Nicolaitans were probably Gnostics. In the ancient Christian sources one named Nicolaus is described as an arch-heretic and a Gnostic.

[34]Was this Onesimus the same as the runaway slave from Colossae for whom the letter to Philemon was written? Many scholars believe it was. If so, Paul's concern for this young slave paid huge dividends for the future church. This may be an example of the fruit that Christian mentoring can bring.

PHILIPPIANS

Bibliography: F.W. Beare, *A Commentary on the Epistle to the Philippians*; J. Finegan, *The Archaeology of the New Testament*; G.F. Hawthorne, *Philippians*; J.L. Houlden, *Paul's Letters from Prison*; J.B. Lightfoot, *St. Paul's Epistle to the Philippians*; R.P. Martin, *The Epistle of Paul to the Philippians*; J.A. Sanders, "Dissenting Deities and Philippians 2:1-11" *JBL* 88 (1969) 279-290; F.C. Synge, *Philippians and Colossians*; C.H. Talbert, "The Problem of Pre-Existence in Philippians 2:6-11" *JBL* 86 (1987) 141-153; M.R. Vincent, *Philippians*.

Founding of the Church

On Paul's second missionary journey, while staying in Troas on the western coast of Asia Minor, he had a vision (Acts 16:8-9). In the vision, a man from Macedonia urged Paul to, "Come over to Macedonia and help us." Paul left soon thereafter to sail across the Aegean Sea, landing at Neapolis (modern Kavalla). At Neapolis began the famous Egnatian Way which ran through both Philippi and Thessalonica. Paul followed this road about nine miles inland until coming to the city of Philippi.

Philippi was first settled in 360 B.C. Philip II, father of Alexander the Great, captured the city in 356 then settled a large number of people there, also building the wall around it which was still present in Paul's day. Philip II also built a theatre which was still in use in Paul's day. In 42 B.C. a major battle was fought just west of the city with Mark Antony and Octavian (later called Augustus) on one side and Cassius (one of the assassins of Julius Caesar) on the other. After the battle — which Antony and Octavian won — many Romans were settled at Philippi and the city became a Roman colony. A Roman style forum was built at that time. The *bēma* or judgment seat where the magistrate would hear court cases was thus where Paul and Silas stood trial (Acts 16:20).

Philippi had only a few Jews — evidently mostly women — as is evident by its lack of a synagogue. Instead, the small Jewish community met by a river or stream for prayer. At one of the Sabbath

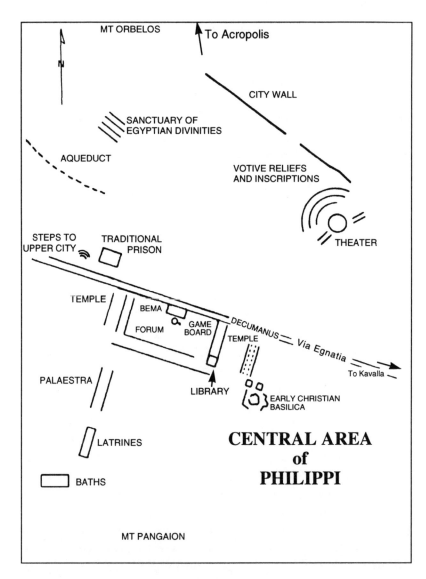

MT ORBELOS

To Acropolis

N

CITY WALL

SANCTUARY OF
EGYPTIAN DIVINITIES

AQUEDUCT

VOTIVE RELIEFS
AND INSCRIPTIONS

THEATER

STEPS TO
UPPER CITY

TRADITIONAL
PRISON

TEMPLE

BEMA

GAME
BOARD

FORUM

DECUMANUS

TEMPLE

Via Egnatia

To Kavalla

PALAESTRA

LIBRARY

EARLY CHRISTIAN
BASILICA

LATRINES

**CENTRAL AREA
of
PHILIPPI**

BATHS

MT PANGAION

prayer meetings Paul and his companions attended and spoke to
the women. Lydia, a somewhat prosperous purple-seller, accepted
Jesus as the Christ and was baptized (Acts 16:13-15). Paul and his
company then lodged at her house until their departure. How long
they remained in Philippi is not clear but we would suppose for
only a few weeks.

Paul cast a demon out of a female soothsayer in Philippi, earning him the anger of her owners. They brought Paul and Silas to court and accused them of being Jewish troublemakers. After the magistrate had them stripped and beaten, they threw them into prison, where during the night they taught the Philippian jailer about Christ (Acts 16:25-34). The traditional site of the prison, a plastered cistern just north of the forum, is very likely, according to Finegan, the actual building. When the magistrates the next day discovered they had beaten Roman citizens without due process, they knew they could be in trouble. Therefore, they escorted Paul and Silas – along with Timothy and Luke[35] – out of town.

Paul visited Philippi two more times after his initial visit. On his third missionary journey, he left Ephesus after an extended stay and traveled through Macedonia "exhorting them with many words" (Acts 20:2). He undoubtedly visited all the churches he had planted in Macedonia: Philippi, Thessalonica, and Berea. He continued on to Corinth where he stayed three months, then retraced his steps back through Macedonia (Acts 20:3) on his circuitous route to Syria. Thus Paul made three trips in all to Philippi.

Occasion for the Letter

The Philippian church has heard about Paul's imprisonment and has sent him money to ease his discomfort (Phil 4:10-14, 18). As a matter of fact, this church established a pattern giving to help alleviate Paul's financial needs. While he was first at Thessalonica, they sent him money (Phil 4:16). Later while he was at Corinth, they continued to share with Paul financially (Phil 4:15; 2 Cor 11:8-9, cf. 2 Cor 8:1-4). Therefore, upon receiving this latest financial gift from Philippi, Paul sent them his epistle as a thank you letter.

---

[35]Luke joined Paul for the first time when he left Troas. This is clear because the "we" passages begin there (Acts 16:10).

Unity and the Hymn about Christ

The Philippian congregation sent the money with Epaphroditus (Phil 2:25; 4:18) who was perhaps an evangelist or prophet. Epaphroditus would have informed Paul of two problems within the congregation. First, there was a problem with disharmony that threatened the unity of the church. Paul urged them to "think the same way" (2:2), to give up "bitter rivalry" (2:3) and that each should think about "the interests (or needs) of others and not just his own interests" (2:4). Possibly the ill-will between Euodia and Syntyche (4:2) was connected to this problem.

Then Paul quotes what may have been a Christian hymn (2:6-11) to illustrate his admonition, "Your attitude should be the same as that of Christ Jesus" (2:5). J. Jeremias[36] has arranged the hymn in three stanzas. C. Talbert and others disagree with Jeremias' structuring of the hymn. At any rate the point of Paul's quoting this hymn (probably written by him) was to show from Christ's life what humility and looking after the interests of others means. Christ was divine and pre-existent but surrendered his heavenly glory in order to save humanity. He even suffered death. As a result of his obedience he has been exalted and given a name above every name. The Philippians should let God exalt them, and not attempt to exalt themselves.

The Judaizers

The second major problem which Paul addressed was that of Judaizers who were trying to compel the Christians at Philippi to submit to circumcision.[37] Paul calls these Judaizers "dogs" (3:2)

---

[36]Given in Houlden's commentary. Jeremias supposed Paul had inserted three lines into the hymn. Jeremias, then, concluded that Paul did not originally compose this hymn. I consider it rather likely that he did, but before he wrote Philippians. Whatever the case, however, Paul accepted and endorsed the message of the hymn.

[37]The abrupt change in tone at Phil 3:2 has led to the following explanations: (a) Paul had just received new information. Perhaps there was also a rather long lapse of time between 3:1 and 3:2. (b) Someone has interpo-

because, like the wild dogs on the streets of many ancient cities, they were scavengers, stealing anything left unguarded. He also called them mutilators (κατατομή, *katatomē*), a jeering word play on the Greek word for circumcision (περιτομή, *peritomē*). True circumcision is in the heart (Phil 3:3; cf. Rom 2:28f; Col 2:11f).

Obviously the Judaizers were not only pressing the Philippians to be circumcised but were boasting in their Jewish heritage. Therefore Paul — in much the same manner as 2 Cor 11 — lists his Jewish pedigree (Phil 3:5-6) and then announces that it is no better than dung (3:8).[38] What Paul really values now is knowing and gaining Christ. To know Christ is to have not one's own righteousness through the law but the righteousness of Christ (3:9). To know Christ is to receive power from his resurrection (3:10), that is, morally transforming power. Third, to know Christ is to share with him in suffering (3:10). The latter is a very common Pauline theme. We must expect to suffer if we live with and in Christ (2 Cor 4:10; Gal 6:17). Finally, to know and gain Christ means to share in his bodily resurrection from the dead (3:11). What could anyone have to boast about — certainly not heritage or religious prestige — compared to the glorious gifts listed above?

Thus the same kind of Judaizers invaded the Philippian church as entered the churches in Galatia. But in this case it appears the congregation was not in as much danger of accepting circumcision. The general tone of the Philippian letter is not hot and urgent like that of the Galatian letter.

---

lated a fragment from another Pauline letter. (c) Someone has combined two of Paul's letters.

[38]The Greek word σκύβαλον (*skybalon*) is a very strong slang word for the filth of the streets. See *BAGD*.

COLOSSIANS

Bibliography: F.F. Bruce, *Colossians*; H.M. Carson, *Colossians and Philemon*; J. Crouch, *The Colossians Haustafel*; J. Eadie, *Commentary on the Epistle to the Colossians*; Guthrie, *NTI*; J.L. Houlden, *Paul's Letters From Prison*; S.E. Johnson, "Laodicea and Its Neighbors" *BA* 13.1 (1950) 1-18; J.B. Lightfoot, *Colossians and Philemon*; E. Lohse, *Colossians and Philemon*; R.P. Martin, *Colossians*; C.F.D. Moule, *Colossians and Philemon*; P.T. O'Brien, *Colossians*; J.C. O'Neill, "The Source of the Christology in Colossians" *NTS* 26 (1979) 87-100; J.M. Robinson, "A Formal Analysis of Colossians 1.15-20" *JBL* 76 (1957) 270-287; F.C. Synge, *Philippians and Colossians*.

Founding of the Churches of Colossae, Laodicea, and Hierapolis

Evidently the churches in the three cities of close geographical proximity, Colossae, Laodicea, and Hierapolis, also worked closely together in the dissemination of the gospel. Paul writes that Epaphras, their minister who is with Paul in Rome at the time, labors very hard for the churches in those three cities (Col 4:13). He was evidently an evangelist making a circuit among the three. Paul also admonishes the Colossians to have their letter read before the believers in Laodicea and to have the Laodicean letter[39] read in Colossae (Col 4:16). Indeed he refers to Laodicea rather often (also see Col 2:1; 4:15).

But was Paul ever in this area? The book of Acts never explicitly says he was and passages such as Colossians 1:4 and 2:1 lead us to believe he was not. It seems rather likely that Epaphras was the founder of these three churches in the Lycus valley (see Col 1:7; 4:12-13).

---

[39]Is this letter: (a) A letter written by the Laodiceans to Paul? (b) A letter written by Paul from Laodicea to some unknown destination? (c) A letter written by Paul to the Laodiceans? (d) Paul's letter to Philemon? (e) Paul's letter to the Ephesians? (f) A letter from John the Apostle (see below, Chapter 11, for John in Ephesus) to the Laodiceans? There is also an apocryphal letter by this name.

At any rate, Paul's authority as an apostle seems to have been recognized by Epaphras, who has come to Rome to ask Paul about the heresy at Colossae. Perhaps Archippus (Col 4:17) was left in charge back at Colossae. Paul then wrote the letter to the Colossians and sent it with Tychicus and Onesimus, along with the letters to the Ephesians and to Philemon (Col 4:7-9). Epaphras chose to remain with Paul in Rome for a while and join Paul's other associates, Aristarchus, Mark, Jesus Justus, Luke, and Timothy (Col 1:1; 4:10-14).

Authorship and Date

As early as 1836 the genuineness of this letter was challenged. Since then several scholars have concluded that Paul did not write it, but someone else at a later time who falsely attributed the letter to Paul. The reasons most commonly given are as follows:

1. There is un-Pauline thought in this letter and conversely much of his theology is absent. The doctrine of justification by faith and the problem of the law are missing. Further, the statement that Christ is the head of the church (1:18; 2:19) is not usual for Paul.

But one should not expect Paul always to write with the same theological emphases. He was flexible and adaptable. He tailored his letters to fit the problem or problems of the recipients. In addition, Paul does show a belief similar to that of Colossians 1:18 (Christ is the head of the body) in Romans 12:4-5 and 1 Corinthians 12:12.

2. The Gnosticism alluded to in the letter (i.e., the Colossian heresy) looks rather too late to have existed during the life of Paul.

But it is very difficult to date ideas. Gnosticism or proto-Gnosticism did not suddenly spring to life in the late first or early second century. Thus many of the allegedly late-looking ideas could very easily have existed long before we meet them in the classic formulations of Gnosticism.

3. The author uses many words and phrases that are uncharacteristic of Paul's other letters. There are (see *FBK*) 48 words in Colossians not found in other Pauline letters, not to mention some

unusual stylistic and grammatical constructions. This argument is the one most commonly used to reject the Pauline authorship.

But we must be very cautious in appealing to vocabulary and literary style to reject authorship. It is well known to scholars of the classics, for example, that the Latin historian, Tacitus, wrote in two distinctly different styles. His work, the *Dialogue on Oratory*, was written in the style standardized by Cicero called concinnity or careful arrangement. But in Tacitus's other works, the *Annals* and *Histories*, he used a style known as inconcinnity which sought intentionally to avoid the stylistic regularities of Cicero.

Another example from classical philology is given by G. Highet with reference to the Roman poet Juvenal:

> About a hundred years ago the German scholar, Otto Ribbeck, conjectured that half a dozen of the later satires were not by Juvenal at all but by a forger who copied something of his manner without equalling his spirit. He was right, but the copyist was Juvenal himself, imitating his earlier work after the passion that inspired it had died away (quoted in R.M. Grant, p. 215).

Therefore, we should counsel caution in assuming we can rule a document inauthentic on the basis of vocabulary or style or both.

Writing styles can change dramatically when the author intends to do so. Anyone as flexible as Paul could change his treasure chest of vocabulary to fit the occasion. Paul has evidently used the words and slogans prevalent among the Colossian errorists much the same as he did with the Corinthians.[40]

The Colossian Heresy

The problem at Colossae involved a new heretical teaching

---

[40]Cf. 1 Cor 6:12 for example. It is also interesting that R. Jewett suggested that Paul picked up the word "conscience" (συνείδησις, *syneidēsis*) from the Corinthians since he first used it in his Corinthian letter and subsequently in his letter to the Romans written at Corinth (1 Cor 8:7, 10; Rom 2:15). See Jewett, *Paul's Anthropological Terms*.

based on a syncretistic religion. This heretical teaching had begun to make inroads in the Colossian church. But to accept its teachings was to abandon historic Christianity.

The religion was syncretistic because it meshed together Greek philosophy (2:8), Judaism (2:11-14, 16; 3:11), and the mystery religions (1:26f; 2:2f; 4:3). The references to the elements of the universe (1:16; 2:8, 15, 20), which are connected with angelic powers (2:18), may also have strong influences from magic. In addition, the emphasis on knowledge and wisdom (2:3, 23) and the "fullness"[41] (Greek πλήρωμα, *plērōma*; 1:19, 2:9-10) sounds very much like a proto-Gnostic influence.

The practices of this religion involved worshiping angels (2:18) or doing cultic acts for those spiritual beings believed to be controlling the universe. They also practiced a kind of asceticism, debasing themselves (2:18, 23) in some fashion. They kept to strict regulations regarding food and drink (2:21) and gloried in severity or harshness toward the body (2:23).

Can we be more precise in identifying the errorists? The following are the most commonly accepted suggestions:[42]

1. Those propagating the heresy in Colossae were Essenes.

2. The heretics were influenced by a pagan Mystery cult.

3. The heresy is a syncretism of Gnosticized Judaism and pagan elements.

4. The problem was a Judaizing syncretism.

5. The false teaching resulted from a Jewish Christian mystical asceticism.

It is probably impossible to ascertain with certainty the origin of the heresy. There seems to be little difference between hypotheses 3, 4, and 5 anyway. On the whole, the present author would say, hypothesis 3 covers the bases better than the others but this is hardly a specific identification. Thus the Colossian heresy was an early form of Gnosticism somewhat more advanced than that in Corinth.

---

[41]The "fullness" was the Gnostic word for the archons or lesser gods that inhabited the cosmos.

[42]See the survey in O'Brien.

The Hymn about Christ

Colossians 1:15-20 (some say 1:15-18) contains a passage that looks like it was originally a hymn. As with the case of the Christ hymn in Philippians, scholars organize — and interpret — this hymn variously.[43]

Did Paul quote the passage or write it? Some scholars say the hymn is not Pauline but was written by someone in the early Greek-speaking church.[44] Other scholars believe Paul wrote it as a hymn either before this occasion — a hymn used in the worship services in Asia Minor — or specifically for this letter. The present writer is inclined to conclude that Paul wrote the passage earlier than the Colossian letter and quoted it to them here. Regardless of the origin of the passage, Paul endorsed it and its theology for his letter.

The passage exalts Christ as absolutely pre-eminent and sovereign over the universe. He is the "image" (v. 15). God is invisible and cannot be seen but Christ, the God-Man, represented and manifested God on earth. He is the "first born of all creation" (v. 15) not because he was the first created being but because he is unique. This expression ("first born of all creation"), known from other ancient literature[45] means not that Christ was created but that he is pre-eminent and sovereign over all creation. Verse 16 supports this conclusion for it states that Christ has created everything on earth and in heaven — even the cosmic powers. Christ as creator holds the universe together (v. 17). He makes the universe a "cosmos" not a "chaos" (Lohse). Christ is over all and pre-eminent (v. 18). He is over the church and is the first to be raised from the dead with a glorified body. Further, all the "fullness" (v. 19) dwells in Christ.

---

[43]Robinson believed several lines to have been added to the original hymn. Robinson also rearranged verse 18, putting part of it after verse 20. Compare also Lohse's and Martin's poetic structuring.

[44]Those that deny the Pauline authorship of Colossians of course also deny that Paul wrote this hymn. Still others believe that Paul wrote Colossians but some later copyist inserted the hymn. There is, however, absolutely no manuscript evidence for such a conclusion.

[45]See Philo, *Questions on Genesis* 4.97; *De Agricultura* 51; *De Confusione Linguarum* 146; *De Somniis* 1.215.

That is, all that is God is in him, as opposed to the Gnostic conception of several emanations from God. Finally, Christ has reconciled and made peace for all things on earth and in heaven (v. 20). The alienation and disharmony of the universe is being changed into reconciliation and harmony through the work of Christ. Thus the message of the Christ hymn is that subservience to the supposed cosmic powers — the worship of angels (2:18) — is in vain. Christ is *the* power of the universe.

PHILEMON

Bibliography: S. Bartchy, *First-Century Slavery and 1 Corinthians 7:21*; H.M. Carson, *Colossians and Philemon*; J. Knox, *Philemon Among the Letters of Paul*; J.B. Lightfoot, *Colossians and Philemon*; E. Lohse, *Colossians and Philemon*; C.F.D. Moule, *Colossians and Philemon*; N.R. Peterson, *Rediscovering Paul: Philemon and the Sociology of Paul's Narrative World*.

The letter to Philemon has to do with a runaway slave named Onesimus. He has robbed his master, Philemon, and fled from Colossae to Rome. In Rome he came into contact with Paul and was converted (v. 10). Paul then persuaded Onesimus to return to Philemon — along with Tychicus and two other letters (Col 4:7-9; Eph 6:21) — carrying this letter which he hoped would move Philemon to accept Onesimus without punishment. Thus the date for this letter is the same as for Ephesians and Colossians: A.D. 61-62.

Slaves ran away often in the ancient world. When that happened a warrant would be issued for the slave's arrest. Some of these ancient warrants have been found among the papyri of Egypt. They usually give the name of the slave and the slave owner, a description of the slave, a description of the articles the slave has stolen in his flight and tell what the reward is for the slave's return.

It is not unusual that Paul interceded on Onesimus' behalf. Since the slave owner could legally punish runaways at his own discretion, severe punishments were sometimes meted out. Thus slaves would appeal to men of influence to plea for them. One very strikingly similar parallel to Paul's letter was written by Pliny the Younger in the early part of the second century A.D. (quoted in Lohse). In the letter Pliny intercedes on behalf of a freedman who has somehow displeased one Sabinianus, evidently the freedman's employer. He has perhaps stolen from him and fled to Pliny for refuge. As Lohse insightfully points out, Pliny pleads in his letter for clemency toward the freedman — a Stoic virtue — but Paul pleads for love toward Onesimus (vv. 5, 7, 9).

The letter is a good example of Paul's masterful pastoral ability.

He never orders Philemon to show love to Onesimus but hints strongly that it would be a personal favor to him if Philemon would (vv. 17-20). As Christians we should see our relationships differently. Now Philemon and Onesimus are brothers in Christ (v. 16).

Some have criticized Paul for not ordering Philemon to set Onesimus free. But Paul never sought to change the social order (or the social conventions between husbands and wives). Paul looked forward to the Second Coming when Christ would do that. Then everything would submit to him (1 Cor 15:25). Until then to desire to restructure the social order is futile (1 Cor 7:17-24, 29-31).

Yet, while not changing the social convention, Paul did insist on individual Christian transformation through love (ἀγάπη, *agapē*). Everything must be based on that motive.

THE THESSALONIAN CORRESPONDENCE

Bibliography: E. Best, *A Commentary on the First and Second Epistles to the Thessalonians*; L. Boettner, *The Millennium*; F.F. Bruce, *The Acts of the Apostles*; Idem, *1 and 2 Thessalonians*; R.F. Collins, *Studies on the First Letter to the Thessalonians*; K.P. Donfried, "The Cults of Thessalonica and the Thessalonian Correspondence" *NTS* 31 (1985) 336-356; R. Jewett, *The Thessalonian Correspondence*; J.E. Frame, *A Critical and Exegetical Commentary on the Epistles of St. Paul to the Thessalonians*; A.J. Malherbe, "Gentle as a Nurse" *Novum Testamentum* 12 (1970) 203-217; Idem, *Paul and the Thessalonians*; I.H. Marshall, *1 and 2 Thessalonians*; M.W. Meyer, *The Ancient Mysteries: A Sourcebook*; L. Morris, *The First and Second Epistles to the Thessalonians*; W. Neil, *The Epistles of Paul to the Thessalonians*; M.J. Vickers, "Hellenistic Thessaloniki" *Journal of Hellenic Studies* 92 (1972) 156-170.

The City and the Founding of the Church

Thessalonica was founded in 316 B.C. and became the capital city of the Roman province of Macedonia in 146 B.C. Not only was Thessalonica an active seaport, but the famous Egnatian highway, which connected the Aegean and Adriatic seas, ran through it. Its population, estimated at around 200,000 in antiquity, made Thessalonica the largest city in all of Macedonia. The city included not only Romans, Greeks, and Macedonians, but a large number of Jews. Archaeologists have also recently discovered evidence of a Samaritan synagogue in the city.

The Egnatian highway ran through Thessalonica near the harbor. Thessalonica had at least one *agora* or marketplace in the center of the city and probably another one south of the Egnatian way. Probably there Paul had a tentmaking shop (1 Thess 2:9; 2 Thess 3:8) as he did in Corinth (Acts 18:3) and preached and taught passers-by as well as customers. The *agora* was a center not only for commerce but for the exchange of ideas. There one could find a host of products and services sold. Some shops in the *agora* were part of large stone buildings called *stoas*; others were wooden shacks or open air stands. One could find cobblers, box makers, statue carvers, pig sellers, leather workers, wine shops, fish shops, barbershops, and perfume shops among others. In addition to the shops that hawked their wares, public buildings and law courts stood in the *agora*. The ancients liked to congregate in public buildings and shops (barbershops and perfume shops were favorites) and talk about everything from street gossip to philosophy and politics. Not only did vendors and shop keepers sell products; philosophers and religious preachers "sold" their ideas in the *agora*. Since Paul used the marketplace at Athens to find an audience for preaching (Acts 17:7) it is likely he did the same wherever he traveled.

Paul founded the church at Thessalonica on his second missionary journey. His preaching resulted in the conversion of several Jews as well as many Greeks who attended the Jewish synagogue. The majority of Paul's converts, however, were formerly worshipers of pagan gods (1 Thess 1:9) and these presented Paul with the most difficulty in nurturing them into mature Christians.

Soon the Jews were upset at having some of their synagogue members taken from them and erupted into mob violence. A group of ruffians sought out Paul and when they could not find him snatched instead Jason, in whose house Paul was residing, and dragged him and a few other Christians before the magistrates. After giving "security" Jason was released (Acts 17:1-9). Paul and his companions left Thessalonica by night, apparently to avoid further trouble for the newly-born Christian community.

Paul moved on to the city of Berea where he encountered more opposition from Thessalonian Jews and was forced to move again. He came south to Athens, at which point he sent Timothy back to inquire after the Thessalonians (1 Thess 3:12). Paul continued on to Corinth and it was probably there that he wrote 1 Thessalonians in A.D. 50 or 51 and 2 Thessalonians presumably shortly thereafter.

The account of the founding of the Thessalonian church in Acts 17:1-9 lays stress on Paul's converting Jews and Gentile "God-fearers." But from what Paul says in the Thessalonian correspondence these must have been in the minority in the church. Paul recalls in 1 Thess 1:9 that they had "turned to God from idols," and in 1 Thess 4:5 he admonishes each of them to "control his own body" in holiness and "not in passionate lust like the heathen, who do not know God."

Ancient Thessalonica was of course overwhelmingly pagan with only a small percentage of the Gentile population attending the Jewish synagogues. As in all non-Jewish cities, the pagan religions were varied and numerous. The ancients saw no problem in belonging to several heathen religions at the same time.

In addition to evidence showing worship of the popular civic deities such as Zeus and Aphrodite and the popular god of healing, Asclepius, strong attestation exists for Roman emperor worship. From the time of Julius Caesar on the emperors were honored in Thessalonica as god and called "Benefactor" and "Savior." A temple was built in honor of Caesar and coins minted in Thessalonica acclaimed him god.

Apparently an oath of allegiance was required of the inhabitants of Thessalonica in which they promised not only obedience but reverence toward the emperor. Some think the charge that Christians defied the "decrees of Caesar" at Thessalonica (Acts 17:7) refers to their refusal to take such an oath.

The Content of the Letter

It is quite possible that Paul is referring in 1 Thess 5:3 to the alleged "peace and security" provided by the emperors as Benefactors of the city (see Donfried). Such a claim was made for Caesar Augustus in an inscription found in Asia:

> Divine Providence . . . has now crowned our life with the best by bringing in Augustus and has filled him with noble concern for the welfare (benefaction) of all humanity and has sent him to us and to those who come after us (as a Savior) who will put an end to war and set every thing in order . . . (trans. in Danker, p. 7).

Paul writes that "when they say peace and security then comes sudden destruction on them." The prosperity and safety that the emperors of Rome can provide are only illusory. The second coming of Christ — who comes as a thief in the night — will bring tribulation and judgment and will expose all man's deceptive claims of self-sufficiency.

Probably most popular were the mystery cults, so-called because of their secret initiation rites. In general they were frenzied and orgiastic. Some involved self-mutilation and many participated in drinking and sexual licentiousness. The cult of Dionysus, the god of wine and fertility, was especially notorious for drunken debauchery. The original rite apparently involved tearing a live animal to pieces and consuming the raw flesh in a frenzied outburst of emotion. By the New Testament period the savagery of the cult had cooled but the uninhibited nature of the rites remained, especially regarding excesses in wine and sexual looseness.

Even more popular at Thessalonica, as the pictures on coins show, was the cult of the Cabiri. This cult shared many of the same characteristics as the Dionysus cult such as feasting, drinking, and moral debauchery. In addition, the Cabiri were believed to provide safety for sailors and benefaction to manual laborers.

Surely into such a context one should place Paul's admonition against sexual licentiousness and drunkenness (Donfried). Paul writes in 1 Thess 4:4 that he wants each man to "learn to control his own body in a way that is holy and honorable, not in passionate lust like the heathen." The new Thessalonian Christians had for the most part come from pagan backgrounds where sexual debauchery was commonplace. Further, they were continually confronted with such practices especially during pagan feasts when almost the whole city must have taken part in some sense. The temptation must have been intense to continue in such immorality. Probably some Thessalonian Christians even saw little wrong with continued participation in immorality. Paul's response is that the Christian is to live in holiness and honor. Something new has happened to these people. They have been called not "to be impure, but to live a holy life" (1 Thess 4:7) and thus their old lives are left behind.

When Paul uses the term "called" he is describing the new status and new relationship of the Thessalonians. Paul employs this term repeatedly to describe Christians (Rom 8:30; 9:24; 1 Cor 1:9; 7:15;

Eph 4:1; Gal 1:6; 5:13). Even the Greek word rendered "church" in English comes from the same root as the word "called," so the church is literally "the called out."

Paul's language is probably based on Isaiah, especially the Greek version of Isaiah. In Isa 41:8-9 God says, "You, Israel, my servant, Jacob whom I chose, the seed of Abraham whom I loved, whom I took hold of from the ends and corners of the earth and *called* . . . ." In Isa 42:6 God says, "I the Lord your God *called* you in righteousness . . ." (also 46:11; 48:12; 51:2). Here the term refers to God's gracious invitation to salvation, service, and a new relationship of covenant.

Paul probably refers to the mystery cults' nocturnal excesses of drinking in 1 Thess 5:5-8. As children of God due to their relationship with Christ, the crucified and risen Lord, they can have no place for any other god and the sinful practices associated with that god. For Christ has "died for us . . . so that we might live together with him" (1 Thess 5:10).

Clearly while Paul and his associates Silas and Timothy were still at Thessalonica they made a beginning in teaching doctrine and ethics. But because Paul had had to depart so abruptly he could not lead the Thessalonians as far as he wished. Moreover the visit of Timothy was necessary to "strengthen them and exhort them" (1 Thess 3:2). Timothy would help complete the job of maturation among the Thessalonians.

But Timothy's presence alone would not be enough. The new believers would want their beloved apostle and "father" in the faith (1 Thess 1:11) to be present in some sense. Paul then sent the letters to assist in nurturing the Thessalonians. Teachers and philosophers commonly used letter writing in antiquity to maintain friendship with their students and to deliver further instructions. The writer would give assurance that he had not forgotten his students and ask that the letter substitute for the time being for his presence. Paul's letters to Thessalonica functioned similarly. They gave the Thessalonians contact with Paul and allowed for more teaching and reinforcing what he had already taught.

Paul constantly reminds the Thessalonians of what he had taught them in his short stay at Thessalonica. In 1 Thess 4:1-2 he urges them "to live and please God . . . even as you learned from us." In 2 Thess 2:15 and 3:6 Paul speaks of "traditions" which the Thessalonian must keep. These traditions are moral and doctrinal teachings which have been handed on by word of mouth from teacher to student. The early church then had a set body of doctrine and moral teaching which was memorized and then taught to new converts. Paul's letters are to remind the Thessalonians to a large extent of the "tradition" which he had taught them.

One of the teachings Paul calls to mind is "to lead a quiet life, to mind your own business, and to work with your hands" (1 Thess 4:11). The reasons they should pursue such a lifestyle are so they can gain the respect of "outsiders" (non-Christians) and not be dependent on anyone. Here Paul is undoubtedly referring to the practice of ancient religious leaders and philosophers of refusing manual labor as beneath them and, instead, spending their days meddling in everyone else's affairs and expecting the populace or a wealthy patron financially to support them (see Malherbe).

One ancient critic sarcastically quoted such a meddlesome teacher as saying:

> I hold it unnecessary to be a merchant or a farmer or a soldier or to follow a trade; I shout, go dirty, take cold baths, walk about barefoot in winter, wear a filthy mantle and like Momus carp at everything the others do (Lucian, *Icaromenippus* 31, trans. Malherbe p. 100).

The Thessalonian believers are not to follow the bad example of Greek philosophers (Cynics) who publically meddle in the business of everyone else and refuse to work. Rather they should live a quiet life, minding their own business, not stirring people up, and they should work at their trade, not live by begging or charging for their teaching of the gospel.

Probably Paul's instructions in 1 Thess 5:14 "to warn those who are idle" relates to the same problem as 4:11. Likewise are the references in 2 Thess 3:6, 11 to stay away from idlers and busybodies and not to feed them. Perhaps the problem grew even worse by the time 2 Thess was written. The heightened fervor for the second coming of Christ must surely have intensified the Thessalonians' belief that they need not work at their trades any longer.

In several places, Paul urges the Thessalonians to greater love of each other. He knows that they have already displayed love (1 Thess 3:6; 4:10) but admonishes them to show even more love (1 Thess 4:10; 5:13). They must care for the weak and faint-hearted (1 Thess 5:14) and nurture them and they must love their church leaders (1 Thess 5:13). Paul also paraphrases the words of Jesus (1 Thess 5:15; see Matt 5:39 and Luke 6:27) with respect to shunning vengeance. Rather they should do good to all people.

The ancient churches were islands of love and concern in a hostile world. There the outcasts and the lowly, as well as the troubled and the fearful, found refuge, acceptance and comfort in a community of people that loved them. The church gave the new Christians status as children of God, loved by God and fellow Christians alike. Jesus' admonition for his disciples to love one another (John 13:35; 15:12) was never forgotten by the early church.

Another teaching of which Paul reminds the Thessalonians is concerning suffering and affliction. He reminds them that they received the gospel "in spite of severe suffering" (1 Thess 1:6) and have suffered even as the Jewish Christians of Judea (1 Thess 2:14). In 1 Thess 3:4 he recalls that when he was still with them he warned them that afflictions would come. In his second letter he uses in addition the words "persecutions" and "trials" (2 Thess 1:4-6).

What caused the suffering among the believers at Thessalonica? Possibly the suffering was internal. The new Christians experienced anguish over being rejected by family and friends because of their new lifestyle. The use of the term "persecutions" in 2 Thess, however, makes it clear that most of their suffering was external and the result of persecution.

Probably the same persecutors that drove Paul out of Thessalonica and later Berea have turned their guns on the church he left behind. One commentator (Bruce, p. 327) even suggests that the references to Satan preventing Paul from returning to Thessalonica (1 Thess 2:18) means these persecutors through whom Satan was working.

Whatever the source, Paul considered suffering a natural part of the Christian life. If they would truly imitate Paul and Christ ("the

Lord" 1 Thess 1:6; 2:14-15) they must expect to suffer. They have entered into a union with Christ so close and so intimate that they will reenact in their own lives his life and death. That is what Paul means when he writes in Phil 3:10 that he wants to know "the fellowship of sharing in his sufferings, becoming like him in his death." So too Paul can say that as a result of his suffering he "bears the marks of Jesus" (Gal 6:17).

Paul's main purpose, then, in writing the Thessalonian letters was to nurture them in the faith by reestablishing contact and reminding them of the instruction he had given them. But he had another purpose as well: to defend his ministry. First Thessalonians 2:1-12 clearly contains a defense of his missionary activity at Thessalonica. Paul states that (v. 3) his preaching at Thessalonica has not been based on error, uncleanness or deceit. He did not speak to please men (v. 4) nor flatter people to become popular and to profit financially (v. 5). He has never sought to glory from men (v. 6). Rather Paul was affectionate and gentle with them like a nurse (vv. 7, 8) or like a father (v. 11). Paul worked at his trade night and day so that he might bring the gospel to them without receiving any financial support (v. 9).

Why did Paul deem this lengthy defense necessary? He was not the only one preaching religion and philosophy in the ancient world. Cities such as Thessalonica would be teeming with preachers and teachers all claiming to offer peace of mind, wise living, or an awakened moral consciousness. Not all these peddlers of philosophy were honest. Then as now many saw the possibilities for enriching oneself. Others preached out of pride, to make a name for themselves. W. Neil's description of this situation is an apt one:

> Holy men of all creeds and countries, popular philosophers, magicians, astrologers, crack-pots and cranks, the sincere and the spurious, the righteous and the rogue, swindlers and saints jostled and clamoured for the attention of the credulous and the sceptical.

Two kinds of these preachers were especially common in antiquity. The first kind was only interested in convincing ignorant people to give them money by using deception and flattery. They "stand at street corners in alley ways and temple gates, they pass around the hat and deceive lads and sailors and crowds of that sort by stringing together puns and philosophical commonplaces and ribald jokes of the marketplace" (Dio Chrysostom, trans. in Malherbe). Paul would not be thought of as such a preacher. On the contrary, he worked at Thessalonica at his trade and took no money for preaching. No one could accuse Paul of being deceitful and greedy.

The other kind of preacher attempted not to use flattery but harshness to secure the admiration (and financial contributions) of the crowds. They would rail at the audiences with a constant stream of abusive language hoping to cloak by their harshness the lack of content of their speeches. As one might expect, this kind of preacher usually could not stay in any one town for very long since after a while the crowd grew unimpressed with such verbal abuse and turned on the preacher. Quick getaways were essential in this line of work.

Paul had not ministered to the Thessalonians in such a way. Rather he was "gentle" as a nurse and "like a mother caring for her little children" (2 Thess 2:7). Certainly Paul must have corrected and rebuked the Thessalonians, but he did so in a loving and gentle manner. He could neither condone their sin nor attack them viciously in the manner of many philosophical preachers. Paul was not interested in "telling them off" but in guiding them toward maturity.

Who accused Paul of being like the charlatans? We think immediately of those from the synagogue that drove him from Thessalonica. Perhaps they have attempted to win back some of their losses by attacking Paul. After all, had he not left Thessalonica rather suddenly as many of the pagan preachers were wont to do?

Paul's response is simply to remind the believers of his conduct in Thessalonica. No one who worked with his hands night and day so that he could bring the gospel to them free of charge and who lived among them and spoke to them as a "nurse" or "mother" could have anything but their best interest at heart.

The Thessalonian letters then not only give us insights into the nature of the church and its beliefs in the mid-first century; they also give us a glimpse of Paul's method of ministry. As in all things Paul based his actions on the model of Christ the servant and in the motivation of love.

The Misunderstanding over the Second Coming of Christ

The teaching in 1 and 2 Thessalonians about the second coming (παρουσία, *parousia*) of Christ is significant enough that it deserves a special section of its own. Clearly the Thessalonian Christians (or at least some of them) held misconceptions about the second coming or parousia of Christ, but how serious were the misconceptions? Many commentators answer that the misconceptions were very serious and that they can be theologically connected with other problems to which Paul refers, such as sexual looseness (1 Thess 4:3-6) or the idler (1 Thess 5:14; 2 Thess 3:6, 11).

In an attempt to get a clearer picture, some commentators have looked for examples in both ancient and recent history of religious groups which they think must have had similar ideas to the Thessalonian error. These other groups which can be studied in more detail can then be compared with the Thessalonians as we have them depicted in the letters.

One popular example-group is the enthusiast group (taking the word "enthusiast" in its original meaning as one who has an infusion of God or the Spirit in his person). Commentators who use this example see the problem in a group at Thessalonica which supposed they, by possessing the gifts of the Spirit, had already experienced the *parousia*. Their spiritual experiences led to such a fervor that they could not believe anything better could be awaiting them in terms of a literal coming of Christ. Christ has already come again in the Holy Spirit (2 Thess 2:2). No further coming is needed, they thought. Furthermore, if there will be no literal second coming of Christ neither will there be a literal resurrection of the dead.

But then one or some from the group at Thessalonica died. If no literal resurrection can be expected then the separation of the church member through death is permanent. Thus Paul must teach otherwise in 1 Thess 4:13.

Commentators using this example to understand the Thessalonian church claim the "idlers" were the members of the enthusiast group. They were "busybodies" (2 Thess 3:11) in the sense that they tried to convince everyone else in the church to accept their views.

Other students of the New Testament use ancient Gnosticism as the model for understanding the Thessalonian letters. Gnosticism was never one organized religion and so took many forms in various regions. In general, however, one can say that Gnostics believed in some sort of salvation by knowledge (γνῶσις, *gnōsis*) and had a disdain for this physical world and all that is in it (even their own physical bodies). Obviously, then, such people could not believe in the literal resurrection of the body. Some Gnostics also tended to live morally loose lives due to their disdain of the flesh. Since the physical body was of no importance one could do with it as one pleased. Thus Paul, these commentators maintain, must correct their immorality in 1 Thess 4:3-6.

A third model or example-group used in studying the Thessalonian heresy is the millennarian model (see Jewett). These are groups which date from the Middle Ages to recent times and who believe so fervently and earnestly that an era of paradise is near they cease all normal activities. People have been known to abandon their homes and leave their farms untended. One group even killed all their cattle in an act of fanaticism, since they believed they soon would not be needing them. Others give away or quickly spend their life savings. People quit their jobs and wait.

Such a model would seek to explain why Paul says the second coming will not occur until the "rebellion" comes, the "man of lawlessness" (2 Thess 2:3). The Thessalonians must not necessarily assume the end is near. This model would also explain the existence of the idlers. People in such millennarian groups commonly abandon their jobs and live in idleness waiting for the new age to come. Perhaps one can even explain the reference to immorality (1 Thess 4:3-6) with this example-group since occasionally such groups live without moral restraints.

If one has to choose, the third model is probably the best. The extreme sense of urgency of the typical millennarian group and their idle waiting for paradise to dawn accords well with the situation at Thessalonica.

We must be very careful, however, with models. While they can help us understand some otherwise inexplicable phenomena, they may not be identical to the Thessalonian situation. It does not necessarily follow that there was an organized group of millennarians so that all Paul says about the second coming (1 Thess 4:13-5:3; 2 Thess 2:1-12) is in rebuttal of them. Perhaps there are several small groups or individuals with different misconceptions. It also does not necessarily follow that what Paul says about immorality (1 Thess 4:3-6) has anything to do with a fanatical belief in the second coming. These may be two unrelated errors which Paul addresses. Even the idlers probably should not be *totally* explained by the millennarian example-group since we can explain them just as well from Greco-Roman culture (see above). To make all of Paul's teachings in 1 and 2 Thess corrections of one homogeneous, heretical group, whether enthusiast, gnostic, or millennarian, is unwarranted.

Furthermore, if a group did exist similar to one of the suggested models and if it were so dominant in the Thessalonian church as to evoke two letters from Paul dealing exclusively with it, we should expect a somewhat more irate tone from Paul. Paul's letters to the Galatians and Corinthians (2 Cor) for example are hot and urgent. He must deal with a dangerous and threatening heresy. Those letters seem to picture one heretical group, theologically homogeneous, which is threatening the church.

But few would say the tone of the Thessalonian letters is similar to Galatians or 2 Corinthians. Paul commends the Thessalonian believers for being examples to all of Macedonia and Achaia in sending forth the gospel to others (1 Thess 1:7, 8). Paul has heard from Timothy the good report of their faith and love (1 Thess 3:6). He basically finds the church commendable but needing Paul to "supply what is lacking" (1 Thess 3:10).

It is in view of correcting such deficiencies that Paul wrote 1 Thess 4:13-5:3. Evidently, at least some Thessalonian Christians believed the new age was about to dawn. But some of their fellow Christians had died ("fallen asleep") and so they concluded that their dead brothers and sisters in Christ would miss the kingdom.

They seem to have had no knowledge of the general resurrection.

Thus Paul wrote about the second coming of Christ in 1 Thessalonians to correct a misconception over the dead saints. Christians should not worry about their loved ones who sleep in the Lord. The dead will participate as well as those left alive at the *parousia*. The death of some church members should not discourage the Thessalonian believers but rather they should remain ready and eager for Christ's coming, who comes as a thief in the night.

It appears that Paul's letter worked too well. His admonition to be ready for the thief in the night has "encouraged an overly heated expectation of an imminent event" (Jewett, p. 187). One can see how the Thessalonian Christians could read too much into 1 Thessalonians so that they would become more certain that the day was close. Paul's urging for them not to be discouraged over the death of some of their members made them even more fanatically expectant of the *parousia*.

Paul wrote 2 Thessalonians to correct these misconceptions. 2 Thess 2:3-10 gives signs attending the *parousia*. Since certain events must take place before or along with the *parousia* and since they were not yet taking place it would be erroneous to claim that the *parousia* had come.

(2:3) "Unless the rebellion occurs (the *parousia* will not come) . . . ." The words in parentheses are not in the Greek text but are clearly implied and something similar can be found in almost every translation. The word "rebellion" is normally used for political rebellion but comes to mean religious rebellion in the New Testament (Acts 21:21; Heb 3:12; 1 Tim 4:1). Some commentators believe Paul is referring to the Jewish rebellion against Rome which began in A.D. 66. Most, however, see this as a religious rebellion against God.

". . . and unless the man of lawlessness is revealed, the man doomed to destruction. . . ." The man of lawlessness (a better translation than "the man of sin") will apparently lead in this rebellion. He will have no regard for God's commandments, laws or morality and thus is called lawless. His description "son of destruction" (the exact expression used of Judas in John 17:12) indicates his end.

Who is the man of lawlessness? Many answers have been given to this question throughout history:

1. Many early Christians and some moderns say it was Nero or some other persecuting Roman emperor.

2. In the Middle Ages he was identified with Mohammed.

3. The reformers and many moderns say he is the Pope of Rome.

4. In the nineteenth century some claimed Napoleon was the man of lawlessness.

5. In the twentieth century many named Hitler or Mussolini as the man of lawlessness.

In addition, many premillennialists hold that the man of lawlessness is identical to the Beast of Revelation 13. He will be a worldwide dictator that will deceive many into worshiping him. He will be in power, according to dispensationalists, during the seven years of tribulation.

Amillennialists often say the man of lawlessness could be a movement, an institution, or an individual. This movement may begin as a principle of evil, but grows until it is embodied in a specific group or person just before the *parousia*.

(2:4) "He will oppose and will exalt himself over everything that is called God or is worshiped." The man of lawlessness will oppose religion of any kind, not just Christianity — except, as we shall see, worship of himself. He will allow no rivals in religion.

". . . so that he sets himself up in God's temple." Does this refer to the literal temple at Jerusalem? Most premillennialists believe it does and expect the temple to be rebuilt so this can happen. Others say this refers to the church (1 Cor 3:16-17; 2 Cor 6:16; Eph 2:21) and see the man of lawlessness leading a great falling away from Christ's church. Still others say this whole clause is purely figurative and stands for the pretensions of the man of lawlessness. He will try to take the place that rightfully belongs to God.

". . . proclaiming himself to be God." The language is reminiscent of Ezek 28:2, Isa 14:13 and Dan 11:36. These passages describe ancient near eastern kings who exalted themselves to the level of gods. But as the true God humbled each one of them, so he will do with this usurper.

(2:5) "Don't you remember that when I was with you I used to tell you about these things?" The Greek indicates Paul had several lessons on this topic while at Thessalonica. Much of this section is then a reminder (see Chapter 1 on this).

(2:6-7) "And now you know what is holding him back, so that he may be revealed at the proper time. For the secret power of lawlessness is already at work; but the one who now holds it back will continue to do so until he is taken out of the way." In these two verses Paul refers to a restraint (neuter gender, v. 6) and a restraining person (masculine gender, v. 7). These restraints prevent the man of lawlessness from coming onto the stage of history. Only when the restrainer is "out of the way" (or "is removed" or "leaves the scene") will the man of lawlessness arise.

(2:8) "And then the lawless one will be revealed, whom the Lord Jesus will overthrow with the breath of his mouth and destroy by the splendor of his coming." Paul paraphrases Isa 11:4 to show that at Christ's *parousia* or second coming he will destroy the leader of the lawless rebellion instantly. His mere coming will bring this about. The vaunted opponent of God will perish at the command of the coming king.

(2:9, 10) "The coming of the lawless one will be in accordance with the work of Satan displayed in all kinds of counterfeit miracles, signs, and wonders, and in every sort of evil that deceives those who are perishing. They perish because they refused to love the truth and so be saved." The man of lawlessness will have Satanic power to do deceptive miracles (Matt 24:24; Rev 13:13) and hoodwink those that do not believe in Christ. In their rejection of truth (that is, the gospel) they have become more susceptible to a lie.

Notice Paul never offered a timetable for all these events. He neither said when they would happen nor how long they would endure. His purpose was to cool some of the millennarian fervor for the second coming. The day of the Lord had not come since the man of lawlessness and his destruction had not yet come first. Thus the Thessalonian believers should go about their daily tasks, working in quietness and waiting patiently on the Lord. Since no timetable is available for the parousia there is no place for "idlers" (2 Thess 3:6-12). These people only stir up trouble and create a burden on others to feed them. The proper Christian attitude is to wait joyfully yet patiently for Christ's coming.

THE PASTORAL EPISTLES:
1 AND 2 TIMOTHY AND TITUS

Bibliography: C.K. Barrett, *The Pastoral Epistles*; M. Dibelius and
H. Conzelmann, *The Pastoral Epistles*; G.D. Fee, *1 and 2 Timothy and
Titus*; R.M. Grant, *A Historical Introduction to the New Testament*; D.
Guthrie, *NTI*; Idem, *The Pastoral Epistles*; W. Hendriksen, *Exposition
of the Pastoral Epistles*; J.N.D. Kelly, *The Pastoral Epistles*; W. Locke, *A
Critical and Exegetical Commentary on the Pastoral Epistles*; D.R.
MacDonald, *The Legend and the Apostle*; B. Metzger, "A Recon-
sideration of Certain Arguments Against the Pauline Authorship of
the Pastoral Epistles" *Expository Times* 70.3 (1958) 91-94; D.C.
Verner, *The Household of God: The Social World of the Pastoral Epistles*.

Authorship and Date

Four arguments have been advanced against the authenticity of
the Pastoral letters, although all of the letters claim to have been
written by Paul (1 Tim 1:1; 2 Tim 1:1; Titus 1:1).

A. First, scholars point out the historical problems with the
events alluded to in these epistles. The letters indicate that Paul
traveled to Macedonia, leaving Timothy behind in Ephesus (1 Tim
1:3), that Paul has been to Crete and left Titus there (Titus 1:5)
while he himself went on to Nicopolis (Titus 3:12), and that Paul has
recently visited Troas (2 Tim 4:13) and Miletus (2 Tim 4:20). In
2 Timothy, further, Paul is in prison in Rome (1:8, 16-17) and Titus
is in Dalmatia (4:10). Although some of these events might be harmonious with the events recorded in Acts, others must have happened after the story of Acts ends. When did Paul visit Crete other
than as a prisoner? When was Paul at Nicopolis? When did Titus
leave Crete for Dalmatia (or vice versa)? It is universally agreed that
none of these situations fit into the life of Paul from his conversion
to his journey to Rome recorded in Acts (see *FBK*).

Thus two solutions are usually proposed: (1) The Pastorals are
pseudonymous or written by someone other than Paul but falsely
attributed to Paul. But this conclusion is based on the assumption

that Paul was executed in A.D. 62 at the end of his two-year imprisonment (Acts 28:30) and thus could not have been released for
further missionary activity. Such an assumption is unwarranted. The
ancient sources (see Chapter 8) never indicate that Paul was executed so early. (2) The Pastorals were written after the history narrated in Acts ends. Paul was released after his two-year imprisonment in Rome and then traveled and taught widely, dying by
execution, according to one view sometime in A.D. 64-65 and
according to another view in A.D. 68.

B. Second, scholars cite ecclesiastical reasons for doubting the
Pauline authorship of the Pastorals. The church organization, it is
claimed, is too advanced, too similar to the organization of the
second century. The bishop is a man of high authority in these
letters as he became in the second century.

But the bishop is not really described in the same terms in the
Pastorals (1 Tim 3:1-7) as in the second century letters of Ignatius
and Polycarp. The latter describe a monarchical episcopate. That is,
only one bishop rules over a congregation and he has great authority and prestige. The same cannot be said for the bishops described
in the Pastorals (also called "elders" in Titus 1:5-9). Nowhere do
these letters state or imply that only one bishop ruled the congregation.

C. Third, scholars suggest certain doctrinal problems. The use of
the word "faith" is especially problematic because the author uses it
not to mean "faithfulness" or "trust" but to mean a body of dogma
(e.g., 1 Tim 4:1). Many are turning from "the faith" or rejecting true
doctrine. This usage is allegedly not Pauline. But Paul was a very
eclectic person when it came to words. If this concept was becoming
in vogue at this time, he could easily have employed it. People, especially good writers like Paul, are not as rigidly predictable as historians often assume.

D. Fourth, some scholars assert that the vocabulary of the
Pastorals is un-Pauline. As we maintained above, however, with
regard to Colossians, Paul was quite capable of reflecting the vocabulary of his opponents in formulating his counter arguments.
Basing conclusions on vocabulary is very tricky in general and especially so with documents as small as the Pastoral Epistles. R.M.

Grant warns about the difficulties of proving non-authenticity by statistics.[46]

In conclusion, the case against the Pauline authorship of the Pastorals is not convincing. Paul should therefore be assumed to have been the author.

The dates conservatives have traditionally assigned to these letters are from A.D. 66-68. But we can see no convincing historical explanation as to why Paul would have been executed in A.D. 68. Much more likely is A.D. 64-65 (see Chapter 8) as Paul's date of death. Thus 1 Timothy and Titus were written between A.D. 62 — when Paul was released from his first Roman imprisonment — and 64 or 65 — his second imprisonment in Rome. 2 Timothy was written in late A.D. 64 or 65, shortly before Paul's death.

The Heresy at Work in the Congregations

A similar false teaching was at work both on the island of Crete and in the area of Ephesus. This false teaching is called "doctrines of demons" and the false teachers follow "deceiving spirits" (1 Tim 4:1). The teachers are liars and their consciences have been so scarred or cauterized that they no longer function. They do not tolerate sound or healthy doctrine (2 Tim 4:3). Thus the errorists are teaching doctrines which are causing great turmoil in the churches.

The content of these doctrines is as follows: The errorists evidently taught that creation was evil (1 Tim 4:7) since Paul defends it as good, and they may have taught that there was more than one God (1 Tim 2:5). They denied that Jesus truly lived in the flesh (1 Tim 3:16) in his earthly life, and claimed that the general resurrection at the last day had already happened metaphorically or spiritually (2 Tim 2:18). They must have attacked the authority and inspiration of "Scripture" (i.e., the Old Testament, see 2 Tim 3:15-16). The errorists were fascinated with "myths and genealogies" which somehow related to Judaism (1 Tim 1:4; 4:7; 2 Tim 4:4; Titus 1:14; 3:9). Some scholars see these myths and genealogies as stories and

---

[46]As Grant notes, there are in all 901 different words in the Pastorals. Of these, 306 words are not found in any other Pauline letter.

genealogies from the Old Testament (Kelly). Others maintain they are Gnostic stories about the descent of the gods (Dibelius). Further, the errorists practice asceticism of the body, forbidding marriage (1 Tim 4:2-3) and restricting certain foods, saying that they are unholy (1 Tim 4:3-5). These restrictions evidently included wine (1 Tim 5:23).

What is this teaching? The combination of denigration of creation, despising the flesh and the Old Testament, asceticism, the use of myths and belief in other gods — or perhaps emanations — sounds too much like Gnosticism to look any further. Like the Colossian heresy this Gnosticism was mixed with certain Jewish elements.

The Church Organization Represented in the Pastorals

In 1 Timothy Paul refers to bishops (ἐπίσκοποι, *episkopoi*), elders (πρεσβύτεροι, *presbyteroi*), deacons (διάκονοι, *diakonoi*) and widows (χήραι, *chērai*).[47] In his letter to Titus (1:5-9) he gives the qualifications of elders but also calls them bishops. In general those who hold one of these offices must have good moral character, be reliable and in control of their emotions.

It is interesting to note that Paul gives two lists of qualifications for the bishops or elders,[48] but the various qualifications in 1 Tim 3:2-7 and Titus 1:5-9 are not identical. Some of the same qualifications are found in both lists, some are similar but not identical and others are completely different. The lists of qualifications for elders (and for deacons) should therefore be viewed as general guidelines. Otherwise Paul would have used the same qualifications in each list. This conclusion should prompt caution in too rigid an application of any specific qualification. It is the general thrust of these qualifications or the qualifications taken as a whole that should be emphasized.

---

[47]1 Tim 3:1-13; 5:3-20.

[48]It is better to assume these two titles were used for the same office. In Titus 1:5-7 Paul seems to use the two terms interchangeably.

Comparison of qualifications lists

1 Tim 3:2-7	Titus 1:5-9
irreproachable	*blameless*
husband of one wife	**husband of one wife**
temperate	*having faithful children*
prudent	not accused of debauchery
respectable	not disobedient
hospitable	**not drunken**
skilled in teaching	**not pugnacious**
not drunken	*not fond of dishonest gain*
not pugnacious	**hospitable**
gentle	loving what is good
peaceful	**prudent**
not greedy	just
managing his own household well	holy
having his own children in subjection	self-control
not newly converted	*holding to the faithful word*
	according to the teaching

Key: **identical words**; *similar ideas*; different

Was there an office for women known as "widow"? Giving the qualifications seems unusual unless these are qualifications for an office (1 Tim 5:5-16). It is also interesting in this connection that an important Christian writer of the second century A.D., Polycarp of Smyrna, gave a somewhat similar list of qualifications for widows (Polycarp, *Letter to the Philippians* 4:3).

2 Timothy

The last letter that Paul wrote — at least the last one we possess — was 2 Timothy. In this letter Paul shows clearly his prescience about his coming death. He firmly believes he will be executed. His most touching words come in 2 Tim 4:6-8: "For I am already being poured out like a drink offering, and the time has come for my departure. I have fought the good fight, I have finished the race, I have kept the faith. Now there is in store for me the crown of righteousness, which the Lord, the faithful judge, will award to me on that day — and not only to me, but also to all who have longed for his appearing."

Shortly after writing this letter and sending it to Timothy, Paul was led out along the Ostian Way and beheaded (see Chapter 8).

CHAPTER 10

THE GENERAL EPISTLES

The New Testament, according to most ancient manuscripts, contains two collections of letters: those of Paul and seven others called the Catholic (meaning "universal") or General Epistles (James; 1 and 2 Peter; Jude; and 1, 2, and 3 John). The latter were so named because they were considered to have been originally circular letters for the church as a whole and not sent to a specific congregation. Paul's letters, on the other hand, were sent to Corinth, Thessalonica, etc. The designation "General" or "Catholic," however, only fits some of the seven letters. 1 Peter, 2 John and 3 John are addressed to specific locations (see 1 Peter 1:1; 2 John 1; and 3 John 1), thus they are not really general letters.

We will nonetheless treat 1 Peter in this chapter since it is almost always still considered as a general epistle. The Johannine letters, however, will be handled in Chapter 11 along with the book of Revelation.

One additional epistle, the Epistle to the Hebrews, will be discussed in this chapter. Although Hebrews was, in antiquity, usually placed among the Pauline epistles, the author probably was not Paul. Therefore some include Hebrews in the General Epistles; others put Hebrews in an appendix to the Pauline letters.

HEBREWS

Bibliography: H. Attridge, *Hebrews*; F.F. Bruce, *The Epistle to the Hebrews*; G.W. Buchanan, *To the Hebrews*; Guthrie, *NTI*; O. Hoffius, *Katapausis*; P.E. Hughes, "The Epistle to the Hebrews" in E.J. Epp and G.W. MacRae, eds., *The New Testament and its Modern Interpreters*; W.L. Lane, *Hebrews*; W. Manson, *The Epistle to the Hebrews*; N. Lightfoot, *Jesus Christ Today*; R. Milligan, *Commentary on Hebrews*; H. Montefiore, *A Commentary on the Epistle to the Hebrews*; Y. Yadin, "The Dead Sea Scrolls and the Epistle to the Hebrews" in C. Rabin and Y. Yadin, eds., *Aspects of the Dead Sea Scrolls*.

Authorship

The author of this epistle did not sign his name. Therefore we are left to speculate about his identity. The following are the three most commonly suggested authors:

A. Paul. Many in the ancient church of the eastern Greco-Roman world, notably Clement of Alexandria (A.D. 200), believed Paul was the author. But most modern interpreters — both liberal and conservative — would argue that Paul did not write this letter. Too many typical Pauline features are absent from this letter (e.g., the greeting, the thanksgiving, exposition followed by exhortation, and the signing of his name) for it to be Paul's. In addition, the Greek style is totally different from Paul's. Still, it is possible that an amanuensis wrote the letter for Paul as Origen (A.D. 220) first suggested.

B. Barnabas. Barnabas, Paul's sometime missionary associate, is the other ancient suggestion. Tertullián of North Africa (A.D. 200) first attributed the epistle to the Hebrews to Barnabas. This suggestion is better than the first one since there is nothing that prevents us from accepting Barnabas as the author. The attestation for Barnabas' authorship is very slim, but it evidently goes back before the time of Tertullian.

C. Apollos. Martin Luther first suggested that Apollos, the eloquent Alexandrian missionary (Acts 18:24), wrote this epistle. His speculation was based evidently on the supposed Alexandrian Greek style of the letter (see below). This is a plausible hypothesis but lacks any ancient attestation. Yet if Apollos did not write this epistle, someone very much like him did.

D. Other names that have been posited as the author of Hebrews are: Luke, Clement of Rome, Silvanus (Silas), Timothy, Epaphras, Philip the Evangelist, Priscilla, and even Mary the mother of Jesus!

We are left to conclude that we do not know the name of the author, but we do know what kind of person he[1] was. He was educated, cultured and able to write in eloquent Greek. He was steeped in the Old Testament and had knowledge of the temple. He was deeply committed to the Lordship of Christ and was probably a Christian preacher of great influence. Finally, the author was a companion of Timothy (Hebrews 13:23) and so probably was an associate or former associate of Paul.

Date

Since Clement of Rome has so many allusions to the epistle to the Hebrews in his own letter, Hebrews must have been written before A.D. 95 (the date of 1 Clement). Second, since Hebrews omits any reference to the destruction of Jerusalem and the temple — an event that would have made his argument about the abrogation of the temple worship much more forceful (see Hebrews 9 and 10) — the epistle must have been written before A.D. 70.

Further, if the letter was sent to Christians in Rome about to suffer persecution under Nero (see below), then a date around or just before A.D. 64 is required. Thus, we conclude that Hebrews was written certainly before A.D. 70 and possibly around A.D. 64.

Destination

Numerous suggestions have been offered as to the destination of this epistle. Most of the suggestions concern the eastern half of the

---

[1]As Attridge points out, the gender of the participle referring to the author in 11:32 is masculine. Thus the author was male.

Roman Empire. Alexandria, Ephesus, Colossae, Corinth, Caesarea, and Antioch of Syria have all been proposed by one scholar or other as the place to which Hebrews was sent. Yet by far, most historians argue for either Palestine or Rome as the destination.

A. Palestine. Many of the older commentators (e.g., Milligan), assuming that the recipients were Jewish Christians who were tempted to apostasize to Judaism, believed that the letter was sent to Palestine. Many of these commentators also concluded that Barnabas was the author. A more recent scholar, Y. Yadin, has maintained that the letter was sent to Palestine to converts from the Essenes at Qumran. These converts had retained some of their previous beliefs, wrote Yadin, and therefore needed further instruction.

The main problem with the Palestinian view is the nature of the letter itself. It is perhaps the most literary and eloquent of all the New Testament documents. Would such a letter be sent to Jewish Christians of Palestine where Greek was at best a second language and for many unknown or only crudely known? In addition, as Guthrie points out, the apparent generosity of the recipients of this letter (Heb 6:10; 10:34; 13:16) does not harmonize well with the poverty of the Jerusalem church.

B. Rome. Because of the reference to Italy in Hebrews 13:24 ("those *from* Italy greet you"), many modern scholars (e.g., Bruce, Lane) have concluded that the letter was sent to Italy with the Italians in the author's company sending their greetings. If the letter had been written in Italy — say, to Palestine — with the Italian Christians sending greetings, the author would have written "those *in* Italy greet you."[2]

Further, the details of the persecutions alluded to in Hebrews fit

---

[2]The author could, of course, have sent the letter to Palestine while himself being in a location outside of Italy and addressing the greeting, for some unknown reason, of Italian Christians in his company. But such a scenario is less likely.

[3]The King James Version accepted an inferior manuscript reading here and so translated "you had compassion of *me* in *my* bonds" (10:34) as if the author had been in prison. But the word "my" is not found in most of the best manuscripts.

the situation in Rome. First, they had some years earlier suffered the loss of their property and were put in prison (Heb 10:32-34).[3] This persecution described in Hebrews accurately reflects the situation in A.D. 49 when the Jews — including of course Jewish Christians — were expelled from Rome by Emperor Claudius. The problem seems to have stemmed from riots between Jews that had accepted Christ and those that had not. Suetonius, the Roman historian records: "Because the Jews at Rome caused continuous disturbances at the instigation of Chrestus, (Claudius) expelled them from the city (of Rome)" (*Claudius* 25; trans. by R. Graves).

Evidently Claudius thought Chrestus (or Jesus Christ) was actually in Rome stirring up the riots since the Jews were arguing and rioting over him. Jewish Christians had been evangelizing in the Jewish quarter of Rome and this caused the riots. To keep the peace, Claudius expelled all Jews from Rome — including believing Jews — and confiscation of their property also took place. The leaders were apparently even imprisoned (see also Chapter 9, Romans).

All of this happened years before the epistle was written. The Jewish Christians had by now been allowed to return to Rome. But then (around A.D. 64) another persecution, that of Nero, seemed imminent. The author wrote that the recipients of the letter had "not yet resisted to the point of bloodshed" (Heb 12:4), meaning that no one had yet been executed for his faith. But "not yet" implies martyrdom could be soon to come. He urged the readers to persevere and not shrink back (Heb 10:36-39) and to endure hardship as a discipline (Heb 12:7). He held up for them as models the heroes of the Old Testament who suffered terrible persecutions (Heb 11:34-38) and especially the life of Jesus who suffered the cross (Heb 12:3). Clearly the author was bracing his readers for a horrible persecution.

The historical situation in Rome — that is the expulsion of the Jews in A.D. 49 and Nero's fire and persecution of Christians in A.D. 64 — fits nicely into the background of Hebrews. In addition, Hebrews was first quoted in antiquity by Clement of Rome (in A.D. 95). Thus it seems plausible that the letter was first known there. We conclude, therefore, that Rome is the best choice for destination of the epistle.

Purpose

The following reasons have been suggested for writing the epistle to the Hebrews (see Guthrie):

A. The epistle was written to warn Jewish Christians against apostasy to Judaism. The title ("to the Hebrews") of the letter was known by the Alexandrian author, Pantaenus (A.D. 180), Clement of Alexandria (A.D. 200) and Tertullian (A.D. 200). In addition, the oldest manuscript of Hebrews (P46 from A.D. 200) has the same title. Thus, if the title was original, we should conclude, according to this view, that the readers were Jewish Christians.

B. The letter was written to counteract an early heresy such as Jewish Gnosticism, according to others. But the evidence of Gnosticism is very tenuous. The author's assertion that Jesus is above angels (Heb 1:4) need not mean that some were worshiping angels as at Colossae (Col 2:18).

C. Still others affirm that Hebrews was composed to announce the absolute character of Christianity to mainly Gentile Christians. The author surely wanted to prove — from Old Testament quotations and analogies — that Christianity is not just another religion. Rather it is the unique and perfect way.

D. Finally, it is posited by some that the letter was to encourage Christians enduring persecution (see above).

There were probably several motives behind the letter. Indeed all of those listed above, except perhaps the second, are plausible. We should probably emphasize, however, that the recipients were in the main Jewish Christians under persecution who were in danger of giving up the faith. To encourage and strengthen them the author used the greatly loved institutions of the Old Testament religion — the temple, the priesthood, and the sacrifices — to demonstrate Jesus' superiority in comparison.

Background

Did the author of Hebrews come from a specific group within Judaism and therefore employ some of the ideas and vocabulary of his background? Scholars have argued for one of two — probably mutually exclusive — backgrounds for this letter: Philonic Judaism and Qumran Judaism (for general information on Philo, see Chapter 7; for Qumran, see Chapter 2).

A. Philo. Commentators of a century ago often argued that the author of Hebrews was a student of Philo and was merely trying to Christianize Philo's Jewish theology. There certainly are some interesting parallels: similar Greek words and phrases, similar ways of citing the Septuagint, use of Melchizedek as a type (Heb 7) and other parallels (see Guthrie and Attridge). But most modern commentators would deny that our author was actually Christianizing Philonism or even that he had been a student of Philo. The significant differences — the author of Hebrews believed for example, in the endtime but Philo did not — would compel us to dismiss any direct connection between Philo and the author of our letter.

Nevertheless, as Attridge suggests, the similarities do suggest a similar general background to Philo. Thus the author was a Greek-speaking, rhetorically educated Jew like Philo. We are impressed at how well Apollos fits that description.

B. Qumran. As noted above, Yadin believed strongly that the author was writing to Christians that had come out of Qumran Essenism and that he himself had been an Essene. Again Attridge notes in his commentary many interesting parallels between Hebrews and the writings of the Dead Sea Scrolls. But many of these parallels are not peculiar only to the Qumran sect. They are found generally in Judaism. Therefore, we should be very cautious in finding any Essene background in Hebrews.

Content

The epistle contains four sections:[4]
   I. Christ the Leader of our Salvation (1:1-2:18)
  II. Exhortation to Persevere (3:1-4:16)
 III. Christ our High Priest (5:1-10:18)
 IV. Exhortation to Persevere (10:19-13:22)
    (13:23-25 concluding remarks)

---

[4]For other views on the structure of the letter, see Attridge and *FBK*.

Section one explains that Christ, the Son of God and the radiance of God's glory (1:3) is above even angels (1:4). Indeed everything is subjected to him (2:8). Yet he lived on earth as a human, even suffering death so that he could be the leader of salvation (2:10). Section three expounds on Christ, the High Priest after the order of Melchizedek — that is, an eternal High Priest — who is greater than the Jewish High Priests (7:1-28). The risen Christ has entered the tabernacle in heaven offering his own blood as expiation for sin (9:11-14), for Christ is not only the heavenly High Priest but also the sacrifice for sin. He was the perfect and final sacrifice (10:12).

The parenetic sections admonish the readers to hold fast to such a Savior. It would be folly to abandon commitment to Christ since he is the exalted Son of God and the final sacrifice for sin.

Literary Form or Genre

Many commentators have concluded that the epistle to the Hebrews was originally a sermon. The epistle begins without any greeting but with a long, rhetorically decorated sentence (1:1-4 is one sentence in Greek). In addition there are telltale signs that this epistle, or part of it, was first delivered as a sermon. Heb 11:32 says, "Time fails me to tell . . . ," indicating the kind of Greek language normally used in a speech. In Heb 13:22 the author calls the epistle a "word of exhortation." This phrase in Acts 13:15 clearly means a sermon (see Lane).

Yet Heb 13:22-25 is the kind of ending one would have in a letter, with information about individuals and with greetings given. In addition, in 13:22 the author says, "I have written you briefly." Thus Hebrews was probably originally a sermon but was later sent as a letter, probably to Rome, to Jewish Christians about to suffer — or just beginning to suffer — the persecution of Nero.

JAMES

Bibliography: J.B. Adamson, *The Epistle of James*; P.H. Davids, *The Epistle of James*; M. Dibelius, *James*; Guthrie, *NTI*; M. Hengel, "Der Jakobusbrief als antipaulinische Polemik" in G.F. Hawthorne and O. Betz, eds., *Tradition and Interpretation in the New Testament*; S. Laws, *The Epistle of James*; B.A. Pearson, "James, 1-2 Peter, Jude" in E.J. Epp and G.W. McRae, eds., *The New Testament and Its Modern Interpreters*; B. Reicke, *The Epistles of James, Peter and Jude*; J.H. Ropes, *St. James*; R.V.G. Tasker, *The General Epistle of James*.

The epistle of James presents us with primarily three problems: Who was the author (and therefore when was it written)? What is the literary genre of this letter? What is the background to the letter?

The Author

The author identifies himself simply as "James":[5] "James, servant of God and the Lord Jesus Christ, to the twelve tribes in the dispersion. Greetings" (1:1). He must have been well known to the recipients of the letter since he gives no other identifying names such as "son of so and so" or "the apostle."

Only two men named James were ever this well known in the first century church: James the son of Zebedee, who was also the brother of John and an apostle, and James the brother of Jesus. Since James the apostle died in A.D. 41, this early date probably rules him out as the author. That leaves only James, the brother of Jesus, as a likely candidate for the author.

Many have accepted this conclusion, especially many conservative scholars, but some have rejected it. First of all, the Greek is considered too good for a Galilean peasant. The style is frequently cultured and the vocabulary is large (see Dibelius). We should probably agree that a Galilean peasant could not write Greek this well but we should

---

[5]Actually his name was Jacob (Heb יַעֲקֹב, *Ya'akob*; Gk Ἰάκωβος, *Iakōbos*) which is usually rendered into English as James.

bear in mind two considerations. Much of the epistle of James is traditional material, as Dibelius himself argued. Thus the language is not necessarily always from James. Also, we must not overlook the influence of an amanuensis (see below under 1 Peter). It is quite possible that James would use a Greek expert to polish a letter to be sent to Greek-speaking Jewish Christians in the dispersion.

Second, some deny that the Lord's brother wrote this letter because there are no references to Jesus' life. As a matter of fact one scholar, F. Spitta (in 1896), maintained that the epistle was originally a Jewish tract which some Christian appropriated by merely inserting two references to Christ (at James 1:1 and 2:1). But there are many allusions to Jesus' teachings in the epistle (cf. 5:12 with Matt 5:37; 1:5 with Matt 7:7; 1:22 with Matt 7:24; 4:12 with Matt 7:1; see Guthrie) and Jews were often more inclined to remember the words of the sages than their deeds. The Talmud, for example, records many of the sayings of the rabbis but only a handful of events. Thus it should not be surprising that James offers no anecdotes about the life of Jesus.

Therefore, we see no convincing argument that the author could not have been Jesus' brother, James. James was a pillar of the Christian community in Jerusalem (Gal 1:19; 2:9) who had seen the risen Christ (1 Cor 15:7) and who had made a decisive and influential speech at the Jerusalem council (Acts 15:13-21). He was certainly known and respected enough to write to Jewish Christians in the dispersion and sign his name merely "James."

The importance of James for the early Christian church in Jerusalem is also confirmed by sources outside the New Testament. James was significant enough to be mentioned by Josephus: "(Albinus the procurator) brought before (the Sanhedrin) a man named James, the brother of Jesus who was called the Christ, and certain others. He accused them of having transgressed the law and delivered them up to be stoned" (*Ant* 20.200, trans. by L.H. Feldman).

James' death in A.D. 62 is described more fully by an early Christian author, Hegesippus (second century A.D.) who writes that the Jews conducted James into a wing of the temple and demanded that he should renounce the faith of Christ before all the people.

But instead he confessed that Jesus Christ was the Son of God. Thereupon they threw James off the temple. Since he was not dead from the fall, they began to stone him and one man, a fuller, beat him to death with his fuller's club (see Eusebius, *H.E.* 2.23).

Hegesippus's version of James' death may have some legendary elements in it but Josephus's and Hegesippus's accounts do agree about one item. James was so well known to Jewish authorities and considered so important that they executed him in the hope that the new sect, Christianity, might be stopped. Thus we should probably conclude that James was one of the four great leaders of the primitive church along with Peter, John, and Paul. Any letter signed merely "James" should *a priori* be considered as written by the Lord's brother.

If James was the author of the letter, as we have concluded, it was written before A.D. 62 and probably after the Jerusalem council in 49. After the council, Peter and John left Judea to preach in other parts of the Greco-Roman world. Peter went to Antioch, to Corinth, and finally to Rome (perhaps also Asia Minor, see below under 1 Peter); John went to Asia (see Chapter 11). That left only James of the pillars in Judea and thus his importance was gradually elevated to what we see just before his execution. We would be inclined to date the epistle sometime in the late fifties or perhaps as late as A.D. 61.

The Literary Genre

Ostensibly this is a letter written to a definite group of recipients. But there is nothing said about the recipients, there is no news given and there are no greetings or messages offered at the end of the document. Therefore we are probably correct to conclude that the epistle of James is not really a letter at all but merely a tract published as a letter. Such publications were certainly known in the ancient world.[6] Epicurus, the philosopher, wrote several "epistles"

---

[6]For this phenomenon in antiquity see M.L. Stirewalt, Jr., "The Form and Function of the Greek Letter-Essay" in K.P. Donfried, ed., *The Romans Debate.*

(three of which have survived) which were really philosophical tracts. The same thing is true of the Christian documents, the epistle of Barnabas and 2 Clement. There was apparently no definite destination for these epistles. They were merely published as epistles.

James addressed his "epistle" to the "twelve tribes in the dispersion," or to Jews living outside of the land of Israel. The contents of the letter as well as the identity of the author make it clear this was a document for Jewish Christians. Thus the epistle of James was a moral tract written for Jewish Christians in general who lived in the dispersion.

Within this moral tract are found numerous individual aphorisms grouped often with no apparent thematic purpose. Martin Luther, who disliked this epistle and assigned it a secondary place in the New Testament, complained that it is too disorganized (unlike the highly structured epistle to the Romans).

M. Dibelius has helpfully analyzed the epistle of James as an example of the genre of parenesis or admonition. Several Jewish writings, both from the dispersion — and thus written in Greek — and from Palestine — written in Hebrew — display similar characteristics both in style and in content. An example will be given here, from Ps. Phocylides 9-22, a dispersion document from the first century A.D. There are several direct parallels to James.

> Always dispense justice and let not your judgment be influenced by favor. Do not cast down the poor unjustly, do not judge partially. If you judge evilly, subsequently God will judge you. Flee false witness; award what is just. Watch over a deposit, and in everything keep faith. Give a just measure, and an extra full measure of all things is good. Do not make a balance unequal, but weigh honestly. And do not commit perjury, neither ignorantly nor willingly. The immortal God hates a perjurer, whosoever it is who has sworn. Do not steal seeds. Cursed is whoever takes (them). Give the laborer his pay, do not afflict the poor. Take heed of your tongue, keep your word hidden in (your) heart. Neither wish to do injustice, nor therefore allow another to do injustice. Give to the poor man at once, and do not tell him to come tomorrow (trans. by P.W. Van der Host in *OTP*, Vol. II).

Dibelius found five characteristics in this and similar Jewish parenetic works which are also in James:

A. There is a lack of continuity. The aphorisms seem often to be thrown together chaotically (from a thematic standpoint).

B. The sayings are, however, often connected by a catchword. Note the following example from James: "My brothers, count it all joy when you fall into various *trials*, knowing that the *trials* of your faith produce *patience*. But let *patience* have her perfect work that you may be perfect and *lacking* nothing. But if any of you *lack* wisdom let him ask of God . . ." (1:3-5). See also 1:12-13.

C. Jewish parenesis often repeats the same admonition in another place in the same document (cf. 1:2 and 1:12, 22; 4:11 and 4:17).

D. Admonitions often do not apply to a single audience and a single set of circumstances. This observation is very important. If this material is put together on a different basis than theme, we should be cautious about trying to detect the background of the recipients from reading between the lines of the epistle.

E. The material is traditional. As one can see from the above example from Ps. Phocylides, several similarities with James in content are evident. James has not copied from such books but he did know well the Jewish parenetic tradition. Thus admonitions about being slow to speak and slow to anger (1:19) do not necessarily point an accusing finger to any particular group of quarreling Christians. These are common moral parenesis. We all need to be told to hold our tongues.

The epistle was written, then, by James, the brother of Jesus, in the late fifties or early sixties to Jewish Christians in general outside Palestine. James probably used an amanuensis or secretary to polish his Greek and he wrote in a typically Jewish style using many common parenetic admonitions but fitting them, under the guidance of the Holy Spirit, to Christian teachings.

Content

The main debate about the content of James is whether or not the epistle was written to contradict Paul's theology of justification by faith. James writes in 2:14, 20 and 24: "How does it help, my brother, if someone says he has faith but has no works? Can faith save him? ... Don't you know, you vain man, that faith without works is useless? ... You see that from works a man is justified and not from faith alone."

Contrast these verses with Paul's important statement in Romans 3:28: "For we reckon that a man is justified by faith apart from works of the Law."

Furthermore, James cites Abraham as an example of someone's being justified from works (2:21-23), whereas Paul refers to him in two of his letters (Gal 3:6-9; Rom 4:1-22) as the example of one who was justified by faith.

M. Hengel has recently maintained that the entire epistle of James is a polemic against Paul. James still believed in keeping the Old Testament Law, maintains Hengel, and thought Paul was deeply in error. Thus Hengel sees in many other passages in James — in addition to 2:14-24 — a refutation of Paul. James 1:13, according to Hengel, is in response to Romans 9:17-18. James 4:13-16 is a rebuke of Paul and his missionary companions who travel from place to place "getting gain" in the sense that they win converts. James 3:1-12, the warning that teachers are subject to greater judgment, is directed at Paul, says Hengel. Even the exhortation to the elders in James 5:13-16 to pray for the sick and anoint their heads in order to heal them is a rebuke of Paul who suffered his thorn in the flesh and in spite of his prayers was not healed (see 2 Cor 12:7-9).

On the other hand, numerous recent monographs have been devoted to showing that James was not refuting Paul at all but at most was only refuting some people who misunderstood Paul (see Pearson's survey of works). These authors maintain that Luther misunderstood the epistle of James and that Luther's influence has clouded our thinking. Luther called this letter a "straw epistle" (which means something like "the letter of an emptyhead"). He believed it was too Jewish and not worthy of the exalted theology of Paul. Many modern interpreters, especially German Lutherans, have followed Luther's lead.

The problems with the view of Hengel (and a host of authors before him) are:

A. The supposed refutations of Paul in the epistle of James are not obvious. James' admonition in 4:13-16 against boastfully making long range plans to "carry on business and make money," is easily understood in its literal sense. There is no good reason for seeing this language as a metaphorical reference to Paul's missionary plans. The same can be said for virtually every one of the alleged attacks on Paul's theology and lifestyle in the epistle of James.

B. Even (what is to Hengel) the clearest contradiction of Paul — James 2:14-24 — is not really what Hengel makes of it. Paul contrasted faith with works of the Old Testament law (Rom 3:28). James never used the term "works" in that sense. On the contrary he refers only to the "law of freedom" (1:25; 2:12) or the law which brings freedom, and the "royal law" (2:8) which is: "you shall love your neighbor as yourself." James certainly, then, was no legalist. His "works" would be roughly equal to Paul's "fruit of the Spirit" (Gal 5:22-23).

Further, James uses the term "faith" more in the sense of belief in a proposition since even demons can have faith in this sense (2:19). But for Paul faith is defined as something more dynamic. It is faith in the cross of Christ which brings about one's dying and rising with him. Thus the two were using different definitions for their terms but actually saying the same thing. Both required good deeds (Gal 5:22-23; James 1:27) but neither one taught salvation by keeping the Old Testament law.

Another possibility is that Paul was referring to works in the sense of absolute righteousness while James was referring to works in the sense of relative righteousness. Paul was saying that no one can be justified by works because in the absolute sense a person must be completely righteous in order to be justified, but all have sinned. James was speaking of works or righteousness only in the relative sense, not in the sense of absolute perfection but in the sense of the general conduct of one's life as compared with what the Bible calls the wicked (see J. Cottrell, *God the Redeemer*).

C. Finally, if Dibelius was correct, it is difficult to determine any specific background to this epistle. The letter is general ethical and spiritual parenesis directed to Jewish Christians living outside Palestine, not a personal attack on Paul or on any other specific group.

1 PETER

Bibliography: F.W. Beare, *The First Epistle of Peter*; C.A. Bigg, *A Critical and Exegetical Commentary on the Epistles of St. Peter and St. Jude*; F.F. Bruce, *Peter, Stephen, James and John*; O. Cullmann, *Peter: Disciple-Apostle-Martyr*; J.H. Elliott, *A Home for the Homeless*; E.J. Goodspeed, *An Introduction to the New Testament*; J.N.D. Kelly, *The Epistles of Peter and Jude*; J.R. Michaels, *1 Peter*; J. Moffatt, *The General Epistles*; E.R. Richards, *The Secretary in the Letters of Paul*; E.G. Selwyn, *The First Epistle of St. Peter*.

The Author

The first verse of the epistle indicates that Peter the apostle wrote it and this claim was accepted apparently by everyone in the ancient church. Irenaeus of Asia Minor and Gaul (A.D. 180), Tertullian of Carthage (A.D. 200), Clement of Alexandria (A.D. 200), and Theophilus of Antioch (A.D. 200) quoted the letter as Peter's.

But more recently some scholars have challenged the Petrine authorship. It is doubted first of all because of the fluent Greek style of the letter (e.g., by Beare). These scholars maintain that a Galilean fisherman could not have written such good Greek. Therefore, the letter cannot have been Peter's.

But these critics overlook two important facts. It is very likely that Peter knew at least some Greek. Palestine was certainly a bilingual (even trilingual) area and anyone living in Capernaum and involved in a fishing business, as did Peter, must have been able to transact business in Greek. This knowledge, however, would not have made Peter necessarily fluent in the language and certainly not a good stylist.

The second fact of importance is that people very often used a secretary or amanuensis to help polish a letter or other document (see Richards). These secretaries were more than people with good handwriting or ability to take dictation in shorthand (both of which were considered important). They could also be skilled in the language and thus help in writing good Greek or Latin.

Josephus, the Jewish historian, for example had the help of Greek stylists in the production of his works since "his own knowledge of Greek was probably never more than mediocre, especially when he was preparing his own work" (J. Goldin, "Josephus" in *IDB*). Josephus, as a matter of fact, wrote his first work, the *War*, in Aramaic and was assisted by his Greek secretaries in translating it into Greek (*War* 1.3; *Apion* 1.50). In Josephus' magnum opus, the *Antiquities*, he admits that he does not have a thorough knowledge of Greek and therefore writing this work in Greek was difficult (*Ant* 1.7; 20.263-65). Thus if even Josephus needed help in writing in Greek, it is not to be doubted that Peter would use such helpers.

Peter's amanuensis may have been Silvanus (1 Pet 5:12) since he writes that the letter was "by Silvanus." Since he was the companion of Paul on his second missionary journey (Acts 15:40; 1 Thess 1:1), Silvanus (or Silas) was probably of a background similar to Paul's. He was probably a diaspora Jew, fluent in Greek and as much at home in the Greek world as the Palestinian. He seems to have been a Roman citizen like Paul (Acts 16:37-38).

Second, the authorship of 1 Peter is doubted (by Beare and others) because of historical considerations. Indications from the letter are clear that the Christians living in Asia Minor, the destination of the letter (1 Pet 1:2f, or specifically the provinces of Pontus, Galatia, Cappadocia, Asia and Bithynia) were undergoing persecution (1 Pet 1:6; 2:12, 18-21; 3:13-17; 4:12-16). Critics claim there is no evidence that the Roman government was persecuting Christians in Asia Minor during Peter's lifetime. This persecution, it is claimed, sounds more like that perpetrated under Emperor Trajan in the year A.D. 112. The persecution under Trajan is described in a letter from the proconsul of Bithynia, Pliny the Younger, to the Emperor asking for advice on how to punish Christians (written A.D. 112):

It is my rule, Sire, to refer to you in matters where I am uncertain. For who can better direct my hesitation or instruct my ignorance? I was never present at any trial of Christians; therefore I do not know what are the customary penalties or investigations, and what limits are observed. I have hesitated a great deal on the question whether there should be any distinction of ages; whether the weak should have the same treatment as the more robust; whether those who recant should be pardoned, or whether a man who has ever been a Christian should gain nothing by ceasing to be such; whether the name itself, even if innocent of crime, should be punished, or only the crimes attaching to that name (translation in H. Bettenson, *Documents of the Christian Church*; Pliny, *Epistles* X.96).

Clearly by the time of Trajan Christians were being freely and enthusiastically persecuted. Interestingly, a person could be punished merely for being a Christian or for having "the name itself." This situation, say some critics, reminds one of 1 Peter 4:16: "If someone suffers as a Christian, do not be ashamed but glorify God in this name." Thus these scholars do not allow that 1 Peter could have been written in the first century A.D.

But there was certainly a persecution under the emperorship of Nero (A.D. 64-65). How wide this persecution spread is unknown. Nevertheless it is certainly unwise and unnecessary to jump to the conclusion that 1 Peter must have been written after Peter's lifetime. Rather, 1 Peter should be taken as evidence that Nero's persecution did spread outside the environs of the city of Rome. The persecution referred to by Pliny seems to have been in existence for some time. He writes of "customary penalties," (*puniri soleat*) and that he has "never been present at any trial of Christians," as if trials had been going on for some time. These references imply that the persecution under Trajan was not a new policy toward Christians. It is possible that since Nero's persecution the Roman government had been generally hostile toward Christianity. There is no good reason to doubt that the government program against Christians happened in Asia during Peter's lifetime. Thus we should date 1 Peter sometime around A.D. 64, perhaps soon after the beginning of the persecution.

Nevertheless, though Pliny's letter is some 50 years after 1 Peter, it is still of interest in that it shows how a Roman bureaucrat would deal with the persecution of Christians and how Christians would react to being persecuted. Thus we quote more of Pliny here to illustrate the background of 1 Peter:

Meanwhile, this is the course that I have adopted in the case of those brought before me as Christians. I ask them if they are Christians. If they admit it I repeat the question a second and a third time, threatening capital punishment; if they persist I sentence them to death. For I do not doubt that whatever kind of crime it may be to which they have confessed, their pertinacity and inflexible obstinacy should certainly be punished. There were others who displayed a like madness and whom I reserved to be sent to Rome, since they were Roman citizens.[7]. . . All who denied that they were or had been Christians I considered should be discharged, because they called upon the gods at my dictation and did reverence, with incense and wine, to your image which I had ordered to be brought forward for this purpose, together with the statues of the deities; and especially because they cursed Christ,[8] a thing which, it is said, genuine Christians cannot be induced to do (translation in Bettenson, *Documents*; Pliny, *Epistles* X.96).

Thus those in Pliny's time who would not deny Christ, even curse him, and worship other gods, were executed. Such was probably the case in Nero's persecution.

A recent challenge to the conclusion that Peter wrote to a church under stress of persecution comes from Elliott's work, *A Home for the Homeless*. Elliott surmises that 1 Peter was written between A.D. 73 and 92 to tenant farmers in Asia Minor who were socially inferior to others and thus socially ostracized or persecuted. The main problem with Elliott's thesis is identifying the situation of 1 Peter as social ostracism. The letter speaks of being proven by fire (1:7; 4:12), of Satan's trying to devour them (5:8-9), and of following Christ's example who was put to death in the flesh (2:21; 3:18; 4:13). Elliott's suggested background seems unlikely in light of the description of the harsh and life-threatening persecution in 1 Peter.

Third, some have alleged (e.g., Goodspeed) that the epistle is too imitative of Paul, both in style and in theology, to have been written by Peter. The letter is very similar to the theology of

---

[7]Compare Paul's being sent to Rome to be tried because he was a Roman citizen (Acts 25:11-12).

[8]Is this the background of 1 Cor 12:3? The Latin terms are: *male dicerent Christo* "to speak evilly to Christ."

Romans and Ephesians and there is nothing in 1 Peter that is un-Pauline. But as Selwyn points out, it is more likely that the "Pauline" language represents a common theological background. Both Paul and Peter were Christian missionaries who traveled extensively in the Greco-Roman world, preaching to both Jews and Gentiles. Why should we think similarities remarkable? Further, since Silvanus was both the companion of Paul and the amanuensis of Peter, we should hardly be surprised to find similarities in language. Finally, we must beware in concluding that Peter must have been so antagonistic to Paul that he could not have adopted Pauline expressions and metaphors.

The arguments against the authorship of 1 Peter are not compelling. Therefore, we will conclude that the apostle Peter authored the letter, with an amanuensis, sometime during the Neronian persecution — which could have lasted several months or even a year or two — in A.D. 64 or 65.

Content of the Letter

Although we cannot agree with Elliott's date for this letter, we do find an important contribution in his monograph: 1 Peter is written to support Christians under great stress by raising their self-esteem and sense of solidarity with the rest of Christendom. Peter does this by reminding the Christians in Asia Minor about their new status in Christ. They are now holy, that is, separated for God, not common or profane (1:13-21). They must now live according to this new status by remaining holy: (1) because God is holy (vv. 13-16), (2) because judgment is coming (v. 17), and because of gratitude, for they have been ransomed by the precious blood of Christ (vv. 18-21). Further, they also enjoy the new status of chosen people and royal priesthood (2:9-10) like the Israelites of old (Isa 43:20; Exod 19:6; Hos 2:23). The Christians in Asia Minor that are being so fiercely persecuted and devoured by Satan (5:8) should not feel that they are criminals or worthy of punishment in spite of what unbelievers say about them. They are people of special status in God's eyes.

Several scholars have suggested that Peter used a liturgical document — perhaps a baptismal liturgy — as the basis for part of his epistle. A liturgical document would be a text that describes a customary worship service, in this case, a typical baptismal service. Selwyn sees 2:6-10; 3:10-12, and 3:18-22 as liturgical fragments. J.N.D. Kelly agrees that there are several "traditional elements" in the letter including liturgy and catechetical materials. It must be remembered, however, that the existence of such earlier materials is only hypothetical.

Peter's Death

Peter probably died and was buried in Rome as a result of Nero's persecution sometime in late A.D. 64 or, more probably, 65. The scriptural, traditional, and archaeological evidence show this. In 1 Peter he indicated he was in "Babylon" when he wrote (1 Pet 5:13). Babylon was a common Jewish pseudonym for Rome (Rev 14:8; 17:5; 2 Baruch 11:1, 67:7; Sibylline Oracles 5.143, 159; see *OTP*, Vol. I). 2 Peter 1:14 and John 21:18-19 seem to indicate that Peter would be crucified ("stretch out the hands") and that he knew of this prophecy.

1 Clement 5-6 says Peter was martyred in a time of persecution. The Acts of Peter (see *NTA*, Vol. II, p. 319), an apocryphal work of the second century A.D., as well as Eusebius (*H.E.* 3.1) say he was executed by crucifixion with his head downward.

Peter's grave is clearly in Rome. Gaius, a second century presbyter of Rome, wrote that one could still see in his day the grave marker of Peter in the Vatican (quoted in Eusebius, *H.E.* 2.25). Further, as Finegan points out, excavations in the Vatican have found several graves from the first century. Over one ancient grave had been scratched "Peter is within."

Thus Peter died in the persecution of Nero at about the same time Paul died. Since Paul was a Roman citizen, he could not be executed by crucifixion. But Peter, the Galilean fisherman, died in the same manner as his Lord. Shortly before his death, however, Peter wrote — with the help of an amanuensis — his two epistles.

2 PETER

Bibliography: C.A. Bigg, *A Critical and Exegetical Commentary on the Epistles of St. Peter and St. Jude*; *FBK*; Guthrie, *NTI*; J.N.D. Kelly, *The Epistles of Peter and Jude*; B. Reicke, *The Epistles of Peter, James and Jude*.

Authorship and Date

The authorship of 2 Peter is challenged today by the majority of biblical scholars. Several details in the letter have led them to conclude that the letter was actually written in the early second century A.D. and thus could not have been written by the apostle Peter, who probably died in A.D. 64 or 65.

A. First are the historical problems (see Guthrie). 2 Peter 3:4, it is alleged, indicates the first century of Christianity has passed because people say, "Where is the promise of his (second) coming? For since the fathers have fallen asleep, everything remains as in the beginning." But this verse does not necessarily point to the second century. Paul's letter to the Thessalonians shows that Christians as early as A.D. 52 worried about the delay of the second coming and the fact that some Christians had fallen asleep (1 Thess 4:13-18).

Further, 2 Peter 3:15 refers to Paul's letters ("all his letters") as if they had already been collected. Surely, it is argued, that collection did not happen in the first century. But why would Paul's letters not have been collected almost immediately? It is clear, for example, that the letters of Ignatius — an early second century Christian bishop from Antioch — were being collected almost as fast as he wrote them. Polycarp, the bishop of Smyrna, wrote to the Philippians in A.D. 110: "We send you, as you asked, the letters of Ignatius, which were sent to us by him, and others which we had by us. These are subjoined to this letter, and you will be able to benefit greatly from them" (*Philippians* 13.2; trans. by K. Lake in *LCL*). The striking thing about this collection of Ignatius' letters which Polycarp is sending on to Philippi is that Ignatius was still alive at the time and most of the letters were only very recently written! Yet already they were being collected and disseminated to other churches. It is certainly then a historical fallacy that Paul's letters could only have been collected many years after his death. Thus Peter, even well before A.D. 64, could easily have referred to "all of Paul's letters."

It is also maintained that 2 Peter was combatting second century Gnosticism. We will point out parallels below with various Gnostic groups from the second century. But these groups may well have had roots in the first century. We should be cautious about assuming that the second century Gnostic sects arose full grown without first century antecedents.

B. Second, scholars point to stylistic differences between 1 Peter and 2 Peter. The Greek of 2 Peter is awkward with a paucity of connecting particles. The Greek of 1 Peter is smooth and fluent. But we argued that 1 Peter was probably written with the help of an amanuensis who not only physically wrote the words of the one dictating but also helped polish the letter.

C. Third, scholars ask questions about the clear literary relationship between 2 Peter and Jude. But we will argue (see below on Jude) that Jude probably used 2 Peter because he wrote later to address the same problem.

There is really no compelling reason to deny the Petrine authorship of 2 Peter. Peter evidently wrote the letter just before his death as 2 Peter 1:14 indicates. Thus the date of the letter should be A.D. 64 or, more likely, 65.

Background to the Letter

J.N.D. Kelly rightly suggests that a Gnostic sect was the troublesome heresy that Peter battled in his second letter. His suggestion further, that this sect was similar to — but not necessarily identical with — one of the sects listed below, known from Irenaeus (c. A.D. 180), Ps. Tertullian (c. A.D. 200) and Origen (c. A.D. 225), is also probably correct.

The three sects of interest to students of 2 Peter and Jude are:

A. The Ophites. The Ophites worshiped the serpent (ὄφις, *ophis*) of the garden of Eden instead of God. He was, they taught, the real hero and God was the villain. Consider the following statements:

> Besides these there are those heretics who are called Ophites. For they exalt the serpent to such a degree that they prefer him to Christ himself. For it was he, they say, who originally gave us the knowledge of good and evil (Ps. Tertullian, *Adv. Omn. Haer.* 6; trans. in J. Stevenson, *A New Eusebius*).

> There is a certain sect which does not admit a convert unless he pronounces anathemas on Jesus; and that sect is worthy of the name which it has chosen; for it is the sect of the so called Ophites, who utter blasphemous words in praise of the serpent (Origen, *Catena fragm.* 47; trans. in J. Stevenson, *A New Eusebius*).

B. The Cainites. The Cainites — in similar fashion to the Ophites — thought that Cain was the hero and Abel was the villain. They taught that angels had placed restrictions on humans to bring them into servitude. The truly free person must defy the angels by committing every sin. Whenever one commits a sin, an angel is present and he who commits it must address the angel and reproach him. Irenaeus says they taught:

> Not otherwise can one be saved than by passing through every action. . . . At every sinful and infamous deed an angel is present, and he who commits it . . . addresses him by his name and says, "O thou angel, I use thy work! O thou Power of such-and-such, I perform thy deed!" And this is the perfect knowledge, unafraid to stray into such actions whose very names are unmentionable (Irenaeus, *Adv. Haer.* 1.31.2; trans. in H. Jonas, *The Gnostic Religion*).

C. The Carpocratians. This group was very similar to the Cainites. It was notorious for its sexual indulgence and its general desire to experience every sin in order to be free.

The Heresy

The group of errorists practiced a lifestyle of sexual immorality (2 Pet 2:2, 7, 10, 12-14, 18-19). This wanton and arrogant display of lust was carried out on a regular basis and involved also homosexuality (cf. also Jude 4, 8).

Second, the errorists "deny the Master" (= Christ; 2 Pet 2:1; Jude 4). How they did this is not clear but the Gnostic practice of cursing the earthly Jesus (see above) and exalting the serpent over Christ may give us some clue.

Third, the errorists "despise authority" and "slander celestial beings" (2 Pet 2:10 and cf. Jude 8). The context (see 2:11) indicates that these celestial beings and authorities were angels. Thus the errorists verbally attacked angels. The practice of the Cainites (see above) comes immediately to mind (see Jude 11).

Fourth, the errorists evidently taught "cleverly invented stories" (1:16). These myths were probably Gnostic speculation about the emanation of the archons (see Chapter 7 on Gnosticism), those lower deities which — Gnostics believed — sought to prevent souls from rising at death to the high God.

Fifth, the errorists taught that there would be no second coming (3:3-4). Such teaching is consistent with other Gnostic denials known elsewhere in the New Testament (cf. 1 Tim 2:16-18).

Thus the heretical group which 2 Peter seeks to oppose probably was a first century Gnostic sect or perhaps a sect strongly influenced by incipient Gnosticism.

JUDE

Bibliography: C.A. Bigg, *A Critical and Exegetical Commentary on the Epistles of St. Peter and St. Jude*; Guthrie, *NTI*; E.F. Harrison, *Introduction to the New Testament*; J.N.D. Kelly, *The Epistles of Peter and Jude*; B. Reicke, *The Epistles of Peter, James and Jude*; B. Weiss, *A Manual of Introduction to the New Testament*; T. Zahn, *Introduction to the New Testament*.

The Author

The author of this letter calls himself Jude and he says he is the "brother of James" (v. 1). He was clearly identifying himself by the name of his more famous brother and the natural conclusion would be that this James was the "Lord's brother" (Gal 1:19), a pillar of the Jerusalem church (Gal 2:9; Acts 15:13-21). This James was martyred in A.D. 62 (see above under James).

Others deny that Jude, brother of James (and therefore also of Jesus) could have still been living when this letter was written. This conclusion of course rests on the date one assigns to the letter. If the date of A.D. 75, which we will offer below, is correct — and it seems to fit the historical situation — then Jude, the brother of James and Jesus could easily have been alive when the letter was written and thus was probably the author.

Literary and Historical Questions

Two overriding problems present themselves to the student of the epistle of Jude.

A. The first problem is that Jude seems to have quoted from the pseudepigraphical books of 1 Enoch (Jude 14-15) and the Assumption of Moses (Jude 9). How can a writer who quoted an apocryphal book be inspired?

The quotation from the Assumption of Moses cannot be considered. Although Clement of Alexandria, Tertullian, Jerome and

Augustine maintain that Jude quoted from this document, not enough remains of the document to confirm their statements. The Assumption of Moses which has survived in fragmentary form does not contain the alleged quotation in Jude 9 (see "Testament of Moses" *OTP*, Vol. I).

First Enoch has fared better with the copyists. It is extant in numerous Ethiopic manuscripts, one large Greek fragment, and numerous small Aramaic fragments. The alleged quotation is found in both the Ethiopic manuscripts and the Greek fragment. Since the Ethiopic translation was made from the Greek, the Greek fragment probably represents the text Jude would have known (see "1 Enoch" *OTP*, Vol. I).

The solutions which have been proposed for this problem are as follows:

1. If Jude quoted from 1 Enoch, then 1 Enoch must be inspired (Tertullian).

2. If Jude quoted from 1 Enoch, then Jude must not be inspired.

3. Jude quoted an oral tradition which preserved a true saying of the Old Testament character, Enoch (many nineteenth century conservatives).

4. Jude quoted the book of 1 Enoch much the same way that Paul quoted the Greek poets Aratus (Acts 17:28), Epimenides (Titus 1:12), and Menander (1 Cor 15:33). Paul may have also quoted a Jewish Midrash in 1 Cor 10:4 and probably has used a pseudepigraphical work — "Jannes and Jambres" — at 2 Timothy 3:8 (see Harrison and Guthrie).

Although many have accepted the third hypothesis, it is unlikely. Would an oral tradition persist for thousands of years (Enoch must have lived at least 3000 years before Christ)? The close parallel in 1 Enoch 1:9 to Jude 14-15 suggests Jude is quoting from the pseudepigraphical book. He does not quote 1 Enoch as scripture but as illustration, the way Paul quotes from pagan poets. Thus we hold to the fourth view.

B. The second major introductory problem of Jude is the possibility of a literary relationship between Jude and 2 Peter 2. Scholars have proposed four different hypotheses to explain the similarities between Jude and 2 Peter:

1. The author of 2 Peter used Jude (i.e., he copied from Jude's epistle).
   a. Jude is smaller than 2 Peter, thus it is more likely that the former has been expanded.
   b. Jude is harsher. Apparently the author of 2 Peter thought Jude needed toning down. For example 2 Peter telescopes Jude's metaphors (2 Pet 2:17 and Jude 12, 13).
   c. The vocabulary of 2 Peter argues that Jude is prior. Weiss explained:

But above all, dependence on the description in the Epistle of Jude is seen in this, that wherever the expression coincides with Jude it is unique in our Epistle, whereas when it is changed or added to, it immediately finds parallels in the independent parts of the second Epistle or in the first (Vol. III, p. 158).

2. The author of Jude used 2 Peter.
   a. Jude may refer to 2 Peter (Jude 4, 17).
   b. 2 Peter used the future tense in speaking of heresy (e.g., 2:1, 2, 13) but Jude used the present tense (e.g., 8, 10) as if 2 Peter predicted what occurred in the days of Jude (see Guthrie).
3. Both Jude and 2 Peter have employed a common source. The evidence for this hypothesis is slight. Most scholars believe the similarities are too close to have come from a common source.
4. There is no literary relationship.

Hypothesis number two seems to be the best. The prophetic nature of 2 Peter argues for its priority. The following best explains the sequence of events: Peter wrote his epistle A.D. 65 to a group of congregations to condemn a heresy which was beginning to develop there. Jude wrote his epistle to the same group or region upon learning of a revival of the immoral practices and unscriptural teachings a few years later (c. A.D. 75). He used many of the illustrations that Peter had used before to recall the apostle's letter, and even referred to the apostle's prediction of that situation.

CHAPTER 11

THE JOHANNINE LITERATURE

THE EPISTLES OF JOHN

Bibliography: A.E. Brooke, *The Johannine Epistles*; R. Brown, *The Epistles of John*; F.F. Bruce, *The Epistles of John*; R. Bultmann, *The Johannine Epistles*; Guthrie, *NTI*; M. Hengel, *Johannine Studies*.

The Author

The close similarity between the author of 1 John and the author of the Gospel of John with respect to language and theology is recognized by virtually all scholars. Guthrie (p. 877) lists the following parallels:

1 John	Gospel of John
1:2, 3	3:11
1:4	16:24
2:11	12:35
2:14	5:38
3:5	8:46
3:8	8:14
3:13	15:18
3:14	5:24
3:16	10:15
3:22	8:29
3:23	13:34
4:6	8:47
4:16	6:69
5:9	5:32
5:20	17:3

Many scholars, therefore, regard the Gospel and 1 John — and therefore also 2 John and 3 John since the style is identical also in them — as written by the same person. Some, however, such as Brown say the epistles were written by a student of the author of the Gospel or a member of the same religious community as the author of the Gospel. But the latter view becomes a very fine distinction. All agree that the Gospel of John and the letters are very similar but scholars such as Brown say they are not quite similar enough (Brown admits the differences in style and theology are minor). The reliability of such distinctions must rightly be questioned. There is really no good reason for spinning a hypothesis of another author for the letters.

The first letter begins in 1 John 1:1: "That which was from the beginning (cf. John 1:1), which we have heard, which we have seen with our eyes, which we have looked at (John 1:14) and our hands have touched — this we proclaim concerning the Word (John 1:1) of life (John 1:4)." Thus behind the author, stood an eyewitness. 2 John and 3 John were signed, however. He called himself "the elder" (2 John 1 and 3 John 1). Because of this, we have concluded (p. 152 above) that John the Apostle was the eyewitness but John the elder was the author.

Date

Some place the letters before the Gospel but most date them after the Gospel. One does notice a more pronounced development in the heretical problem which the apostle dealt with. Therefore we would be inclined to date the epistles a few years after the Gospel (c. A.D. 100).

Occasion

The problem with docetism which was seen reflected in the Gospel is also refuted in the first and second epistles (1 John 1:1-4; 2:22; 4:2; 5:6; 2 John 7). In the letters, however, one gets the impression that docetism threatens to lure away many members of the true faith. A small group of docetic believers has split from the main Johannine Christian community ("They went out from us but they were not of us," 1 John 2:19). This group, probably influenced by the archheretic, Cerinthus (see p. 154), is attempting to pull the faithful away with them (2 John 10). But the faithful must not fellowship with the heretical group at all (2 John 10-11) but must test every spirit according to whether he confesses Jesus came in the flesh (1 John 4:1-2).

Content of 1 John

1 John is the only unsigned letter in the New Testament except for the epistle to the Hebrews. Many scholars think both of these "epistles" were originally sermons. 1 John has no references to any specific addressees but only to types of people (fathers, young men, 1 John 2:12-14). More often the author calls the recipients "my dear children" (1 John 2:1, 12, 28; 3:7, 18; 4:4; 5:21). The epistle has numerous admonitions from the beginning of the text on (e.g., 1 John 1:6-10; 2:1-6, 7-11, etc.) in the manner of a homily. There is neither a typical epistolary greeting at the beginning of the letter or an ending.

The letter moves in a sequence of propositions regarding proper Christian conduct and confession. Conduct and confession are closely tied together. The sequence is as follows:

Fellowship (1:3) = Abiding in God (1:6-7) = the Proper Ethical Lifestyle (2:3) = Love of Others (2:7-11) = the Love of God Which You Receive (3:14-16) = Response in Faith to God's Love in Sending His Son (4:7-10) = Proper Confession (4:13-16).

Fellowship or union in common faith with others is only possible if we abide in God. But to abide in God one must practice the proper lifestyle, that is, keep God's commandments, which can be summarized as loving others. To understand love properly, however, one must know and believe in God's love for us manifest in Jesus Christ. Knowing and believing this love means accepting Jesus as the Son of God and making the proper confession. Thus fellowship, love, doctrine, and faith are all tied together.

Content of 2 John

Second John repeats the themes found in 1 John. The author, who calls himself merely "the Elder," writes to the "elect lady" (i.e., the congregation). He admonishes them to do two things: First, they must love each other. Second, they must avoid those deceivers that deny that Jesus came in the flesh.

Content of 3 John

Although 2 John concerns the same topic as 1 John, the third epistle handles a different problem. The missionaries of Asia Minor were traveling from city to city to evangelize. They were dependent on the hospitality of the local believers for their lodging and meals. But in a certain locality one Diotrephes refused to accept and help the missionaries. The elder, who wrote 3 John, called Diotrephes, "One who likes to be the head" (v. 9). Thus Diotrephes' motive seems to have been jealousy, that centuries-old blight on the ministry. Further, Diotrephes even refused to receive the elder but rather spoke to him in offensive words (v. 10). The elder, however, commends Gaius, the recipient of the letter (v. 1), for his hospitality and general Christian character.

REVELATION

Bibliography: G.R. Beasley-Murray, *The Apocalypse of John*; R.H. Charles, *The Revelation of St. John*; A. Yarbro Collins, *Crisis and Catharsis: The Power of the Apocalypse*; J.N. Court, *Myth and History in the Book of Revelation*; Guthrie, *NTI*; J. Massyngberde Ford, *Revelation*; C.J. Hemer, *The Letters to the Seven Churches of Asia in Their Local Setting*; M. Kiddle, *The Revelation of St. John*; R.H. Mounce, *The Book of Revelation*; W.M. Ramsay, *The Letters to the Seven Churches of Revelation*; E. Scheussler Fiorenza, *The Book of Revelation: Justice and Judgment*; H.B. Swete, *The Apocalypse of St. John*; M. Tenney, *Interpreting Revelation*; J.F. Walvoord, *The Revelation of Jesus Christ*.

Authorship

The book of Revelation identifies its author as a man named John: "I, John, your brother and fellow in tribulation, in the kingdom, and in endurance in Jesus was on the island of Patmos on account of the word of God and my testimony about Jesus" (Rev 1:9). The author was so familiar with the addressees of Revelation — the seven churches of Asia — that he needed no further identification than "John."

Several important early Christian authors believed this John to be the apostle. Justin (A.D. 140 in Asia Minor), Irenaeus (A.D. 180 in Asia Minor and Gaul), Clement of Alexandria (A.D. 200 in Egypt), Origen (A.D. 220 in Egypt), Tertullian (A.D. 200 in Carthage) and Hippolytus (A.D. 200 in Rome) maintained that the apostle wrote Revelation. The second century attestation of authorship is widely dispersed geographically.

The opponents of apostolic authorship, however, came from two sources: Gaius, a presbyter of Rome in A.D. 200, and Dionysius of Alexandria in A.D. 240. Gaius intensely disliked what seemed to him the worldly imagery of Revelation (the kingdom of God's being on earth for 1000 years, for example, Rev 20:4). He therefore charged that all of the Johannine literature — the Gospel, epistles and Revelation — was written by Cerinthus, the archheretic referred to above, who also taught a crude millennialism. Gaius and his followers were called "the alogoi" because they rejected the *logos* doctrine of the Johannine literature (John 1:1; 1 John 1:1; Rev 19:13).

Dionysius, an Alexandrian deeply influenced by Greek philosophy and also opposed to millennialism — or "chiliasm" as they called it then — also challenged the apostolic authorship of Revelation but accepted John the apostle as the author of the Gospel and epistles. Dionysius argued that the vocabulary and style of Revelation were different from the Gospel and epistles — though he also admitted some similarities as well. The Gospel and letters are written in correct Greek, observed Dionysius, but Revelation is full of grammatical *non sequiturs* (or *anakoloutha* in Greek). Thus Dionysius concluded that another person named John wrote Revelation, while John the apostle wrote the Gospel and epistles.

Certainly *anakoloutha* are very common in Revelation[1] (but they are found here and there throughout the New Testament too). They are the kind of grammatical *non sequiturs* that one would make if one's mother tongue were Aramaic. It appears that the author of Revelation spoke Greek understandably though not fluently[2] and that his native language was Aramaic.

What best explains the facts? We concluded above (p. 150) that although John the Apostle was the eyewitness behind the Gospel of John, a different John, "the Elder," was probably the author. But the Apostle John, himself, wrote Revelation directly as he was instructed to do (Rev 1:11, 19). This solution explains the differences in language, and yet the common testimony that all of this literature is linked to John the apostle.

Revelation is clearly Johannine. First it has many of the same important terms: *logos* (Word) in John 1:1 and Rev 19:13; Lamb in John 1:29 and Rev 5:12 (although the Greek words for lamb are different); Shepherd in John 10:1 and Rev 7:17; Manna in John 6:31

---

[1]See F. Blass, A. Debrunner and R.W. Funk, *A Greek Grammar of the New Testament*, paragraphs 466-470 for examples. Also see R.H. Charles's commentary and Guthrie.

[2]J.A.T. Robinson's (*Redating the New Testament*) assertion that the author of Revelation spoke only "pidgin" Greek is an exaggeration.

and Rev 2:17. Most scholars would agree that Revelation is closely related to the Gospel on the basis of vocabulary.

Second, Revelation is addressed to seven churches in Asia: Ephesus, Smyrna, Pergamum, Thyatira, Sardis, Philadelphia, Laodicea. Since ancient sources indicate that John the apostle had a lengthy ministry in western Asia Minor, we should see this book as a part of that ministry.

Date

Irenaeus (V.30) wrote that John wrote Revelation toward the end of the reign of emperor Domitian (A.D. 81-96). This date would seem confirmed by several other considerations as well. First, as R.H. Charles noted, the church at Smyrna did not exist until the sixties. Thus a date earlier than, say, the late sixties for Revelation would be improbable (see Rev 2:8-11). The presence of the Nicolaitans (Rev 2:6, 15) in two of the churches may also point to a later date. These were a Gnostic sect well known to second century authors (Irenaeus, Clement, Hippolytus, Tertullian) thus suggesting it developed toward the end of the first century A.D.

Perhaps the most important consideration for date is the references to emperor worship: Rev 13:4, 15-16; 14:9-11; 16:2; 19:20; 20:4. Emperor worship (see Chapter 7) was done as early as Julius Caesar but Domitian was the first one consistently to seek to enforce his divine status (although Caligula and Nero also did so to some extent).

The evidence taken cumulatively points to a date for Revelation of around A.D. 95. Thus we suggest the following dates for the Johannine literature: Gospel of John, 90; Revelation, 95; epistles of John, 100.

Occasion

The purpose and occasion for the Revelation was to address problems in the seven churches of Asia. These were problems of false doctrine, laxity in commitment to Christ, and immorality. In some cases there were troublers that had insinuated themselves into the congregation (2:6, 14, those that hold the teachings of Balaam; 2:15, the Nicolaitans; and 2:20, "Jezebel").

But the main problem is persecution: 2:10, 13; 3:10; 6:9; 17:6; 18:24; 19:2 and 20:4. This persecution either has caused or will cause the martyrdom of many saints. The persecutor is the Dragon and his henchman, the Beast, evidently symbols for Rome and the emperor respectively.

The reign of Domitian was an especially bloody and dangerous one for many subjects. People were executed, exiled, and their property confiscated by the jealous and paranoid megalomaniac. Christians were also persecuted as Eusebius narrates:

> Domitian, indeed, having exercised his cruelty against many, and unjustly slain no small number of noble and illustrious men at Rome, and having, without cause, punished vast numbers of honourable men with exile and the confiscation of their property, at length established himself as the successor to Nero, in his hatred and hostility to God. He was the second that raised a persecution against us, although his father Vespasian had attempted nothing to our prejudice (*H.E.* 3.17; trans. in Cruse, *Eusebius*).

The recipients of the Revelation, the seven churches, were also enduring a severe persecution. The purpose of the book, therefore, was to comfort the believers by holding out to them the hope of heaven and eternal peace while also promising that evil will meet the justice of almighty God.

Schools of Interpretation

Revelation can be a very puzzling book to understand. One can be even more puzzled about how the commentaries on Revelation disagree with each other. If the reader will bear in mind, however, that there are basically four ways of interpreting this document, the commentaries may be more understandable (see Tenney):

A. Preterist Interpretation

This way of understanding Revelation maintains that the symbolism in the book relates only to the events of the day in which it was written. Revelation, according to this view, has no bearing on the future (see R.H. Charles and most liberal interpreters).

B. Idealist Interpretation

This view states that Revelation is a symbolic picture of the enduring struggle between good and evil, or Christianity and paganism. The symbols are not describing actual events (either past or future). This view focuses on the ethical and spiritual truths of Revelation.

C. Historicist Interpretation

According to this school of interpretation Revelation outlines in symbolic form the entire course of the history of the church from Pentecost to the second coming of Christ. Thus the seals symbolize the breakup of the Roman empire, the locusts from the bottomless pit symbolize the Muslim invasions, and other scenes picture symbolically the Papacy and the Reformation. (Most of the reformers held this view and many older commentaries will advocate it. Martin Luther, however, was not very fond of Revelation.)

D. Futurist Interpretation

Futurists maintain that the first three chapters of Revelation are about the day in which Revelation was written or possibly the seven churches stand for seven eras in church history. But from Revelation 4:1 on, the symbols deal only with events that will take place in the Great Tribulation just before the return of Christ. This Tribulation will last either $3\frac{1}{2}$ or 7 years. Thus most of the book, according to this view, is about the events of the second coming of Christ. (J. Walvoord is an example of a Futurist.)

Millennial views also play a role in interpreting Revelation. Futurists and some Historicists would be also Premillennialists. Amillennialists and Postmillennialists would tend to be Idealists.

Literary Genre

Revelation is an apocalypse (Greek ἀποκάλυψις, *apokalypsis*, "uncovering"). It shares, therefore, certain literary characteristics with other apocalypses of the Old Testament (especially Daniel but also parts of Ezekiel and Zechariah) and of intertestamental Judaism (see Chapter 2). But Revelation differs from the apocalypses, at least those of the intertestamental period, in one important point. The intertestamental apocalypses are pseudonymous. They attribute authorship to Enoch, Ezra, Baruch, or Abraham among others. Revelation was written by a person named John. There is no attempt to claim a great figure from the Old Testament as its author.

Content

The drama of Revelation moves forward by the employment of the number seven (cf. the seven signs of Jesus in the Gospel of John). First there are letters sent to seven churches (1:11-3:22). Then the seven seals on a scroll are broken, one at a time (5:1-8:1). Next seven angels blow seven trumpets (8:2-11:19). Finally seven angels empty seven bowls (15:1-16:21). Each of these events brings a series of judgments on earth. Are these series of judgments repetitious or progressive? In other words are the judgments of the seven trumpets the same as those of the seven seals — thus emphasizing that judgment is sure — or are they new judgments? Commentators debate the issue.

The drama reaches its high point when in chapters 17-19 Rome (the Harlot, Babylon the Great) is destroyed and from heaven rides victoriously the King of Kings and Lord of Lords on his white horse (19:11-16). Chapters 20-22 describe Christ's reign of peace and joy in the Millennium and in the new Jerusalem.

Throughout Revelation one is struck by the many similarities to the Old Testament. For example, Rev 4:7-8 is very much like Ezek 1:6 and 10. Rev 6:1-8 (the four horsemen) is reminiscent of Zech 1:8-17 (and cf. Zech 6:1-8). Rev 13:1-10 is like Dan 7:2-8. The symbols are never exactly the same in Revelation but certainly they are influenced by the Old Testament.

Regardless of how one chooses to interpret Revelation, the bottom line is the same. Christ will be the victor and will grant his saints eternal reward. Our present stress may be a trial but eternity will be an unending time of joy, love, and light in the presence of God:

> No longer will there be any curse. The throne of God and of the Lamb will be in the city, and his servants will serve him. They will see his face, and his name will be on their foreheads. There will be no more night. They will not need the light of a lamp or the light of the sun, because the Lord God will give them light. And they will reign for ever and ever (Rev 22:3-5).

CHAPTER 12

THE TEXT AND CANON
OF THE NEW TESTAMENT

What happened to the New Testament books after they were written? The study of the text of the New Testament deals with how the documents were copied and disseminated to other churches in other localities, and with the methods used to reconstruct the exact wording of the original "autograph" of each book. The study of canon concerns a book's acceptance among the churches as genuine and inspired.

TEXT

Bibliography: K. Aland and B. Aland, *The Text of the New Testament*; J. Finegan, *Encountering the New Testament Manuscripts*; J.H. Greenlee, *Introduction to the New Testament Textual Criticism*; F.G. Kenyon, *Our Bible and the Ancient Manuscripts*; B.M. Metzger, *The Text of the New Testament*; B.H. Streeter, *The Four Gospels*; L. Vaganay and C.B. Amphoux, *An Introduction to New Testament Textual Criticism*.

Writing Materials and Methods in Antiquity

Ancients could write documents on clay tablets, wood, stone, pieces of pottery, animal skins (parchment) and papyrus. But almost all of the manuscripts of the New Testament are on either parchment or papyrus. Parchment (also called vellum) was made from the skins of cattle, sheep, goats, and antelopes. Several very old parchment manuscripts of the New Testament have survived, along with a host of later ones.

Papyrus was manufactured mainly in Egypt from the papyrus

plant. This plant, which could grow 12 to 15 feet tall, was cut lengthwise into thin sections about a foot long and crisscrossed with another layer. These were then pressed together to form a writing surface not unlike our paper. Many papyri have been found in the dry sands of Egypt. These documents on papyrus range from literary works (including N.T. books) to personal letters and legal notices. The oldest extant N.T. manuscripts are on papyrus.

Most ancient literary works were published in the form of a scroll. Papyrus leaves would be glued together or parchment would be sewn together to create a scroll up to 35 feet long. Works needing more length would be published in several volumes. The two longest N.T. books, Luke and Acts, would have required, according to Metzger, a scroll of 31 feet each.

But sometime early in the second century many copyists began publishing N.T. books in the codex form. This form more closely resembles our present books with many smaller pages or leaves. Such a form made it easier to look up a specific passage in Scripture rather than unrolling the large scrolls.

Handwriting in antiquity could take one of two forms. The cursive style was used to write rapidly any everyday document. But literary works were written in the uncial style in which each word was written in capital letters. The N.T. was copied in the uncial style of writing until the ninth century A.D. when handwriting went through a reform and smaller letters were used, called minuscules. Thus the designation, uncial, means both a writing style (used on both papyrus and parchment) and specifically the parchment manuscripts in capital letters as opposed to the later minuscule manuscripts.

Important Greek Manuscripts

A. Papyri

1. $\mathfrak{P}^{52}$ — The Rylands fragment of John 18:31-33, 37-38 is the oldest copy of any part of the New Testament. It dates around A.D. 125-150.

2. $\mathfrak{P}^{45}$ — The Chester Beatty papyrus is a codex, in some parts

badly preserved, of the Gospels and Acts. It was produced in the first half of the third century A.D.

3. $\mathfrak{P}^{46}$ — The second Chester Beatty papyrus contains the Pauline letters. It was produced around A.D. 200.

4. $\mathfrak{P}^{47}$ — The third Chester Beatty papyrus is a copy of Revelation dating to the latter part of the third century.

B. Uncials

1. Codex Vaticanus or "B" is considered one of the two best and oldest parchment codices. It dates from the fourth century A.D.

2. Codex Sinaiticus or "‫א‬" (the Hebrew aleph) is the second of the two most accurate manuscripts. It also dates from the fourth century.

3. Codex Alexandrinus or "A" dates from the fifth century.

4. Codex Ephraemi or "C" dates from the fifth century.

5. Codex Bezae or "D" is from the sixth century.

6. Koridethi codex or "Θ" is from the ninth century.

7. Washingtonianus or "W" is from the fifth century.

8. Regius codex or "L" is from the eighth century.

C. Minuscules

1. Minuscule 1, from the twelfth century, is one of the more important manuscripts.

2. Minuscule 33, from the ninth century, is considered one of the most accurate manuscripts.

The following table from K. Aland and B. Aland can indicate the number and type of surviving New Testament manuscripts:[1]

Distribution of Greek Manuscripts by century

Century	Papyri	Uncials	Minuscules
		Text Manuscripts	
2nd	1	—	—
ca. 200	4	—	—
2nd/3rd	1	1	—
3rd	26	2	—
3rd/4th	7	2	—
4th	13	14	—
4th/5th	7	8	—
5th/6th	3	10	—
6th	6	50	—

---

[1]Aland and Aland, *The Text of the New Testament*, p. 81. Used by permission.

Century	Papyri	Uncials	Minuscules
6th/7th	5	3	—
7th	8	26	—
7th/8th	2	1	—
8th	1	26	—
8th/9th	—	1	—
9th	—	46	13
9th/10th	—	—	3
10th	—	18	122
10th/11th	—	1	8
11th	—	—	428
11th/12th	—	—	33
12th	—	—	553
12th/13th	—	—	25
13th	—	—	544
13th/14th	—	—	27
14th	—	—	508
14th/15th	—	—	8
15th	—	—	240
15th/16th	—	—	4
16th	—	—	134

When scholars examine these manuscripts to determine what was in the original autograph of a N.T. book, they ask not only which manuscript is older but which was made by the more careful scribe. They ask not only which reading has the most manuscripts supporting it but which reading has the best manuscripts supporting it.

Important Ancient Versions of the New Testament

The New Testament was rather early translated into other languages, for although Greek was the universal language of the Roman empire, by no means could all people speak it fluently. The oldest translations can be helpful to scholars who reconstruct the Greek text as it was in the original autograph. The following are the most important:

A. Syriac translations
    1. The old Syriac version was made about A.D. 200.
    2. The Peshitta version was prepared around A.D. 400.

B. Latin translations
    1. The old Latin version dates from A.D. 150.

2. The Vulgate (Vg) was made by Jerome in A.D. 384.

C. Coptic translations (the native language of Egypt)
1. The translation into the Sahidic dialect of Coptic was made in A.D. 325.
2. The Boharic dialect version of the New Testament was made in A.D. 400.

Manuscript "Families"

Textual critics discovered after years of painstaking analysis that one could group the Greek manuscripts and the versions into families. If ten copies are made from one manuscript, then all ten copies will have some of the same characteristics as the model manuscript. If in turn five copies are made from one of the ten prior copies, they too will have most of the characteristics of the model manuscript. Thus all sixteen documents comprise a family.

The analysis of B.H. Streeter is standard and we give it below. Streeter has grouped the more important manuscripts and versions into their respective families. Most of the abbreviations and symbols in the table were explained above.

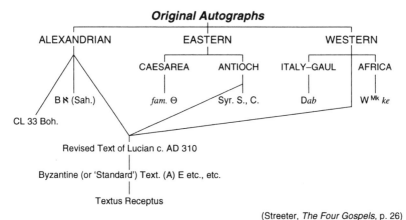

(Streeter, *The Four Gospels*, p. 26)

Sometimes the work of the textual critics involves hotly contested passages. The reader is encouraged to turn to Mark 16:9-20 and John 7:53-8:11 to see two of the most debated textual decisions of the New Testament. Most modern translations now either omit these passages or bracket them off with a warning that the best ancient manuscripts of Mark and John do not contain them.

But most of the work of the textual critic is to decide much more mundane issues such as the spelling of a word, or the precise wording or word order of a sentence. Very few of the textual differences affect an important matter of doctrine. As a matter of fact, the surprising thing is how uniform the manuscripts are, considering all the theological controversies the church went through during the early centuries of its existence. The reader has only to compare the old King James Version (made in 1611) with the New International Version. The latter has had use of all the latest manuscript finds. Nevertheless, most of the differences between these two versions are due to translation matters, not textual matters. The texts are remarkably similar.

Finally, one must compare the vastly better attested New Testament with other ancient documents. Aland and Aland (see above) list 2,980 Greek manuscripts of the New Testament, not to mention hundreds of manuscripts of the early versions and the 2,095 lectionaries (collections of New Testament passages in Greek to be read on Sundays). Many of these manuscripts date only two to three hundred years after the New Testament was written. When one considers that Caesar's *Gallic War* has only ten good manuscripts and the oldest of these came 900 years after the work was written, one can see how extremely reliable our text of the New Testament is. Livy's Roman history has survived in only 20 manuscripts and Tacitus's works have survived in only two manuscripts from the ninth and eleventh centuries. Thucydides' works are only extant on eight manuscripts, the earliest of which is from A.D. 900. Still no classicist would assail the authenticity of these works based on such manuscript evidence. The student of the New Testament can be remarkably assured then that we have a reliable text of what the inspired authors have written.

THE CANON OF THE NEW TESTAMENT

Bibliography: F.F. Bruce, *The Canon of the New Testament*; J.W. Mc-Garvey, *Evidences of Christianity*; B. Metzger, *The Canon of the New Testament*; M. Tenney, *New Testament Survey*; B.F. Westcott, *A General Survey of the History of the Canon of the New Testament*.

The word "canon" (Greek κανών, *kanon*, "measuring stick") was used in antiquity to refer to a list of books that measured up to a standard of genuineness. The N.T. canon became an issue first in the second century when the archheretic Marcion (A.D. 150) made known which New Testament books he accepted — the Gospel of Luke and the ten Pauline epistles, minus the Pastorals — and when so many apocryphal and Gnostic gospels began appearing.

Historians trace three phases in the process of canonization. First certain of the documents of the N.T. were collected locally and quoted in works of theology without any thought of having to argue their genuineness. Second, in response to Marcion and the spurious Gnostic texts, Christian leaders began to investigate the canon and to publish lists of genuine books. Finally, church councils met to decide between genuine and spurious books.

Collections of N.T. books must have been made very early. If the letters of Ignatius (A.D. 110) are similar, the N.T. documents were collected almost immediately after being written, for Polycarp (A.D. 110) indicated he was making a collection of Ignatius's epistles. We read that one of the martyrs in Scilla in 188 held a satchel full of Paul's letters. When standing before the Roman proconsul, he was asked what was in the satchel. He replied, "The books and letters of Paul, a righteous man" (text in *FBK*). Such collections of New Testament books were probably in existence in the first century A.D.

The lists of the church leaders (next page) seem quite different at first. But there are some constants here. Almost all of these lists include the four Gospels, Acts, thirteen Pauline letters, 1 Peter, 1 John and Revelation. None of our present N.T. books were labeled by these writers as spurious, though some of them were questioned for a time. The disagreements stemmed mainly from geographical considerations. What might be read and accepted in one locality, might also be looked upon with caution in another for a while. The later councils — in Carthage in A.D. 397 and in Hippo in A.D. 419 — settled on the present twenty-seven books of the New Testament.

What is important to bear in mind is that "The church did not *determine* the canon; it *recognized* the canon" (Tenney, p. 405; emphasis is his). It was a process of investigation of genuineness, not a process of choosing what one liked.

Second, the disputed books were mostly the very short letters — 2 John, 3 John, and 2 Peter — or the Jewish Christian letter of James which might appeal less to Greek Christian readers. Our New Testament was substantially agreed upon from the beginning with variations in the canon due to local situations. When Christian leaders began investigating the canon on a broad geographical basis, there was general agreement.

(Ir=Irenaeus; Ter=Tertullian; Cl=Clement of Alexandria; Mur=Muratorian Fragment; Or=Origen; Eus=Eusebius)

	Ir	Ter	Cl	Mur	Or	Eus
4 Gospels	x	x	x	x	x	x
Acts	x	x	x	x	x	x
13 Pauline letters	x	x	x	x	x	x
Hebrews	?	?	x	0	?	x
1 Peter	x	x	x	0	x	x
2 Peter	?	0	x	0	?	?
James	?	0	x	0	?	?
Jude	?	x	x	x	0	?
1 John	x	x	x	x	x	x
2 John	x	0	x	x	?	?
3 John	?	0	x	0	?	?
Revelation	x	x	x	x	x	x
Epistle of Barnabas	0	0	x	0	0	•
Apocalypse of Peter	0	0	x	?	0	•
Gospel of the Hebrews	0	0	?	0	0	•
Gospel of Egyptians	0	0	?	0	0	0
1 Clement	0	0	x	0	0	0
Didache	0	0	x	0	0	•
Shepherd of Hermas	0	0	x	?	0	•
Epistle to the Laodiceans	0	0	0	•	0	0
Epistle to Alexandrians	0	0	0	•	0	0
Acts of Paul	0	0	0	0	0	•

Key

x	Included	?	Undecided or disputed
0	Not mentioned	•	Considered spurious

APPENDIX I
NEW TESTAMENT CHRONOLOGY

Political Events	–	Events of Christian History
	–	5 B.C. (spring) Jesus' birth
4 B.C. Herod the Great dies	–	
	–	
	–	
	–	
A.D. 18-37 Joseph Caiaphas is High Priest	–	
	–	
A.D. 26-36 Pontius Pilate is Procurator	–	A.D. 27 John the Baptist begins preaching
	–	A.D. 28 Jesus is baptized and begins his ministry
	–	
	–	A.D. 30 Jesus' crucifixion
	–	
	–	A.D. 32 Stephen is stoned, Saul of Tarsus is converted
	–	
	–	
	–	
	–	A.D. 46 Paul goes up to Jerusalem after 14 years to bring famine relief (Gal 2:1; Acts 11: 27-30)
	–	A.D. 47-48 First Missionary Journey
	–	A.D. 48 *Epistle to the Galatians*
	–	A.D. 49 The Jerusalem Council (Acts 15), Second Missionary Journey
	–	A.D. 50 In Thessalonica
A.D. 52 Gallio Proconsul of Achaia	–	A.D. 50-52 In Corinth, *1 and 2 Thessalonians*
	–	A.D. 50-55 *Gospel of Matthew*
	–	A.D. 54 *1 Corinthians*
	–	A.D. 55 *2 Corinthians*
	–	A.D. 56 *Epistle to the Romans*
	–	A.D. 55-56 *Epistle of James*
	–	A.D. 58-60 *Gospel of Luke*
	–	A.D. 61-62 *Epistles to the Philippians, Ephesians, Colossians, Philemon*
	–	A.D. 62 *Acts*

	– A.D. 62-65 *1 Timothy, Titus*
	–
A.D. 64 The great fire of Rome and	– A.D. 64 *Epistle to the Hebrews*
the subsequent persecution of	–
Christians lasting possibly until	–
late 65	– A.D. 65 *2 Timothy, 1 Peter, 2 Peter*
	–
A.D. 66-73 (74?) The Jewish War	– A.D. 66 *Gospel of Mark*
in Palestine	–
	–
	–
	–
	–
	– A.D. 75 *Epistle of Jude*
	–
	–
A.D. 81-96 The Reign of Domitian	–
	– A.D. 90 *The Gospel of John*
	–
	–
	– A.D. 95 *Revelation*
	–
	–
	– A.D. 100 *The Epistles of John*

APPENDIX II
THE TEN MOST IMPORTANT ARCHAEOLOGICAL FINDS
FOR NEW TESTAMENT STUDY

A. Material Remains

1. The bones of a crucified man were found in a tomb near Jerusalem. For the first time historians could examine the nature and effects of crucifixion on an actual victim. See Chapter 4; and N. Haas, "Anthropological Observations on the Skeletal Remains from Givat ha-Mivtar" *IEJ* 20 (1970) 35-59.

2. Excavations around the temple mount have revealed the colossal size of its foundation stones, the main entrances and exits to the mount, and assorted inscriptions and buildings around it. See Chapter 2; and M. Ben-Dov, *In the Shadow of the Temple.*

3. Excavations in the Jewish Quarter of old Jerusalem have brought to light many houses of the first century A.D. well-to-do Jews. One of these houses, the huge 6000 square feet mansion, may have belonged to one of the High Priests. Another, the so-called "Burnt House," certainly belonged to a member of one of the High Priestly families for inside it was found the inscription "son of Kathros." See Chapter 4; and N. Avigad, *Discovering Jerusalem.*

4. Capernaum, Jesus' main base of operations, has also been excavated. One can see the foundations of the synagogue that was there in Jesus' day and possibly even — if certain archaeologists are correct — the house of the apostle Peter. See Chapter 4; and V. Corbo, *The House of St. Peter at Capharnaum.*

5. The digs at Sepphoris — only 3 or 4 miles from Nazareth — are also resulting in important finds such as city streets, houses, mosaics, and a theatre. Surely Jesus visited there often and possibly even worked there as a carpenter. See Chapter 2; and R.A. Batey, *Jesus and the Forgotten City.*

6. In a tomb just south of Jerusalem have been found recently the bones of the High Priest, Joseph Caiaphas, the first High Priest's tomb ever discovered. See Chapters 2 and 4; and R. Reich, "Caiaphas' Name Inscribed on Bone Boxes" *BAR* 18/5 (1992) 28-45.

7. In the area outside Palestine one of the most important excavations has been that at ancient Corinth which revealed important

inscriptions, the agora, the shops, the judgment seat (or Bema), and the temples, all of which played a role in Corinthian Christianity. See Chapter 9; and J. Murphy-O'Connor, *St Paul's Corinth*.

8. Excavations in modern Salonika (ancient Thessalonica) have also produced some material remains helpful for interpreting the Thessalonian correspondence. See Chapter 9; and K.P. Donfried, "The Cults of Thessalonica and the Thessalonian Correspondence" *NTS* 31 (1985) 336-56.

B. Literary Remains

1. By far, the Dead Sea Scrolls, found in the caves around Wadi Qumran, have been the most important literary finds. We have been enriched in knowledge of ancient Judaism as well as knowledge of the text of the Old Testament. See Chapter 2; and W.S. LaSor, *The Dead Sea Scrolls and the New Testament*.

2. The second most important literary find was at Nag Hammadi in Egypt where numerous texts in the Coptic language were unearthed. These texts were mostly Gnostic. Therefore our understanding of Gnosticism was dramatically broadened. In addition, documents such as the Gospel of Thomas have proven valuable to scholars of the Gospels. See Chapter 7; and A.K. Hembold, *The Nag Hammadi Gnostic Texts and the Bible*.

APPENDIX III
RABBINIC LITERATURE AND THE DEAD SEA SCROLLS

A. Rabbinic Literature
1. Rabbinic Generations
    a. Tannaim — A.D. 10–200 — The producers of the Mishnah, Tosephta and Tannaitic Midrashim
    b. Amoraim — A.D. 200–500 — The producers of the two Talmuds
    c. Gaonim — A.D. 500–800 — Late rabbinic scholars
2. The Mishnah's six orders or divisions
    a. Zeraim (seeds)
    b. Moed (feasts)
    c. Nashim (women)
    d. Nezekim (damages)
    e. Kodashim (hallowed things)
    f. Tohoroth (cleannesses)
3. Definitions
    a. Tosephta — "addition," materials from the Tannaim but not in the Mishnah
    b. Baraita — "outside," materials preserved in the Talmuds but from the age of the Tannaim
4. Tannaitic Midrashim (A midrash is an exposition of the Old Testament.)
    a. Mekilta — on Exodus
    b. Sifra — on Leviticus
    c. Sifre — on Numbers and Deuteronomy
5. The Talmuds
    a. Jerusalem Talmud (Yerushalmi) — Compiled in Palestine
    b. Babylonian Talmud (Bavli) — Compiled in Mesopotamia
(Each Talmud consists of the Mishnah and the Gemara — a commentary on the Mishnah by the Amoraim.)

B. The More Important Documents of the Dead Sea Scrolls
1. The Rules
   a. The Community Rule (1QS) or Manual of Discipline —
      Early first century B.C. MS, other fragments in caves 4 &
      5. Date of the document is c. 125 B.C. — a collection of
      regulations for the community.
   b. The Damascus Rule (CD) or Zadokite Document —
      Preserved on two incomplete medieval MSS of the tenth
      century and twelfth century A.D. discovered in the Cairo
      Geniza, and on fragments found in caves 4, 5 & 6 (dated
      early first century B.C.). It contains exhortations to remain
      faithful to the covenant followed by statutes arranged top-
      ically, and Essene halacah.
   c. The War Rule (1QM) — Probably composed in the late
      first century B.C. or early century A.D. — concerned with
      the eschatological war and the tactics to be used.
   d. The Temple Scroll (2Q Temple) — (Herodian script, 20
      B.C.-A.D. 70) probably composed from 125 to 75 B.C. It
      has four sections: rules of purity, festivals, building the
      temple, the king and his army.
2. Poetic and Liturgical texts
   a. The Hymns (1QH) — Script from first century A.D. —
      resembles the Psalms
   b. Four Apocryphal Psalms — These were previously known
      from the Greek, Latin, and Syriac Bibles — Script is from
      second century B.C.
3. Bible Interpretation
   a. Genesis Apocryphon (1QapGen) — Script is from first
      century B.C. and composition second century B.C. In
      Aramaic, it covers the birth of Noah to Abraham's
      covenant with God.
   b. Habakkuk Pesher (1QpHab) — Applies first two chapters
      of Habakkuk to the sect's history
   c. Targum of Job (2QtgJob) — Composed 100 B.C., script of
      MS is first century A.D.
   d. Messianic Anthology (4Q175) — Testimonia or scriptural
      texts on the messianic teaching of the community (e.g.,
      Deut 18:18-19, Num 24:15-17, Deut 33:8-11)

4. Miscellaneous
   a. The Copper Scroll (3Q15). A list of real or imagined trea-
      sures in Mishnaic Hebrew
   b. Horoscopes (4Q186) — Written in Hebrew but from left
      to right using both archaic and square letters; associated
      spiritual qualities with physical ones.

GLOSSARY

Agora — the marketplace in ancient Greek cities.

Apocalyptic — (literally: "revelation") a term used to describe a type of literature which claims to be revelations of hidden knowledge written by an inspired seer.

Apocrypha — (literally: "hidden") a term used by Protestants to denote those books appearing in the Roman Catholic Old Testament which they do not accept as canonical.

Canon — (literally: "a measuring stick") a closed body of writings considered to be inspired and authoritative.

Catechism, Catechetical — (literally: "instruction") having to do with instruction given to those about to undergo Christian baptism.

Christology — the study of the doctrine of Christ.

Diaspora — (literally: "dispersion") the dispersion of Jews from Palestine into the Greco-Roman world.

Eschatology — (literally: "study of the end") the study of the end-time, for Christians the second coming.

Gemara — commentary on the Mishnah (literally: "completion").

Haggadah — (literally: "narrative") nonlegal materials in the rabbinic literature.

Halacah — legal materials in rabbinic literature (literally: "walking," hence rule of conduct).

Hasmonean — the family of Hasmon, the best known figure of which is Mattathias, the father of Judas Maccabeus.

Hanukkah — (literally: "dedication") the feast of dedication begun when Judas Maccabeus recaptured and cleansed the temple.

Liturgy — (literally: "service") the standardized order and vocabulary of the Christian worship service, written down in various forms from the second century on.

Macellum — the meat market in Greek and Roman cities.

Midrash — (literally: "searching") study; also interpretation of the Old Testament.

Mishnah — (literally: "repetition") a written codification of the Pharisaic oral law, completed in A.D. 200.

Parenesis — (literally: "exhortation") exhortation, advice, or instruction.

Pericope — a small literary unit such as a narrative or a form of teaching.

Pseudepigrapha — (literally: "false writings") those ancient Jewish texts, often with Christian interpolations, not accepted today in any canon.

Septuagint — (literally: "seventy") the Greek translation of the Old Testament supposedly done by seventy translators.

Talmud — (literally: "learning") the Jewish oral law in its final form, including both Mishnah and Gemara. Completed by A.D. 500.

Targum — (literally: "translation") translation of the Old Testament into Aramaic, originally done orally, later written down.

Torah — (literally: "instruction") The Old Testament Law; also (for Pharisees) the oral law.

Vulgate — (literally: "common") Jerome's Latin translation of both the Old and New Testaments.

Yahweh — the personal name of God in the Hebrew Old Testament (sometimes spelled Jehovah in old English versions).

INDEX

INDEX OF MODERN AUTHORS

SUBJECT INDEX